Second Edition

CREATIVE
PLAY
DIRECTION

Robert Cohen
University of California at Irvine

John Harrop
University of California at Santa Barbara

PRENTICE HALL, Englewood Cliffs, New Jersey 07632

Library of Congress Cataloging in Publication Data

COHEN, ROBERT
   Creative play direction.

   Bibliography
   Includes index.
   1.– Theater—Production and direction. I. Harrop,
John   II.–Title.
PN2053.C58–1984   792'.0233   83-2417
ISBN 0-13-190926-6

Editorial/production supervision by Joyce Turner
Manufacturing buyer: Ron Chapman
Front cover photo: Ruth Walz
Back cover photo: Mark Taper Forum
Cover design: Diane Saxe

© 1984, 1974 by Prentice-Hall, Inc.
A Simon & Schuster Company
Englewood Cliffs, New Jersey 07632

Printed in the United States of America

20 19 18 17 16 15 14 13 12

ISBN 0-13-190926-6

Prentice-Hall International (UK) Limited, *London*
Prentice-Hall of Australia Pty. Limited, *Sydney*
Prentice-Hall Canada Inc., *Toronto*
Prentice-Hall Hispanoamericana, S.A., *Mexico*
Prentice-Hall of India Private Limited, *New Delhi*
Prentice-Hall of Japan, Inc., *Tokyo*
Simon & Schuster Asia Pte. Ltd., *Singapore*
Editora Prentice-Hall do Brasil, Ltda., *Rio de Janeiro*

CONTENTS

Preface   vii

ONE   The Directorial Function   1

The Director in History   2
The Prehistory of Directing: 5000 B.C. - 1850 A.D.   2
Actor-Managers   3
Director-Managers   6
The Director Today   9
So What Do Directors Do?   10

TWO   Interpreting the Script   12

Overall Versus Moment-to-Moment Interpretation   13
Intrinsic Versus Extrinsic Interpretation   14
"Right" Versus "Vital" Interpretation   15
Moral Imperatives in the Director-Author Relationship   18
Intrinsic Interpretation, Moment to Moment   18
Dramaturgical Analysis   22
Breakdown of the Script   25
Outside Resources for Study   29
The Overall Interpretation—Intrinsically Derived   34
Working Extrinsically   37
Summary of Interpretation   39

THREE Composition—Design 40

Production Design: Theater Forms   41
Basic Theater Designs and Their Utility   41
A Director Chooses a Theater   55
The Staging Area   58
Violating the Stage   59
The Scenery System   63
Scene Changes   79
The Quality of the Design   84

FOUR Composition—The Ground Plan 87

Choosing a Ground Plan   90
The Ground Plan Accommodates the Action of the Play   90
The Ground Plan Forcefully Projects the Action of the Play   90
The Ground Plan Encourages the Pattern of Movement   94
The Ground Plan Encourages Effective Tableaux   97
The Ground Plan Stimulates Effective Improvisation   99
The Ground Plan Creates Focus   100
The Ground Plan Creates Atmosphere   101
The Ground Plan is Dynamic   101

FIVE Composition—Blocking 102

Terms   102
Called-for Stage Actions   103
The Chosen Actions   104
Blocking Creates Clarity   104
Blocking Creates Focus   106
Blocking Establishes Credibility   115
Blocking Establishes and Heightens the Inner Action   119
Blocking Creates Behavior   123
Blocking Creates Special Effects   126
Blocking Creates Aesthetic Effects   127
Compositional Aesthetics   130
Blocking Creates Variety   135
Blocking Creates Abstract Effects and Symbolic Patterns   135
The Director's Blocking Tools   136
Blocking Terms   137
Working Out the Blocking   137
Recording the Blocking   140

SIX Composition—Lighting 146

Lighting Instruments   148
Lighting Control   148
Effects of Lighting   149
Lighting the Action   150
The Effects of Controlled Lighting   153
The Director Works on Lighting the Play   154

SEVEN Composition—Sound 156

Rhythm   157
Pace   159
Music   161
Sound Effects   165
Integration of Sounds and Sights   167

EIGHT Working with Actors 168

Background   168
Systems and Studios   172
Rehearsal Techniques   198
Auditions and Casting   224
Rehearsal Rhythms   228

NINE Styling the Play 233

Fitting the Style to the Period in Which the Play Is Set   241
Setting the Play in the Period in Which It Was Written   242
Contemporizing the Play   243
Setting the Play in an Arbitrary Period   253
Aesthetic Styles   257
Alternative Theater   263
Example—*Macbeth*   277
Realism and Naturalism   282
Summary   285

TEN Putting It Together 287

First Period: *Speculating*   288
Second Period: *Planning*   299
Third Period: *Creating*   307
Fourth Period: *Consolidating*   317
Directing a Scene for Class   321
Directing a Musical Production   323

Bibliography 326

Index 329

Preface

There is an adage in the theater that you have to learn the rules before you can break them. But are there "rules" in the theater? Louis Jouvet, the great French director, once said that "There is only one rule of the theater: success." Jouvet did not just mean critical or commercial success; he meant that there was one irreducible demand of the theater—that it attract, stimulate, and satisfy an audience. Are there really any other rules besides Jouvet's?

Probably not. There is *craft*, which has been developed over more than two thousand years of theatrical achievement, and there is *creativity*, which is the theater's leap, from moment to moment, into new forms, new ideas, and fresh originality, but there is no predetermined way of bringing these two things together.

All great theater is a blend of crafts—"what works," as derived from theatrical experience—and creativity, which leads to the unexpected. And it is the role of the director to be both craftmaster and creative innovator.

The director must understand and have a working knowledge of *all* the crafts of the theater: the time-honored disciplines of playwriting, acting, designing, and staging; the management techniques of planning, organizing, scheduling, and controlling; the theatrical technologies of lighting, sound, and special effects; and the elusive art of dealing effectively with people—both as individuals and as functioning ensembles. And the director is also a creator, who understands craft in order to use it—and transcend it. As a creator, the director must reexamine the theatrical heritage, must redefine the theatrical disciplines, and must, to some degree, re-create the very nature of theater with each directorial effort. The director is, therefore, both a follower and a leader: a follower of the theatrical past, and a pioneer in the exploration of the theater's potential. It is this combination that makes the theater a conservative craft and a radical art at the same time.

Creative Play Direction was conceived and first drafted during the late 1960s and early 1970s—catalyzed to some degree by the radical directorial experiments of those times. Nudity, group improvisation, gymnastic contortions, audience "invasions," psychological mayhem, spatial anarchy, sexual audacity, and language previously considered unthinkable for the theater became the radical components of a self-proclaimed "new theater" seeking—often successfully—to displace the old while reflecting the revolutionary social attitudes of the time. Creativity was very much the dominant force in the directorial art, and considerations of craft were often dismissed as reactionary and obstructive.

Times have changed. The passage of a decade or so has seen continued experimentation—if at a lower level—in the American theater: writer-directors such as Robert Wilson and Richard Foreman have received great acclaim for highly inventive works, and many of the avant-garde directors of the 1960s have been "mainstreamed" into the establishment bastions of New York's Lincoln Center, Los Angeles's Music Center, and Minneapolis's Tyrone Guthrie Theatre. In Europe, too, a radical directorial creativity dominates the theater in almost every company. However, the 1980s have also seen a return to tried and true principles of craft and professionalism, redressing the balance significantly since the "new theater" heyday. The great rise of regional and repertory theaters in this country; the heightened interest in classical revivals, as exemplified by the spread of Shakespearean festivals and public broadcasting versions of classic plays; and the growth of professionally oriented actor-training programs, both academic and commercial, across the country have stimulated a demand for creativity married to excellence of craft—brilliantly innovative directors working with virtuoso actors. A new balance has been established.

The second edition of this book seeks to address the current balance of the theater. Creativity remains of title significance in the work, and we continue to eschew narrow prescriptions about "how to direct" (or, worse, "how *we* direct"). But we have augmented those sections of the book that provide practical discussions calculated to guide the beginning director through the various steps involved in casting, staging, rehearsing, and presenting a play. We have paid more attention to the details of directorial craft and practical ways of working with actors, designers, and production personnel. And we have provided more photographs and diagrams to illustrate the specific problems directors face and the specific ways they go about finding solutions to these problems. These augmentations are to be found throughout the main body of the book—the "four concerns of play directing" (interpretation, composition, acting, and style)—and, most particularly, in a new final chapter on "putting it together."

Our discussions are still not "rules," however. There is simply no "one way" to direct a play, and as joint authors we happily acknowledge that our own directorial methods are quite dissimilar. *Creative Play Direction* remains founded on the concept, expressed in the original preface, that "directing is a creative rather than an imitative art." That statement remains true; it will always remain true: the director will always be the one person in the theater who simply cannot be told what to do. The director must *do*, and in part, must do what has never yet been done. Inheritor of a great theatrical tradition, the director must use it as a springboard for the unexpected: the melding of the theater's elements—time, space, people, fabric, scenic constructs, light, and sound—into a richly satisfying and fundamentally *unique* stage experience. When he or she accomplishes a true marriage of craft and creativity, the director will become a consummate theatrical artist of the first order.

Our thanks to Martha Anne Glantz of the Berliner Theatertreffen for assistance with photographic research, and to the members of the senior acting class, 1982, of the University of California at Santa Barbara, who appear in the workshop photographs.

R.C.
J.H.

ONE

The Directorial Function

What does a director do?

It is commonplace knowledge that directors stage plays; it is also generally recognized that they usually cast them as well, and have a say in the interpretation of the script and the design of the production.

But these are mere aspects of the fundamental directorial function, which is nothing less than to create a theatrical experience; preferably a powerful, witty, exciting, eloquent, hilarious, and/or profound one at that.

Most basically, a director *directs*. That is to say, the director of a play, just like the director of any organization, determines what is to be done, who shall do it, and how. The most important single directorial quality is leadership. The director must initiate, must organize, must arbitrate, and should be able, as well, to command, induce, and inspire. These are the absolutely minimal demands of directing. Without them, the art of directing is no more than textbook theories.

The range of directorial functions varies enormously, depending in part on the medium, the role of the producer, the director's personality, the play, the amount of rehearsal time, and the nature of the artistic and/or commerical challenge. A television director, for example, ordinarily does nothing but stage the action—the actors having been cast long before his or her appointment and the settings fixed for several seasons. On the other hand, the producer-directors of independent companies may find their functions breathtaking in diversity. Louis Jouvet, the great French play director of the era between world wars, took it upon himself, in the productions he directed, to choose the play; collaborate with the author on rewrites; cast the production; hire the actors; interpret the play to the cast; contract for the theater and the rehearsal space; conduct the rehearsals; design the scenery, costumes, and lighting; write the theater program; design the advertisements; and perform the leading role. In other words, he did everything that needed doing—everything that one man can do. Fortunately, we do not all need to have Jouvet's multitalented directorial skills; most directors delegate many of Jouvet's tasks to fellow artists. But the range of directorial functions—that is, of theatrical crafts which must be combined in a theatrical experience and which must be guided by the director—is vast.

THE DIRECTOR IN HISTORY

History has seen a gradually evolving role for the director in the theater. Indeed, the director as an independent theatrical artist did not really appear on the scene until hardly more than a hundred years ago. As the director emerged, through three distinguishable historical periods, the directorial function evolved into its present status as a creative art.

THE PREHISTORY OF
DIRECTING: 5000 B.C.–1850 A.D.

For close to six thousand years of theatrical history—including more than two thousand years of recorded theatrical history—we have almost no knowledge of directing whatsoever. The records of the Greek theater, the Elizabethan theater, and the court theaters of seventeenth-century Europe reveal wonderful plays, some fine actors, but virtually no directors. The staging of plays may have been superb, but no one thought the subject worth writing about; such exceptions as Aeschylus's staging of the entrance of the Furies in his *The Eumenides* (the impact of which caused women to miscarry) is one of the few documented descriptions of a stage effect in those millenia of dramatic grandeur.

Such directing as was performed was ordinarily handled by the playwrights, who would read their manuscripts to the cast, explain any meanings that were unclear, and guide the actors through such movements as the play required. For the most part, such directing would have tended to be quite conventional. Most eras had fixed concepts of staging, scenery, costumes, and properties; lighting effects, in the preincandescent era, were ordinarily nonexistent. Costumes, blocking, and business were generally left up to the actors or to company conventions; in an amusing sketch Molière depicts himself directing his actors to jump up and sit down as they wished, according to their "natural anxiety" in the scene.

Playwrights died, of course, and their plays were restaged by other people; the first independent play directors were probably older or retired stage actors who took charge of the details of staging revivals of the Greek tragedies. These restagings, however, were simply attempts to imitate the original, playwright-staged productions, and there is no record of anything that could be considered reinterpretation or fresh stylization in the prehistory of directing.

The terms used to describe these prehistorical directors show them to be schoolmasters, not artists. The Greek term, *didaskalos,* means "teacher"; the medieval term was *maître de jeu,* or "play master." Teachers and masters, of course, are instructors, and the notion of instruction is that there is something already set that must simply be conveyed to uninitiates. There is no suggestion that the director was expected to make any departure into unknown aesthetic waters or to experiment with theatrical conventions as they then existed. Indeed, the word *unexceptional* turns up as a signal of *praise* in the theatrical criticism of the predirectorial period, implying that something that did not "take exception to" the normal way of doing things was to be highly commended.

It is not to be inferred that directing before the present time was carried out by unimaginative or untalented people. Certainly Shakespeare and Sophocles must have been exciting directors (although it is not known if they ever directed any plays other than their own), and the unlauded directors of the commedia dell'arte must have been inspiring to generations of actors and audiences. But the directors, and their art, remained unremarkable—and they were unremarked upon. The Comédie Française, founded in 1680 shortly after Molière's death, only began to list the director's name in its programs in 1937, indicating the relative recentness of the director's rise from obscurity.

ACTOR–MANAGERS

The precursors of the modern director were a line of actor-managers who dominated the English stage from the time of the Royal Restoration in 1660. English theater had been closed down, and the theaters burned, in 1642 during the Civil War; when they were reopened, in 1660, a whole new generation of actors had come of age. Shakespeare, however, dead for nearly half a century, was much admired, and by the eighteenth century Shakespearean revivals were major theatrical undertakings. At first the actor-managers contented themselves with rewriting the Shakespearean

FIGURE 1. Nineteenth-century staging. Shakespeare's *Henry VIII,* staged by Charles Kean at the Princess Theatre, London, in 1855. Notice the extraordinary attention to historical detail within the formal pictorial composition. (*Crown Copyright Theatre Museum Victoria & Albert Museum*)

plays according to the tempers of the times—and by interpreting the plays as best they saw fit, according to a traditional line. Often, however, they began to call attention to their productions by novel, even shocking, reinterpretations of that line. Charles Macklin, for example, astounded London in 1741 when he reinterpreted Shylock in *The Merchant of Venice* as a sympathetic hero rather than a low comedy buffoon; what Macklin may not have realized is that by doing so he was also reinterpreting the directorial function and breaking new ground on what a director can do with a script.

The next directorial advance of the actor-managers was to create an integrated visual style of production. We should remember that at the time actors could pretty much dress themselves as they wished, and staging[1] was usually a last-minute affair. The actor-managers who first decided to change that tradition did so in the name of a rigid aesthetic: historical authenticity. In the nineteenth century, therefore, English actor-managers like Charles Kean and Samuel Phelps, and the fine American actor-manag-

[1]In her memoirs, Katherine Goodale, who was a juvenile in Edwin Booth's touring Company in 1886, relates that they "rehearsed" *Hamlet, Richlieu,* and *Macbeth* in one day; that supporting actors simply gave their cues to Booth and never practiced their speeches; and that Booth never appeared at rehearsals for a further seven plays they added to the repertory while on tour.

er Edwin Booth, produced glorious Shakespearean revivals dedicated to the accurate protrayal of medieval Denmark, ancient Rome, or Periclean Athens. Whatever one may think about the aesthetic validity of such an effort, it is hard not to admire the great scholarly labors that went into those productions, which were often accompanied by lengthy treatises documenting every costume and property.

Actor-managers, in seeking to create an integrated picture for every moment of the play, assumed an authority over production details previously unknown. Some of them became virtual scholars of the plays they produced; Edwin Booth, in fact, was invited to add several hundred footnotes to the Variorum editions of *Othello* and *The Merchant of Venice* owing to his well-regarded insights into the plays in which he starred. But the actor-managers were, in the end, basically actors, arranging productions primarily as frames around their unique talents. Booth may have contributed to the Variorum *Merchant,* but his own production of that play concluded with his exit (as Shylock) in Act IV; Shakespeare's fifth act was never performed by a Booth company. Moreover, the actual moment-by-moment staging of Booth's production was not in fact handled by Booth,

FIGURE 2.   Nineteenth-century staging. Trial scene from Shakespeare's *A Winter's Tale,* produced by American actor-manager Edwin Booth at Booth's Theatre, New York, in 1871. Elaborate historical realism was achieved by an artful combination of painted figures and live actors. Striking as the scene may have been, it was unoriginal, copied to the letter from Kean's 1856 British production. This was typical of the times.

but by Booth's loyal and obscure stage manager, D. W. Waller, despite Booth's citation as director on the theater program. The actor-managers were precursors of our modern director, but they lacked the overall commitment to the totality of the theatrical production that characterized their successors, the director-managers. It was those latter figures, springing forth in Europe and America in the late 1800s, that brought the directorial art into its present eminence and the directorial function into its present wide-ranging complexity.

DIRECTOR-MANAGERS

The first of the director-managers was George II, Duke of Saxe-Meiningen, in Germany. Beginning in 1866, and aided by his collaborator, Ludwig Chronegk, Saxe-Meiningen revolutionized the principles of staging with his provincial court repertory theater. In the Saxe-Meiningen productions, there were no stars; instead the leading actors rotated their principal roles with bit parts and walk-ons in the company repertoire; it was the company itself which was the "star." The Duke and Chronegk staged their crowd scenes not in the customary rank-and-file fashion two days before opening night but rather with acute attention to every person's individual movement and behavior, coordinated into a synchronized whole. The tradition of historical authenticity ruled the Meiningen productions, but not as mere background for the star performers; instead the Duke's goal was a dynamic harmony of movement involving individuals and well-rehearsed small groups, integrated in complex kinetic patterns. As a court theater, the Duke's company had the luxury of time and budget; six months were often spent rehearsing a play, and great sums were expended on imported (and authentic) fabrics, chain mails, weaponry, and furniture, all toward the goal of a consummate and authoritative theatrical ideal. The results were revolutionary. From their first tour to Berlin in 1874 to the end of their days in 1890, the Meiningen Players presented over 2,500 performances in thirty-eight cities in nine European countries; they were heralded as the leading avant-garde theater in the Western world. Although they broke no new ground in the interpretation of dramatic literature, their success firmly implanted the concept of a director-manager, supervising all aspects of an ensemble production, as the key figure in the theatrical world to come.

The growing predominance of realism in the late nineteenth century was in part an outgrowth of the Meiningen insistence on authenticity—even regarding crowd movements—and in part a new scientific interest in psychology and human behavior. André Antoine and Konstantin Stanislavski, prototype director-managers, were both devotees of the Meiningen techniques and inventive theorists on the subject of acting and

FIGURE 3.   Sketch by the Duke of Saxe-Meiningen for blocking a crowd scene in *Julius Caesar,* about 1870. The dynamic thrust of the crowd pattern was revolutionary.   *(Deutsches Theatermuseum, Früher Clara Ziegler-Stiftung)*

theatrical "reality." Both began, like the Duke, as amateurs and idealists. Antoine, an employee of the Paris Gas Company, created a dramatic circle from among his friends and fellow workers, which soon sprang to attention as the Théâtre Libre, specializing in naturalistic presentations following the principles set forth by novelist Emile Zola. From its beginning in 1887, Antoine's theater demonstrated a commitment to naturalism in acting, playwriting, and design; Antoine even envisioned a permanent repertory company with directorial control over rehearsal conditions, hiring practices, and theater management. The Théâtre Libre occasioned both praise and ridicule; Antoine's actors coughed, snickered, and hiccoughed their way through squalid, life-imitating scripts with varying degrees of effectiveness, and turned their backs on the audience so often that the Libre became known as the "theater of Antoine's back." The staging copied life in every way possible; for a play about butchers, Antoine built a real butcher shop with real sides of beef (which attracted real flies and gave off real smells), a verisimilitude that many considered foolishly (and unnecessarily) extreme. But the range of directorial authority had unquestionably been broadened.

Stanislavski took directing several steps further. In his Moscow Art Theatre (cofounded with Vladimir Nemirovich-Danchenko in 1898), Stanislavski directed plays according to his evolving theories of acting, which demanded that actors "live the life of the character" during the course of performance. Stanislavski's theories and writings on acting are well known and are still considered controversial in some quarters; what is incontestable is that with the celebrated work of the Moscow Art Theatre came the expansion of the director's role into psychological areas—both analytic and interventional. For if the goal of acting is to discover and embody the character within the actor, then the director is obviously both involved with the exploration of the actor's inner thoughts and feelings and engaged in the shaping of those thoughts and feelings into a meaningful and believable performance. The assimilation of the individual actor into a true acting ensemble, which was another of Stanislavski's goals, further expanded the role of the director, in that no single actor could effectively define the nature of the ensemble—that could only be done by an "objective" director standing somewhat apart from the interactions of the acting company.

The realistic director-managers were limited, however, in their creative options. Insofar as realism was their ideal, their process of achieving verisimilitude verged on the scientific rather than the artistic or imaginative. To many theatrical artists around the turn of the century, naturalism was unbearably pedestrian, and countermovements emphasizing poetic expressiveness and abstract stylization quickly came into vogue. These were mainly led by antirealistic director-managers, among them Aurélien-Marie Lugné-Poë (Théâtre de l'Oeuvre), Jacques Rouché (Théâtre des Arts), and

Jacques Copeau (Théâtre du Vieux-Colombier) in France; Vera Kommissarzhevskaya and Vsevelod Meyerhold in Russia; George Fuchs and Max Reinhardt in Germany; and Harley Granville-Barker in England. Two seminal figures in this development were Adolphe Appia and Gordon Craig, both theorists and practitioners at the turn of the century. Appia's discoveries about the potential of incandescent stage lighting, with shadows, dimouts, blackouts, and selective spotlighting, broadened the director's technological palette in ways undreamed of only years previously. And Craig's insistence on directorial discipline created a model of the director as supreme artist which in many places still obtains today. "I have contempt for any man who fails in the whole duty of the stage director," Craig declared, emphasizing that "whole duty" included disregarding the playwright's stage directions, the actor's egos and ambitions, and the designer's traditional prerogatives—all in the service of an overriding directorial control. "Until discipline is understood in a theatre to be willing and reliant obedience to the director," Craig maintained, "no supreme achievement can be accomplished."

Craig and Appia's influential ideas held; the twentieth century has been one of strong directors taking bold, often nonrealistic concepts and shaping play productions around them. It has been a century of the director; certainly Elia Kazan, Jean-Louis Barrault, Peter Brook, Peter Hall, Peter Stein, John Dexter, Joan Littlewood, Tom O'Horgan, Harold Prince, Alan Schneider, and Jerzy Grotowski have had as strong an influence on the contemporary stage as any group of current writers. Nonrealistic director-managers, freed from the confining restraints of naturalism and empowered to create new theatrical forms and unique theatrical experiences, have gone completely beyond the original concept of the director as *didaskalos* and have brought the directorial function into the realm of a creative art.

THE DIRECTOR TODAY

Historically, we are probably in a fourth period in the director's development, for this is an age of freelance directors. Director-managers still exist, of course; William Ball at the American Conservatory Theatre, Trevor Nunn at the Royal Shakespeare Company, and Judith Malina and Julian Beck with the Living Theatre have endured, at this time, more than a decade of company management and artistic control. Still, most notable directors today rotate among assignments with institutional theaters, with commercial dramatic ventures, and sometimes with films. The premium for freelancing directors is flexibility, for the freelancer must work with a wide variety of actors and designers from different "schools" and with varying ideologies and aesthetic understandings. Certainly the freelance artist demands more collaborative skills than did the director-managers of past generations.

The need for collaboration, and for artful, effective collaboration, has never been more important than in the present age. Indeed, Craig's concept of "willing and reliant obedience" is probably an idea whose time has passed; particularly in Eastern Europe, the modern director is now more regarded as the first among equals rather than the all-important artistic dictator. Tyrone Guthrie, the late British director who worked for many years in Canada and the United States, suggests that being a director is somewhat akin to being the chairman of a board—a person who achieves results mainly by suggestion, implication, and subtle inducement rather than by exercise of authority or power.

But the director's role as an imaginative creator has not diminished— it has increased. The freelance director has perhaps the greatest need for originality; as "guest" directors, or directors hired for a single production, they must develop fresh and unique insights for every production; they must distinguish their production with conceptual specificity and superiority in craft. The contemporary theater rewards a directorial identity, a directorial "stamp" that makes clear a director's artistry and creativity— that demonstrates that the director is not merely an interchangeable staff employee but an original theatrical artist with a unique vision. And artistic vision is the fundamental area in which today's directors are judged.

SO WHAT DO DIRECTORS DO?

So what do directors do? Basically, they do what they decide needs doing.

Directors should know how to do *everything* in the theater. They should know the current state of the art in scenery construction, costume design, lighting technology, and makeup technique. They should have at their command the world's dramatic literature and the critical skills that open that literature to penetrating analysis and interpretation. They should know how to hang a light, fix a flat, run a rehearsal, and stage a curtain call. Whether or not they will use all these skills, whether or not they are expert at performing them, they will ultimately be responsible for getting them done, and getting them done properly and imaginatively.

Directors imagine and initiate a theatrical production. They imbue it with a sense of mission, inspiring their coworkers with a sense of ensemble. They focus the disparate production elements into an integrated and meaningful dramatic experience, communicating strong theatrical forces to an audience. They turn the words of a script into stage actions, and through the process of imagination and collaboration, transform the bare space of the theater into a visual and aural construction of aesthetic harmony and intellectual import. Working with time, space, material, and human beings, they create dramatic events. This takes knowledge, skill, creative imagination, and a great deal of interpersonal effectiveness.

The directorial responsibility is to the production, not to the directors themselves. In other words, a director succeeds when the production is brilliant and when the actors and designers reach levels of artistry that they themselves never even thought possible. The director's authority, for the most part, comes not from the employment hierarchy of the theater but from the actors' and designers' and technicians' essential conviction that the production is being well directed. A director must provide leadership for a vast enterprise, sometimes involving fifty or a hundred individuals, people known throughout history to be highly temperamental. Directors work under constant pressure and are always subject to rigid deadlines. They must be able to communicate, delegate, decide, and when necessary dictate in what are often crises. They must be able to bolster, to teach, to protect, to charm, and to inspire their fellow workers, without the overbearing or patronizing attitude that destroys collaborative involvement. And they must be creative. They must direct toward ends that come at least in part from a visionary sense of what the theater *can* do, not just what it has done before. For there is really no such thing as imitative directing. The people are always new, the situations always different. And the director must always work with fresh perspectives toward surprising results.

TWO

Interpreting the Script

It is a common assumption that script interpretation is the director's first responsibility, because all other directorial decisions, such as questions of stage composition, can be answered only in terms of a preformulated interpretation. In practice this is not always true. At times many directors candidly admit that they have no interpretation of the play as they begin rehearsals and none when the play opens, and plays produced in such a manner have occasionally succeeded enormously. Certainly little is needed of conscious (or self-conscious) script interpretation for most dinner theater sex comedies or Scribian farces, for example, since the single object of these plays is to entertain the audience continually.

Yet it is also fair to state that most plays are approached from a directorial interpretation, even if such an interpretation is unarticulated. The director's interpretation is a set of ideas, images, and feelings that express what the director wants the play to communicate to the audience. This set of ideas includes the director's conception of the play's meaning and whatever additional meanings he or she plans to infuse into the production (or burden the production with, depending on his or her success at blending interpretations).

For simplicity, let us divide the director's interpretational function into two categories—*overall interpretation* and *moment-to-moment interpretation*—and into two sources—*instrinsic interpretation* and *extrinsic interpretation*.

OVERALL VERSUS MOMENT-
TO-MOMENT INTERPRETATION

Overall interpretation is the director's concept of the meaning of the entire play. "*Hamlet* is a play about a man who thinks too much"; "*The Three Sisters* is a play about the coming of the Communist revolution"; "*Othello* is a play about Elizabethan racism and homosexuality." These are three controversial overall interpretations which the director might try to convey to the audience through the implementation of the production. Moment-to-moment interpretation is the director's analysis of the beat-by-beat inner action of the play, what is happening at every moment of every scene in each character. Moment-to-moment interpretation is diagrammatic understanding of motivations, objectives, inner monologues, and psychological understandings, even in nonrealistic plays.

Whether overall interpretation is derived from moment-to-moment analysis or vice versa is an open question. Directors often begin production with a firm overall idea and seek to make every moment in the play conform to that overriding interpretation. Conversely they may begin with only a few scenes visualized and work studiously through rehearsals to develop an overall interpretation from the bits of evidence conveyed by those scenes. Most productions noted for highly original interpretation are deductive; that is, the director begins rehearsals with a carefully conceived overall interpretation. Ellis Rabb's *Merchant of Venice* at the American Con-

FIGURE 4.   Ellis Rabb's 1971 production of Shakespeare's *Merchant of Venice* focused on the affections of Antonio (at right, facing forward), thus bringing new values to the familiar play.   (*Photo by Hank Kranzler, courtesy, American Conservatory Theatre*)

servatory Theatre (1971) is a case in point. Rabb decided at the outset that the play concerned a homosexual elitist society in Venice, with Antonio its chief patron and Bassanio a young man opting (with difficulty) for a bourgeois heterosexual marriage. Rabb's interpretation meant that the most dramatic trial scene occurred not in Act IV (the trial of Shylock) but in Act V (the "trial" of Bassanio), thus lending great theatrical impact to the last act of Shakespeare's play, long considered difficult to bring off successfully. It also added new and poignant meanings to many moments in the play, such as Antonio's recantation during Shylock's trial: "I am a tainted wether of the flock, Meetest for death: the weakest kind of fruit . . ." On the other hand, strikingly original interpretations occasionally call attention to themselves and away from the excellence of the script and the actors' performances. A traditional interpretation has usually become traditional because it receives little resistance from the text; productions celebrated for their naturalism and fine acting usually result from a greater emphasis on moment-to-moment script interpretation than from a strikingly original overall concept. But there is no reason why this is necessarily the case.

INTRINSIC VERSUS EXTRINSIC INTERPRETATION

The directors' two basic sources of interpretative decisions are the text and themselves. The extent to which they use the one rather than the other determines whether their interpretation is basically intrinsic or extrinsic.

Intrinsic interpretation comes precisely from the text and from materials that illuminate the text. Such materials include explanatory remarks by the author, critical remarks about the author and the play, biographical and historical data, and material concerning the play's critical and theatrical history. Intrinsic interpretation seeks to re-create the playwright's world and the play as a part of that world.

Extrinsic interpretation comes from the world of the director and the world of the audience. Whereas intrinsic interpretation attempts to define precisely what the play "means," extrinsic interpretation involves what, in the present production, the director wishes the play to "say." For that reason, extrinsic interpretation is often considered "reinterpretation" or "updating."

We need not justify extrinsic interpretation on the basis that the author really intended these meanings; the script is simply deep and elastic enough both to suggest and to permit them. For example, *Othello* has been produced with implications of American racism, *Hamlet* with a bow to Freudian (Oedipal) theories, and *King Lear* as a paean to existential alienation; such productions can be justified by their dramatic vitality but not by their exact replication of the author's original intentions. Because of their frequent production and consequent overfamiliarity, and their profundity and universality, classics are obviously most subject to extrinsic interpretation.

Critics and even directors frequently assail extrinsic interpretation. The generation of directors after Jacques Copeau followed his maxim *le texte seul compte* ("only the text counts"); thus our generation of directors was preceded by one which asserted that the director's sole function was to elucidate the pure meaning of the text as created by its author. To be sure, Copeau's maxim was honored more in the breach than in stage practice, as any examination of his production books shows, but the maxim remains in theoretical service to this day. It is unrealistic theory, however. Director Peter Brook says, "When I hear a director speaking glibly of letting a play speak for itself, my suspicions are aroused, because this is the hardest job of all. If you just let a play speak, it may not make a sound. If what you want is for the play to be heard, then you must conjure its sound from it."[1]

"RIGHT" VERSUS "VITAL" INTERPRETATION

The transition from intrinsic to extrinsic interpretation, from the director's finding what the playwright "meant" to expressing what the play "says," is largely unconscious, crossing an undefinable line at a hidden point. Certainly we have reached an existential age in which there is no such thing as a right or wrong interpretation. Of course, there are historically correct interpretations, such as the D'Oyly Carte presentations of Gilbert and Sullivan operettas which have been produced intact since their original premieres in the last century; and there are productions which are authorized or certified by the playwright, and even directed by him or her, which have some claim to "correctness." But the vitality of the theater depends on the fact that as times and people change, attitudes do also, and play productions must adjust to those changes if genuine communication is to occur. Because *The Trojan Women, A Midsummer Night's Dream, Hamlet,* and *King Lear* permit reinterpretation throughout the centuries, their impact is as immediate today as it was when they were written.

No director—and no critic, for that matter—can "see" a play exactly as the author intended; directors or critics who assume that they can are guilty of an arrogant lack of perspective. The exactly "correct" production never existed: our perception is limited by restrictions on our imagination and ability to determine the author's intent, and altered by the ideas and imaginative leaps of our sensory apparatus and intelligence. A Hindu para-

---

[1]*The Empty Space: A Book About Theater—Deadly, Holy, Rough, Immediate* (New York: Atheneum Publishers, 1968), p. 25.

FIGURE 5. Benno Besson's production of Shakespeare's *As You Like It* for the avant-garde Théâtre de L'Est Parisien (France) in 1976 was an athletic romp on airbags under a canvas tent. Shakespeare's works, because of their universality, have particularly lent themselves to extrinsic interpretations and "concept productions" in this century. (*French Cultural Services*)

ble tells of eight blind men who felt and then described an elephant. The first felt the tail and exclaimed that an elephant was like a rope; the second felt the animal's hide and insisted that an elephant was like a wall; and so on. In the same way, reality appears different to different people. No single view is exclusively "correct," not even the author's.

The director's aim, then, is a vital interpretation, rather than a "correct" one. Tyrone Guthrie said

> An interpretive artist can only make his own comment upon the work which he endeavors to interpret, and . . . to do so humbly is the only possible attitude to the "creator" (or, more truly, the expressor) of the "original" idea. Throughout my own career I have been criticized for impertinently attempting to express my own subjective, and admittedly limited, comment upon the masterpieces which I have been privileged to direct. I consider such criticism misplaced. I know perfectly well that my comment upon *Oedipus Rex, Hamlet* or *All's Well That Ends Well* is not the final, any more than it is the first, interpretation of these works. My collaborators and I have merely added one more comment to the vast corpus of criticism, admiration, revulsion, rever-

FIGURE 6. A scene from Manfred Karge and Matthias Langhoff's 1982 production of Anton Chekhov's *The Cherry Orchard* at the Schauspielhaus Bochum, one of Germany's most innovative theaters. Chekhovian realism, no less than Shakespearean verse drama, can be interpreted very freely by creative direction. (*Pressbüro, Berliner Theatertreffen*)

ence, love, and so on, with which a masterpiece of human expression is rightly surrounded.[2]

This situation should not alarm the dramatic author. Theater is a collaborative art, most vital when that collaboration is healthy and flexible. Nowhere is there more potential for greatness than in the director-author relationship, even when the author is no longer alive. Some author-director combinations have produced dynamic fusions of talent, such as the long-lasting partnerships of Tennessee Williams and Elia Kazan, Lanford Wilson and Marshall Mason, Harold Pinter and Peter Hall, Jean Giraudoux and Louis Jouvet, Paul Claudel and Jean-Louis Barrault, and Anton Chekhov and Konstantin Stanislavski. Such collaboration, even if stormy, can be a factor in scaling the greatest heights to which the theatrical artist can aspire.

[2]Tyrone Guthrie, *A Life in the Theatre* (New York: McGraw-Hill Book Company, © 1959), p. 139. Reproduced with permission.

MORAL IMPERATIVES
IN THE DIRECTOR-AUTHOR
RELATIONSHIP

Interpretation always comes from both intrinsic and extrinsic sources, that is, from the play and from the director. The ideal is the best of both, the worst of neither. The director is neither an automaton who helps the author technically transform the play from page to stage nor a tyrant who arbitrarily hacks the play to pieces in the act of creating his or her own.

In collaboration with living authors, the director must be guided by ethical considerations. The Dramatist's Guild, which is involved in all contracts for new plays being professionally produced, insists that the author have veto power over the selection of the director and the right to insist on or veto script changes. Beyond the law, a director should treat the playwright as a collaborative artist (presumably the most important one) on the production team.

However, the artistic director of the production has the right to interpret the play as he or she chooses, even if the playwright screams, the actors curse, the producer cuts the budget, and the critics yelp like mad dogs. The theater today seeks vision, vitality, and excitement, and the director has been elected to elicit them. If playwrights want a production of absolute fidelity, they can direct it themselves; Arthur Miller took over the direction of his play *The Price* partly for this reason. The final criterion for measuring interpretation is that it make a production work, engendering what we recall (or fantasize) about a great theatrical experience: catharsis, empathy, understanding, astonishment, hilarity, awe—feelings that can be powerfully communicated from the stage to the audience. If a play works, no one will complain about the director's reinterpretation of the text; if it fails to work, no amount of critical commentary by the director in the program note can persuade the audience not to remain indifferent. Propriety and nicety have never been very helpful in theatrical interpretation. They certainly are not now.

INTRINSIC INTERPRETATION,
MOMENT TO MOMENT

Although no firm line separates intrinsic and extrinsic interpretation, it is clear that the director can analyze either intrinsically or extrinsically; that is, the play can be approached from these two vantages (not necessarily simultaneously) with an eye toward their coalescing in the final interpretation. Ordinarily the director begins by thinking intrinsically, because only when there is a firm grasp on the play's intrinsic moment-to-moment action and overall theme can he seriously begin to apply externally derived interpretive ideas. (For example, it would be impossible for a director to decide to produce a Marxist *Hamlet* if he had not read the play.) We will follow the director's normal method of organizing sources of information to arrive at an interpretation.

Study of the Text

A first quick reading of any play reveals only a fraction of the action occurring within it. Even in a simple play the inner action is complex; the changing interrelationships of characters and situations are found only through several readings, each from a somewhat different point of view. The directors' familiarity with the inner action, which is ordinarily at the heart of their overall interpretation, must be developed in painstaking detail. This is easily overlooked. Examine, for example, the opening scene in *Hamlet* (I. i. 1–15).

Enter Bernardo and Francisco, two sentinels.

BERNARDO.   Who's there?
FRANCISCO.   Nay, answer me: stand, and unfold yourself.
BERNARDO.   Long live the King!
FRANCISCO.   Bernardo?
BERNARDO.   He.
FRANCISCO.   You come most carefully upon your hour.
BERNARDO.   'Tis now struck twelve; get thee to bed, Francisco.
FRANCISCO.   For this relief much thanks; 'tis bitter cold,
                       And I am sick at heart.
BERNARDO.   Have you had quiet guard?
FRANCISCO.   Not a mouse stirring.
BERNARDO.   Well, good night.
                       If you do meet Horatio and Marcellus,
                       The rivals of my watch, bid them make haste.
FRANCISCO.   I think I hear them. Stand, ho! Who is there?

The scene looks simple, but appearance is deceptive. We recognize that Bernardo is replacing Francisco at the sentry post, that Francisco has had a quiet guard, and that others are coming, but there is much more to the scene. Follow the example of scene interpretation closely to see the level of detail which must be pursued.

"Enter Bernardo and Francisco." Shakespeare (or the editor) fails to say from where the characters enter, but it is obvious that they do not enter at the same time or place. In a modern production, with lights and/or a curtain, Francisco can be "discovered" at the rise of the curtain. Nor need the dialogue or Bernardo's entrance follow immediately. The director may wish to indicate mood, time, action, or character by inventing business for Francisco as he awaits his replacement. Francisco might be pacing out his

sentry duty, sleeping against a post, warming his hands against a fire, reading a book, even relieving himself behind the battlements.

"BERNARDO. Who's there?" This is a highly uncharacteristic line which must be carefully interpreted. Ordinarily the on-duty guard challenges the newcomer, not vice versa. A few lines later Francisco does his job correctly, hearing Horatio approach and challenging him immediately. But here Francisco apparently does not hear Bernardo before he arrives on stage. Moreover, Bernardo's question is unusual: he knows he is to replace Francisco at this place and time and would ordinarily have no doubts as to whom he was seeing.

Uncharacteristic dialogue should alert directors that a between-the-lines explanation is needed; in interpreting a moment in a play they must not only find out what is happening but also what is *not* happening, why a character says something unexpected. A possible interpretation and staging of Bernardo's opening line follows.

> Bernardo, arriving alone for guard duty, is aware of the possibility of the ghost's appearance and is therefore in a highly alert and frightened state. Francisco, on the other hand, has not been told of the ghost's appearance the previous night. (Later in the play it becomes clear that only Horatio, Marcellus, and Bernardo know of the ghost, and Francisco does not reappear in the play after this scene). Francisco is therefore carrying out his guard duty perfunctorily. At the end of his long tour at the sentry position he is sitting against the battlement wall, huddled in his blanket, tending a fire. Bernardo, tiptoeing to his post, does not see Francisco at first, and Francisco is so enclosed by his blanket that he does not hear Bernardo. Suddenly Francisco rises to poke the fire. Bernardo sees the blanket move and in his agitated state is alarmed at the prospect of seeing a ghost. He nervously cries, "Who's there?"

"FRANCISCO. Nay, answer me: stand and unfold yourself." This should have been Francisco's immediate response: to challenge the arriving guard. He is embarrassed at having been caught derelict in his duty and speaks brusquely to cover his embarrassment.

"BERNARDO. Long live the King." Possibly a prearranged password, although Horatio does not use it later. Bernardo must recover his composure quickly, or Francisco will think something is the matter. Bernardo, it is now understood, wishes to prevent Francisco from knowing about the ghost of Hamlet's father.

"FRANCISCO. Bernardo?" This confirms Bernardo's earlier uncharacteristic behavior. Since he was expected, and since he comes "most carefully upon his hour," Francisco should ordinarily be expected to recognize him immediately, without further questioning. That he does not reflects his puzzlement at Bernardo's original alarm.

"BERNARDO. He." Bernardo confirms his identity, probably with a gesture, handshake, or embrace.

"BERNARDO. 'Tis now struck twelve; get thee to bed, Francisco." The first of three subtle and not so subtle admonitions that Francisco leave before the ghost arrives. That it is twelve the director might wish to confirm by the tolling of a bell in the distance.

"FRANCISCO. For this relief much thanks; 'tis bitter cold and I am sick at heart." An atmospheric line which is all the more poignant when we realize that Francisco knows nothing of the ghost and senses a dread presence merely from the air itself. The line also establishes the physical cold of the surroundings, which the director could confirm by stage business.

"BERNARDO. Have you had quiet guard?" Bernardo is fishing for information without revealing what he knows. Had Francisco known about the ghost, Bernardo would probably have asked him, "Has this thing appeared again tonight?"—which Marcellus asks Bernardo a few moments later. But Bernardo asks a neutral, nonrevealing question and receives a neutral answer: "Not a mouse stirring." Again, we can discover what is happening by examining what is *not* happening.

"BERNARDO. Well, good night." The second admonition for Francisco to leave, perhaps uttered more directly. Why is Francisco lingering? Perhaps to gather up his blanket and other accouterments.

"BERNARDO. If you do meet Horatio and Marcellus/The rivals of my watch, bid them make haste." Bernardo does not want to be left alone with a ghost nearby. Francisco has just served his tour alone, and Bernardo's concern for his companions can be justified only by the particulars of the situation.

"FRANCISCO. I think I hear them. Stand, ho! Who is there?" Francisco calls out as he should, demonstrating that his original behavior toward Bernardo derived from unusual circumstances.

Our interpretation of the first fifteen lines of *Hamlet* is intrinsic— deduced from the lines of the play rather than from any external theory. However, the interpretation is neither exhaustive nor unarguable. Directors with different insights would discover inner actions not suggested, even contradictory to the preceding analysis. Even if our interpretation were followed explicitly, there would be countless ways of implementing it. The point is that the inner action must be studied with extraordinary attention to detail. If the actors performed the opening lines without considering the questions raised by this discussion, the play would open flatly and without definition. True, it is not absolutely vital that the members of the audience involve themselves in whether Bernardo is acting strangely or whether Francisco has been let in on the ghost's appearance; unless they are very familiar with the play they will not even know that they have missed anything by not answering these questions. But without close interpretation and performance, the scene will lack texture, meaning, and definition. And obviously, if that is true of the first fifteen lines of *Hamlet,* it is true of the rest of *Hamlet* and of every other play besides.

Finding the Inner Action

The examination of the text for inner action, or subtext, involves probing the intentions, motivations, and inner monologue of each character during the scene in question. Even a thousand readings by the director could not explain every moment of every character's performance; that is why much moment-to-moment interpretation occurs not in the director's study but in rehearsal. The actor's task is to present a consistent and thoughtful characterization that makes sense to him (the character/actor). Francisco can hardly memorize his lines without wondering how much he is supposed to know about the ghost. Good actors will spend a great deal of time questioning their character's behavior. Directors aid their actors' work in this matter by being ready to answer and initiate questions. "Why are you doing this? What are you thinking about now? What do you want from him?" are the kinds of questions directors frequently ask during rehearsal. The director may not have a ready answer but trusts the actor to come up with something, perhaps through discussion. The important thing is that questions are asked.

Moment-to-moment interpretation takes time. Stanislavski rehearsed plays for over a thousand hours at his Moscow Art Theatre—about eight hours per playing minute—and much if not most of that time was discussion of intentions and motivations. Directors who brag that they can "bring in" a production with just fifty or sixty hours of rehearsal probably "see" only about 5 percent of the subtext of the play. They may win plaudits in the hinterlands, but their work usually dissolves if exposed to intense critical analysis.

DRAMATURGICAL ANALYSIS

Moment-to-moment analysis is not simply an accumulation of unrelated events. Plays are carefully organized presentations of experiences, and the technical name for that organization is *dramaturgy,* the art of dramatic composition. Dramaturgy is the process by which a playwright presents a series of acts, inner actions, revelations, changes in attitude, and thought processes so as to create climaxes and reliefs. In this, the theater differs markedly from everyday life. Arguments in real life are irregular and sporadic; rarely do they rationally come to a satisfying climax. Theater, even in our existential world, rarely permits that sort of frustrating experience. The elements of dramaturgy are usually present in every scene of a play: exposition, inciting action, rising action, climax, and resolution.

Exposition is the introduction or exposure of relevant material. The audience is informed about the individuals who will soon experience a conflict. They are also informed, ordinarily, of the prior conditions which bear on the conflict.

Inciting action is the introduction of a source of conflict among the characters or within a single character. In melodrama, a pure dramaturgical art, the classic inciting action is the detective's entrance to assert, "Dr. Jones did not commit suicide, he was murdered. And someone in this room is the murderer."

Rising action is the detailed struggle of the characters to overcome the conflict. The conflict cannot be easily overcome, and frustration, rage, and fear may grow. The source of conflict becomes more insistently irritating, and the characters grow more desperate to rid themselves of the irritant.

Climax is the identification and exorcism of the irritant through violence, argument, hilarity, or some other means. In melodrama the detective discovers the murderer and kills him or her in a shoot-out. In Aristotelian terms the climax of a tragedy is said to provoke in the audience a *catharsis,* a purging of the emotions and an enlightening of the spirit.

Resolution is the reestablishment of the sense of order and calm that existed before the inciting action. In many Shakespearean tragedies, for example, the last lines are spoken not by the principal characters but by fairly neutral characters whose speeches set the house back in order—a new order, not a reversion to the old one.

Directorial interpretation uses the dramaturgical devices throughout a production, by the moment-to-moment clarification of conflict and inciting actions, the sensitive projection of subtext during rising action, and the induction of catharsis during a well-wrought climax and resolution. Let us examine the opening scene (after a monologue) from Tennessee Williams's modern classic, *The Glass Menagerie.*[3]

> *(Amanda and Laura are seated at a drop leaf table.)*
> AMANDA *(calling).* Tom?
> TOM. Yes, Mother.
> AMANDA. We can't say grace until you come to the table!
> TOM. Coming, mother. *(He . . . takes his place at the table.)*
> AMANDA *(to her son).* Honey, don't *push* with your *fingers.* If you have to push with something, the thing to push with is a crust of bread. And chew—chew! Animals have secretions in their stomachs which enable them to digest food without mastication, but humans beings are supposed to chew their food before they swallow it down. Eat food leisurely, son, and really enjoy it. A well-cooked meal has lots of delicate flavors that have to be held in the mouth for appreciation. So chew your food and give your salivary glands a chance to function!
> *(Tom deliberately lays his . . . fork down and pushes his chair back from the table.)*
> TOM. I haven't enjoyed one bite of this dinner because of your constant directions on how to eat it. It's you that makes me rush through meals with your hawk-like attention to every bite I take. Sickening—spoils my appetite,—all this discussion of animals' secretion—salivary glands—mastication!

[3]Reprinted from Tennessee Williams, *The Glass Menagerie,* © Random House, Inc., by permission of the publisher.

AMANDA (*lightly*). Temperament like a Metropolitan star? (*He rises and crosses downstage.*) You're not excused from the table.
TOM. I'm getting a cigarette.
AMANDA. You smoke too much.
(*Laura rises.*)
LAURA. I'll bring in the blanc mange.

This short scene contains all the classical dramaturgical attributes of a longer play. The exposition, aside from Tom's opening monologue before this scene, is clear simply from the exchange in the first two lines, in which Amanda names Tom, and he replies to her as "Mother," revealing the essential characteristic of their relationship, which is to be explored. The inciting action is twofold: Amanda chides Tom for not coming to the table and for his unrefined eating habits. The situation is not unusual; the audience can respond to the introduction of an obvious irritant in the mother-son relationship.

In the rising action both Amanda and Tom try to justify their points of view, Amanda begging Tom to eat leisurely to better enjoy his meal, Tom begging to be left alone to eat as he wants. Yet we understand from this simple exchange that Amanda is really disturbed at far deeper aspects of Tom's personality than his eating habits; her harping shows us her insistence on babying a grown-up son and her refusal to see the new reality which threatens to engulf her. Tom is irritated not so much at his mother's specific remarks but at his inability to counter them successfully. His frustration intensifies her anxiety, and her anxiety intensifies his frustration, causing a spiraling buildup of dynamic energy that demands release.

The climax of this scenelet is modest: Tom leaves the table without finishing his dinner and lights a cigarette. Amanda's "You smoke too much" is a climactic line which really means "You are not what I had hoped for in a son." The minor climax of this scene prefigures more unrestrained ones to follow; this climax delays the dramaturgical process, allowing the rising action to begin again and again and again until the final climax of the play is achieved. The resolution of this scene is also specific: Laura rises to bring in the blanc mange (the very name of the dessert connotes a cooling off), reestablishing the illusion of harmony which existed before the inciting action occurred. The resolution, like the climax, is not complete, and this is a pattern for scenes and subscenes during the course of the moment-to-moment interpretation. If every scene ended with Oedipus gouging out his eyes, the theater would become very boring.

There is nothing arbitrary about the ordinary dramaturgical process; neither is it restricted to plays. A bullfight follows much the same pattern, with exposition (the procession), inciting action (entrance of the bull), rising action (series of passes, each closer than the last), climax (killing the bull), and resolution (ridding the arena of the bull's carcass and cheers for the matador). Perhaps the dramaturgical process imitates the act of sexual congress, which has been described by modern physiologists as consisting of inciting action (erotic stimulation), rising levels of action (plateaus of excitement), climax (climax, or orgasm), and resolution (detumescence).

The director uses dramaturgical principles by examining his script for incitements to action, climaxes, and resolutions. He examines the rising action to discover at what points the argument climaxes: where Tom feels like continuing his line of reasoning and where he decides to peak and cut it off. He recognizes Amanda's "You smoke too much" as a climactic line and directs the actors accordingly. He analyzes Laura's "I'll bring in the blanc mange" as a premature attempt at resolution. A play that produces an integrated series of incitements, rising actions, climaxes, and resolutions becomes a meaningful communicative experience. One that simply presents the audience with a series of arbitrarily organized phenomena is as dense as a treatise written in a foreign language.

BREAKDOWN OF THE SCRIPT

A play is made up of hundreds of "scenelets," like the one between Tom and Amanda which we have just read, and one of the director's first duties is to break the script down into its constituent elements in order to develop and structure the pieces of mosaic that will comprise the final production.

Most plays are already divided into acts, with intermissions presumably separating each act; additionally many acts are divided into scenes, denoting a brief pause in the action for scene changes or indication of a lapse of time. The designations which the director and actors will make are more subtle:

1. *French scenes,* which begin with the entrance or exit of a character;
2. *Action units,* which are the reasonably complete (although ordinarily inconclusive) interactions between characters; and
3. *Beats,* which are the smallest units of meaning that can be clearly communicated to an audience. The *Glass Menagerie* scenelet, for example, is a French scene (as it begins with Tom's entrance and ends with Laura's exit). It can be construed as having three action units: the first where Amanda calls Tom to the table, the second where she lectures him on chewing, and the third where he argues with her—and she with him—about how each other should behave. Each action unit is filled with beats, such as Tom laying his fork down "deliberately" and Laura's rising; beats are contained in stage movements and "significant" glances as much as in dialogue.

The division of a play into French scenes has immediate practical value in that these are also rehearsal scenes; actors can be called just for those French scenes in which they appear and can have time off during the rehearsal of other French scenes to go off and work on their lines or have a cup of coffee. Additionally, the French scenes make clear an underlying structure of relationships which constitute a play's dramaturgical architecture. Examine, for example, the characters in the French scenes in Shakespeare's *Macbeth,* up through the scene of Duncan's murder (for reference, the Folio act and scene divisions are given in parentheses):

1. (I. i) Three witches
2. (I. ii) Duncan, Malcolm, Donalbain, Lennox, Captain
3. (I. ii) Duncan, Malcolm, Donalbain, Lennox, Ross, Angus
4. (I. iii) Three Witches
5. (I. iii) Three Witches, Macbeth, Banquo
6. (I. iii) Macbeth, Banquo
7. (I. iii) Macbeth, Banquo, Ross, Angus
8. (I. iv) Duncan, Malcolm, Donalbain, Lennox
9. (I. iv) Macbeth, Banquo, Duncan, Malcolm, Donalbain, Lennox, Ross, Angus
10. (I. v) Lady Macbeth
11. (I. v) Lady Macbeth, Messenger
12. (I. v) Lady Macbeth
13. (I. v) Lady Macbeth, Macbeth
14. (I. vi) Duncan, Malcolm, Donalbain, Banquo, Lennox, Macduff, Ross, Angus
15. (I. vi) Duncan, Malcolm, Donalbain, Banquo, Lennox, Macduff, Ross, Angus, Lady Macbeth
16. (I. vii) Sewer and Servants
17. (I. vii) Macbeth
18. (I. vii) Macbeth, Lady Macbeth
19. (II. i) Banquo, Fleance
20. (II. i) Banquo, Fleance, Macbeth, Servant
21. (II. i) Macbeth, Servant
22. (II. i) Macbeth
23. (II. ii) Lady Macbeth
24. (II. ii) Lady Macbeth, Macbeth
25. (II. ii) Macbeth
26. (II. ii) Macbeth, Lady Macbeth
27. (II. iii) Porter
28. (II. iii) Porter, Macduff, Lennox
29. (II. iii) Macduff, Lennox, Macbeth, Porter*
30. (II. iii) Lennox, Macbeth, Porter
31. (II. iii) Macbeth, Macduff, Lennox, Porter
32. (II. iii) Macduff, Porter
33. (II. iii) Macduff, Porter, Lady Macbeth
34. (II. iii) Macduff, Lady Macbeth, Banquo, Porter

*From the moment of Macbeth's entrance in French scene 29, the Porter has no further lines, nor is he mentioned. Most likely, he rings the bell at Macduff's urging in French scene 32; possibly he remains onstage through French scene 37, depending on whether the bell rope is on or off stage. Nonspeaking attendants have been omitted from this list.

35. (II. iii) Macduff, Lady Macbeth, Banquo, Macbeth, Lennox, Porter
36. (II. iii) Macbeth, Lady Macbeth, Macduff, Banquo, Lennox, Malcolm, Donalbain, Porter
37. (II. iii) Macbeth, Macduff, Banquo, Lennox, Malcolm, Donalbain, Porter
38. (II. iii) Malcolm, Donalbain

Notice how the arrangement of French scenes brings Macbeth and Lady Macbeth together alone onstage four times in these first two acts; no other twosome shares the stage alone more than once. Also note Macbeth's pairing with Banquo in the early scenes, and with his wife in the later ones, indicating his shifting allegiance. The twelve French scenes in II. iii indicate the rapid comings and goings as King Duncan's assassination is revealed; Shakespeare's gradual adding of characters to the stage results in a full stage climax at French scenes 36 and 37, followed by the quiet plotting of Malcolm and Donalbain who are left alone onstage at French scene 38 for the first time, given a chance to set in motion the new events which will result in the play's final climax three acts later.

Armed with the French scene breakdown, the director's interpretive job becomes immediately focused. If there are four scenes between Macbeth and his lady before the assassination, what is the importance of each one? What is *different* about each one? Why did Shakespeare write four scenes instead of one? What do the characters learn *between* the scenes to make their situation change? What do *we* need to find out in each scene? Where do the soliloquies fit in the scheme of the play? How do they advance the plot? How do they qualify the developing relationships? Which are the "big" scenes in terms of the number of characters onstage? What lines of action do they develop? What actions do they bring to a head? What is going to be the impact of a soliloquy by a character not previously introduced (the Porter in French Scene 27)?

The French scene breakdown is an essential starting point for the directorial blueprint, and most directors work out such a breakdown at a very early stage in their preparation and conception process. Often directors choose to give each French scene a title (for example, "The murder" or "Macbeth's letter") sometimes the "title" is simply a key line in the scene (for example, "If it were done when 'tis done . . ."). The use of titles can help a director keep the overall focus of a French scene in view, and this can be particularly useful in the heat of rehearsals when discussions and decisions tend to resolve about finer and finer points—to the extent that larger issues of plot and character can be overlooked.

The action units of a play are less easily pinned down, insofar as every director (and actor) will have his or her own scale of determining what actions are reasonably complete. Normally, an action unit is a single dramatic event, something that can be summarized in a sentence, for example, "Lady Macbeth reads her husband's letter"; "Lady Macbeth resolves that her husband shall be king"; "Lady Macbeth worries that her husband is too full of the milk of human kindness"; "Lady Macbeth rehearses arguments to give him courage"; "Lady Macbeth, as if speaking to her husband, urges him to come home and listen to her." These five summarizable action units are all contained in French scene 10, Lady Macbeth's first soliloquy. Clearly, the soliloquy could be divided in other ways equally well; this division, however, provides the director and actor with a logical internal order of actions that will give the speech structure and theatrical meaning. Notice that the action units are expressed in terms of the characters' objectives: Lady Macbeth reads; she then resolves to act; she then debates with herself; she then rehearses what she will say; she finally urges the fates to deliver her husband home. This is mainly inner action, of course, and for that reason structure is particularly crucial to prevent a feeling of mere random talking and rambling monologue. The theater is an arena of actions, and it is the pattern of those actions, ultimately, that produces dramatic meaning; the breakdown of action into action units, therefore, is an essential step in articulating that pattern theatrically.

Action units, like French scenes, may be given "titles" in order to create clear distinct integers of dramatic meaning; or they can simply be identified by their one-sentence summarization. Very few directors will try to do this on paper for an entire play, for the process would be unnecessarily cumbersome, but they generally define action units by notations in the production script and through discussions with actors, particularly in key scenes. It certainly should be done—and done on paper—when student directors begin presenting scenes in class, for it lends crucial definition to scenes not otherwise given the context of scenery, costume, and surrounding scenes of the play itself. The essential aspect of a breakdown into action units is that each unit has a specificity and an identity, that each is distinct from the units that surround it. In linear plays, the units generally lead to the development of plot and "learning" of characters; in abstract, nonlinear plays, the units form patterns which are often more aesthetically whole than informational; still, the distinction of individual action units creates a sense of temporal structure which is essential in the theater. The structure of action units gives the sense of a receding past and an impending future, and it pulls the audience into and along with the course of the play, making even the relative inaction of a *Waiting for Godot* ("Nothing happens, nobody comes, nobody goes . . ." says one of the characters) a complex series of dramatic events that creates true activity, even if circular and finally inconclusive.

The breakdown of an action unit into separate beats is almost never done by a director in comprehensive fashion, for this is basically the actor's job. The director comes into the designation of beats only at key moments—where they are not being articulated in rehearsal or where the director wishes to create, on a beat-by-beat basis, a specific action that the actor would not be expected to play otherwise. "I want a pause here where you think about what to say next," a director might request of an actor: this is to introduce a beat of indecision that is neither indicated nor proscribed by the text. "Look at her before continuing," is a directorial instruction to add a beat in a scene, showing that the speaking actor is, perhaps, encouraged to continue because of the behavior of another character. There are literally thousands of beats in a play, perhaps thousands of beats in a good scene. Each beat conveys information—about plot, about character—and these simple informational units form, in composite, the incredibly complex rhythms and harmonies of scene development. In a well-developed play, slow beats alternate with fast ones, quiet ones with loud ones, subtle ones with bold ones. Great actors, of course, are capable of articulating a higher quantity of discrete beats per scene than beginners; the capability of a John Gielgud, for example, in virtually "packing" meaning into a Shakespearean soliloquy, is an astonishing display of virtuosity that no director can simply will into the production without casting Gielgud himself.

The breakdown of the script, at its three distinct levels, is a critical phase of the interpretive function, for it is precisely the way the various French scenes, action units, and beats are defined that will, in the end, determine the overall meaning of the production; moreover, it is the way that these scenes, units, and beats are integrated that will determine the play's rhythms, its sense of momentousness (its sense that something important is about to happen), and its dramaturgical impact. Once broken down, a play must be put back together. The broken-down elements must be seen, not as autonomous pieces of theater or static, "pure" elements of a mosaic, but as dynamic and ultimately harmonious integers of a dramatic whole, the architectural skeleton of a fully fleshed-out play. Each unit must be seen as springing from the one before, and leading, perhaps inevitably, to the next; until the final beat, every constituent "broken-down" unit of a play is a springboard to further action and further theatrical impact.

OUTSIDE RESOURCES FOR STUDY

Directors often need resources in addition to their intellect and imagination to understand the intrinsic meanings of a text. This is particularly true of noncontemporary and foreign plays, but even a local, contemporary playwright may use allusions and references unknown to the director or anyone else on the production staff. Difficulties in intrinsic interpretation call for the use of external resources, many of which are easily available.

Dictionaries

Obviously the director must know the meaning of every word in the play. Most modern American plays present little problem, at least to a modern American director, but in foreign plays or revivals, words can frequently be a stumbling block. The plays of Shakespeare, for example, are filled with words that have no present meaning or whose present meanings differ from the ones Shakespeare intended. Most editions of Shakespeare include footnotes and/or glossaries that give the sixteenth-century meaning of disputed words, but even these footnotes may be open to question. A helpful resource for the complete understanding of old English words is the *Oxford English Dictionary*, which not only defines every word in the English language but also gives the entire history of each word, tracing its usage from earliest times through Shakespeare's to our own.

One common misconception of a Shakespearean line is Juliet's famous plaint, "Romeo, Romeo, wherefore art thou Romeo?" Incredibly, this line is frequently read with *wherefore* misapprehended as *where*, so that countless young actresses have leaned over the balcony crying, "Wherefore *art* thou Romeo?" as though they were calling a dog home for dinner. Of course, *wherefore* meant (and means, although the word is now generally obsolete) *why*, not *where*, and the line should be read "Wherefore art thou *Romeo*?" Occasionally Shakespeare uses a word that is found absolutely nowhere else, such as *exsufflicate*, in *Othello*, and a meaning must be imaginatively attributed, either through etymological research or analysis of context.

Variant Editions

Older plays often present the problem of differing versions. Most plays in the Shakespearean canon were printed in Quarto editions as well as in the First Folio, and in many cases variant readings exist which editors have tried to collate into an "official" text. One famous variation is Hamlet's line, "Oh that this too too solid flesh should melt," which in two of the three printed versions of the play reads "sallied flesh." To compound the problem, editors throughout the years not only have chosen among variant readings but also have often suggested their own on the grounds that all printings are wrong; one such emendation of the word in question is "sullied flesh." Obviously the interpretation of this key speech will differ, depending on whether Hamlet complains about his "sullied," "solid," or "sallied" flesh. Directors must be careful in selecting edition and editor, if they do not enter the field of Shakespearean bibliography themselves.

From time to time the words of modern plays also need outside elucidation. A production of William Saroyan's *The Time of Your Life* was foundering during rehearsal of a scene in which characters spoke of going "down to the Sunset," until someone explained to the East Coast director that "the Sunset" is a district in San Francisco, the locale of the play. References in the plays of Sean O'Casey and Brendan Behan are unintelligible unless Easter Week and the IRA are explained to the cast. Highly poetic plays like those of T. S. Eliot and Samuel Beckett frequently require the use of dictionaries and encyclopedias if the director is to understand even the surface meaning of the lines. Among the insults Vladimir and Estragon hurl at each other in *Waiting for Godot* are such epithets as *morpion, curate, gonococchus, spirochete,* and *cretin.* In the same play, Lucky speaks of "a personal god, quaquaquaqua, with divine apathia, divine athambia, divine aphasia. . . ." Unless the director's vocabulary equals Beckett's, he or she will have to look up these words and fit their meanings into the context of the play.

Translations

In directing translated plays, directors can usually choose from several scripts, translate the play themselves, or commission someone to translate it for them. They can even choose to collate several different translations and use the readings that they prefer from each. Collation may result in an uneven and jerky script, but it has frequently proven worthwhile.

Some translations severely alter the text and subtext of the play. The first American translations of Giraudoux, for example, so changed the content of his plays that they should instead have been called adaptations: whole characters and scenes were omitted and added; names and ages of the characters, dates, places, language, and meaning were arbitrarily changed. The same is true of many other plays. If directors can read the original, they obviously should, and also incorporate translated versions of disputed passages into their production.[4]

Even if accuracy is not in question, translations should be carefully examined for the nature of the inner action their words transmit as well as for the flavor of the dialogue and poetry. Just as a director collaborates with an author, so does a translator, and though the translators' express purpose can be to transmit the play with total accuracy, they may be psychologically unable to keep their mind and personality out of their work. There is no totally accurate translation of a work of art. Changing one language into another presents a variety of options in every line; a simultaneous examination of two "accurate" translations of any play will produce hardly a single identical line. Translators try to convey not only the meaning of the text but also the diction, rhythm, poetry, and intangible feeling. Some famous translations sound awkward on stage, and some that appear feeble in print achieve great heights in performance. Very few translators—particularly of Greek plays—have much if any experience

---

[4]Commissioning translations or tampering with extant ones may raise questions of royalty payments and infringements of rights, if the play or the translation is protected by copyright.

with the theater, and their translations sometimes prove entirely unactable in the hands of modern actors and directors.

Historical Sources

When producing plays of a bygone age, directors frequently find it invaluable to acquaint themselves and then their actors with the historical perspective of the plays. Trevor Nunn, artistic director of the Royal Shakespeare Company, frequently begins his rehearsal for a Shakespearean play with a lecture on the world of the play, covering Shakespeare, the country in which the play is set, and the music, customs, language, and political situation of the times. Nunn also brings to his first rehearsals voluminous visual materials, pictures not only of the set and costumes but also of the people of the age and their civilization. Nunn's practice is common and usually helpful. Some directors steep themselves in the history of the period, giving their actors books that pertain to it. Actors who play historical characters (for example, Thomas More or Marat) may benefit from reading biographies of their characters, even if the literal biography does not correspond to the central topic of the play. The director should read these books first to determine their pertinence and to incorporate them in his or her interpretation. Many lines in historical plays, and much of their inner action, can be more clearly defined by consulting the sources (or their equivalents) the playwright had when he or she wrote the play.

The word *historical* need not apply only to plays of past centuries. It would be difficult for directors to evolve an excellent production of John Osborne's *The Entertainer* (1957) if they were not familiar with the events leading up to the Suez crisis, the disintegration of the British Empire, the effect of the nuclear bomb on British domestic culture and policies, and the effects of aristocracy and class division in England.

Critical Sources

Dramatic literature includes a large body of written criticism. Only when directing an utterly original play is the director devoid of critical and descriptive material. If possible, the first critical source a director should consult is the author's own words. Published plays frequently include an author's preface, which may give skillful interpretive suggestions; occasionally (as with the plays of Eugene O'Neill) a wealth of critical commentary is written into the stage directions. Most modern playwrights have also written dramatic criticism, at least of their own work; for example, excellent essays on the theater have been written by Arthur Miller, Luigi Pirandello, George Bernard Shaw, John Osborne, Friedrich Dürrenmatt, Eugene Ionesco, Bertolt Brecht, Edward Albee, Jean-Paul Sartre, Rolf Hochhuth, and Peter Weiss. The *New York Times* solicits dramatic opinions from playwrights on the eve of their openings in New York, and various journals and books also feature interviews with and statements from playwrights on their craft and their intentions in any given play.

A second critical source is the works of criticism that have been published about most dramatic authors. Published mainly by university presses, these are available in any major college library. The literature on any established playwright, of course, is voluminous; the material on Shakespeare alone could hardly be digested in a lifetime. Experience leads to judicious selection of helpful material. The worlds of literary criticism and theatrical practice are all too often remote from each other, and critics, who seldom have to test their points in performance, often tend to be overly prescriptive in their interpretations. Criticism can be of enormous value to the director, but it must be auxiliary—it cannot determine the creation of the stage life of a play.

Other Productions of the Play

Seeing an earlier production of the play is of questionable value to the director. Sometimes it is unavoidable, as when the director is asked to direct a play he or she has seen, acted in, or even directed before. Max Reinhardt directed *A Midsummer Night's Dream* many times during his long career in the theater, and each production was different from the last, as he drew on his increasing knowledge of the play. But earlier productions directed by someone else may actually inhibit certain directors' creative powers by subliminally suggesting interpretations, blocking, and business that will come off as borrowed rather than created, part of an earlier plan, not the directors' new one.

Directors who feel secure enough to examine the ideas of other directors can watch prior productions of the plays they are working on. If seeing the production is impossible, the director can study the prompt book, examine photographs, read local reviews, and talk to persons who have seen or worked on the play. The earlier director might be happy to answer interpretational questions. Reviews by New York theater critics are published biweekly in loose-leaf segments which are also bound together at the end of each season, and reviews in the national press can be located in periodical indexes. All such sources may suggest answers to moment-to-moment interpretational questions.

It is often helpful to examine the original production of the play, particularly if the playwright was involved in supervising, advising, or even directing that production. Bertolt Brecht's productions at the Berliner Ensemble are detailed in his *Modellbücher,* which record with text and photographs the blocking, business, settings, properties, and virtually every word of the author-playwright to his actors during rehearsals. Some of Brecht's "model books" are available in published abridgments; others can be had only in East Berlin. But all plays produced since the eighteenth century have some stage history available in libraries, theater collections, and various personal files, and all these premiere production records can further illuminate the intrinsic meaning or interpretation of a script.

THE OVERALL INTERPRETATION— INTRINSICALLY DERIVED

When the director has read the text a number of times—and has carefully studied the meanings of individual words; the moment-to-moment development of character relationships; and the world created by the playwright out of his or her own psyche, political and social interests, and physical environment—the director may want to create an overall interpretation for the new production. This is not simply the sum of the play's moment-to-moment aspects. A play never shows a simultaneous existence, but rather a temporal existence that differs from exposition to climax to denouement. Overall interpretation synthesizes moment-to-moment meanings but also supercedes and is wholly different from them.

It is never absolutely necessary to formulate an overall interpretation, of course. Plays vary in obviousness. The director of a nineteenth-century melodrama may simply forgo considerations of overall interpretation ("This play is about a murder and who did it") and work directly on developing moment-to-moment action and characterization. Or the complexity of a play may elude the director, who unconsciously chooses a simplistic interpretational approach.

Some plays, however, are complex even on the surface. It is difficult to read *Hamlet,* for example, or Molière's *The Misanthrope* without appreciating their apparent ambiguity of approach. We are never entirely certain how seriously to take Hamlet or Arnolphe at any moment, or how we should expect to think of them at the end of the play.

An overall interpretation gives a philosophical direction to the presentation of a complex play. It is not enough that the director and the scholar know what a play is "about"; it is also important that those in the audience, who see the play only once, leave the theater with some concrete ideas about what they have seen. They need not perceive a "message" or a coherent philosophical "position"; the transmission of interpretation may be simply a series of vivid images and feelings, ineffable but highly memorable. In his valuable book, *The Directorial Image,* Frank McMullan suggests that directors interpret plays through imagery rather than ideas and transmit those images intact (visually, sonically, and ideologically) as their "interpretation." Perhaps we can clarify by giving examples of interpretational questions a director might ask of major classic plays.

Hamlet.   Is Hamlet really feigning his madness (he claims to put his "antic disposition" on, as if it were a mask), or is he insane? Does he love Ophelia? How old is he? Why does he delay his assassination of Claudius? (The last question is the most answered in the history of dramatic criticism, and all the answers are different.)

Othello.   Is Othello a Black or an Asian Moor? Does racial prejudice fit into the subtextual character relationships of the play? Why does Iago behave the way he does? Why is Othello so susceptible to Iago's questions? Why does Desdemona so foolishly pursue Cassio's reinstatement? Why does Emilia steal the handkerchief, admitting her guilt only after the damage is done?

A Streetcar Named Desire (Tennessee Williams).   With whom are we supposed to sympathize? Should we feel protective toward the frail, neurotic Blanche, or toward the "normal" married couple, Stanley and Stella? Why does Stanley rape Blanche? Why does Blanche lie to Mitch? What should we feel about these characters and their behavior?

All these questions will lead to an overall interpretation which is well beyond the mere moment-to-moment happenings. If Hamlet is played as mad, the play is one of madness, and the fruits of madness run rampant in a corrupt court. If he is sixteen the play's meaning differs from that if he is thirty. If he fails to kill Claudius because of deep psychological fixations, the play is very different from what it would be if he fails because the opportunity never presents itself.

The overall interpretation should take into consideration the feelings of the audience. Plays can be weighted toward a certain character; for example, Sophocles' *Antigone* has been interpreted to make Creon a noble hero and Antigone a spoiled brat, and one production of Williams's *Cat on a Hot Tin Roof* shows Maggie as heroic and Brick as rotten. Shylock, in Shakespeare's *The Merchant of Venice,* has been played for both sympathy and ridicule, sometimes in simultaneously competing productions. At the level of overall interpretation directors decide how they will present the characters to the audience, and what kind of feelings they will try to engender. When the play is over, the audience will have a patchwork of ideas, images, feelings, and questions. These, in composite, are the interpretations transmitted to them.

Overall Interpretation as Emphasis

Overall interpretation is not just a matter of making yes or no decisions. A more subtle area of overall interpretation is generally much more important than specific decisions about a character's behavior or motivation. This is the matter of *emphasis.* Any complex play has hundreds of themes, subthemes, plots, subplots, character relationships, and character revelations, all of which cannot be equally promoted to the audience. The director selects themes that seem important to him or her and sets them off emphatically to the audience. Other themes he or she underplays or avoids.

The process of emphasis parallels the compositional process of achieving focus. Just as the director focuses the audience's attention on a given actor, so their intellectual attention is focused on a certain theme. *Hamlet* has many related themes, but the director who tried to bring out even a few would find difficulty. Audiences seek clarity. It can be argued that they attend the theater to escape the chaos of mundane existence. The theatrical experience is a programmed one: the director is the programmer. He or she employs exposition, conflict, climax, and resolution. At every stage the audience is moving through an elaborate maze of magic, emotion, ideas, and theatrical devices. When these become confused, the way is lost; despite the excitement of the individual moments, they seem to be going nowhere and the audience grows irritated, then bored. The director cannot say, "That's like life!" when accused of presenting an unfocused and meandering play; life doesn't charge thirty-five dollars a seat.

Directorial emphasis usually falls on one or more lines from the play which can be isolated and used to clarify and intensify the overall interpretation. For example, in Arthur Miller's *Death of a Salesman* Biff Loman says of his father, "He didn't know who he was." Willie's wife, Linda, exclaims, "He's only a little boat, looking for a harbor." Willy himself says, "You know, I feel sort of temporary about myself." King Lear discovers that, like all other men, he is only a "bare, forked animal." Vladimir, in Samuel Beckett's *Waiting for Godot*, cries, "I can't go on!" and then does.

Lines like these are selected as consonant with the overall interpretation and then emphasized through the use of compositional and audial focus. They can be isolated, surrounded by silence (the "pregnant pause"), elevated physically to a position of maximum attention. They stand as a focal point for all the action of the play; such a line is prepared for, and when made, confirmed so that it lingers in memory after the play. A well-directed play communicates its points in small bursts of intelligence that combine the spatial, the sensual, the intellectual, and the emotional. Spectators make their own highly personal synthesis of the bursts, sometimes days, weeks, or months after the actual performance.

Working intrinsically, directors at best become their own literary critic. Some directors, like Peter Brook, write excellent dramatic criticism, and some dramatic critics, like Eric Bentley, make excellent directors. Though the person equally skilled in both areas is rare, it is apparent that one skill complements the other. A director who can find nothing to say with a script can hardly direct, and a critic who has no theatrical sense can hardly analyze a play's dramatic (as opposed to literary) content. The directors' intrinsic interpretation is seen best in their productions, and although they may wish to write a note about the play for the program or for the local papers, it is on stage that their interpretations must be clear to be successful.

WORKING EXTRINSICALLY

Extrinsic interpretation involves the director's desire to create a *specific* interpretational effect on the audience. The operational question for extrinsic interpretation, in contrast to "What does this play mean," is "What *can* this play mean."

Working extrinsically means working inductively, from a basic interpretation down to precise particulars. The directors tailor the moments of the play to cohere with their overall extrinsic interpretation. "Tailoring" the play is a delicate operation. Traditionally, plays are "cut" in the preproduction period. Cutting is the elimination of dialogue, ordinarily because the dialogue is nonessential, time-wasting, or in the director's opinion, simply poor theater. Few plays reach performance with all the words from the original manuscript intact.

Besides reducing a play to manageable proportions, cutting offers directors an opportunity to delete lines that are superfluous to their interpretation. In his "existential" production of *King Lear*, Peter Brook purposely eliminated all signs of Edmund's final recantation and the servant's explanation of how he treated Gloucester's sore eye sockets. More optimistic productions of *Lear* have retained those rather human moments and cut the lines (or even the whole scene) regarding Gloucester's blinding. More dramatic tailoring of script—most critics would call it tampering, not tailoring—is evident in the Joseph Papp production of *Hamlet* (1968), sometimes referred to as "The Naked Hamlet." Thus does Hamlet meet the ghost:

> *Hamlet sits in his coffin-bed, turns on his radio, and begins reading. The radio offers ghostly wailing instead of music, and Hamlet tries to adjust it.*
>
> *A long, green, rubber hand emerges from the bed-clothes and starts to feel its way across the sheets to Hamlet.*
>
> *Audience laughs and gasps. Hamlet looks up and asks the audience what is the matter. The hand touches Hamlet on the shoulder. He leaps out of his coffin and begins flailing with his pillow at the figure which emerges from the bed-clothes.*
>
> HAMLET. Angels and ministers of grace defend us! (*general laughter.*)
> GHOST. Mark me.
> HAMLET. I will.
> GHOST. I am thy father's spirit—(*Hamlet cheers and runs like a scared rabbit out into the audience. He stays there for some time hiding and cheering*) . . . Now, Hamlet, hear. 'Tis given out, that sleeping in my orchard the lightning struck me. (*The Ghost produces a newspaper with the banner headline:* KING STRUCK BY LIGHTNING. . . .)[5]

[5]Reprinted from Joseph Papp and Ted Cornell, *William Shakespeare's "Naked" Hamlet: A Production Handbook*, Copyright © 1969 by Macmillan Publishing Co., Inc. Used by permission of the publisher.

Extrinsic interpretation and script tampering need not go so far as Mr. Papp's, nor need they be so sedate as Brook's selective cutting. Yet even though critics complain that Shakespeare is "rolling over in his grave," it is hard to see that anything but an abstract and outmoded commandment has been offended; rather, new generations of audiences have been exposed to valuable dramatic material, and directors have found themselves able (and audiences willing) to excite new issues with reference to the older ones. Few directors today believe in ghosts, and few fear to add their imprimatur to the dramatic material they prepare for their audiences.

Working with an Extrinsic Interpretation

The sources for extrinsic interpretation cannot be listed in any book, because they are the directors' personal sources. Extrinsic interpretation may come from their experience of political events, philosophy, psychological discovery, religion, science, or any other human area. Creative play directors are not craftspersons working in isolation from their world; they are not so devoted to the theater that they bring nothing with them *to* the theater. Although theater is not a substitute for polemical argument, the artist in the theater (or in any other medium) must ultimately have something to say besides the implicit statement, "I am an artist." The statement need not be verbal, scholarly, unique, or even profound, but if he or she is a great artist it is invariably *there*. Most successful directors today are involved, at least emotionally, in the cultural concerns of their times, in politics, in the sociology of life and art, and in philosophizing about the quality and destiny of human life. Without this involvement, they would be hard put to appreciate, much less direct, the great plays. Though they might be able to "spin out" a passable community theater production of a Broadway sex comedy, they could hardly tackle a play of even moderate complexity, nor could they hope to direct creatively in any way.

The actual extrinsic interpretation occurs on both conscious and unconscious levels. Directors unconsciously project (or introject) their personality and/or subjective ideology into the play. If, for example, they are especially sensitive to racist intimidation, they will emphasize such incidents as they see them in the script when coaching the actors and staging the scenes. As fish are unaware of the current in which they swim, directors are usually unaware of their special prejudices and sensitivities; they may be shocked when critics praise or damn their "unique interpretation," when all along they felt that they were doing the play "straight." Since the unconscious level is always at work, there is no such thing as a "straight" interpretation of a play with any degree of complexity.

At the conscious level, the director may choose a governing idea for the production which, though latent in the material, is beyond the immediately revealed intentions of the author. This governing idea should be general enough to create a universal theme and specific enough to be applied to moments in the playing of the text. It would be folly to produce *Hamlet* as a plea for racial integration unless relevant lines could be found; it would also be foolish to present it as an appeal for a particular city council candidate in a coming election.

SUMMARY
OF INTERPRETATION

The director works with interpretation by focusing the audience's attention first on the moment-to-moment action of the play (its story) and finally on an overall concept, feeling, or theme. In this discussion it has been hard to avoid the theater's only curse word, *message* ("If they want a message, send them to Western Union" is a classic remark), but it is undeniable that a play presents its audience with something more than a random story of random people. It gives them something with shape, a final meaning, and a set of impressions which, because they are organized, make a lasting mark on the mind and memory. We do not remember ordinary experiences; most of us cannot even recall our behavior during a given hour yesterday. But a superbly organized and interpreted play gives us a concise vision of reality which, properly conceived and transmitted, can leave an indelible mark upon us. Whether the interpretive material comes directly from the playwright's imagination and is simply elucidated, clarified, and intensified by the director, or whether it springs wholly from the director's imagination, struck off like a billiard ball from the playwright's cuestick, matters little in the last analysis: the successful production. Interpretation of a play, in one form or another, is a vital and absolute function of the director, and his or her achievement will be measured in that final integration of form with meaning which is the art of dramatic production.

THREE

COMPOSITION—
DESIGN

The term *composition,* as used in this book, refers to the articulation and orchestration of all the sights and sounds of a theatrical presentation. Stage composition is the visual arrangement (placement and movement) of the actors vis-à-vis the scenery and the audience; sound composition is the rhythmic or arythmic flow of sounds that reaches the audience's ears.

Historically, stage composition is the first area in which directors began to assert themselves, and even today there are directors who still consider that there is little else to the director's art. The reason for the directors' relatively quick assumption of the compositional function is obvious: they were the "outsider" in rehearsals who sat back and represented the audience, previewing what it would see. They immediately saw the need to arrange the production as they would like to see it if they were in fact in the live audience.

The goals of stage composition range from the modest ones of orderliness, clarity, and attractiveness to the more theatrically vital ends of dramatic impact, beauty, spectacle, and emotional catharsis. Directors have frequently used compositional techniques to create great emotional climaxes for plays with rather mundane conclusions. Director Peter Hunt, for example, fashioned a successful climax to the musical play *1776* by presenting a tableau showing the signing of the Declaration of Independence, backlit behind a scrim showing the Declaration itself. This arresting, affective composition brilliantly closed the play and engendered a strong emotional response from the audience, which the text alone proved unable to do.

There are four major steps in stage composition: the overall *design* of the entire show, the *ground plan* of the individual settings, the *blocking* of the action, and the *business* of the characters. These are discussed separately, as is *sound composition*. These aspects of composition are, however, interdependent, and all involve various levels of collaboration among the director and other staff members. The design of the production and the ground plan involves collaboration with the designer; blocking and business involve collaboration with the actors; and the sound composition involves collaboration with the music director and/or technicians and engineers. The nature of the collaborations, of course, depends entirely on the wishes, talents, and personalities of the persons involved, but because the director remains responsible for the decisions taken in every area, he or she must be more than simply familiar with the problems and possibilities available in each.

The first area of composition we are going to deal with is the theatrical space itself.

PRODUCTION DESIGN:
THEATER FORMS

The design of a production is a totality of visual and plastic elements which engage the attention of the audience. The first of these elements is the theater itself, more particularly, the theatrical form that the director chooses. Too often, the theatrical form is simply taken for granted—because the director has at his or her disposal some sort of building with a set stage already in place. But nothing, in the theater, should be taken for granted. Even in a classroom scene, chairs can be moved around, out of their "set" position, and a scene can be presented in the round, in a corner, or behind the audience. The theatrical form is always subject to some sort of directorial control and directorial decision, and it is essential, therefore, that the director understand as much as possible what options exist in the area of theatrical forms—and what opportunities for imaginative creativity lie open.

BASIC THEATER DESIGNS
AND THEIR UTILITY

In most theatrical periods, one or two theater designs account for virtually all stage productions. In classical Greece a massive outdoor theater was the home for tragedy and comedy. In Elizabethan times the public theaters—

the Globe, the Fortune, and the Swan—were relatively similar to each other, imposing their particular spatial gifts and limitations on the plays of Shakespeare, Ben Jonson, and John Webster. But there were also private theaters, indoors and intimate, such as the Blackfriars, as well as stages set up in royal palaces, in which the directors produced their shows.

American and European theaters today exhibit one predominant form of working architecture: the *proscenium stage*. Basically this is a rectangular building with the audience at one end and a stage at the other, the division between them marked by a proscenium arch through which the audience observes the action of the play. Prosceniums vary in width from eight feet (a cabaret theater in New Orleans) to a hundred feet (Radio City Music Hall, New York) and in height from eight feet to over seventy. Audiences vary from a handful to several thousand. Ordinarily a curtain divides the audience from the stage between acts, and occasionally a forestage extends beyond the curtain for certain special effects. Virtually all Broadway and commercial European theaters have proscenium stages, with an audience capacity of a thousand plus and a proscenium width of about forty or fifty feet. Most university theaters feature a proscenium stage with similar dimensions. Although the proscenium stage is an out-

FIGURE 7. Proscenium stage: spectacular. The massive proscenium of Radio City Music Hall, New York. The proscenium opening is 60 feet high and 100 feet wide—enough to accommodate a straight-across chorus line of thirty-six Rockettes. The Music Hall, used for variety shows, seats 6,000. (*Courtesy, Radio City Music Hall*)

FIGURE 8. Proscenium stage: intimate. In the tiny proscenium of a cabaret theater in New Orleans, an intimate satirical review plays within arm's length of the spectators. The proscenium width is less than eight feet, but the arrangement of scenery, actors, and audience is not fundamentally different from that of the Music Hall. (*D. J. Benit*)

growth of theater architecture of the sixteenth and seventeenth centuries, and although it had its absolute peak in the nineteenth century, it is in no way outdated as a theater form, and new proscenium theaters are built each year with exquisite refinements, including hydraulic pit lifts, flexible prosceniums, computerized rigging systems, and turntable stages.

The chief characteristic of the proscenium stage is that it presents to the audience (and to the director) a highly controllable stage picture. The proscenium arch acts as a frame which looks roughly similar from all parts of the auditorium. Since the audience is located on only one side of the action, looking in one direction all the time, scenery can be highly illusionistic or realistic. In the proscenium theaters of the seventeenth, eighteenth, and nineteenth centuries, two-dimensional painted scenery had its heyday, and the naturalistic sets of the late nineteenth and early twentieth centuries were ideally suited to proscenium presentation. The box set, with its real walls, ceilings, light fixtures, and furniture, is possible only on a proscenium stage. Scenery in this type of theater can be effectively hidden from the audience between scenes either backstage or in the flies, brought on at will

FIGURE 9.   Thrust staging. Chekhov's *The Three Sisters,* staged by Sir Tyrone Guthrie at The Guthrie Theater, Minneapolis. The action is almost entirely projected into the midst of the audience. The dark patch right center is a vomitorium access to the stage.   (*The Guthrie Theater*)

either behind a closed curtain or in sight of the audience. Stage tableaux can be effectively created, as can effects which depend on the entire audience's seeing a certain actor's eyes or lips at a given moment.

A second form of theater presently in wide use is the *thrust stage*, also called open stage, platform stage, or three-sided arena stage. The stage is a square, round, or trapezoidal platform surrounded on three sides by audience—usually sitting in a highly raked (angled) area—and backed by occasional scenery pieces or a permanent architectural structure. The thrust stage ordinarily has no hanging scenery, and what scenery it does have must be fairly limited. Thrust stages are aided immeasurably by the use of *vomitoria,* entrances through and under the audience (see illustration this page). Newer regional North American theaters rely extensively on thrust stages; notable among them are the Mark Taper Forum in Los Angeles; The Guthrie Theater in Minneapolis; the Stratford Shakespeare Festival Theatre of Ontario; the Long Wharf Theatre in New Haven, Connecticut; and the Pacific Conservatory for the Performing Arts theater in Santa Maria, California. Many universities have built thrust stage theaters to supplement their proscenium stages, and many community and off-Broadway theaters use the thrust stage as their only theater.

The chief characteristic of the thrust stage is that it "thrusts" the performers into the midst of the audience, emphasizing them and their performance rather than the scenery around them. The Elizabethan public theater (for example, the Globe) was basically a thrust stage, and it is not surprising that many of the first thrust stages built in the United States were constructed for Shakespearean revivals. By virtue of having a back wall the thrust stage also retains some of the illusionistic possibilities of the proscenium stage, especially because the members of the audience are all able to see a projection or a set located there. A not inconsiderable feature

FIGURE 10.   Modified thrust staging. Ben Jonson's *Volpone,* staged (and contemporized) by Edward Parone at the Mark Taper Forum Theatre, Los Angeles. The thrust does not extend so far into the audience as at The Guthrie Theater, and many scenic and blocking elements are meant to be viewed frontally, as in a proscenium theater.   (*Center Theatre Group*)

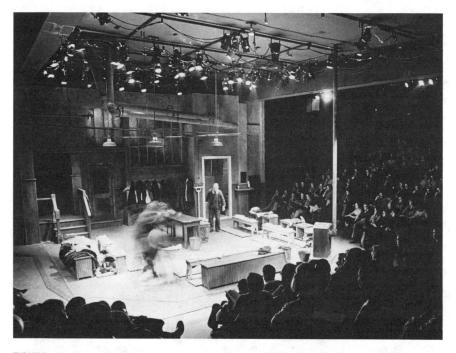

FIGURE 11.   Three-sided arena staging. An extreme thrust stage with the audience arranged in a U-shaped arena around the action, which need not be separated by a raised stage as at the Guthrie. Shown here is a production of David Storey's *The Changing Room,* directed by Michael Rudman at the Long Wharf Theatre, New Haven, Connecticut.   (*Long Wharf Theatre*)

of the thrust stage is that since less scenery is required or expected, productions can ordinarily be mounted at lower cost.

A form of theater architecture which has been much propounded but rarely used is the *arena* theater, or theater-in-the-round. The action occurs in the middle of an arena surrounded by the audience, and the actors enter down the aisles. The Arena Stage in Washington, D. C., has had great success with this form, but it has not grown in popularity relative to its older sibling, the thrust stage.

Arena staging focuses even more on the performer and almost totally eliminates the possibility of solid scenery, since anything over two or three feet high would block the view of the actors from various points in the audience. Arena staging limits the possibilities of spectacle, eliminates linear composition (since everyone in the audience has a different perspective), eliminates tableaux in the ordinary sense, and forces all the actors to have their backs to at least some of the spectators at all times. The benefits of arena staging, on the other hand, are intimacy and a frequently extraordinary intensity, with the audience involved almost in a participatory fashion with the drama. In the 1950s and 1960s, huge arena-style tent theaters

FIGURE 12.   Classic thrust stage. The Globe Theatre of London (1599) in a hypothetical reconstruction by Richard Southern. *(Deutsches Theatermuseum, Früher Clara Ziegler-Stiftung)*

or music tents opened throughout the United States to stage high-budget productions, mostly musicals. Few of these arena stages have outlasted their novelty, however, and the arena form has not reached the widespread potential its adherents anticipated.

Outdoor theaters, or amphitheaters, are probably modeled on the theaters of ancient Greece and Rome. Some are huge permanent structures with stone seats (softened by pillows) and architectural stages, occasionally using buildings as backdrops, as does the Mary Rippon Theatre in Boulder, Colorado. Others are carved out of natural formations—pits, quarries, chasms, and so forth—and seat great numbers of patrons, for example the Red Rocks Amphitheatre in Denver and the Quarry Theatre at the University of California at Santa Cruz. The Hearst Theatre in Berkeley, California, is a replica of a fourth-century B.C. Greek stage. Modified bandstands such as the Hollywood Bowl and the Carter Barron Amphitheatre in Washington, D.C., can be used for staging plays, and in New York City a bankside in Central Park was the original home of the New York Shakespeare

FIGURE 13. Four-sided arena staging. The Arena Stage, Washington, D.C., pioneered in the professional use of "in the round" staging, as this format is occasionally called. Characteristically, scenery is held to a minimum. (*Arena Stage*)

FIGURE 14. A wall-less but otherwise realistic interior setting at the Arena Stage. (*Arena Stage*)

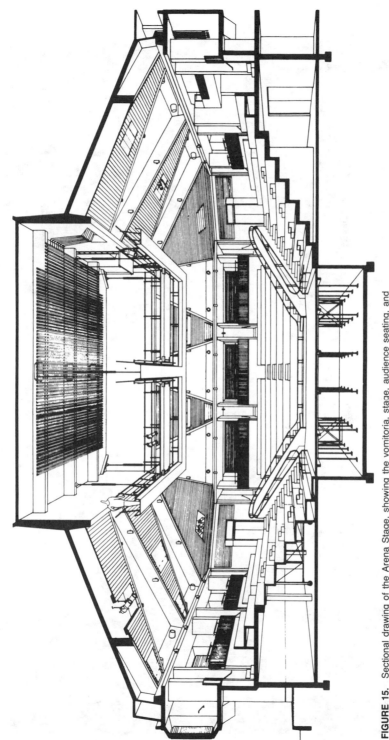

FIGURE 15. Sectional drawing of the Arena Stage, showing the vomitoria, stage, audience seating, and lighting positions. *(Arena Stage)*

FIGURE 16. Each year the city of York, England, mounts a production of its famous medieval cycle play before the ruined abbey on the town's outskirts. Here is the Crucifixion scene as performed in 1981. (*Courtesy of York, Department of Tourism, England*)

FIGURE 17. Street theater. El Teatro Campesino of California in a politically oriented outdoor presentation. (*Centro Campesino Cultural Inc; photo by George Ballis*)

Festival. These giant amphitheaters have proven values for all but the most intimate of plays. European directors, particularly Firmin Gémier, Jean Vilar, and Max Reinhardt, have maximized their possibilities. Huge audiences can be accommodated inexpensively, and spectacular stage effects can be achieved. Some productions have become extremely popular: *Aïda* at the Roman Baths of Caracalla, the Théâtre Nationale Populaire productions in a medieval palace in Avignon, France, all draw thousands of spectators, creating unusual artistic opportunities for the director.

Yet outdoor theaters need not be large. Small *trestle stages*, carried sometimes in a truck and sometimes by hand, can be set up quickly by street theater groups like the San Francisco Mime Troupe or the New York Shakespeare Festival touring company, and in an instant we can have Goldoni in Golden Gate Park or *Romeo y Juliette* in Spanish Harlem. Ben Jon-

FIGURE 18. The Utah Shakespearean Theatre is designed in many respects after Shakespeare's original Globe, with the audience surrounding the stage on three sides, and the structure left open at the top. (*Courtesy, Utah Shakespeare Festival*)

FIGURE 19.   Replica court theater. The Asolo State Theater, Sarasota, Florida, a transplanted eighteenth-century court theater. Pictured here, from behind, a production of *Charley's Aunt.*   (*Asolo, The State Theater Company of Florida*)

son, after all, declared that the theater was no more than "two boards and a passion," and many producer-directors have proved him correct. Guerrilla theater companies often stage plays in shopping centers, using the shops as scenery and the customers as audience. In this practice the theater returns to a form widely popular in the Middle Ages and dormant for centuries.

Finally, *specific* theaters are frequently erected for a single play or style of play. The original Old Globe Theatre in San Diego was roughly a reconstruction of an Elizabethan playhouse, as is the Oregon Shakespeare Festival Theater in Ashland, Oregon. The Asolo Theater in Sarasota, Florida, is a restoration of an eighteenth-century theater, and the Goodspeed Opera House in East Haddam, Connecticut, and Ford's Theater in Washington, D.C., are both reconstructions of working nineteenth-century theaters. Most of these theaters prove hospitable to contemporary plays as well

But no list of forms could exhaust the possibilities of theaters. "I can take any empty space," declares Peter Brook, "and call it a bare stage."[1] The theater is where you stage your play, and it can be designed, or modified, as the director and staff wish. Polish director Jerzy Grotowski creates a new theater for each play. For *Dr. Faustus* the audience sits around a "banquet" table and the action occurs on the tabletop. For *The Constant Prince* the audience peers over a five-foot wall into a deep pit in which the action

[1]Peter Brook, *Empty Space: A Book About Theatre—Deadly, Holy, Rough, Immediate* (New York: Atheneum Publishers, 1968), p. 9.

FIGURE 20.   Uniquely designed theaters. Director Jerzy Grotowski of the Polish Laboratory Theatre designs specific theatrical environments for each of his productions. This picture illustrates the scenic action for *Kordian,* by Slowacki. Spectators, in white, become fellow patients in a mental hospital with the actors, in black.   (*Jerzy Gurawski, architect. Courtesy, Jerzy Grotowski*)

FIGURE 21.   The staging area for Adam Mickiewicz's *Forefathers' Eve,* also directed by Grotowski, with spectators surrounding and occupying islands within the freeform state.   (*Jerzy Gurawski, architect. Courtesy, Jerzy Grotowski*)

FIGURE 22. Environmental theater. Richard Schechner, collaborating with Jerry N. Rojo, the "environmentalist," has directed a series of productions in the Performance Garage, a Manhattan garage fitted out with carpeted scaffolding to serve both as audience and staging area as desired. This is *Dionysus in '69.* Barechested actors at top and bottom interact amid four tiers of spectators. (*Photo by Raeanne Rubenstein. Courtesy, Richard Schechner*)

takes place. In *Forefathers' Eve* the audience is seated in chairs scattered carefully about an otherwise vacant room, and the action occurs in their midst. To employ the possibilities that Grotowski's staging suggests, directors are asking for, and architects are supplying, "bare room" theaters, or theater laboratories, consisting of little more than a big room, a grid for lights, and some platforms for seats and/or stages. Richard Schechner took his New York Performance Group far from the off-Broadway district, into a warehouse district in lower Manhattan, and produced his *Dionysus in '69* in a vacant garage, where three-tiered carpeted platforms served for stage and "house" alike, and the members of the audience were invited to locate themselves wherever they chose. Schechner calls this an *environmental theater,* a phrase which has entered the contemporary stage vocabulary. There is no limit to the possibilities in creating theater: the only rule is that the theater must be successful in housing both audience and play in a vital relationship with each other.

A DIRECTOR CHOOSES
A THEATER

A director does choose, or create, a theater, even if by merely accepting the theater offered. By agreeing to direct a Broadway play, the director chooses a proscenium style theater; by accepting a guest show at a regional or community theater, the director is more or less required to use the existing premises. Frequently the "choice" of a theater is obvious; practical considerations are so overwhelming that there is no conceivable alternative to the "obvious" house. But this section of our book is designed to make a director aware of the possibilities that may be worth exploring.

Most new theater plants house different styles of performing areas. The Krannert Center at the University of Illinois contains four theaters, and most new college plants include three. There are always nearby amphitheaters, either fabricated or natural, and the outdoors holds great potential. Where there seems to be no choice of theaters, the director, working with the production staff, need not take the facilities as he or she finds them. A proscenium stage can be made into a thrust by removing some seats and building a platform. A large theater can be made more intimate by closing off areas, either by drawing a curtain or installing a partition or by isolating the audience. The set and the audience might both be put up on the stage and the auditorium area converted to a maze through which the audience must walk to reach the seats. A modern theater may be "antiqued" by hanging gas lamps and old theater posters in the house, as for example, for a music-hall production of Behan's *The Hostage.* The walls of the theater can be painted, covered, or decorated to make the audience feel part of another era, as was done in the Actors' Studio production of *Mar-*

FIGURE 23. A seatless theater, where the audience stands and moves where the actors direct, was the principal staging feature of this New York revival of *Orlando Furioso*. The actors, sometimes wheeled about on carts, played in the midst of the audience and sometimes surrounded it.   (*Photo by Martha Swope*)

FIGURE 24. For this 1982 production of Aeschylus's *Prometheus Bound*, The Théâtre de L'Est Parisien was completely renovated: the orchestra seats were removed, and bleachers descended from the balcony to the stage—with the line between them blended with tons of real dirt. The shop door (off camera) became the only stage entrance.   (*Courtesy, Théâtre de L'Est Parisien*)

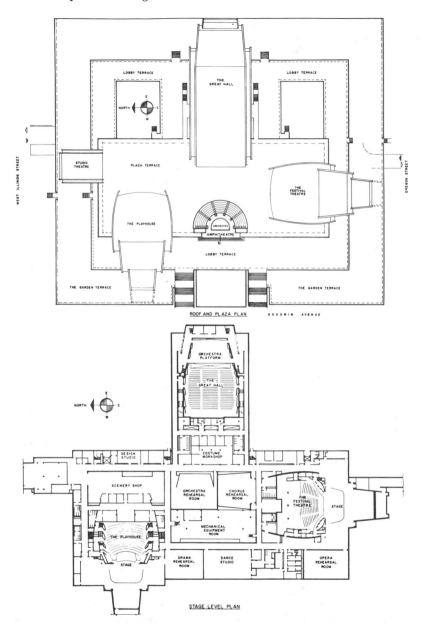

FIGURE 25. Multiple theater complex. The Krannert Center, University of Illinois, allows the director to choose any of five theaters. Above, the three proscenium theaters are separated by a flexible studio theater and an outdoor amphitheater, as well as by plazas and terraces. Below, the five theaters share common backstage facilities. Stages are located at the extremities of the complex to minimize interference and provide the audience with a common lobby area. (*Courtesy, Max Abramowitz and University of Illinois*)

athon 33. Theater walls, layouts, prosceniums, lobby displays, programs, and costumes (and attitudes) of the ushers are not necessarily fixed and can be modified or redesigned as part of the play's overall composition. Directors should avoid the natural tendency to consider the theater as an unchangeable vehicle for their play: they should consider it *part* of their play, and part of their overall concern.

In choosing, creating, or dressing up a theater, directors might ask themselves the following questions:

1. How will the play look and sound in the theater? How will the play act, feel, and project? How can the theater be best arranged to convey what I have in mind? Do I want the people in the audience to be aware of each other or aware of the building? How can I make them more (or less) aware of each other? Of where they are sitting? Of the outside world?

2. Where does the audience I desire for this play live? Where does it go to the theater, if it goes at all? Without patrons, theater does not exist; without the right kind of patrons, a specific play might not succeed. *Little Murders* was a failure on Broadway but a success in Greenwich Village; conversely, *Hair* was only modestly successful in the Village but was a bonanza on Broadway. Some plays, such as the productions of Grotowski, are meant for a small coterie of theater sophisticates (Grotowski hand-selects his audience before every performance). Others depend on a wealthy cultural elite—the Metropolitan Opera, for example. Others, such as street theater, have to be brought, free of charge, to audiences that are unaccustomed to going to them.

3. How big an audience do I want? How many can I get? It is folly to put on a play in a huge auditorium when audiences of fifty to a hundred are all that can be expected; the audience feels adrift in a sea of empty seats. It is also artistic folly to present a delicate, intimate play in a giant theater even if the audience will come, unless measures are taken to ensure that the intimacy of the action is properly conveyed to the far reaches of the house.

THE STAGING AREA

The staging area is where the play takes place: ordinarily on the stage of the theater. But the staging area need not be the stage, nor must a theater have a defined stage.

Richard Schechner's Performance Garage had virtually no stage to define. Many environmental theaters go to this extreme, with the action occurring anywhere on the premises. Other productions feature a defined stage but include other areas of the building in the staging area. The Broadway production of *Hair*, for example, featured actors entering and moving through the audience, down the aisles, and across the rows; hanging from ropes and swinging out over the audience; stepping across the arm rests of the auditorium chairs; and sitting in vacant seats (where there were any) or even on the laps of members of the audience. Though by no means an innovation, this created much of the electric theatricality of that production.

Entrances down the theater aisles are now common, even in proscenium theaters. (That practice, and other, similar ones, are often referred to as "breaking the proscenium arch.") In the Berliner Ensemble production of Brecht's *Das Kleine Mahagonny,* the orchestra sat in a theater box above the audience, drinking beer when they were not playing. In the New York Public Theatre production of *Stomp,* the staging area included a catwalk around the audience and a "stage" amid the patrons; during the course of the play, the actors demanded that part of the audience leave their seats and sit on the "stage," while the actors moved into the space originally reserved for the audience.

VIOLATING THE STAGE

When there is a defined stage and the action occurs outside it, we might say that the accepted stage space has been violated (a more general term than "breaking the proscenium arch"). Violating the stage space may be done for technical reasons: directors may simply want to gain more space for entrances and exits, or similarly, may wish to fill or clear the stage with sudden rapidity. They may, however, violate the accepted stage for aesthetic, theatrical reasons as well—and they will accomplish these ends whether they wish to or not. For violation of the stage creates a different form of audience involvement than does nonviolation, an involvement that directors must reckon with and try to turn to their (and the play's) advantage.

Productions which use a defined nonviolated stage and a defined audience area work within the audience's preconceived expectations and demand greater audience concentration *on* the play, as opposed to participation *in* it. This is virtually essential for illusionistic theater, where the director's intention is to make the audience oblivious of its surroundings and to engulf it with the situations and characters of the play itself. In illusionistic theater the audience is clearly segregated from the action and generally ignored by the actors. Most naturalistic and romantic plays are produced in this manner, the audience viewing the action much as if it was seeing it through a one-way mirror. Naturalistic proscenium staging is often called "the theater of the fourth wall removed," meaning that the audience is examining apparently random behavior inside a room whose fourth wall is imaginary. There are many advantages to working in illusionistic styles. The audience is secure and comfortable; its privacy is not violated; it does not feel compelled to take a position or form a judgment; and it is not "on the spot." The patrons can simply relax and enjoy the play they paid to see. Lulled into a state of secure voyeurism, they can become involved in the story and empathize with the characters to their hearts' content. They can laugh, cry, grow angry, and be charmed without having to account for their emotions—they can fall prey to the magic of the theater. This is an altogether satisfying way of working, and probably 75 percent of play productions in America are basically illusionistic.

Productions which use an undefined or violated staging area (and frequently an undefined audience area thereby) involve the audience in a different way, which we may call participatory. Participatory theater seeks to involve the audience and the actors in a joint experience which takes the audience onstage, the actors offstage, and gives the audience more to concentrate on than a story and some characters. Participatory theater asks the audience to be aware of many disparate things: the actors as people, the actors as entertainers, the political themes of the material, the nature of contemporary society, the elegance of wit and poetry. Bertolt Brecht, the great German playwright and director, wrote and directed plays meant to be seen as nonillusionistic. Brecht believed that theater must rid itself of "magic," creating instead intense political reaction and discussion among its patrons. His theater of *Verfremdungseffekt* (distancing) sought to force his audience to consider the moral, not the story, of his plays. To do this he continually violated the romantic concept of an audience segregated from the actors and propelled the action into the house at every opportunity.

FIGURE 25A.   The action is propelled forth in this East Berlin production of Bertolt Brecht's *Mahagonny*, with one actor (downstage) actually sitting with his legs draped over the footlights, singing directly to the audience.   (*Photo by Arvid Lagenpusch*)

Nonillusionistic theater, however, is not merely political in nature. The classic Greek theater, which used masks, dances, songs, and extraordinary stage effects, was nonillustionistic, as was the Elizabethan, and as is most musical comedy, fantasy, and historical tragedy. There are many reasons why a director may wish to address the audience directly (participation) rather than indirectly (through illusion). Some examples of nonillusionistic theatre using violated stages follow.

Marathon 33, produced by the Actors' Studio at the ANTA Theatre in New York, made the members of the audience believe that they were spectators at a marathon dance contest in 1933. The entire auditorium was decorated as a dance arena, and although the action occurred mainly on the theater stage, which was the dance platform, entrances were made through the aisles, the audience was addressed and commented upon directly by the actors, and entertainment specialties were directed to the "dance" audience.

In *Hello, Dolly* a runway, dressed with footlights, projected into the audience so that the star—played in New York by famous entertainers Carol Channing, Ginger Rogers, Mary Martin, Phyllis Diller, Ethel Merman, and Pearl Bailey—could come right into and over the audience and belt out the title song like a night club number. Pearl Bailey as Dolly even sang some of her own night club routines, which had nothing to do with the show, to a madly cheering audience.

The James Joyce Liquid Memorial Theatre, produced by the Company Theatre in Los Angeles and New York, blindfolds the members of the audience and leads them through a maze in which they are touched, kissed, brushed, and given things to smell, eat, and drink—a "sense bath."

In the 1968 New York production of *Tom Paine,* the cast broke the story of the play and entered the audience to engage spectators in a political discussion ranging far from the points of the play's text.

These examples demonstrate the range of nonillusionistic theater and violated staging areas, though not their limits, which extend as far as a director's imagination can take them.

A word of caution: In discussion directorial options for selecting a theater and explaining a defined, undefined, or "violated" staging area, we have concentrated on the unconventional. By way of reminder, let us state here that most American theatrical productions take place in a "normal" proscenium theater, where the action is confined to the stage and the audience to its seats. We are not exploring departures from this conventional arrangement to suggest that they are improvements. Departures are only possibilities which can be explored; nothing that is creative in the theater should be taken for granted or simply handed down as tradition. In the last analysis the director should be able to defend his choice of theater and staging area on the basis of the play he is directing and the effects he is trying to achieve. He should not simply accept them unthinkingly.

FIGURE 26.   Modified proscenium. The St. James Theatre, New York, altered by the addition of a runway for *Hello, Dolly!* directed by Gower Champion, Pearl Bailey as Dolly.   (*Friedman-Abeles*)

FIGURE 27. The audience area as the stage. The Company Theatre's Los Angeles production of *James Joyce Liquid Memorial Theatre,* in which the audience intermingled with the actors and the "stage" disappeared completely. (*Company Theatre Foundation*)

THE SCENERY SYSTEM

The nature of the scenery vitally concerns the director's composition. In this field the designer's voice is powerful, but directorial initiative and agreement are absolutely essential. Almost all scenery systems can be included among the following categories (and the overlapping categories between them):

1. A single realistic set (representing a real environment, even abstractly)
2. A single abstract set (representing no real environment)
3. Multiple sets, realistic or abstract
4. No set

Frequently the play strongly suggests (one can almost say requires) one form or another. A single realistic set is virtually essential for many modern American plays, such as *A Tale Told, Ladyhouse Blues,* or *American Buffalo.* Multiple sets are invariably called for in musical comedies (*Oklahoma!, Little Mary Sunshine, My Fair Lady*) and two-, three-, or four-set realistic plays (*Heartbreak House, Intimate Relations, The Three Sisters*). Abstract sets seem to be unavoidable in certain more modern plays (*Endgame,*

The Chairs). But there is great freedom of choice among the possibilities, and in working out the variations of the possibilities, for nearly all theatrical productions.

We can examine the possibilities that have opened up in designing scenery systems by looking at the history of English Shakespearean revivals. Seventeenth-, eighteenth-, and nineteenth-century revivals of Shakespearean plays were staged on a series of "realistic" sets. *Hamlet* had first a representation of battlements, then a throne room, then battlements again, then a room in the palace, then the king's study, then the queen's closet, and so forth (although the texts of the plays were frequently rearranged for the convenience of the designer and the scene shifters). It was discovered late in the nineteenth-century, however, that this was contrary to the original Globe staging for which Shakespeare wrote, and in the "Shakespearean revival" that occurred around the turn of the century, Shakespeare's plays were performed on a permanent architectural, non-scenic setting that seemed to be an accurate re-creation of the original stage. Now we witness complete variety of methods of staging Shakespeare. Both the nineteenth-century series of realistic sets and the Shakespearean revival staging are used (though the former is increasingly rare). Single abstract settings are also used, as in Peter Brook's *King Lear,* played against two giant sand-colored panels and three hanging thundersheets.[2] Multiple abstract sets with turntables, flying walls and banners, elevator stages, wagon stages, and actor-bringing-on-the-set staging patterns are often used. Every known scenery system has been used for Shakespearean revivals in our day, and the end is not in sight. For most plays directors can now choose from a number of possibilities. Their directing should be consistent with the nature of the scenery they select: this is one of their earliest choices in terms of how they do the play. Staging in the Forest of Arden will vary depending on whether the trees simulate real trees or are hanging ropes, magically rising cylinders, or steel sculptures.

A Single Realistic Set

Does the play seem to require, or does the director desire, a single realistic set? If so, certain considerations should be worked out with the designer at an early stage of production: how realistic? Is the scenery to be heavy, with platforms, doors that slam convincingly, bookshelves with real books, bannisters that can be sat upon, windows that open, steps that can be ascended? Or is it to be fragmentary and airy, a room delineated by a few hints of walls, indications of corners, openings for doorways, and fragile, stylized furniture? The audience will accept either, but each will lead to a different kind of composition, and thus of production.

[2]London, 1962. See also Brook's set for *A Midsummer Night's Dream,* page 68.

Realistic scenery is obviously associated primarily with naturalistic plays. In the early days of naturalism, "authentic" settings were de rigueur. David Belasco, an American producer of the early twentieth century, was greatly admired for having a dining room at Childs Restaurant (including walls and fixtures) precisely copied down to the last detail of furniture, linens, china, and tableware. Realistic scenery in a proscenium theater creates the strongest possible illusion of scenic naturalism.

A second attribute of realistic scenery is that it allows an actor to relate physically to the scenic artifacts in a way difficult or impossible to achieve on other sets. Some productions depend at least in part on the actors' ability to leap bannister rails, pound or bang into walls, slam doors, and throw furniture. Directors may wish to leave the specific activity uncharted in rehearsal, and even in performance. (This may be an unwise decision, but they should have the right to make it.) The only way they can do so freely, of course, is to assure themselves beforehand that the scenery can take it.

A set can still be considered realistic even when the actual scenery is somewhat stylized or simplified. Audiences are trained to theatrical conventions, and they will accept many modifications of actuality without even thinking about them. Walls may be built of muslin, bookcases and books

FIGURE 28. A single realistic set. The interior setting used in Frank Gilroy's realistic play, *The Subject Was Roses,* directed on Broadway by Ulu Grosbard. The illusion of day-to-day reality is total; the photo appears to be a candid snapshot of a family at breakfast, rather than of actors on a Broadway stage. (*Friedman-Abeles*)

FIGURE 29.   A single realistic set: fragmentary. For this 1982 production of *What the Babe Said,* The Denver Theatre Center provided selected fragments of a realistic interior: floor, furniture, a door, some appliances, and portions of walls. Individual elements are naturalistic, but the overall set is abstracted from reality.   (*Courtesy, Denver Theatre Center; photo by Nicholas de Sciose*)

may be painted, furniture arrangements may be realistically unorthodox, but the setting still appears realistic. It is even possible, within this general context, simply to indicate the walls with linear structures, overhead beams, or cardboard cutouts. This must be done in arena staging and is the usual practice on a thrust stage, where walls would entirely block the view of the stage. The audience's imagination will fill in the rest.

There is a frequent cost advantage in simplifying scenery, but the major difference is aesthetic. Simplified scenery tends to make its point and be forgotten; the audience does not linger over the many details of a natural setting but focuses on the actors and the action instead. Further, the stylization of scenery may be enchanting, moody, lively, vibrant, and so on without breaking completely away from simplified realism. The designer can be wildly creative, emphasizing the elements of or in the setting which he or she feels are worth an added touch. A wall can be made out of plastic, a tree of concrete, a crown of rusted spoons, yet the basic arrangement will still be only a modification of a realistic one. The basic decision concerning the single realistic set—how real it is to be—must be made early in the production planning.

The Abstract Set

Many plays call for an abstract or unlocalized setting. Samuel Beckett's plays, for example, are set in locales which cannot be considered interiors or exteriors; they are more like stage sculptures. August Strindberg's fantasies, Alfred Jarry's *Ubu Roi,* and Jean Cocteau's *Orphée* require, according to their authors, scenery which is unlike anything appearing in the everyday world.

Many plays for which realistic scenery could be used have been successfully, even brilliantly, produced on abstract sets. Peter Brook's *Midsummer Night's Dream* and *King Lear* have already been mentioned. John Gielgud's production of *Hamlet* was performed on a gray-black stage with several platforms, black flats, and drapes scattered about in a seemingly aimless arrangement. Paul Sill's *Story Theatre* takes place on a painted but otherwise bare stage, in front of a screen onto which are projected colorful abstract designs. Peter Stein's magnificent 1980 *Oresteia,* in Berlin, was performed in front of the stage, with the proscenium closed off by a massive, flat-black wooden backdrop, pierced by an unadorned door. During the final intermission, the backdrop was spray-painted white, so as to serve as backdrop to the final play of the trilogy.

Unlocalized sets are not a modern creation. All ancient theater was performed on what we would today call abstract settings, since realistic scenery is a relatively modern innovation. Ancient Greek dramas were performed in front of a permanent scene building, the *skene,* which represented interior and exterior locales with a minimum of literalness. Medi-

FIGURE 30.   A single abstract set. The setting for Samuel Beckett's *Waiting for Godot* in its original 1953 Paris production, directed by Roger Blin.   (*Photo by Photo Pic, Paris*)

FIGURE 31.   A single abstract set used for multiple scenes. Sally Jacob's setting for Peter Brook's celebrated 1970 production of *A Midsummer Night's Dream*. Three white walls, two doors, a catwalk, some swings, ladders, and aluminum coils were used in various combinations to suggest the palace or the forest. Here, the "mechanicals" rehearse while Titania swings overhead.   (*Joe Cocks Studio*)

eval pageant plays and mystery plays were performed in and about stage areas that were only modestly defined in terms of naturalistic detail. The Elizabethan theater was an architectural masterpiece which permitted interior and exterior scenes to flow rapidly without extensive scenery or scene changes. In all these theaters the stage itself was the setting, and the setting was a stage; there was no attempt to define the literal location in detail. Sometimes symbolic indications would be employed: it has been conjectured that the Elizabethan stage used banners and signs to indicate place or country, and revolving triangular prisms (*periaktoi*) on either side of the stage effected changes of situation in Greek plays. Oriental theater has been purely symbolic throughout its long history and has developed beautiful and poetic stage symbols, such as a waving piece of cloth for a river.

The development of realistic scenery can be traced to the court stages of the Italian Renaissance, when for a period the theater became a form of living pictorial art, used by architects and painters to amuse and amaze the nobility with their realistic copies of everyday physical surroundings. The English theater of the Restoration period saw the development of painted and architectured realism, and by the nineteenth century most plays were performed in front of elaborately painted two-dimensional sets.

Naturalism brought with it the box set and the "real" set in the late

FIGURE 32. Peter Stein's 1980–81 *Oresteia* production utilized a setting of purely structural elements. *(Pressbüro, Berliner Theatertreffen; photo by Ruth Walz)*

nineteenth and early twentieth centuries, so that any director requesting abstract settings from a designer today does so by choice. Today's abstract sets are intentionally, not traditionally, abstract. They may borrow from traditions—for example, Shakespearean stage replicas or Brecht's use of Oriental staging conventions—or they may create new traditions.

The movement toward intentionally abstract settings began in the late nineteenth century in response to the rigidity and "nonartistry" of realism. In 1890 Paul Fort developed in Paris his "Théâtre d'Art" (Theater of Art) to compete with Antoine's naturalistic Théâtre Libre. Fort performed his plays in front of abstract designs by friends of his: Pierre Bonnard, Odillon Redon, Maurice Denise, the leading impressionists of the day. He also performed plays in front of settings made from wrapping paper and indifferent collages of scrap materials. Later the coming of expressionism led to a greater sophistication of such abstract settings.

In Paris, in the second decade of the twentieth century, Jacques Copeau created his Théâtre du Vieux-Colombier, a neo-Elizabethan architectural stage, to present the poetic plays of Middleton, Shakespeare, and Claudel, which he considered the only true theater. All over Europe, the designs of Adolphe Appia, Gordon Craig, and Leopold Jessner, relying on giant sprawling staircases, rotating neutral screens, and great geometrical patterns, revolutionized scenery. Even American designers did not ignore this movement, and Broadway audiences of the 1920s were familiarizing themselves with the radical new abstract settings of Lee Simonson and Robert Edmond Jones, which featured sharply angulated and broken walls, deep shadowy recesses, unorthodox bolts of light. Theatrical virtuosity was the order of the day.

The effect of an abstract setting today, since it is obviously the product of the director's and designer's choice, is to announce to the audience that "there is more than just a story here." Abstract sets emphasize the theatricality of the theater: that it is an art form as well as a form of direct communication and not merely the depiction of ordinary events calculated to create an empathetic response. Abstract settings state, "The specifics of locale, period, and time of day are not important here." They lend a feeling of universality and broad relevance.

Abstract settings have enormous appeal to directors and designers. For designers the appeal is a chance to transcend the simple depiction of reality, to make a personal statement about the theme of the play. It is a chance to create a genuine stage sculpture, as opposed to a simple piece of interior design. For the director, an abstract setting offers the immediate opportunity to have the play appreciated as a major creative effort.

However, these appealing factors can accompany enormous liabilities. Direction must be consistent with the entire production plan; the director must use his setting as imaginatively as the designer has drawn it. A misused abstract set can easily come off as pretentious, even shabby if it seems

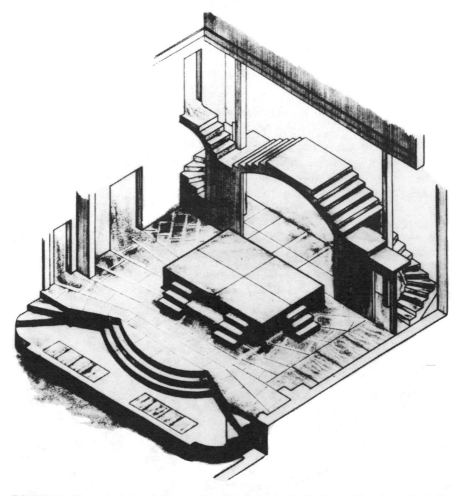

FIGURE 33. The "naked stage." Jacques Copeau's design for the Théâtre du Vieux-Colombier in Paris (1913) featured an architectural arrangement, which by the occasional addition of curtains and masking units, could be used for the productions of many plays of differing periods. (*Centre National de la Rècherche Scientifique*)

to be a substitute for something more difficult to make. Without a clear sense of its effect in terms of the play's statement, a director would be foolhardy to agree to an abstract setting for a play which does not intrinsically support one.

Multiple Sets

Today most plays are presented on multiple sets, by which we mean any setting which contains or presents numerous locations, either simultaneously or in sequence. The most conventional format of multiple set productions is a series of sets brought in during intermissions in the action. But multiple sets can be created organically in a single setting, either by simple juxtaposition or by *a vista* (not concealed) scene changes.

Sequential settings became the norm with the development of wing and drop proscenium theaters in the seventeenth century. Sets were created from flat painted scenery brought in on grooves in the stage floor. Scenery was shifted by sliding one set of wings and backflats out and another set in. Modern proscenium houses modify this technique with elaborate variations. Huge turntables can hold three completely different sets for a three-act show, and can change them in a matter of seconds. Fly galleries can hold vast stores of flat scenery which can be whisked in or out in a second or two. "Wagons" transport whole sets on from the side or

FIGURE 34.   A more concrete multiple set. Director Gordon Davidson used a single multilevel environment in his production of Shakespeare's *Henry IV*, Part I, at the Mark Taper Forum in Los Angeles. Lighting changes define action in various areas of the stage for interior scenes, or over the entire stage area for the battle scene shown here.   (*Center Theatre Group/Mark Taper Forum, Los Angeles. By permission*)

FIGURE 35. The Jo Mielziner setting for the original Broadway production of Arthur Miller's *Death of a Salesman,* directed by Elia Kazan (1949). Shown here is the basic setting, with all rooms visible simultaneously. *(Courtesy, Jo Mielziner; photo by Peter A. Juley & Son)*

fragmentary set pieces from any direction. These wholesale scene changes permit the use of any form of scenery, realistic or abstract, limited only by the facilities of the particular theater.

Sequential settings have many advantages. They allow for rapid change of mood as well as locale, and can create great audience excitement. Cecil Beaton's *My Fair Lady* settings drew gasps and bravos from the audience as one beautiful scene followed another on the stage. For spectacular musical productions like *My Fair Lady* a series of lavish settings is ordinarily de rigueur. Although sequential sets are important in realistic plays to convey vital plot points, they may also convey a symbolic point. In Anton Chekhov's *The Three Sisters,* the action occurs first in the salon, then in Irina's bedroom, and finally in front of the house, demonstrating the sisters' expulsion from their family home.

Organically multiple settings are more difficult to work out than sequential settings, but they may be superior for many plays. The most common form of an organically multiple set is the *simultaneous setting,* akin to those used in medieval European plays, where several locations coexist on the same stage, with most or all of the action occurring on one part of the set at a time. Action in *The Good Woman of Setzuan* occurs in a tobacco shop, a woman's house, a hut, a tobacco factory, a barber shop, a street, and in front of several doors, yet a striking design once combined all these locations on a single multiple set less than thirty feet across. Parts of the set were illuminated only as needed, and the theatricality of the playscript

FIGURE 36. A memory scene from *Death of a Salesman,* created by lighting projections (also designed by Mielziner) on a translucent backdrop. *(Courtesy, Jo Mielziner; photo by Peter A. Juley & Son)*

allowed the audience to accept the conventions of the setting. A superb simultaneous set was designed by Jo Mielziner in collaboration with director Elia Kazan for the Arthur Miller classic, *Death of a Salesman.* Kazan, Miller, and mainly Mielziner created a two-story house, with a couple of side stages for Willie's office and Charley's home, allowing the play to take place, in Miller's words, "in a mobile concurrency of past and present." Miller had originally conceived the play as staged with sequential, realistic settings; the simultaneous set of Mielziner allowed Willy to putter about the kitchen while his sons talked about him above; it gave the play a cohesive style which undoubtedly added to its success.

Simultaneous sets give the audience the entire picture of the play at first glance, although portions can be partially withheld by selective lighting. There are few if any scenic surprises. The simultaneous set seems to have great effect in preordained tragedies, especially such self-admitted ones as Anouilh's *Antigone,* since the setting itself discloses a certain preordained fatality. Simultaneous sets also allow "dormant" characters to remain on stage, their mute behavior observable by the audience and by other characters.

A final type of organically multiple set is *evolving sets.* One set, by the addition, rotation, or elimination of certain parts, becomes another in full view of the audience. One example is the Christopher Morley set for Trevor Nunn's Royal Shakespeare production of *The Taming of the Shrew.* In that production the curtain opened on the exterior of a tavern. When Christopher Sly was revived by the lord he was brought into the tavern,

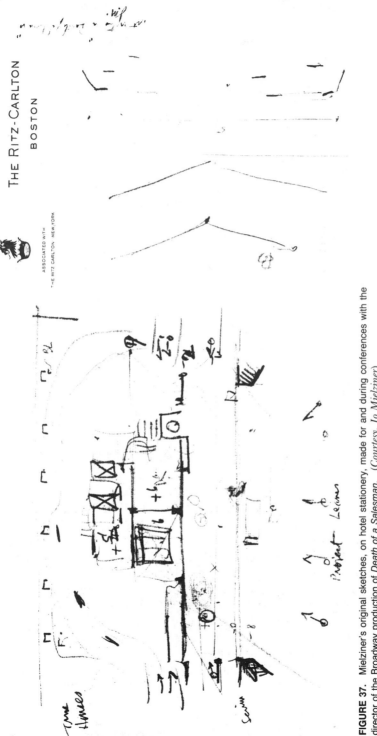

FIGURE 37. Mielziner's original sketches, on hotel stationery, made for and during conferences with the director of the Broadway production of *Death of a Salesman.* *(Courtesy, Jo Mielziner)*

which, mounted on two turntables, opened its inside out, revealing the entire cast reveling and dancing inside. Then the "play" began.

Turntables, stage wagons, and fly galleries are the most common elaborations of evolving scenery. Typically there is a basic set, with a backdrop which remains permanent and some set wings or side scenery. Other elements drift in and out, turn around, come up from traps or down from the flies. In the Joe Layton production of *No Strings* the scenery was mainly an assortment of wheeled, colored screens which whizzed in and out, flipped end over end, and defined whatever setting was necessary to the text. Ming Cho Lee's set for the New York Shakespeare Festival's *Peer Gynt* was a huge turntable containing a mammoth scaffolding arrangement. With a simple turn of the table, entirely different arrangements of steps and open spaces faced the audience. Director Gerald Freedman took great advantage of this feature, painstakingly rehearsing his cast to enter the turntable in mid-rotation and arrive simultaneously at their positions as the set turned.

Evolving sets allow for changes without intermissions or lost time. More than any other staging form, they reveal the theatricality of the medium, as the audience actually watches the machinery of the theater produce the changing illusion. They can unify a production by showing that each scene in a play is integral to the whole. They require enormous advance planning, since every prop and furniture piece must somehow be accounted for at every moment, but for many productions the fluidity, fascination, and stylistic excitement of evolving scenery is well worth the trouble.

The final choice open to the director is *no scenery*. Many plays dictate this choice; others can be performed that way. Frequently stage directions merely request "bare stage." *Six Characters in Search of an Author* is one of the most famous of these; *Our Town, The Serpent,* and *Impromptu* are others. *Six Characters* and *Impromptu* are set in theaters, so the theater itself may act as the "set." *Our Town* occurs in a small town, but the author, to indicate the play's universality, decided to let the actors create the scenery with the aid of a few ladders and properties. Shakespearean plays are frequently done on Elizabethan replica stages with no additional scenery, and some scholars suggest that this is how they were originally performed.[3] Many plays are successfully produced without scenery in low-budget theaters and workshops, before audiences willing to go along with them.

The liabilities of a bare stage are obvious. The audience may grow tired of the bleakness of the bare walls. Conventional audiences may miss the opulence they are accustomed to. They may become confused about the time, place, and period of the play, and they may resent the stinginess

[3]There are also suggestions to the contrary. For a summary of opinions see Alois M. Nagler, *Shakespeare's Stage* (New Haven, Conn.: Yale University Press, 1958).

FIGURE 38. Robert Benedetti's production of the medieval *Everyman* at the Tyrone Guthrie Theatre in Minneapolis was staged on the bare floor of the Guthrie stage. (*Courtesy, The Guthrie Theatre*)

of the management vis-à-vis their visual entertainment. The absence of scenery can confuse actors as well, and if the bare stage is not intrinsic to the particular play and production, it may have a harmful effect on their performance. It is not beyond an actor's ability to imagine the door he is supposed to be going through, but he cannot get the feeling from slamming an imaginary door behind him that he would from a real door or even a stage door. Bare stage directing takes skill; it can rarely be accomplished simply by informing the actor that he is to "pretend" the scenery.

But there are considerable assets to bare stage producing: first, it relies explicitly on the actor and the text. It was to emphasize the actor that Copeau designed his architectural Théâtre du Vieux-Colombier in Paris with its *tréteau nu* "naked platform." Bare stage designing merely carries this concept to its conclusion. *The Emergence,* produced by the Company Theatre of Los Angeles, is a superb example of the theatricality that can be achieved on a bare stage; in that production, which featured only a few unpainted blocks on an otherwise naked stage, masks, costumes, lighting effects, music, ensemble acting, dancing, and extravagant special effects made scenery, for the time being, unnecessary. The eyes always could return to a naked stage to realize that the "magic" of the theater was being created by living actors.

Bare stage producing also indicates universality, the frank admission that the performance is occurring on a stage and has relevance to life. It uses the stage as a neutral platform for the presentation of a theatrical

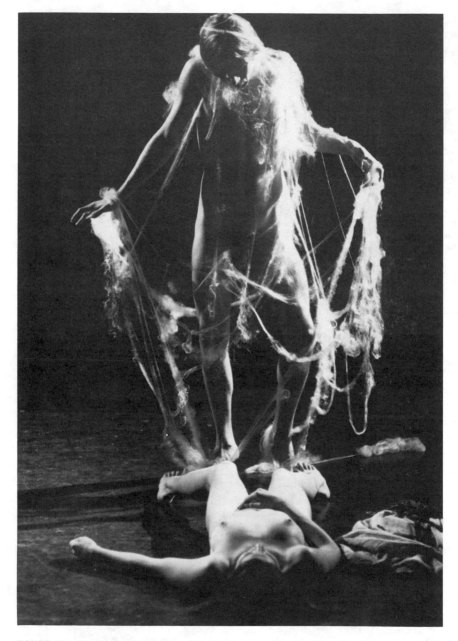

FIGURE 39. *The Emergence,* produced by the Company Theatre of Los Angeles, was created by the company for a bare-stage production. Costumes, bold lighting, nudity, and smokey laser effects had a substantial visual impact. *(Company Theatre Foundation)*

experience. It also candidly drives home the point that the production is not expensive and must therefore be appreciated for values other than lavish effects. The same approach was used in the 1950s and 1960s by film producers who made their "artistic" films in black and white, even though they could easily have afforded color. Some directors feel that the use of bare stage creates an increased receptivity on the part of the audience for poetry, art, and philosophy. It is worth noting, however, that filmmakers had almost entirely abandoned black and white in the 1970s, and this justification for bare stage producing may also have reached its limit. There seems to be no intrinsic reason why a bare stage should call for more "artistic" appreciation. It is the manner in which staging artifacts are used that will determine their impact.

The director should be involved in the matter of selecting a scenery system. He may be forced to accept a theater and a stage, but he should never be forced to accept a scenery system he does not want. The director can never put his head in the sand at the design stage and expect to have any control over the composition of his production. The scenery system is a primary factor in stage composition, therefore its conception is largely a directorial responsibility.

SCENE CHANGES

Integral with the scenery system is *how* the scenery is to change. In a conventional play using a single set or series of sets divided by intermissions, the scenery and properties are changed by stagehands behind a drawn curtain, or during a blackout if there is no curtain. In the case of multiple organic scenery the settings are changed *a vista*, and they must be planned. *A vista* scene changes are ordinarily accomplished in one of three ways: by stagehands, by actors, or by hidden mechanical means.

Stagehands are persons qualified to move scenery. They can be costumed however the director chooses and rehearsed like actors to move scenery quickly, efficiently, and on cue. They need not worry about getting their costumes dirty, being out of breath in their next scene, or breaking character. Needless to say, if stagehands are used to move scenery in front of the audience, they become actors, albeit mute ones. They must be costumed; they cannot wear whatever is at hand unless that is the desired effect. Some plays make explicit use of neutral stagehands. *The Fantasticks* uses a mute actor to distribute properties, move set pieces, and act as a wall between two characters. *Muzeeka* is performed with four stagehands who impersonate telephones, carry identifying signs, move set units, and occasionally take a part in the action. Oriental theater, such as the Nō and Kabuki theaters of Japan, uses such devices extensively.

The use of actors to change scenery is a frequent practice. Actors

FIGURE 40.   The working part of the *Sweeney Todd* set, as used by director Hal Prince in the musical's 1979 Broadway production, was a rolling "cube" that could be brought onstage by the actors and rotated to create, by turns, a pie shop, a parlor, a bakehouse wall, and a barber shop (upstairs). Other units moved mechanically; a great crane above delivered the play's important prop: a barber chair.   (*Martha Swope*)

playing speaking characters set and remove scenery pieces between or during scenes, bringing their chairs on with them, moving flats around, and so on. The obvious liabilities are implied above: actors are concerned with much more than scene changes and are not always happy to move scenery before their big scenes. They may not do it very well, nor are they dressed properly for it. In addition, the effect of an actor concluding an emotional scene and then stooping to strike a chair can destroy the mood of the scene. Complete stage blackouts are difficult if not impossible to achieve, as obligatory fire exit signs, aisle lights, shoe squeaks, and actor noise conspire to let the audience know what is happening on stage as the scenery is shifted.

The use of actors as stagehands, however, has some important virtues. Like evolving scenery, the practice helps to unify a production. It emphasizes that the actors are actors—stage people, not just "characters."

It is fully in the spirit of most improvisational theater, comedia dell' arte, Shakespearean comedy, and modern "theatricalist" productions. It communicates from the actors to the audience a feeling that "we are putting on a show for you," which is frequently desirable. *The Emergence*, mentioned previously, used actor stagehands in this way with excellent results.

Frequently the moving of scenery systems can be justified realistically by having actors who play waiters move the dining table and chairs, butlers move furniture, and other characters naturally pick up a chair from one side of the stage and bring it to another, to seat themselves there. This method might cover awkward scene shifting situations. More often, the actors move the scenery with no realistic justification, merely to serve a theatrical purpose. The audience is generally willing to accept this, as long as it is done with sureness and is consistent with the scenic style.

Mechanical scene shifting can be stunning and need not be enormously expensive. Scenery that evolves *a vista* by hidden means can create electric audience response. This is not because the audience is fooled by magical effects—ordinarily the mechanical means to move scenery are quite obvious. But the effortless shifting of sets with actors simultaneously moving over them and action occurring as they shift creates a fluid cinematographic effect which is lively and enchanting. Though engaged, audiences are never distracted by the nature of the scene shifts; their concentration on the play and its characters can be uninterrupted. Mechanical scene shifting is as old as the theater: the ancient Greek *exostra, ekkyklema, periaktoi,* and *mechane* operated grandly to reveal new scenes and tableaux to the audience.

New variations of mechanical shifting are explored every day. There is no limit to the possibilities for a skilled technician and an imaginative designer or director.

Although we shy away from drawing "rules" for directing, two principles may be safely established concerning scene shifting. First, whatever method that is employed should look intentional. If the actors are to change sets and props, they must look as if they know exactly what they are doing, and the director must make the shift completely consistent with the total composition and style of the production. All *a vista* scene changing must be rehearsed to absolute perfection, or it can be a worse disaster than actors going dry on their lines. Nothing in the staging of a play for which an audience pays admission should look makeshift simply because no one had the imagination or the time to devise something better.

Second, the director must recognize that scene changing is a vital part of the scenery system. The decision on scene shifting must be made at the time the scenery is agreed upon. It is not a last-minute decision, but a fundamental one. If it is left until the last minute to decide to have scenery changed in view of the audience, the director faces a mishmash.

FIGURES 41, 42. Evolving sets. Two scenes from Trevor Nunn's Royal Shakespeare Company production of *Coriolanus* at Stratford-on-Avon. Huge moving blocks, electronically operated, move in and out, to define walls; up and down, to create staircases and platforms. Above, the Romans and the Volscians (with head-dresses) battle before the gates of Corioli. Below, Menenius addresses the plebeians.   (*Joe Cocks Studio*)

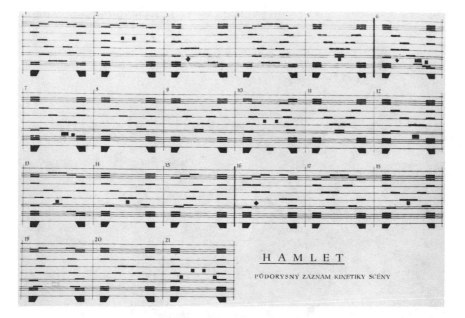

FIGURES 43, 44. Evolving sets. Josef Svoboda's design for a Czech production of *Hamlet,* using highly polished vertical screens which move mechanically to twenty-one different positions, each defining a different staging space. Above, configuration number 11, viewed from the audience. Below, the different configurations of screens, shown in ground plan. *(Art Centrum, Prague)*

THE QUALITY OF THE DESIGN

In collaborating on the play's basic design, directors must be concerned with its quality. If they like and trust the designer, a few words are often sufficient. They want the set light and airy, dark and damp, constricted, cluttered, towering, rustic, ethereal, pop/op, futuristic, spiral, naturalistic, shallow, antique, or whatever. The designer will expect them to describe what they want with words, images, references, and sometimes details. Set quality has to do with style as well as composition, of course, but it is central to composing a stage picture. The quality of the design is, after all, what the audience will see on stage, apart from the actors, and the movement and placement of the actors must be related to the nature of the set design.

The quality of design is also seen in the design of costumes and properties. Although these are ordinarily not as crucial to the director as the design of the scenery (as they do not determine the spatial patterns), they do play an important role in the overall composition. First, simply by color and shape, costumes, props, and accessories form elements in the stage picture which may be by design harmonious, contrasting, dramatic, awkward, or arbitrary. Certain directorial compositions may require specific color combinations or contrasts which must be envisioned and planned at the design stage, not midway through rehearsals. Second, the style, shape,

FIGURE 45. Quality of design. A portfolio of contemporary stage designs by Josef Svoboda, showing technological constructions which create striking qualities. Here, mirrored hexagonal surfaces reflect the actors and sculptural scenery in Karel Capek's *The Insect Play.* (*Art Centrum, Prague*)

FIGURE 46. Down lights and step levels used in John Dexter's Berlin production of Verdi's Sicilian Vespers. (*Art Centrum, Prague; design by Josef Svoboda*)

FIGURE 47. Textured cubistic construction for Otomar Krejca's Brussels production of *Hamlet*. (*Art Centrum, Prague; design by Josef Svoboda*)

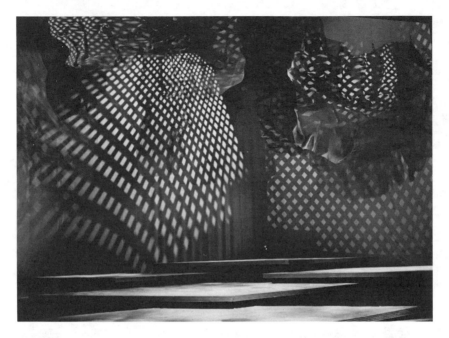

FIGURE 48.   Platforms, projections, and abstract hangings for a Prague production of *As You Like It,* directed by J. Pheskot.   (*Art Centrum, Prague; design by Josef Svoboda*)

design, and fit of costumes and properties can (and presumably should) affect stage movement. The same costuming that makes for breathtaking entrances may not be suitable for falling over sofas; and a Louis XVI sofa may not be suitable for falling over. Staging effectiveness depends on everything that is on the stage.

Some directors design their own scenery. Franco Zeffirelli's *Romeo and Juliet,* though controversial, was certainly a masterfully consistent Shakespearean production. Zeffirelli's designs were meant for his blocking and his blocking for his designs, and the effects were astonishing. Small wonder that directors often team up for years with designers whom they find sympathetic. Trevor Nunn and Christopher Morley are one team; Tyrone Guthrie and Tanya Mosievitch were another. Like all other artistic collaborations, the director-designer relationship can be delicate, and sympathetic teamwork based on concrete artistic goals is essential to the successful production.

FOUR

Composition—
The Ground Plan

Technically the ground plan is part of the production design, but it is such a key part from the director's point of view that it rates special consideration. Frequently the director has ground plans in mind before the scenery is designed; often a basic ground plan inspires a design built around it.

The ground plan, also called floor plan, is the stage and set as seen from above. More literally, it is a draftsman's illustration of the set as it intersects the floor of the stage. Its importance is enormous insofar as it determines the visual shape of the play's action, specifically the movement (blocking) of the actors. A character cannot enter upstage center if the doorway is downstage right, and a bedside assault cannot occur downstage right if the bed is upstage left. Create a good ground plan, and the action can almost block itself; create a bad one, which will soon be made permanent in the shop, and the blocking genius of a Tyrone Guthrie could not save the performance.

For this reason, the design or selection of a ground plan is a task in which the director's primary participation is essential. Directors often design their ground plans before the designer has been chosen or hired, and then present the directorial ground plan as the first input of the director-designer collaboration. This is not, of course, to belittle the designer, who may be equally as—perhaps even more—alert to the overall shape of the

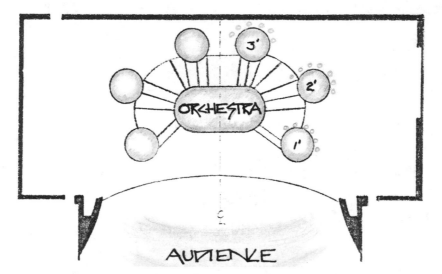

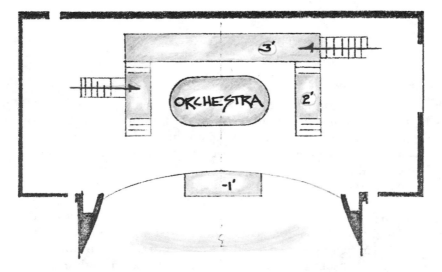

FIGURES 49, 50, 51. A series of ground plan designs for the Bertolt Brecht-Kurt Weill musical play, *The Threepenny Opera,* showing the evolution of a ground plan from director-designer discussions. Figure 49: The director has envisaged a production in which the orchestra sits center stage, with the orchestral group surrounded by "cages" that will be used as minor acting areas. The cages exemplify the oppressive social conditions that Brecht was writing about. Figure 50: After further discussion, the designer turns the "cages" into interconnected areas that provide upstage movement and entrance areas to downstage. A platform is added at the front of the stage for a "Brechtian" presentation of musical numbers. The evolving design intensifies the harsh, angular quality of the play, but it has lost some of the "cage" motif. Figure 51: The final ground plan synthesizes the earlier sketches and creates an integrated series of platforms and steps. The orchestra platform and the downstage singing platform are each trifurcated, and wagon stages are added for individual scenes. Elevations are noted in circles, as is customary. (*Designs and drawings by Charlotte Stratton*)

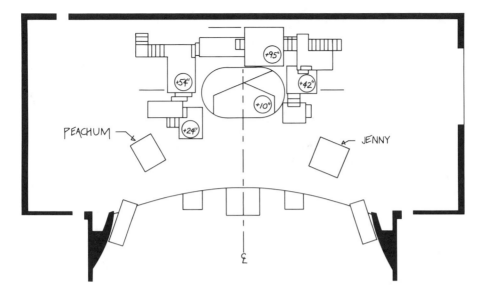

action as the director; rather it indicates the need for directorial input and final judgment on the specific structure of the setting upon which he or she will be directing.

Collaboration with the designer, assuming there is a separate designer who has independent artistic prerogatives, is probably most delicate at the ground plan stage. The director must approach the designer with a fairly complete knowledge of the play's staging requirements and a fairly sure sense of how he or she wishes the play to move. Platforms, doorways, windows, walls, and furniture arrangement must always be examined from the standpoint of how they will be used, not simply how they will look. Directors must have a firm sense of where entrances and exits will be made; how many people will be entering the stage at any time; and how many specific staging requirements, such as duels, battles, dances, hiding-in-closets, and so on are to be accommodated by the sets they are asking to have designed and built. They must have an overall vision of the movement in the play, both in terms of spatial direction and vigor, which they must convey specifically to the designer.

The sensitive collaboration between director and designer at this point will probably involve several meetings, some mutual rethinking, and some compromise. The nature of the collaboration depends, obviously, on the talents and mutual regard of each party; the most profitable collaborations involve a general sharing of ideas and aesthetics. Like all collaborations to which the director is a party, it is ordinarily most fruitful when uninhibited by artistic arrogance.

CHOOSING A GROUND PLAN

The director will consider the following aspects when examining or drawing up a ground plan:

1. Does it allow for the action of the script?
2. Will it allow the action to be forcefully projected?
3. Does it encourage desirable movement? Tableaux? Improvisation?
4. Does it provide mechanisms for establishing focus?
5. Does it communicate the atmosphere of the play? The inner world of the play?
6. Is it dynamic?

The first criterion establishes the basic qualifications of the competent ground plan; the remaining criteria, those for the better than competent one.

**THE GROUND PLAN
ACCOMMODATES THE ACTION
OF THE PLAY**

Accommodating the action is, of course, a prime function of the ground plan. If, for example, we are dealing with a realistic play, performed "by the book" on a single realistic interior set, then we must have doors for people to enter through, chairs to sit on, beds to lie on, and enough furniture to make the setting plausible and the actors comfortable. The ground plan must also provide the necessary crossover (backstage) space. If a character enters from outside, goes into a bedroom and then into another bedroom, and then comes out of the bathroom, there will have to be four doors in some kind of architecturally proper pattern if we are to understand what is going on. Designing a ground plan of this sort, the director must read through the play with nothing else in mind but what is needed in the way of functioning scenery. Sets have been completely built without the window through which Uncle Harry is supposed to be seen coming up the walk.

**THE GROUND PLAN
FORCEFULLY PROJECTS
THE ACTION OF THE PLAY**

This second task of the ground plan is much more than a technical operation. There is obviously more to designing the plan than arranging the doors, windows, and furniture in an obliging pattern. The placement of all the objects on the set determines in advance the positioning of the actors at many crucial scenes, particularly entrances, exits, and scenes involving furniture. These placements must be figured out with great care, ordinarily before rehearsals have even begun; they certainly cannot be changed at the whim of a director after the design has been built.

Let us first examine the problems involved in a single realistic interior which is to be used in a standard proscenium theater, the set appearing upon the raising of the curtain and the scene ending when the curtain falls. The ground plan will ordinarily be located in the trapezoidal space bounded by the curtain, the rear wall of the theater, and two lines, which are extensions of a line drawn from the last seat on either side of the first row of the audience to and past the nearest proscenium edge. These lines are not truly perpendicular to the curtain line, but are "raked" inward about ten degrees. This is because in most theaters some audience seats are positioned beyond the width of the proscenium. Scenery or action located outside these raked lines will be invisible to a portion of the audience.

Obviously the ground plan need not be absolutely bound to these perimeters. The left and right boundaries may be broken at will as long as total visibility from every seat in the house is not of major concern. The curtain line is not an absolute limit; scenery or furniture can be placed on whatever apron lies in front of it. Even the rear wall is not particularly sacred if an alternative can be fashioned. Alexander Dean, in a production of Pirandello's *Six Characters in Search of an Author* in the early years of the Yale Drama School, made use of the fact that the scene shop was located immediately behind the stage. He raised the huge loading door and then opened the tiny door at the rear of the shop, more than a hundred feet behind the curtain line. Through this tiny door came the six characters, who walked mysteriously into and through the shop, through the loading door, onto the stage, and down to the curtain in a staging that has been remembered ever since.

The director must first define the usable perimeters, whether or not they are entirely within the trapezoid, and then form a ground plan within them. If the job were merely functional, this would be easy. The director would simply make the back wall of the set parallel to the back wall of the theater (allowing sufficient crossover space behind), make the side walls follow the raked sight lines, and puncture the set with as many doors and windows as the script requires. He would then place furniture in the classic position (two chairs and a table stage left, a sofa stage right, both canted slightly inward, and perhaps occasional chairs at one or both far downstage corners) and let the designer "dress" the set with pictures, bookcases, fireplaces, and a raised landing or two. Perhaps half of the amateur productions of modern drama in the United States are designed in such a way.

However, this form of ground plan design does nothing to project the specific action of the play. Implicit in its statement is that all plays and all interior sets are the same; that whether the play is a farce or a melodrama, a classical domestic tragedy or a Neil Simon comedy, the same set can work. Nothing could be less creative or farther from artistic truth.

A ground plan must be designed, first and foremost, for the play being produced. What does the play say? What does it mean, or existentially, what does it *do?* These questions of interpretation are vital. Whether the interpretation actually precedes the design in the director's mind is a moot point, for different directors work in different ways, and it is certainly possible for directors to conceive of a ground plan before they have consciously articulated their interpretation. Still, at the unconscious level at least, the directors' ground plan is based on their concept of what the play is about and how it is to be presented to the audience. The movement from interpretation to ground plan design can be either inductive or deductive.

Inductive ground plan design.   Sometimes directors work inductively; that is, in their minds they "see" the entire play. They "see" the kind of room (assuming the scene involved is a room, of course), its shape and configuration vis-à-vis the audience, its style, its levels, its overall atmosphere. Inductively, the whole play dictates the whole set, at least in its broadest details, and then the design is more precisely articulated as the director goes through the play's action and shapes the setting around it. One can imagine the Kazan-Mielziner set for *Death of a Salesman* being created in this manner, Kazan deciding that it would be theatrically expedient (and artistic) to show the entire house simultaneously, rather than in sequential scenes, and building a ground plan which would show the bedroom over the living room for that purpose.

Deductive ground plan design.   Occasionally directors choose to work deductively. They have no general idea of what they want for the whole play or scene, but they isolate in their minds from one to a dozen vital moments in the play and "see" them as occurring in specific places with regard to the audience. These moments could be simple ones, such as vital entrances or exits, or moments of great dramatic action, such as Hamlet's killing of Claudius or Orgon's hiding under the table (in Molière's *Tartuffe*). They could also be repeated moments, like the comic entrances in Neil Simon's *Barefoot in the Park.* Or they could be entire subscenes revolving around a piece of furniture for example, the scene by Leslie's bed in Brendan Behan's *The Hostage* or the scene between Joan and the dauphin on the throne in Shaw's *St. Joan.* The placement of these scenes, and the furniture necessary for them, can be determined first and the ground plan designed around that placement.

Why is one placement better than another? Why would a director visualize a scene in one place instead of another? Why would one placement project a scene to the audience better than another? Successful staging in principle means that the audience sees what it is supposed to see, hears what it is supposed to hear, and most important, feels what it is supposed to feel. The goal of the ground plan in these respects is to create movement and positioning which will make the characters face the audience, naturally, as much as possible. For this reason the classic position of furniture is, as described, a sofa downstage center left and a chair-table arrangement downstage center right (or the reverse), both canted slightly inward toward center for maximum visibility. Characters seated on the sofa and chairs face not only each other but the audience as well, at least in a proscenium stage setting. It is the director's business in blocking the play to have the actor's faces as visible to the audience as possible, not only for visibility and audibility but also so that the audience can "read" the emotions on the actors' faces. The ground plan lies at the heart of the blocking. Obviously if the sofa and chairs faced upstage, actors sitting on them and talking would be closed off from the audience.

The actual implementation of this principle, however, allows great leeway for experimentation, and the classic furniture position is so far from sacrosanct that it is often considered a last resort. Novelty and visual excitement, which are highly desirable theatrical attributes, suggest more vital ground plan arrangements than the symmetrical and undynamic "classic" one.

So far we have considered relatively arbitrary interiors. However, realistic plays frequently call for specialized ground plans, such as a courtroom or the interior of a railroad car, requiring great care and ingenuity from director and designer. Courtroom scenes are common in contemporary plays. Such scenes usually involve a jury box, a judge's bench, and a witness stand. In a proscenium theater this arrangement presents no problem. But sometimes an "audience" is also required (in addition to the theater audience), as are tables for counsel, a stenographer, and the press. To crowd all these on stage and still open up the action requires great skill on the part of the director. In such matters his or her advice to, and authority over, the designer become especially vital, because the ground plan will virtually dictate the staging.

Realistic plays must conform to realistic conventions—unless a deliberate choice to use more abstract forms is made—and that means a basic adherence to normal architecture for ground plans. In designing ground plans for nonrealistic plays the director can be more flexible in projecting the action, since scenery does not have to conform to normal architectural relationships. The custom in Japanese Kabuki theater of thrusting one or two gangways (*hanamichi*) from the stage into the audience can be adapted to many Western plays that involve direct audience-actor rapport (*The Hostage*, for example). Many ground plans for nonrealistic plays use similar devices to bring the play directly forward to the audience and project it without the guise of natural placement.

THE GROUND PLAN
ENCOURAGES THE PATTERN
OF MOVEMENT

The third task of the ground plan is to encourage movement. In most plays movement is desirable, and in plays in which it is not, the ground plan should encourage the desired stasis. But ordinarily we enjoy in the theater a fluid, mobile play whose actors meaningfully create outward action that helps transmit the play's inward action. Actors like to move and audiences like to watch them move.

In a realistic play the ground plan is an essential element in starting up the pattern of movement. In real life people tend to move very little for long stretches of time. They eat leisurely dinners around a table, each in his or her own chair; they converse while sitting around a fireplace for hours on end, without anyone going anywhere but to the bathroom; they quietly plot assassinations, love affairs, and coups d'état across a counter with barely a toss of the head. On stage, however, a lack of physical action can produce boredom, and playwrights and directors are usually well advised to get their plays moving. The director uses first whatever the playwright provides. Phones ring and are answered. Drinks are mixed, served, and consumed. Books are taken from bookcases, cigarettes from cigarette cases, and clothes from suitcases. Even in Samuel Beckett's *Waiting for Godot*, the classic play of inaction, people come in and go out, eat carrots, fall to the ground, run off stage to relieve themselves, do exercises—hundreds of physical acts. All the stage actions specified in the script (we shall call them *obligatory stage actions* since the playwright has required them) can be performed quietly or theatrically, according to the sense and imagination of the director. When directors are given obligatory business by the playwright, they have an initial ready-made pattern of movement which they can either elaborate or leave alone.

Even in a realistic play there may be little obligatory movement, however, so most of a director's blocking is self-initiated. In these cases as well, an effective ground plan can stimulate realistic business. A bar, a box of cigars, a telephone, a mirror, a photograph on the wall—such items of scenery or properties can be situated and used with great finesse to create a fluid, motivated movement pattern in a naturalistic play, even though they are not directly mentioned in the text. A good ground plan liberates business and behavior on stage; it does not box it in between pieces of furniture or set it upstage.

No ground plan is "best" for getting a play to move; like everything else in the design, the ground plan must be shaped to the specific play, theater, interpretation, and occasionally even to the intended cast. Still, to provide a fluid movement pattern a ground plan should be laid out in terms of its dynamic use rather than its static appearance. Important set

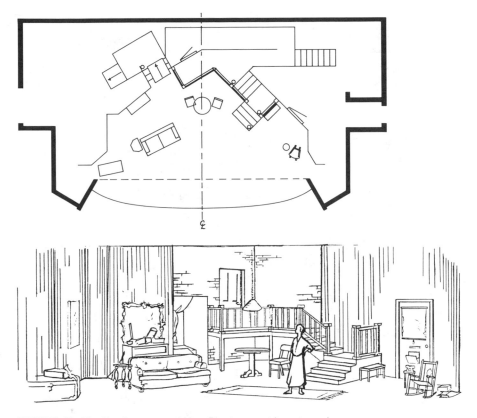

FIGURES 52, 53. Reading a ground plan. Directors must learn to read a ground plan just as musicians must learn to read music. Thus a director should be able to look at the schematized ground plan on paper and "see" scenery. Although models and drawings make this "seeing" process easier, they are not always available, particularly during a play's planning period. The ground plan above is Charlotte Stratton's rendition of a set for Paul Zindel's *The Effect of Gamma Rays on Man in the Moon Marigolds*. Below, Stratton's drawing of the same set, with a character drawn at center stage. Study the relationship between the two illustrations.   *(Designs and drawings by Charlotte Stratton)*

and prop pieces should be spread about the stage, not cluttered in one corner. Similarly, entrances and exits should create movement. Many real-life rooms have two doors next to each other; however, this is rarely useful on stage. The setting should provide movement in three dimensions as well as two; it is not impossible to conceive of entrances up through trapdoors or down stairways, ladders, ropes, or firepoles.

Furniture can be butted against a wall or located so that it can be walked around as well as toward, creating greater movement possibilities. Telephones can have long cords so that actors can walk while talking on them; chairs can swivel, bars can roll, railings can be sat on, and windows can be entered through. It is vital that the director anticipate at the design

FIGURE 54. Five different acting positions on Charlotte Stratton's *Man in the Moon* . . . set, utilizing different levels, pieces of furniture, and architectural units in the setting. (*Drawings by Charlotte Stratton*)

stage the movement patterns he or she will use, and not wait for the blocking rehearsals, so that the ground plan can include enough movement possibilities and so that shop technicians can build the scenery sturdy enough to support or accommodate the anticipated movement. A railing cannot be sat on if the stage carpenter builds it of cardboard, assuming that it will be a "nonpractical" piece of decor.

THE GROUND PLAN
ENCOURAGES EFFECTIVE
TABLEAUX

A *tableau* is a frozen stage picture in which the arrangement of actors and scenery conveys a striking impression or effect. The golden age of tableaux was the nineteenth century, when almost every scene ended with one; imagine, for example, Hamlet staring off after the departed ghost, wringing his hands, while Horatio and Marcellus kneel beside him, swearing on the hilt of the sword which has been plunged, crucifix-like, into the stage floor. As the characters freeze with appropriate devotion on their faces, the curtain falls and the audience applauds madly. Today's tableaux may seem more subtle to us, but in fifty years they will presumably appear as contrived as earlier ones do now. The tableau is used today for much the same reason for which it was originally invented: to put into visual terms a vivid moment, thought, or feeling.

Technically, a tableau is a frozen moment, a framed picture. The film medium has turned to the tableau with great relish in the past decade, with the freeze-frame becoming a common method of terminating a scene or a film. But the freezing need not be unnatural (as in the freeze-frame, or with actors suddenly becoming, to all appearances, lifeless); it can be realistically performed, as in the conclusions of the films *Midnight Cowboy* and *The Graduate*—both tableaux occur in the back seat of buses—or of the famous nude scene that terminates the first act of *Hair.*

Tableaux may occur throughout a play to mark significant dramatic points such as an entrance, a departure, a revelation, an introspection, a kiss, a touch, or any other emotional transfer. For a moment, a single beat, the characters stop and think; audiences think too, and the picture of the setting and the characters is etched (we hope indelibly) on their minds. Then the action continues.

A good ground plan encourages tableaux to be memorable and effective. In a proscenium theater the goals are similar to those of pictorial composition: the stage picture should have balance, focus, dynamism, and inner life. The last of these is most important, the inner life in a frozen situation. It is not accidental that paintings of immobile objects are called still lifes, for the interaction of the objects, which may not themselves be alive, creates an artistic vitality akin to life itself.

If the ground plan is deductively designed, it will probably derive from the director's envisioning several tableaux throughout the play, or possibly just one or two vital ones. But the staging must of course be effective in the quieter moments of the play as well. Stage composition is a fluid enterprise that when properly handled creates exciting stage pictures throughout a production, not just at its crucial moments. Thus the ground plan must be examined in relation to every moment in the play, to deter-

FIGURE 55.   Effective staging of the party scene in Chekhov's *The Three Sisters,* directed by William Ball at the American Conservatory Theatre in San Francisco. Note that thirteen of the fifteen characters on stage can be fully seen; in real life, of course, fewer than half would be. The placement of the table and chairs on the set is critical, as is the decision about where each character sits or stands.   (*Courtesy, American Conservatory Theatre*)

mine where a character can enter, stand, sit, talk, listen, and exit so that words and feelings are strikingly conveyed to the audience.

The compositional goals of balance and focus are so vital that several books have been written to explain them in precise mathematical detail,[1] and many studies on compositional instruction have been published over the past 150 years. Yet this is a subject that is probably as much intuited as learned; the factors in creating vivid stage tableaux can never be successfully reduced to mathematics or rigid academic strictures, and no working professional director today operates within formalistic limitations of this sort. To create successful tableaux, the director tends to rely on his informed aesthetic taste and judgment, abetted by his familiarity with a wide variety of options and models from all media.

[1]The classic example is Alexander Dean and L. Carra, *Fundamentals of Play Directing,* rev. ed. (New York: Holt, Rinehart and Winston, 1965).

THE GROUND PLAN
STIMULATES EFFECTIVE
IMPROVISATION

Improvisation means that some movements, business, and stage behavior are left up to the actors to work out, usually in rehearsals in which they are encouraged to initiate movements instead of being told what to do. All productions are to some degree improvisational, and some are overwhelmingly so; in recent years improvisation has become much more common in professional theater, and occasionally entire "plays" are improvised, dialogue and all, night after night.

The ground plan can stimulate improvisation, particularly in realistic plays, by being as real as possible. If the setting is a room, the ground plan represents a real room with real furniture scattered about in relationships different from the "classic" stage positioning. Set pieces are chosen or built strong enough to do what their real-life counterparts would: windows can be opened, hanging chairs can be swung on, doors can be slammed. This is not always practical or economical, but the improvisational dividends are high. In improvisational rehearsals the director wants the actors to be as free as they would be in an equivalent real-life situation; they cannot be so if they must worry continually about which walls they can lean against. Similarly, fine improvisational results can be obtained by placing furniture in nonclassic positions, for example, a sofa that forces a traffic detour, a chandelier that people run into, a chairless room that forces people to sit on kitchen counters, the floor, or bedrails. Actors improvise not merely with the text, but with the setting, and if the setting contains elements that lack fixed functional purposes (such as the nineteenth-century use of andirons downstage center, so that the principal actors could come down front to warm their hands over a make-believe fire) the actors will be able to create novel and exciting movements and tableaux.

It is often said that a ground plan should provide for free, unhindered movement and that the primary goal of ground plan design is to create a large, unobstructed acting area. This is rarely if ever helpful advice for a creative production. Some of the best ground plans, on the contrary, intentionally create obstacles. Actors, particularly good ones, tend to follow their intentions in a straight line, with regard to both movement and inner action. One of the goals of directing, however, is to put obstacles in their way, to force those dull straight lines into more theatrically exciting curved or broken ones. In a film chase scene, the characters never chase each other down a straightaway track; their path follows as varied a path as the director can contrive. Similarly, in the tiny confines of a stage, the ground plan should allow nothing to be too simple, lest the directness of the movement imply a dullness and simplicity in the inner action. The audience wishes to see not only the intention of the character but also the contour of his or her path in pursuit of that intention; the director frequently has to create that contour, or at least elaborate on it, by placing hindrances, generally physical ones, in the actor's path.

THE GROUND PLAN
CREATES FOCUS

A ground plan creates focus even if no actors are on stage. Some elements of the stage are more important than others. There may be an empty throne, as in *St. Joan;* a doorway behind which lives a character who never comes on stage, as in O'Neill's *Touch of the Poet;* or a doorway through which someone is expected to enter (*The Inspector General*) or through which someone does enter.

The director often determines at some point in the design process what is the most important element in the setting. In most cases he or she wants to assure that it has spatial prominence and is not lost in the back-

FIGURE 56. The ground plan of Feydeau's great farce, *Hotel Paradiso,* as staged at the American Conservatory Theatre in 1979, uses stairs, doors, railings, and below-stairs entryways to create a flurry of farcical movements. (*Courtesy, American Conservatory Theatre*)

ground. Elements in the stage set that have a sense of mystery should be presented with that mystery intact, so that it tantalizes the audience until it almost begs to have the mystery revealed.

THE GROUND PLAN
CREATES ATMOSPHERE

The ground plan helps to create the atmosphere not only of the setting but also of the play. If the setting is a cramped attic apartment, for example (as in Henrik Ibsen's *The Wild Duck*), the ground plan must be contained in size and probably jumbled with architecturally superfluous levels, steps, and obstructions. If the atmosphere of the play, moreover, is of cramped minds and limited vision, the ground plan must go even further. Ground plan atmosphere is left largely to the designer, but it is a good idea for the director to use many adjectives in describing what he or she wants. A room can be stifling or airy, comfortable or restricted, expensive or cheap, lofty or dreary, light or dark, peaceful or frenetic, cluttered or spare. These qualities will be built into the architecture of the set, not just into its decoration, and they are a matter for agreement and creativity at the level of ground plan design. They create the inner world of the play at an exterior level.

THE GROUND PLAN
IS DYNAMIC

Dynamism is the synthesis of all the other ground plan design elements. The plan must be fluid and encourage fluidity; it must be meaningful in itself and encourage meaningful activity; it must convey a sense of the inner world of the play while the play moves within it. It must place the actors in dynamic relationships with each other, perhaps along diagonals, up and down different levels, confronting each other while running up steps or ramps, leaping down from railings, or swinging on ropes. In a different kind of play, it may do this by setting the actors adrift on a bare platform in the midst of an audience.

In addition, the ground plan must place the actors in a dynamic relationship with the audience. That makes of the audience either participants (for example, in some forms of communal, environmental, or improvisational theater) or voyeurs. In either case, the play must be dynamically projected to the audiences; it must open out to them, reach across to them, seize their emotions and their minds, and give them an experience they have never had or felt before. This is the function of theater and the final goal of the ground plan which helps to achieve it.

FIVE

Composition— Blocking

Once there is a cast, a ground plan, and a rehearsal space, the director can proceed to block the show. In this one task there is complete freedom. Blocking is the one duty of the director that has not traditionally been collaborative, and many directors still define the sum of their responsibilities as blocking and taking occasional notes.

TERMS

Blocking is not synonymous with movement, although they are occasionally used interchangeably (with confusing results). Characters may be blocked to sit about a table and not change their positions for an entire act—this is still blocking. *Movement,* as used here, refers to the major spatial changes as a character moves from one place on the stage to another—entering, crossing, standing, sitting, lying, exiting—and not to the character's individual movements—breathing, head scratching, moustache twirling—which are called *business. Blocking* refers to the placement and movement of all characters on stage at any time. *Business* is dealt with separately.

CALLED-FOR STAGE ACTIONS

Called-for stage actions are the external actions that define the plot events of the play, such as Hamlet killing Claudius in the last act. They are the actions which, if you were attending a play in the company of a blind person, you would have to explain so that he or she would understand the story line. Story-telling actions such as these ordinarily involve a small fraction of playing time; still, since they are generally the key moments in every play, they must be accomplished with utmost clarity and with powerful theatrical effect.

Let us make this clear by example. Consider the scene in *Hamlet* (III. ii) where the "Murder of Gonzago" is being performed by itinerant players to "catch the conscience" of Claudius. Hamlet has inserted dialogue into this play-within-the-play to see whether Claudius reacts guiltily to the performance of an assassination similar to the one he instigated earlier. Hamlet has also asked Horatio to note Claudius's reaction. At the moment of the reenacted killing of Gonzago, the Shakespearean text reads as follows:

> HAMLET. He poisons him i' the garden for his estate. His name's Gonzago: the story is extant, and written in very choice Italian; you shall see anon how the murderer gets the love of Gonzago's wife.
> OPHELIA. The King rises.
> HAMLET. What, frighted with false fire!
> QUEEN. How fares my lord?
> POLONIUS. Give o'er the play.
> KING. Give me some light. Away!
> POLONIUS. Lights, lights, lights.

Then, presumably, everyone leaves the stage except Hamlet and Horatio.

Notice the number of discrete events we (the audience) must see clearly at this moment. Above all, we must see that Claudius's action stops the show. This is not as easy as it might seem. First, recall that the stage is filled with people, the entire court as well as the king and queen, Polonius, Ophelia, Hamlet, Horatio, and the players—perhaps thirty people or more. Then realize that (in a modern production, at least) the lights are dim and focused on the players; otherwise the king's cry for light makes little sense. Then realize that the audience is supposed to be watching the performance of the players, not of Claudius. Claudius has no words to speak during the moment of his deepest revelation, which is that Hamlet has somehow discovered his regicide. Amid all this confusion and split focus, the audience must clearly see the dramatic inner torment of the king, and that it is his silent perturbation which forces Polonius to abort the performance of "Gonzago." Then the king, whose sole line is "Give me some light. Away!" must hurriedly leave the stage, confirming our knowledge that he now understands the reason behind Hamlet's feigned madness.

But that is not all we must see. We must also see the reactions of Gertrude, Hamlet, Horatio, and Polonius, whose later actions make sense only in terms of what they observe here. Even the courtiers and players must have an observable reaction to this series of events, for their behavior and lives are also to change because of the happening. Not a few professional productions have bungled this scene entirely, and audiences have questioned each other during intermission (or worse, during the playing of the following scene), asking, "What happened?" In such scenes, successful blocking is utterly vital to tell the playwright's story. If the blocking fails, even the most brilliant interpretation of the events will be wasted.

THE CHOSEN ACTIONS

Most blocking is chosen by the director in the absence of ruling stage directions; it is not called for by the playwright, but simply arbitrary from the point of view of story telling. This is a different kind of blocking; it is one thing to block Claudius stopping the show and another to show Laura (in *The Glass Menagerie*) having her feelings hurt. About 95 percent of a director's blocking serves purposes other than gross story telling, instead heightening the inner actions and character relationships which form the greater part of the fabric of a play.

BLOCKING CREATES CLARITY

Blocking is the director's prime device for making the action (inner or outer) clear to the audience, which is, after all, the sine qua non of successful directing. We have already discussed clarity in terms of the principal actions of a play, the called-for actions. But clarity is vitally important for the inner action as well. At any moment in the course of a play the audience will want to know, "Did he hear her line?" "Does he realize what she means by that?" "Does she know that a man is behind her?" "Where is he going?" and so on. One of the worst pitfalls in directing is to develop too great a familiarity with the play. By the final dress rehearsals an inexperienced director may "read in" answers to these questions that a first-time audience cannot begin to answer.

Suggestions for Clarity in Blocking

• Make the actors visible. For example, when Claudius stops the play, he should be visible from every seat in the house. He should be higher than anyone else or downstage (in a proscenium theater) of everyone else, and he should be illuminated enough to be seen. Ideally, all the actors should always be visible to the entire audience. Although this may be impossible with a large cast or in a large pillared theater, it is ordinarily a good rule of thumb.

• Make the focal actor's face visible. If Claudius is stopping the play, and his reaction is important, then his face should be seen. This is difficult to arrange in arena staging, but at a key moment like this it would not be out of place for Claudius to say his line while turning 360 degrees and speaking it to everyone on stage, thereby showing his face to everyone in the audience. It is always preferable to let the audience see the actors' communicative tool, whether it be their face, body, or voice. Their dialogue is more understandable if we can see their lips as they speak.

• Isolate the beats in the scene. Beats are moment-to-moment actions, miniscule events. For example, after Polonius says, "Give o'er the play," the following beats could occur:

1. Hamlet and Horatio exchange a glance.
2. Claudius observes Horatio.
3. Claudius follows Horatio's gaze and sees Hamlet.
4. Horatio raises his eyebrow as a sign to Hamlet that the king is looking at him.
5. Hamlet turns his head and smiles at Claudius.
6. Claudius gives Hamlet a look that says, "I know what you've done and I'm going to kill you for it."
7. Hamlet laughs, mocking Claudius. His gaze lands on Gertrude.
8. Gertrude looks at Claudius, inquiring, "What's going on between you two?"
9. Claudius grabs Gertrude's arm to lead her away from her son's influence, crying, "Give me some light. Away!"
10. Gertrude glances over her shoulder at Hamlet in despair.
11. Hamlet points his finger at Claudius as if to tell Gertrude, "He's the man who killed your husband."
12. Polonius, realizing what has just happened, shouts for lights to distract the others.

This series of beats is hypothetical. None is specified in the script, so they must be considered discrete subtextual events. All the same, it is entirely possible for experienced actors under expert direction to convey these twelve events or beats accurately in the two-second pause between Polonius's cry and the king's exit. (In film, of course, it would be comparatively easy to do this.) The beats convey clearly what the text does not: that Gertrude is only now made to suspect that Claudius killed her husband, that Claudius is now conscious that Hamlet knows of his crime and is plotting against him, that Hamlet will try to enlist his mother's help, and that Claudius knows that Hamlet and Horatio are together against him. To make these points (which are, of course, a matter of interpretation), the director must say to the actors, "I want to see all twelve of these beats." And the actors, probably at "walk through" pace at first, will play them.

• Discuss the action of the play fully with the cast. It is useless to ask the actors to play the twelve beats just enumerated if they do not fully understand them. Clarity cannot be achieved through blocking if the actors do not understand the action as the director has interpreted it. The director should ask the actors to explain the beats to him or her; they may see things that he or she does not.

• Isolate the principal actors. In the scene from *Hamlet* we have only a fraction of a second to follow Claudius's gaze to Horatio, Horatio's to Hamlet, Hamlet's back to Claudius, Claudius's back to Hamlet, Hamlet's to his mother, Gertrude's to Claudius, Gertrude's to Hamlet, and Hamlet's back to Gertrude. The human eye works with lightning speed, but all will be lost if the characters involved are hidden in a crowd of lookalikes.

• Make the actors take definite movements and positions. Each action should be able to be defined in terms of its intention. Avoid aimless movement (movement without communicative function), as it will only blur the focused movements and confuse the audience. Make the blocking points register by setting them against a fixed background.

• Check the clarity of the blocking. Invite friends unfamiliar with the play to rehearsals to see if the points are coming across. Do not rely on generalities, but ask them direct questions that they can answer only if they have really understood ("What do you think Gertrude feels after the king stops the play?"). If they cannot tell what the director thinks he or she has put into the scene, it has not yet succeeded.

BLOCKING CREATES FOCUS

Focus is the means by which the director "orders" the audience's attention to the line, face, or gesture which is most important at a given moment. Consider the difficulties stage directors face in contrast to their film counterparts. Film directors (together with their editors) can aim their camera at as large or as small a subject as they wish. When a character speaks a line, the camera can follow with a closeup of another character's reaction. The camera can zero in on a prop, a clenched fist, a pained expression, or a two-shot (isolating a glance between two characters), or it can draw back to show the whole scene at once. The cameraperson can also convert to slow motion (within most contemporary film styles) or freeze frames without breaking the stylistic realism of the scene, thereby fixing the audience's attention on an action of supreme importance or emotional content. Imagine the possibilities open to the film director in the "mousetrap" scene in *Hamlet,* just discussed: closeups of the king's face, of his hand clenching the arm of his throne; two-shots between Hamlet and Claudius exchanging potent looks, between Claudius and Gertrude, between Horatio and Claudius, between Hamlet and Horatio. By contrast, stage directors are faced with a full setting all the time, and if they want the audience to look at Hamlet instead of Polonius, they have to contrive that it does so.

Focus is just as important, however, in relatively simple and outwardly nonactive scenes. A scene with only two characters on stage, for example, is ordinarily watched as one watches a tennis match; the audience has eyes only for the speaker, and shifts back and forth as the characters exchange lines. But a scene is not a tennis match; sometimes its central points are made "between shots." Sometimes a character's line is the most important focal point of the moment, but sometimes a director would rather have the audience see the other character's reaction. The director must then find ways to interrupt the audience's natural desire to follow the dialogue and focus its attention instead on the more important event taking place. Antigone is arguing with Ismene; does the director want the audience to watch Ismene develop her line of reasoning or watch Antigone quietly considering it? Lear is jesting with the fool; should we watch the fool's antics or the reactions they are drawing from the tormented king? These are questions the director must answer and then implement, or the play's internal workings will be muddled and arbitrarily presented. In scenes with three, four, or a dozen characters, the problems of achieving valid focus grow exponentially. Fortunately, the director has many ways of handling them.

Principles of Focus

More than any other staging accomplishment, focus requires the complete compliance of the audience. Ultimately the audience will decide for itself what it wants to see, and if the production is dull, the audience may choose to focus on the patrons instead of on the actors—in most cases a disastrous occurrence. In Elizabethan times, we are led to believe, it was a major accomplishment if the play drew the patrons' attention to the stage, away from the galleries.

Directors collaborate with the playwright as well as with the actors and designers to induce the audience to see and hear precisely what they want it to. Theater conventions will help them, of course; the houselights will ordinarily be darkened, the ushers dressed in muted tones and speaking discreetly; the patrons, by common consent, will keep their thoughts and words to themselves, except for periods of applause and laughter, and stay in their seats. Of course this custom varies with cultures and climes (in gold rush days, mining camp theaters pleaded with patrons not to stamp on the floor or stand on the chairs), but certainly in today's American and English theater directors can expect compliance with their task. The rest is up to them and their production.

The principles that govern focus are complex, because manifold factors come into play. We shall list a number of these factors, roughly in descending order of importance. Those listed first, therefore, can in most cases override those following, all else being equal.

Focus Intrinsic to the Script

The first principles of focus are instrinsic to the script itself and to the story. Ordinarily the audience is more interested in the story of the play than in what the director does with or to it, and for this reason focus intrinsic to the script overrides all other forms.

A character has focus when he or she is *vulnerable*. This trait depends on the situation of the play more than on the blocking. Just as in the tennis match, where the spectators all watch the person to whom the ball has just been hit instead of the one who has hit it—so in the theater we always focus on the character who has been asked an important question or required to perform a risky task. This result is largely intrinsic to the inner action of the play, but the director can, by enhancing the inner action, create a stronger focus.

A character has focus when he or she has a *stronger intention* than the others. In the scene before the arrival of Othello's ship at Cyprus, for example, Iago, Desdemona, Emilia, Cassio, and various others are engaging in what appears to be small talk. Because Iago's known (to us) inner intentions are so fierce, he will have focus no matter what staging is used.

A *title* character will have focus, as will a principal character or a star performer. This is partly justifiable; if the play is called *Othello*, Othello has focus by dint of his name, since we assume the play is going to be about him and we will have to watch him closely. And when Katharine Hepburn steps on stage, we watch her because we know she is being paid a fortune for her efforts and we want to get our money's worth. Little can be done about this phenomenon, so the director had better accept the situation.

Focus Intrinsic to the Staging

Purely compositional methods of achieving focus can overrule the preceding, but they are most often used to supplement and enhance them, as well to determine focus when the already mentioned factors are not in play or are self-canceling, as is frequently the case. These compositional methods follow in rough order of their potency.

A character "pointed at," all else being equal, has focus. The pointing need not be literal; in fact, it usually involves simply having the other characters look at the focal character. This is one way of throwing the ball to him or her.

A character speaking, all else being equal, has focus. If the actor clears his or her throat or stammers first, he or she will have focus before the first word. This is ordinarily a cheap trick—and if initiated by the actor, an offensive bit of upstaging—but it is frequently the only way of drawing sudden focus to a character who is in no other way the point of attention. Some actors have made this stratagem a stock in trade.

A character facing the audience, all else being equal, has focus over those not facing the audience. Again, if initiated by the actor, this move can be considered upstaging. (The term means that the upstager moves with respect to the upstaged so that in a face-to-face confrontation the upstager is facing the audience and his or her smoldering colleague presents a back.) Upstaging arranged by the director is perfectly correct, though it occasionally causes bruised nerves. A character delivering a long speech to another is frequently blocked upstage center with the other downstage left, for example, since it is desirable at that point to see only the speaker's face. When the listener's reaction becomes important, he or she can turn to face the audience; the scene is what is called in films a two-shot, with both faces pointing to the audience. (See the photograph on page 111.)

A character moving, all else being equal, has focus over those who are still. Movement attracts attention, and even the most free, improvisational directors sometimes stop actors from moving about while others are supposed to have focus. In most productions calling for large numbers of actors on stage, the less important characters are told to freeze during their still moments; even a fidgeting finger can steal the focus from Hamlet if it is within the peripheral vision of the audience. Major movements, such as entrances, exits, full stage crosses, or anything done rapidly, are certain attention getters on stage, proving it desirable for directors to externalize inner actions as much as possible. Finally, a brief movement before a line, like a stammer, will draw focus before the actor's first word and is a common technique.

A character who is isolated, all else being equal, has focus. If ten actors are on stage right and one on stage left, the one on the left has a high degree of compositional focus. The same principle applies if ten are on the stage floor and one is on a raised platform or vice versa, or ten are upstage and one is downstage.

A character who is moving in a different pattern from the others, all else being equal, has focus. If he limps and the others stride, if she runs and the others walk, he or she will be looked at.

A character who is more brightly lit or is placed in a more interesting part of the stage or has a more exciting costume has focus. Actors have been known to make friends with lighting technicians and costume designers for this purpose. If a large canopied chair downstage left remains unsat in for a while, the first actor to sit in it will tend to draw attention.

An actor who is downstage, all else being equal, has focus. Early textbooks on directing laid great stress on areas of the stage that had high innate compositional focus, judging that downstage center had the highest, followed by upstage center, downstage right, and downstage left. We find this fairly arbitrary. Of course, if six actors stood motionless and impassive, all facing the audience, one in each of the six main areas of the stage, we would tend to look at those in the first row more than those in the second because the former were closer. We might look first at the one downstage center, because we are trained to look there, but our eyes would finally come to rest on the one closest to us: the actor downstage right for those on house left. and the actor downstage left for those on house right. If one of the actors was somewhat more attractive than the others, we would probably stare at him or her wherever he or she was located. The point is that, while focus by stage area has theoretical truth in a static situation, in practice almost any other focal principle overrides it.

We have cautioned throughout, "all else being equal," knowing of course that all else is not equal. Obviously, if Marlon Brando, playing Molière's Tartuffe, enters (after a big two-act buildup from the other characters) in his all-black costume, strides gallantly to an otherwise unused, raised downstage chair as the other actors stare at him, cries, "Where is my hair shirt and flagellator?" and is illuminated by a 5000 watt followspot as he sits down, he will have focus. But invariably focal matters are more complex. One character is speaking, one moving, one looking at someone else, one isolated in a corner, one downstage center, yet focus must still be achieved. The director works this out by understanding the principles of focus, knowing which ones are strongest in various situations. The synthesis of these principles is not scientific; it comes from an understanding of the theater itself—even of life itself—and from intuitive and experiential knowledge of which principle will override in each case. In this area, too, the director should check his choices against the findings of visitors at rehearsals if he is at all diffident about the validity of his intuition.

The fourteen photographs on the following pages illustrate various stagings from the contemporary theater—analyzed here for their illustrations of aesthetic and dramatic principles of focus.

FIGURE 57. With actors in the same plane and area, the man receives greater focus because of his more open stage position and slight height advantage. (*Courtesy, American Conservatory Theatre*)

FIGURE 58. With actors in different planes, the downstage actor has greater focus because of his closeness to the audience (here exaggerated by the camera). Compare with photograph below, however. (*Courtesy, Royal Shakespeare Company*)

FIGURE 59. With actors in different planes, the upstage actor has focus because of her open position, higher level, and the reinforcement of the "pointing" lines of the deckchair. (*French Cultural Services*)

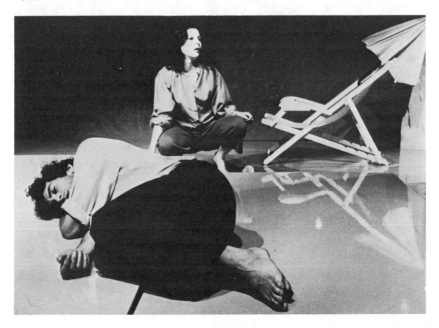

Upstaging

Actors are intuitively aware of devices to attain focus, and many try to use them, either consciously or unconsciously. Actors should not be condemned, of course, for what is a vital ingredient of an actor's talent. A highly mobile and exciting actor may be a dream as Hamlet, however, and a curse playing Horatio opposite a phlegmatic prince. The old actor who cagily lights a cigarette while another is speaking, the five-year-old girl who rolls her eyes at the audience while the leading lady is pontificating, even the novice actor who drifts upstage in a face-to-face scene to "see" the audience better are all upstaging and should be checked; if they are doing so involuntarily and cannot stop, they should be removed or the play is doomed. Incidentally, some actors continually upstage themselves, for various psychological reasons; for the production this can be just as disastrous as an actor who upstages others (though it causes fewer hurt feelings among the cast).

FIGURE 60.   Triangularity. The higher figure has focus because of his level, mass, and position at the apex of the triangle, in this French production of *Falstaff,* after Shakespeare, directed by Marcel Marechal.   (*French Cultural Services*)

FIGURE 61. Triangularity again, with the focus shared by the standing man and center woman. The man at the top has the higher level, but the woman has costume contrast, an interesting body position, and is framed by the men. From a Parisian production of *Proust.* (*French Cultural Services*)

FIGURE 62. Triangularity and the use of line. The focus goes to the actor at the apex of the triangle formed by the two pointed staves, which is reinforced by the focus of the other actors and by the separation of the pointed-at actor from the two masses of characters. It would be difficult to give a stronger focus. From the American Conservatory Theatre production of *Julius Caesar.* (*Courtesy, American Conservatory Theatre*)

FIGURE 63. Vertical emphasis. The striking sweep of the curved stairs, emphasized by the Gothic spires and reflective mirrors, utilizes great differences in level and plane. From a production of the National Theatre of Strasbourg (France). *(French Cultural Services)*

FIGURE 64. Horizontal emphasis. Formal but not stiff staging of a 1978 British National Theatre production of *The Cherry Orchard* directed by Peter Hall. The audience's interest is maintained by small variations in body positions. The focus is shared by actresses at left center and right center on the downstage plane: the actress on the right (stage left), by her separation from the others; the actress on the left (stage right), by her open facial position. Both actresses are also reinforced by the light colored objects next to them. The overall composition is balanced by the actress at the far right of the picture and the greater mass of the actors at the left—whose aesthetic weight is appropriately diminished by their upstage positions and dark costumes. *(Courtesy, National Theatre of Great Britain)*

FIGURE 65. Staging in depth. A subtle and interesting use of line is demonstrated in this Comédie Française production of Racine's Britannicus. The upstage center actor has focus because of his centrality, height, and open body position; by the line and focus of the other actors; and by the apposition of the statue at the right of the photograph. (*French Cultural Services*)

BLOCKING ESTABLISHES CREDIBILITY

The problem of achieving credibility for a character is to a certain extent an acting problem, a problem for the director insofar as he or she is working with the actor. But blocking is also an integral part of credibility; the greatest naturalistic actor in the world would be hamstrung if directed to stand, sit, and cross like no real person. Actors represent people, and in most dramatic situations people move and position themselves in response to the situation. In any play which is directed within a framework of realism, characters should move as we expect people to move; they should sit when they are tired, stand when they are excited, run when they are in a hurry, cross to someone when they want to make love. The *arbitrary* (and we emphasize arbitrary) disregarding of these and similarly obvious principles leads to noncredible action and is never tolerated by audiences, or for that matter, by actors. Again, in plays directed more or less realistically, the most theatrically effective bit of staging will collapse if it makes no sense to execute it at that moment.

Although we have considered only realistic plays to this point, the principle of credibility applies to all styles and forms of theater. No one would call *Hamlet* a realistic play—it is written in verse, for example—yet in all but the most abstractly styled production we expect Hamlet and the other actors to be credible. We want to see them walk, sit, and stand like human beings, and we expect that when Hamlet crosses to the audience to deliver a soliloquy, he crosses to us because he has something important to say to us. Even in the wildest theater of the absurd, we expect the actors to be credible within the context of the style of the play. The director must block the play to ensure that ultimate consistency of credibility.

Considerations of credibility in blocking must be carefully weighed against considerations of focus and clarity, for whereas credibility requires an attempt to simulate real-life behavior, clarity tries to make inner actions clear to an outside observer, which is not a consideration in real life. An outsider could observe a heated family argument without ever getting the gist of the disagreement or the internal shifts, but this must not happen in the theater. Clarity must always prevail, even at the possible risk of loss of credibility. But a loss of either is urgently to be avoided, and can be avoided by careful staging. Just as in a naturalistic play the playwright tries to shape

FIGURE 66. This National Theatre production of Tom Stoppard's *Jumpers* illustrates the strongest possible use of level: the raised actor has extreme focus because of height, perpendicularity, the strong contrast with the low supporting mass, centrality, costume, and lighting. (*Courtesy, National Theatre of Great Britain*)

FIGURE 67. More uneven form adds a sense of the dynamic to the composition in this photograph of Terry Hands's production of *The Changeling* for the Royal Shakespeare Company in 1978. The focus rests on the kneeling actor in the center because of his body position and the strong visual line from the lying woman and the standing man. A secondary focus rests on the lying woman because of her interesting body position. The standing man at center, despite being at the apex of a triangle, tends to be a part of the mass, framing the action rather than taking focus. (*Courtesy, Royal Shakespeare Company*)

FIGURE 68. In Michael Bogdanov's 1978 production of *The Taming of the Shrew* for the Royal Shakespeare Company, fairly compact mass and even form give a sense of relaxation. The body of each actor adds interest. The focus rests on the central actor because of framing, costume, and body position. (*Courtesy, Royal Shakespeare Company*)

FIGURE 69. In this photograph of a French production of Bertolt Brecht's *Arturo Ui,* focus within a dispersed mass of actors goes to the actor (center right in the photo) with his arms raised, because of framing by other actors, reinforcement by table and chairs, and the focus of other actors. A secondary focus rests on the actor seated at down right (left in photo), who receives primary focus if he moves while the other actors freeze. *(French Cultural Services)*

FIGURE 70. Philip Prowse's production of the Jacobean *Painter's Palace of Pleasure* for the Citizens' Theatre Company of Glasgow, Scotland, achieves an interesting aesthetic balance with the full use of stage areas. The focus goes to the actor downstage center because of the area and his body position; a secondary focus goes to the actor in armor because of his costume, his mass, and the line of the pointing hand. Note the interestingly varied positions of the hooded figures, giving tertiary focus to the woman in the open position upstage. An easy flow of the eye from body to body gives a smooth yet dynamic rhythm to the scene. *(Citizen's Theatre Glasgow. The Citizens' Company in PAINTER'S PALACE OF PLEASURE by Ford & Webster, directed and designed by Philip Prowse. March/April 1978. Photograph John Vere Brown)*

and compress the dialogue into a telling two-hour product, so the director must eliminate extraneous movement and try to make directorial points through credible human physical actions. For ultimately, if the blocking and acting are not credible, the failure of the play will be as great as if it is not clear.[1]

Method of Blocking for Credibility

• Familiarize the actors with the set and the situation. This is ordinarily the first task of a director trying to achieve any kind of naturalistic performance. If the setting is an interior room, for example, make it as easy as possible for the actors to feel at home in the room (particularly if it is supposed to be their home). Because rehearsals rarely take place on a prebuilt set (and the results are extraordinary when they do), arrange the rehearsal space to resemble the set as closely as possible. Use furniture that resembles the stage furniture (or use stage furniture) so that the actors can use it as they will in performance. Let them practice living in the set, using its doors, furniture, fireplace, bookshelves, and so on. Improvise scenes not in the play that could take place on the set. Give directions in terms of the set as a room rather than as a stage ("Go to the bathroom" instead of "Exit upstage left door"). Give the actors the props they will use. Let them bring in set dressing and furniture if possible and use it in the performance, too.

• Work with the actors on establishing their characterization down to the details of ordinary living: how would they sit in a chair, set the table for dinner, brush their teeth, and so on. Have the actors do these routine things on the set or the set simulation.

• Use set pieces with the structural counterparts of the real objects they represent. If you are doing *Zoo Story,* which takes place on a park bench, obtain a bench on the back of which Jerry can sit, as he could on a Central Park bench. If the set has wide window sills and there are teenage boys in the play, have the carpenter build the set so that the boys can sit on the sills as they could or would do at home. Use furniture that is not too fragile to experiment with—couches that the actors can climb on, trip over, sit on the arms of, and so on.

• Let the actors improvise much of their blocking. Credibility is the one directorial objective which the actors, if they are good, can probably establish better through their movement than you can.

BLOCKING ESTABLISHES AND HEIGHTENS THE INNER ACTION

Blocking intensifies the inner action of a play (see Chapter 2). Inner action is the emotional or intellectual (mental) shifts within characters: realizations, resolutions, alterations of plans, alterations of attitudes, and so on.

---

[1]We admit exception to this. Countless Broadway plays, especially when well into their runs, are performed with only the vaguest simulation of credibility. Regardless of theoretical considerations, audiences seem not to mind. What they do find intolerable, however, is not knowing what is happening or not being able to hear. This state of affairs is painful to anyone concerned with the art of the theater, but it exists and bears reporting. Still, we are concerned with the art of directing, not the practices of a commercial industry, and we stick by our point.

Falling in love, for example, is an inner action which does not necessarily correspond to any outward physical activity, yet it must in some way be made apparent to an audience if the story of the play depends on it. The following scene from *Othello* contains intense inner action unaccompanied by any specified outer action.

> IAGO. My noble lord—
> OTHELLO. What dost thou say, Iago?
> IAGO. Did Michael Cassio, when you wooed my lady
>   Know of your love?
> OTHELLO. He did, from first to last. Why dost thou ask?
> IAGO. But for a satisfaction of my thought;
>   no further harm.
> OTHELLO. Why of thy thought, Iago?
> IAGO. I did not think he had been acquainted with her.
> OTHELLO. O, yes, and went between us very oft.
> IAGO. Indeed?
> OTHELLO. Indeed? Ay, indeed! Discernst thou
>   aught in that? Is he not honest?
> IAGO. Honest, my lord?
> OTHELLO. Honest? Ay, honest.
> IAGO. My lord, for aught I know.
> OTHELLO. What does thou think?
> IAGO. Think, my lord?
> OTHELLO. Think my lord?
>   By heaven he echoes me,
>   As if there were some monster in his thought
>   Too hideous to be shown. Thou dost mean something . . .

On one level, nothing is happening except talking. On an intellectual and emotional level, however, Othello's entire psychic foundation is being attacked, and his life will never hereafter be the same. Similarly, Iago is for the first time taking criminal risks with his security to plant the seed of jealousy in the Moor's ear. The nature of the action is in fact as urgent and compelling as Hamlet's killing of Claudius, but it is entirely mind-to-mind, not body-to-body.

The inner action of a scene is occasionally called its subtext. Although it might be valuable to distinguish these terms (an inner action may be fully textual, for example, as in a soliloquy), for most purposes they are the same. Subtext involves all the inner action of a scene or play which is not specifically noted in the text; it is under (*sub*) the text, there to be found by the diligent interpretive study or intuition of the director and actors. It is also there for the study and intuition of critics and audiences, so the director must work carefully to avoid universal censure.

The subtext of a given moment is the composite of three components which, in the lazy parlance of the theater, are frequently mistaken for the whole thing. They are not, and they should be precisely understood:

1. The character's intention (what he wants to do)
2. The character's motivation (why he wants to do it)
3. The character's inner monologue (what he is thinking when he does it)

The subtext of a play, therefore, is a highly complex network of conscious and unconscious impulses that are as real and theatrical as the external actions. The text is the mere external tip of a giant iceberg of inner action.

As an example of the complexity of this problem, let us look at Othello's single line, "Indeed? Ay, indeed!" A possible interpretation of the subtext of that moment follows.

> Othello's intention: to make light of Iago's hint by mocking Iago's unusual inflection, thereby diverting Iago from continuing.
>
> Othello's motivation: to prevent himself from hearing what he dreads to hear.
>
> Othello's inner monologue: "What the hell is he driving at?"
>
> Iago's intention (while listening to Othello's line): to note how much the hint rattles Othello.
>
> Iago's motivation: to see how fast and hard he should pursue this line of hinting without overstepping his bounds.
>
> Iago's inner monologue: "Yes, he's upset; he's going to pursue this."
>
> The subtext of the moment: Othello, frightened by the possibilities that Iago's hint has opened to examination, tries to avoid further discussion of the subject by the psychological defense mechanism of mocking his subordinate. Iago, a superior psychological analyst, sees through Othello's mechanism, recognizes it for what it is, and discovers that the Moor is open to further suggestion.

Multiply this subtext by every definable moment in the play and every character on stage at every moment, and the magnitude of the subtextual play becomes apparent.

The director "finds" or "chooses" the interpretation of the play and its moments (see Chapter 2) and communicates it to the actors so that they can think about it, feel it, and play it (see Chapter 8). No matter how great the contribution of the actors in this regard, the director is still responsible for the understanding and projection of every action, inner and outer, in the course of the play. Blocking is one of his or her major vehicles in this task.

Blocking intensifies inner action by making it outer action. Blocking is the principal mechanism by which a play moves off the page into the theater. It gives life and fullness to dialogue, demonstrating that something important is happening. It is entirely possible for guests at an intimate cocktail party to sit in the same positions without moving for an hour at a time, even if their discussion leads to shattering revelations and emotional shifts. But stasis is rarely successful in the theater, because plays usually involve dramatic confrontations causing characters to become highly disturbed and active. The audience expects the characters to become deeply involved in the situation; if the characters are not involved, why should the audience be? Character involvement is usually communicated across the footlights by movement, by doing things and by physically reacting to stimuli. Even when the entire point of a play is stasis (as in Chekhov's *The Three Sisters*) directors ordinarily find that movement which can be shown to be self-defeating is the most effective way to project the stasis. Only rarely (we are reminded of Ralph Richardson and John Gielgud in *Home*) can even superior actors remain still on stage for long periods of time and hope to engage the audience with philosophical reflections and internal reactions. The plays of George Bernard Shaw, filled as they are with rhetorical dialect and devoid of external action, are usually most successful when staged with movement to emphasize the "points" of the playwright.

Thus a play's blocking creates a sense that things are happening. A familiar adage in the early days of cinema was that "moving pictures move." The same is true, perhaps to a lesser extent, in the theater. Placement and movement tell not only the external story of the play but also the characters' thoughts and feelings. A well-blocked production can be attentively (if not perfectly) followed even if the dialogue is in an unknown foreign language; for proof of that one need only attend productions of the late Bertolt Brecht, still playing at his Berliner Ensemble in East Berlin.

Methods of Blocking to Heighten Inner Action

• Establish the inner action precisely in terms of beats. Discuss the beats with the actors to make sure that you and they see them the same way.

• Externalize inner action. If an actress is saying, "I want to get out of here, Charlie," it might be effective to have her back toward the door, facing Charlie, while she speaks. If, on the other hand, she is saying, "I'm going to kill you, Charlie," she can emphasize her inner action by reaching for a weapon.

• Dramatize inner shifts of emotion. It is possible, sometimes even likely, that real-life people would remain outwardly impassive while their world is crumbling. It is also possible that they would externalize the inner shift through movement. A director is free within the bounds of credibility to choose either course; the latter is ordinarily more theatrical. When Juliet first hears that Romeo is a Montague, for example, she could make no visible response. But she could also run downstage, throw herself on her bed, pound on the bedstead, whirl back at the nurse who has informed her, and finally bury her face in the pillow. The first reaction may be considered more naturalistic and the second more melodramatic, but each is reasonable for a fourteen-year-old girl, and each has a valid place on the stage.

All mechanisms for intensifying stage action can tend to lead to melodramatic spectaculars, mugging on the part of the actors, and empty theatrics. They must be used with caution or they will be laughable. Once clarity is achieved, the level of intensification is a variable that directors should handle with care, but they should not be afraid to use it. Actors, particularly those trained in naturalistic styles, often wish to play their scenes with an outward display of cool dispassion. When this tendency is uncorrected, the inner action the director wants to project may remain in the actors' minds and not reach the audience's emotion.

BLOCKING CREATES BEHAVIOR

This is one of the least understood yet most important aspects of blocking; it is fair to state that few directors until the last two or three decades have even been aware that blocking creates behavior. Yet it is a major part of most contemporary professional directing. As Elia Kazan noted, "Directing finally consists of turning Psychology into Behavior."[2]

Behavior is movement on stage which is not called for in the script and which seems to have no direct correlation with the play. It is movement for actors to "play against," rather than with which to express themselves and their feelings directly. It allows them to set up a pattern of audience expectations through which, by making deviations, they can allow their deepest feelings to be inferred.

For example, consider a meaningful but not climactic speech in the middle of a modern play, a speech that could (and with an unimaginative director certainly would) be delivered straightforwardly from the middle of the stage. Now imagine the same speech delivered while the actor crosses to the bar, mixes himself a Manhattan, drops a cherry into it, crosses back downstage, and concludes the line by taking a drink. Consider the possibilities of subtextual communication this bit of blocking provides. The actor's inner action, which could otherwise be conveyed only by his inflections and facial expressions, which can easily become mugging, can now be revealed by his manner of walking to the bar (compulsively? casually? is he comfortable in this room? is he uptight?); by how he pours the drink (do his hands tremble a bit? is he composed enough to measure the vermouth carefully?); by how he drops the cherry (is he trying to show how composed he is by adding that little extra, perhaps victorious, touch? or is he trying to disguise his worry about his drinking by elegantly plopping in the cherry to show that he retains his control?); or by how he crosses back downstage (triumphantly? nervously? proving something?) and takes the first swallow (desperately? savagely? savoring the taste?). What a wealth of inner action such a minor piece of blocking can convey!

[2]Elia Kazan, "Notebook for *A Streetcar Named Desire*," in Toby Cole and Helen K. Chinoy, *Directors on Directing*, rev. ed. (Indianapolis: The Bobbs-Merrill Co., Inc., 1963), p. 346.

Consider the possibilities of staging the scene from *Othello*. Suppose that in an experimental modern dress production or a rehearsal for a more traditional production, Othello is lifting weights while Iago sits at his feet. Imagine Othello pausing, the weight in midair, as he ponders Iago's point, then renewing his workout with greater energy as he tries to shake off Iago's comments. Imagine Othello playfully tossing Iago one of the weights, and Iago redoubling his efforts because of the discomfort the Moor's action causes him. Imagine the lines spoken as the two men jog around the stage, drink at a bar, or fire at a rifle range. The creation of behavior can unlock all sorts of internal feelings that mere face-to-face confrontation, and even the abstract "cross left, cross right" directing, cannot.

The creation of behavior is inextricable from the creation of style, and it is not normally considered under the general heading of stage composition. But ultimately the director's blocking creates it. In this area, within the bounds of what will be effective, the director can make an enormous contribution to the play. Behavior is a director's creative option because he or she is invariably the one who invents it; actors are trained to follow their intentions without deviation; and behavior will tend to be an obstacle to, rather than an intensifier of, their intentions.

Methods of Blocking
to Create Behavior

• Consider creating obstacles. Suppose a character receives an onstage telephone call in the midst of a conversation. If he is next to the phone when it rings, it must be made to ring just as he completes his last sentence. He picks up the receiver and answers. Consider this alternative: the character, standing behind a sofa at upstage right, is talking to a friend who is sitting on the sofa. The phone rings in mid-sentence, and still talking, he crosses down left to the telephone, picks up the receiver, and begins to speak. The action is more fluid, more interesting (more credible, for that matter), and more open to subtextual acting. Now suppose that during the phone conversation he reaches into his pocket and pulls out a cigarette. He fumbles for a match but has none (the obstacle). His friend, seeing his distress, picks up a lighter from the coffee table. The actor on the phone picks up the body of the telephone and, still talking, crosses back to the sofa, where his friend lights the cigarette. At that point the person on the other end of the line says something of great importance. "What?" exclaims our actor, wheeling back to a full-face position. Talking furiously on the phone, he crosses urgently back to the telephone table, where the ashtray is located. Finally he sits by the phone while his friend lights a cigarette of his own. This staging sequence is arbitrary, to be sure, but it can greatly heighten the excitement of the scene. The obstacle has forced the actor to move, to turn, to be frustrated (at not having a match), to be satisfied (with his first pull on the cigarette), and to further identify his relationship with the other actor on stage, who has demonstrated some empathy by realizing that his friend needed a match, but not enough empathy to cross to him and light his cigarette. Only in action can we discover the full measure of a character.

• Think of the possibilities for behavior suggested by the setting. Are there dishes to be cleaned, ashtrays to be emptied, pillows to be fluffed, a floor to be swept? Tennessee Williams's plays are filled with marvelous behavior that renders the subtext vividly. Recall the scene in *The Night of the Iguana* in which Maxine and Hannah are having a life-and-death struggle, in utterly quiet tones, while setting the tables for dinner. The handling of knives and forks and the rattling of dishes becomes the prime vehicle whereby the actors reveal what is on their minds. Recall also the scene in Arthur Miller's *The Death of a Salesman* in which Willy accidentally turns on the wire recorder and struggles insanely to turn it off.

• Consider the possibilities for behavior suggested by the characters. What is Othello doing when Iago accosts him? Standing around waiting to be accosted? Think creatively: what *could* he be doing? "Enter Hamlet reading on a book," says Shakespeare in one of his few behavioral stage directions. How is Hamlet reading it—avidly, absent-mindedly, discovered at a desk, in a chair? What are Benvolio and Mercutio doing as they jest with Romeo? Playing catch? Practicing their dueling skills? Carrying each other on their backs?

• Stretch the actors' capacity. In the tea scene of Giraudoux's *The Madwoman of Chaillot*, for example, there may be pressure to use imaginary tea and no cream, sugar, or lemon. This pressure may come from the prop department (it would mean less work and expense), but it might also come from the actors, who may consider that the real props "get in the way." "In the way of what?" the director should ask. No play is simply the sum of its verbal content. Imagine the possibilities for hilarity, as well as for character revelation, when the three old madwomen struggle with tea, an antique teakettle and teakettle warmer, china teacups, cream, sugar, spoon, lemon, napkins, spills, mop-ups, burned tongues (too hot), wry faces (too much lemon), and satisfied, semisenile sighs (just right).

• Think imaginatively about where a scene is set. Elizabethan and multiscene plays in particular provide a great deal of choice in this matter. The so-called "First Court Scene" in *Hamlet*, for example, Shakespeare calls simply "scene two." No lines specifically define the setting as a court, so why could it not be set in a meadhall? Claudius, a heavy drinker, could receive Cornelius and Voltimand wherever he chooses; the play is full of lines and imagery about drinking (Hamlet: "They klepe us drunkards"), so why not play the scene among courtiers carousing over pints of ale? Imagine Claudius's effect when, red-faced and befuddled, he turns half-drunkenly to Hamlet (a nondrinker?) and says, "But now, my cousin Hamlet, and (burp) my son."

• Set up behavior opposite to the inner action of the scene. Interrupting or shifting the behavior will make the drama of the scene more chilling or poignant. In *Romeo and Juliet*, Paris finds Juliet apparently dead on her wedding day. In Mel Shapiro's production of the play at the Old Globe Theatre in San Diego, Paris came in with a hired group of strolling musicians, who played their joyous serenade right down to the discovery of the presumed corpse. This practice parallels what the actor calls "playing against the obvious," whereby a character who is supposed to cry tries instead to laugh, yet his or her tears show through the laughter for greater poignancy. Blocking against the obvious means blocking against the normal system of intensifying the inner action; the actress who says, "I'm going to kill you, Charlie" does not in this case cross to the rifle rack but backs timidly toward the door. The effect is one of surprise, intrigue, and a feeling that something unknown is going to happen. (Of course, something should then happen, or the movement will look absurd.)

The danger in blocking to create behavior is that it might appear gimmicky. In classical productions (as of Shakespearean plays) some critics will attack anything other than the actors standing and delivering their

FIGURE 71. Food props and real table settings provide hilarious opportunities for staging the comic banquet scene from Molière's *The Bourgeois Gentleman* in Jerome Savary's 1982 production for the Théâtre de L'Est Parisien. (*Courtesy, Théâtre de L'Est Parisien; photo by Enguerand*)

lines straightforwardly ("It might be theatrical, but it certainly isn't Shakespeare," or "Imagine old Will rolling over in his grave"). Of course behavior can be gimmicky, as can anything in the theater, which after all is only humanly created illusion. Transparency in a director's achievement is rarely commendable; if the audience dismisses a bit of created behavior as a cute directorial device, the bit will fail because it has not satisfied its primary objective: to project character and action more deeply than would a line reading. Still, the creation of behavior may ultimately be that which gives a produced play its greatest sense of vitality, and it should be creatively, and intently, pursued.

BLOCKING CREATES SPECIAL EFFECTS

So far we have been speaking mainly in terms of the goals of blocking in serious, realistic plays, since those general principles apply to almost all theatrical modes. But much blocking is executed for what we might call special effects, especially for farcical effects. Pratfalls, for example, are blocked actions which cannot really be justified on the basis of clarity or credibility and can only by stretching the point be considered to derive from the director's wish to heighten inner action. A pratfall is staged for one reason, to make the audience laugh, although it is selectively employed to make a statement about the character who falls. In plays that permit or require them, extensive chase scenes, slapstick beatings, characters backing into each other, speeded-up motion or slow motion, and wildly exaggerated tantrums can produce the same effect. Although these farcical staging bits are as old as Aristophanes, they are frequently employed today with great effect, in the appropriate stylistic circumstances.

Blocking can also create nonfarcical theatrical effects. Slow motion and nonnaturalistic freezes can delineate dramatic confrontations superbly. Actors advancing en masse on the audience can be chilling, as in Peter Brook's *Marat/Sade*. Actors accomplishing seemingly superhuman feats, as in the Polish productions of Jerzy Grotowski, can be awesome and thrilling. Blocking which fills the stage with hundreds of extras, horses, and elephants, such as the summertime Roman production of *Aïda*, can be breathtaking. Blocking for these purposes, needless to say, involves a high level of advance planning and consideration of the style of the production.

This sort of blocking also involves the most delicate originality. Although books of comic *lazzi* (time-honored comic bits) and spectacular staging effects could be compiled, the success of these special feats is in their newness; in their appropriateness to the play and the character involved; and in the unique imagination of the director, playwright, and cast.

BLOCKING CREATES AESTHETIC EFFECTS

Historically, one of the first goals of a director was to arrange the actors in an aesthetically pleasing composition. In the nineteenth century the models of this sort of composition were art masterpieces such as Raphael's *The School of Athens,* which displays dozens of men and women grouped so that the canvas is balanced and the focus is on the central group. There is a danger, however, in seeing stage composition in precisely similar terms. In the first place, it speaks only to proscenium staging and may be inapplicable to thrust, arena, or environmental staging. Second, it assumes a single vantage point (the center of the auditorium) from which the stage picture is perfect. But even proscenium theaters have two features that Raphael did not have to contend with: a multiplicity of vantage points and a real (not simulated by perspective) depth of stage (versus canvas). The stage director's goals are partly shared by other visual artists, but they are also partly different and their implementation is considerably so.

FIGURE 72. Comic business from traditional vaudeville is up to the invention of the actors and director Roger Planchon in this Théâtre National Populaire production of *Bourgeois Follies,* staged in Paris in 1977. (*French Cultural Services*)

FIGURE 73. Ships at sea are created by sheer stylization of movement in this Denver Theatre Center production of *Moby Dick.* (*Courtesy, Denver Theatre Center*)

FIGURE 74.   Absolute contrast in position, level, and costume characterizes
this scene from Aragon's *The Clocks of Basle,* as adapted and staged by the
French director Antoine Vitez.   (*French Cultural Services*)

The compositional subgoals of a director might be to create

1. Balance (or imbalance)
2. Visual focus (or mass confusion)
3. Sweeping movement (or formal stasis)
4. Use of all stage areas (or of one stage area)
5. Prettiness (or ugliness)
6. Dignity (or grotesquery)

COMPOSITIONAL AESTHETICS

Balance is a particularly important element in composition. There is a need for balance, gravitational stability, in the human makeup. A picture hung unevenly can be disturbing; things off-kilter can set up an uncomfortable, even irritating response. A director can, of course, use such compositional effects to create particular moments that illustrate disturbing action; but for the most part a director wants the audience to feel comfortable with the stage picture so that the action may be directly communicated. Balance does not, however, have to be even and symmetrical. Symmetrical balance, that is, mass equally distributed on either side of a center line, is the most comfortable; but it is, equally, monotonous and unimaginative and will give a rather flat and linear quality to composition that is particularly unsuitable

FIGURE 75. Symmetrical balance. The near-exact symmetry of this composition—from a French production of Harold Pinter's *No Man's Land,* directed by Roger Planchon—underscores the stasis of personal relations, which is the play's subject. *(French Cultural Services)*

FIGURE 76. Assymmetrical balance. The tall figure on the platform at the right of the photograph balances the seated figures facing him diagonally and provides a stable tableau. (*Courtesy, Denver Theatre Center*)

for realism. Asymmetrical balance uses the weight of space to achieve balance between unequal masses, which allows for much more interesting compositional effects: one person against a mass, two persons against three, two and three persons against a mass, and so on. Finally, what a director is trying to achieve is total aesthetic balance: the use of the stage space in such a way as to achieve focus and communicate the dramatic action, by balancing against each other all the factors we have discussed—area, plane, body position, level, line, mass, symmetrical and asymmetrical balance—so that they create the most comfortable, interesting, and dynamic impact on the audience. (See again, figures 57–70 on pp. 110–18.)

This may sound daunting enough in itself, but so far we have been dealing with the basics of composition; the whole business becomes both more complex and interesting when the basics are used to build a complete aesthetic vocabulary, in which line, mass, and form, in and of themselves, create particular responses in an audience. In any given culture, human beings share an experiential iconography. They are moved in particular and consistent ways by rhythms and images. These are learned associations stored over millenia in what the psychologist Jung termed the "collective unconscious." For example, darkness is frequently associated with fear and evil—an atavistic response to the vulnerability and unprotectedness felt by our distant ancestors in their dark caves through long unlit nights. By contrast, fire, in the context of a hearth, has connotations of home and comfort. Fire is also associated with passion, because of its heat, and danger, because of its destructive power. The color white can call up age, winter, and death and also purity in its unblemished form.

The rhythms of human existence also produce particular responses: life is seen as a movement from birth to death, as night follows day (night = darkness = death); spring turns to summer, fall, and winter. The waning of the moon and the turning of the tide all produce rhythmical responses in us. Along the east coast of England it was long-established folklore that a person only died as the tide was going out: Shakespeare made reference to this belief in *Henry V* (II. iii), speaking of Falstaff's death "e'en at the turning o' the tide." Shakespeare also made frequent use of storms, with their connotation of God's wrath, and the disruption of nature, as in the first scene in *Macbeth* and the conspirator's scene in *Julius Caesar*.

Whether aware of it or not, directors constantly make use of this shared human vocabulary in creating stage effects; indeed it is an absolutely fundamental part of their communication with the audience. They are turning the signs and symbols in the text—in which the playwright has lodged his or her flesh-and-blood ideas and emotions—into signs and symbols on the stage which will create a flesh-and-blood response in the audience. Mass, line, and form—the shape that mass and line take—create very strong emotional responses and communicate a great deal to an audience quite apart from any intellectual content or statement they may be making. The whole principle of abstract art is built on this phenomenon. Line, mass, and form are seen as images which produce an emotional response or evoke a mood in the spectator. The weight of mass may be oppressive, a feeling one sometimes gets walking between high skyscrapers; or it may be light and delicate, with a great deal of free space. The line may be aspiring, as the delicate, perpendicular spires of Gothic cathedrals; it may be aspiring but threatening, as the larger perpendicular mass of a mountain.

To simplify and focus this discussion, the following are some responses a director may expect from the audience to the use of certain lines and forms in stage compositions:

- Horizontal lines, with little mass, can create a restful, calm, monotonous effect.
- Perpendicular lines can express aspiration, dignity, rigidity, grandeur—again depending on the weight of mass.
- Diagonal lines can be dynamic, forceful, eccentric, cutting, harsh.
- Straight lines convey strength, formality, regularity.
- Curved lines connote fluidity, flexibility, gracefulness, freedom.
- Broken lines have the effect of informality, disorder, individuality.

The same exercise may be done with form:

- Regular or symmetrical form produces formality, hardness, calculation.
- Irregular form is more realistic, informal, unrestricted in its quality.
- Compact form suggests strength, power, energy, determination.

- Diffuse form creates the response of diversity, individuality, casualness, lack of discipline.
- Shallow form, within a single plane, induces artificiality, monotony, superficiality.
- Depth of form, more than one plane, expresses warmth, richness, a realistic effect.

Of course, not everyone will have precisely the same response to these compositional aesthetics, and a director will be working with combinations of line, mass, and form which may very well induce mixed emotional responses. This is absolutely as it should be; little interesting dramatic action is one-dimensional, and the director can produce dynamic tensions by balancing line against mass and form. For example, an irregular compact form is quite different in its impact from either a regular compact form or an irregular scattered form. Again, a regular form with perpendicular lines contrasts strongly with a regular form that has horizontal lines or an irregular form with perpendicular lines.

Directors will produce their own balances in accordance with the way in which they "see" the play, but there are one or two rules of thumb:

- Tragedies, or serious dramas, are likely to have fairly large mass, compact and regular form, and perpendicular line—because of the strength, dignity, and formality of their environment and characters and the lofty nature of the issues involved.
- Comedies will tend toward curved and possibly broken lines (depending on how physical they are), delicate mass, and diffuse, somewhat shallow form—which helps to communicate the sense of ease, freedom, fluidity, and positive, optimistic outlook on life which informs the comic sensibility.
- Contemporary realistic plays probably have broken line, irregular and deep form, and moderate mass—projecting the informal, individualistic, and scattered but reasonably substantial nature of modern life.

A very simple series of exercises to demonstrate and test the validity of these propositions is to have a group of actors set up and improvise scenes with a very specific quality, for example,

A patio party in a warm climate
Tourists in a medieval cathedral
A presidential inauguration
Sunday teatime in England
The greenroom on opening night
The same greenroom in the second month of the run

Because of their experiential background, actors will tend automatically to set up situations whose line, mass, and form fall somewhere within the expected parameters. For example, the green room on opening night will probably have a rather deep, irregular form and broken line and mass; this suggests the somewhat nervous, anticipatory, wrapped-up-in-one's-tensions quality of such an occasion. Two months later the line will be more horizontal, the form more shallow and regular, and the mass possibly more compact—suggesting the ease, calm, and even monotony that now predominates. Understanding the principles we have just discussed can be very useful to directors, as it will help them realize the feeling of a scene in terms of shape and rhythms. The qualities of the scene will suggest composition, not in minute-to-minute detail, but broad balances of line and form. Then, given a floor plan that allows such shape to evolve and a few general suggestions to the actors, the director should find that the details follow and fall comfortably into place, arising from the actors' intuitive sense of the action taking place. All very simple, "all else being equal," which, however, as we suggested at the beginning of this section, it never is.

So as not to confuse the discussion, we have been talking so far in terms of still-frame composition; but of course the picture is constantly dissolving and reforming, and we are going to close this section with a brief look at the impact of movement on composition. Fundamentally, movement on a one-to-one basis will always take focus over stillness. However, with six persons moving on stage, one still person would have focus by contrast. Movement itself has relative strengths and weaknesses: moving downstage tends to be stronger than moving upstage—because of stronger plane and body visibility; standing up or moving up onto a level is stronger than sitting or moving off a level. Long movements are initially dramatic, but they lose strength if prolonged beyond the audience's interest or pass through strong areas into weaker ones. Strong exits which entail movement to upstage doors are difficult, for the reasons we have just suggested—which is why the convention of pausing, and taking the last line at the door, grew up; today this is considered "stagey," but if well done it can be effective. Movement before a line emphasizes the line—the movement draws focus to the line; conversely, movement after a line emphasizes the movement.

Movement is derived from understanding the demands of the dramatic action. Again, if the director has a good ground plan and the actors well understand their characters' action, the actors will constantly feel impulses toward movement from the text. Very simplistically, disgust, embarrassment, and rejection will create impulses to move away; joy, love, hope, and so on will suggest movements toward. Just how these movements are taken, at what tempo and rhythm, will depend on the character and situation. Occasionally it will be necessary for a director to ask an actor to move simply to balance the composition. This movement might be anything from a simple counter to an inconspicuous move of several feet. Such adjustments, though technical, must seem natural to the character in the situation, and a good actor will always be able to find an adequate motivation:

after all, in life we are always adjusting our balance and vantage point when in groups.

BLOCKING CREATES VARIETY

There is no question that blocking creates variety, but whether movement should be injected into a production for that reason alone is debatable. Many directors insert a series of sits, stands, and crosses simply to keep the audience alert; perhaps nothing is more indicative of poor directing, in fact, than to see the characters moving aimlessly around the stage because the director told them to do so. It is not enough merely to remind the director that every move must have a motivation from character; every move on stage should have a directorial purpose, more than for variety. Indeed, if a play is creatively blocked to clarify the external action, to intensify the inner action, and to develop credibility, behavior, and the desired special effects—and if the play is a good one to begin with—it is difficult to conceive that the necessary variety will not be present.

The theater has no innate need for movement. Samuel Beckett's short play, *Play*, requires three characters to be immersed to their necks in urns for the play's duration, and to remain impassive and expressionless to boot. In *Home*, John Gielgud's most vigorous movement during the entire play was to stretch his legs. One should not underestimate the audience's ability to stay involved, *as long as valid action is taking place on stage.*

Still, not all plays are devoid of dull passages, and the director may be said to have a responsibility to enliven these with effective movement. No one really questions this use, in practice; still it seems far more effective for directors to find something in the inner action, or to create some behavior, than simply to say to themselves, "They've been sitting there long enough. I'll move them over to stage right." Such arbitrariness can often bewilder the audience as well as the actors, leaving the audience more bored than before.

BLOCKING CREATES
ABSTRACT EFFECTS
AND SYMBOLIC PATTERNS

We have mentioned a few cases where directing creates special effects, such as actors moving en masse toward the audience. Particularly in non-naturalistic plays directors often create what we must consider nonnatural character movement or placement for abstract purposes. For example, in the last scene of Dürrenmatt's *The Visit*, as staged by Peter Brook, the actors formed a perfect semicircle around Anton Schill, then slowly converged on him as he was killed. This not only created an abstract feeling of horror, it also conveyed the symbolic meaning that people can be turned into machines, given proper stimulus (in this case, money). Otherwise, the action of this play was realistically directed.

When abstract or symbolic movements repeat or reverse themselves, the director is using a blocking pattern. In comedy or farce, this practice is familiar as the running visual gag: an actor always trips on the last step of the stairway, always knocks over the same chair. In highly stylized plays, the pattern may be consciously symmetrical; for example, actors on opposite sides of the stage rise simultaneously and cross to meet each other at exact center stage. Other patterns are much more subtle; for example, one character may always move in a circular fashion whereas others are blocked back and forth in straight lines. In styles that permit it, actors can move simultaneously, as in *The Visit*, or with identical strange mannerisms, such as goose-stepping, to indicate a greater than normal sense of menace. Or an actor can be positioned in a realistically abnormal manner, such as at the proscenium edge or in the audience, to establish a relationship with the audience that exceeds the limits of the regular play. An actor can establish one area of the stage as "his," thereby making his presence felt even when he is not on stage.

Abstract and symbolic blocking can be received with enormous approval or disapproval. On the positive side, they may be considered the director's great contribution to the play, as memorable as Alexander Dean's entrance of the six characters, mentioned earlier. Or they may be quickly dismissed as meretricious, the director's "showing off." They may also sound exciting in theory yet be lost on the audience. More than one director has proudly said, "What a great idea! See, she comes in that door in the first act and goes out the same door in the last act!"—and the point is completely wasted because no one else noticed it, even subliminally.

The most that can be said about abstract movement patterns, in terms of a director's goals, is that the best of them are sensational, many are a waste of time, and the worst are utterly disastrous. They are risky (particularly because they are so easy) and should be considered and even reconsidered carefully.

THE DIRECTOR'S BLOCKING TOOLS

To accomplish all blocking goals the director has only two tools: actor placement and actor movement (including direction, velocity, and manner). However, if we consider that in a three-hour Shakespearean play with an average of six people on stage at a time, the director stages over 1,000 person-minutes of stage time, we realize that a lot of blocking goes on in the theater. Even a much smaller play involves thousands of moment-to-moment blocking decisions on who is where, who moves where, how fast, and in what way.

BLOCKING TERMS

The director communicates blocking to the actor by using a set of accepted terms. Actors stand, sit, lie down, fall to the floor, enter a room, or exit just as they would if asked to do so in real life. If they are told to move left or right, they do so from their vantage point, not the director's, which of course means that a director in a proscenium theater who wants an actor to move left must ask him or her to move stage right. If that seems confusing, there is no need to worry; directors who have been in the business forty years get confused, too. If directors wish the actor to move away from them, they ask the actor to move upstage; if they wish the actor to come forward, they request downstage. This terminology originated in the seventeenth century when stages were raked (angled) toward the audience to reinforce "perspective," so that the back part was actually higher than the front; today the terms are firmly fixed in theatrical jargon. Occasionally it is unclear, as when an actor who is asked to "come down" from a platform instead comes forward and remains on it. The terminology is still in common use, however—though a few directors simply say "come forward" or "go back." *Above* and *below* are terms used to mean on the upstage or downstage side, as in "cross above her." The terms are used together in most stage directions, for example, "cross down left and sit in the upstage of the two chairs there." This theatrical shorthand is useful in making immediate communication with new actors, but directors can use any terminology as long as they are clearly and quickly understood.

In the illustration on page 131 for example, focus goes to the man on the platform downstage left (DSL). Other characters are distributed from downstage center to upstage right. Most stage directions are given in terms of course rather than destination; a character who is up left is asked to cross down right but may end up at center. The direction means down right *from where the actor is now,* unless he or she is told to go *to* down right.

WORKING OUT THE BLOCKING

There are an infinite number of ways of working out the blocking of a play, but they fall within two fairly well-defined extremes. The authoritarian director (and this term is not meant to be pejorative but simply to indicate strictness of directorial control) preblocks the show, and the improvisational director allows the actors to block themselves. Most directing, of course, falls between these two poles.

In preblocking a play authoritarian directors prepare a promptbook well before the first rehearsal; they also work out every detail of the setting, lights, and costumes with the designers and note them in their book. Many directors prepare their production book with a mimeographed copy of the ground plan facing every page of text—or every half or quarter page. The ground plan is complete, with every piece of furniture drawn carefully to scale. Then the directors plot on paper every movement and position that the audience will see three months hence. The more they put into the book, the more they are preblocking; and the more they put down in ink rather than in pencil, the more they are rigidly preblocking.

The improvisational director, in the extreme case, assembles the cast even before the set has been designed. Together they read the play and then improvise staging for it. If a chair is desired, a chair is added to the prop list. If a wall is desired, or a door, the designer is informed. Gradually, and simultaneously, a set and a production are created.

The advantage of preblocking, in theory at least, is that the production is plotted out with the extreme intellectual care that can be attained only in the director's study. The performance will come off with precision and polish. The design staff is delighted, for they have months to build their scenery and hang their lights without fear that design changes will send them into overtime. The advantage of improvisational blocking, again in theory, is that the production achieves greater spontaneity, charm, delight, and above all, honesty. It is not compromised by earlier design decisions, and the actors' and director's on-the-spot creativity is unrestricted. Additionally, if a new and desirable interpretation is found during rehearsals, it can be implemented without destroying a preconceived network of blocking. The qualification "in theory," however, must be kept in mind, for occasionally the very opposite results occur.

There are now few extremists in the directing trade, however. Even the most dedicated of the "old school" directors (who are considered the most authoritarian) have come to realize the value of improvisational blocking, at least with experienced actors; and even the most dedicated improvisationalists have bowed to the pressure of production deadlines and the actors' inherent desire in many cases to be told what to do or which action is better than another. Today directors we would call authoritarian still direct from a promptbook, but they discuss their blocking with the actors and probably change it when something better is proposed. And directors we would call improvisational usually work within a predesigned set and at a certain point in rehearsals begin to help the actors choose among the various improvised actions they have attempted in rehearsal. So most plays, once they reach the stage, are fairly well formalized into a set blocking pattern, no matter how it was arrived at. Both systems, for that reason, have to find methods for achieving spontaneity as well as precision and polish.

Which method works best? There is no answer to this question: excellent directors work both ways. There are many determining variables: the play, the set, the actors' experience with each other, the director, the director's self-confidence, the number of called-for actions, the number of people on stage, the length of the rehearsal period, and so forth. Obviously a beginning director working on a complex set with thirty beginning actors in what is to be (hopefully) a new interpretation of *King Lear* (with two weeks rehearsal time allotted) had better do some preblocking before the rehearsals begin. In that extreme case, as a matter of fact, the director had best preblock the entire show. On the other hand, if you are Mike Nichols directing Alan Arkin, Eli Wallach, and Anne Jackson in the three-character comedy *Luv,* you might very well come to the first rehearsal and say, "Well, let's see what this play is all about," and proceed from there. Nichols apparently did just that and won every directorial award in New York that year.

Ordinarily beginners are cautioned to preblock. First, the rehearsal time is limited. Until a director is fast enough to come up with blocking spontaneously, much time could be lost in pondering blocking decisions while the actors cool their heels. But a more important reason is that the successful attainment of directorial objectives takes careful creative thinking, which may be impossible for the beginner (or anyone else) under the pressure of rehearsals. An inexperienced director who comes to rehearsal without some fairly firm planning may be unable to generate ideas on the spot. The rehearsal is chaotic and the blocking is put off for another day, and then another. Actors tend to lose patience with, and confidence in, directors who do not seem to know what they want; and even though that may be the directors' privilege, they are foolish to exercise it wantonly. Most directorial goals require a good deal of directorial homework, and if the blocking is to achieve clarity and telling effects, the director almost certainly has to plan it.

Experienced directors tend to do much *gross* preblocking, often in their heads with a note or two in their promptbooks. Entrances and exits are plotted, key scenes are diagrammed, certain effects are planned, and suggestions for behavior at various moments are at the ready. The scene is blocked roughly and then refined, changed, and supplemented during the course of rehearsals. This is probably the most common method of blocking in use today.

Improvisational methods in blocking are also widespread today, especially as a modification of gross preblocking. Old-school directors usually sat in the middle of the house and dictated the movements authoritatively. Many contemporary directors sit in the first row or on the stage itself and continually engage in dialogue with the actors at this point in rehearsals. Such directors suggest movements ("Why don't you move to the bar and get a drink?") or ask the actors to suggest them ("What do you think he would do here?"). They may ask some actors to suggest placements or movements for others ("Where would you like her to sit when you say that?"), or they may put the actor on his own ("Block yourself in this speech"). Some directors remove themselves entirely from the blocking of certain scenes (such as between two characters) and ask the actors to go to another room and work out the blocking for the scene, then come back and demonstrate it on stage. All these methods have been used successfully, even within the framework of a grossly preblocked show, and may be recommended to those who wish to try them.

Finally, however, directors must take responsibility for the blocking. Only they, sitting in the audience (and they should sit in every possible area of the theater during rehearsals), can judge whether the blocking objectives of clarity and dynamic communication are being met.

RECORDING THE BLOCKING

No matter how it is derived, the blocking is usually set (fixed) at a certain point in rehearsals. This can be done immediately, in the case of a minutely preblocked production, or in the final dress rehearsals of an improvised one. Some directors prefer never to set the blocking, to let it change ad lib each performance, but this practice is rare except in the case of totally improvised shows, where the dialogue and action change night by night as well. The time-honored way of setting the blocking is to record it in a production book. This task is ordinarily done by the stage manager, who keeps a book of the play which includes all technical cues (sound, light, and scene shifting) as well as a detailed notation of the blocking.

Blocking is recorded for two reasons. First, the director and actors might work very hard at selecting the best blocking for a moment and then forget, the next day, what they had arrived at. Ordinarily this does not happen (most directors have total recall of their blocking, even years after the production), but rehearsal fatigue should not be overlooked as a reality of play direction. Unusual and intricate blocking patterns should be carefully noted so that if the directors forget, perhaps in a late rehearsal, what they set up, they need not reconstruct the entire scene in their mind to recall it and so that they will not resort to a less interesting blocking pattern because they are too tired to remember the original. The second reason for recording blocking is to establish a workable production book for the play. This proves invaluable when in late rehearsals or during the run of a show a new actor is substituted for another or a stage manager has to be replaced. The production book is also necessary for understudy rehearsals and in Broadway theater for rehearsing road companies. Finally, when the production has closed, the production book can be filled with photographs,

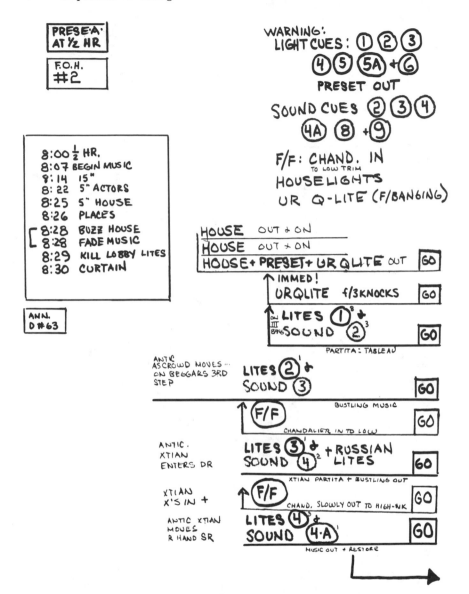

FIGURE 77. Promptbook pages from ACT's 1973 productions; William Ball was the director, James Haire the stage manager. Above, cue sheet for the beginning of *Cyrano de Bergerac*. Light, sound, house, and timing cues are recorded in different colors. Here, light and sound cues are both numbered. Some stage managers prefer to give letters to one of these, to avoid confusion in calling cues. (*Courtesy, William Ball, General Director, American Conservatory Theatre*)

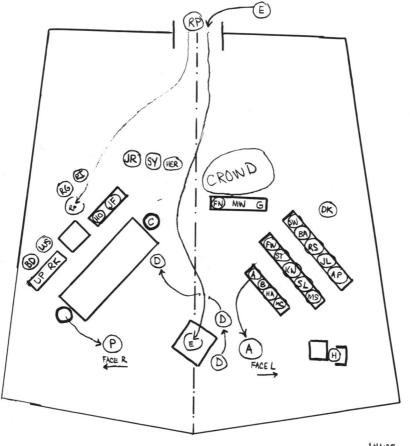

FIGURE 78. Blocking for Elizabeth Proctor's entrance in Act III, *The Crucible*. All actors are placed exactly (A is Abigail, D is Danforth, E is Elizabeth, P is Proctor), their moves indicated by arrows. (*Courtesy, William Ball, General Director, American Conservatory Theatre*)

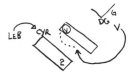

I-22 Revised
9/20/72 (HAIRE)

VALVERT
Observe: I myself will proceed to put him in
his place.
(*TAPS CYR ON SHOULDER*)   (Walks up haughtily to CYRANO)
·Ah, sir, ~~your nose...ah~~..your nose is...rather large.

CYRANO
TURNS (coolly)
Is that all?

VALVERT
(Turning away with a shrug)
Well, of course...

oh no young sir, why WASTE CYRANO   *· PUSHES V--WHO SITS DS 2 BENCH*
~~What? Nothing more?~~ ~~With~~ such an opportunity for
eloquence? Consider all the things you might have
said! For example, *THE* AGGRESSIVE ~~approach~~: Sir,
if that nose were mine, I'd have it amputated on
the spot! DESCRIPTIVE: 'Tis a rock, a crag, a
cape! A cape? Nay, say rather a peninsula!
KINDLY: Ah, do you love the little birds so much
that when they come to sing ~~to you~~, you give them
this to perch on! *HE HE HE HE*   *HO HO HO HO*
HUMEROUS: ~~INSOLENT~~: Sir, when you smoke, the neighbors must
suppose your chimney is on fire! *CAREFUL WHEN YOU TURN YOUR HEAD*
CAUTIOUS: ~~Take care when you walk. With all that~~ *YOU MAY CLUB*
~~weight in front, you could easily fall head first~~ *ME WITH IT,*
~~into the street!~~
PEDANTIC: Does not Aristophanes mention a
mythological monster called the Hippodragonocamelephantos?
Surely we have here the original! *DO YOU MIND IF I*
FAMILIAR: Hey, ~~that thing must be convenient to~~
hang ~~your~~ *by* hat on. *IT?*   *(STANDS ON 4 STAGE -- +5 STEPS)*
ELOQUENT: When it blows, the typhoon howls! When
KNEELS L   it bleeds, the Red Sea!
OF VALVERT ENTERPRISING: Stripe it -- you've got a barber's pole!
└─·INQUISITIVE: What do they call the monument? *MAN OF PROMINANCE*
RESPECTFUL: Sir, I recognize in you a ~~forward-looking man!~~
RUSTIC: What? You call that a nose? What kind of
a fool do you think I be? That ain't no nose--it's *A NEW KIND OF*
~~se~~ bulbous cucumber!
MILITARY: The enemy is charging! Fire your cannon!
PRACTICAL: At least it keeps your feet dry in the
STEP SON· rain!   Or, parodying Faustus in the play, "Was this
DS EDGE the nose that launched a thousand ships and matched
#2 BENCH the topless towers of Illium?"· These, my dear sir,
are things you might have said, had you some tinge
of letters or of wit to color your discourse. But
wit? Not so -- you never had an atom! And of letters
you need but three to write you down -- an ASS!
└ *SITS DS*   *LE BRET*
  EDGE #2 BENCH   *X'S DSR*

FIGURE 79. Annotated and cut text from Scene 1 of *Cyrano*. Stage furniture is numbered; actors' moves are
recorded by abbreviations (DSR is downstage right, and so on). (*Courtesy, William Ball, General Director, American Conservatory Theatre*)

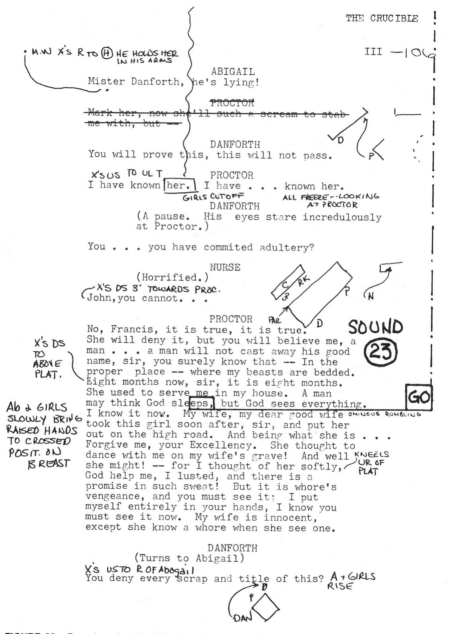

- M.W X'S R TO (H) HE HOLDS HER
  IN HIS ARMS

THE CRUCIBLE

III — 106

ABIGAIL

Mister Danforth, he's lying!

~~PROCTOR~~

~~Mark her, now she'll such a scream to stab~~
~~me with, but --~~

DANFORTH

You will prove this, this will not pass.

X'S US TO UL T

PROCTOR

I have known her. I have . . . known her.

GIRLS CUTOFF   ALL FREEZE--LOOKING
                      AT PROCTOR

DANFORTH

(A pause. His eyes stare incredulously
at Proctor.)

You . . . you have commited adultery?

NURSE

(Horrified.)

X'S DS 3' TOWARDS PROC.

John, you cannot. . .

PROCTOR   PAR

No, Francis, it is true, it is true.

SOUND
(23)

X'S DS
TO
ABOVE
PLAT.

She will deny it, but you will believe me, a
man . . . a man will not cast away his good
name, sir, you surely know that -- In the
proper place -- where my beasts are bedded.
Eight months now, sir, it is eight months.
She used to serve me in my house. A man
may think God sleeps, but God sees everything.

GO

Ab & GIRLS
SLOWLY BRING
RAISED HANDS
TO CROSSED
POSIT. ON
BREAST

I know it now. My wife, my dear good wife   OMINOUS RUMBLING
took this girl soon after, sir, and put her
out on the high road. And being what she is . . .
Forgive me, your Excellency. She thought to
dance with me on my wife's grave! And well   KNEELS
she might! -- for I thought of her softly,   UR OF
God help me, I lusted, and there is a   PLAT
promise in such sweat! But it is whore's
vengeance, and you must see it; I put
myself entirely in your hands, I know you
must see it now. My wife is innocent,
except she know a whore when she see one.

DANFORTH

(Turns to Abigail)

X'S US TO R OF Abagail

You deny every scrap and title of this?   A + GIRLS
                                            RISE

FIGURE 80. Page from Act III of *The Crucible* showing diagrammatic recording of blocking and exact moment when sound cue 23 is to be taken. (*Courtesy, William Ball, General Director, American Conservatory Theatre*)

reviews, and set and costume designs and bound as a book. It becomes the director's only tangible record of the production, and a possible asset in getting future work.

Blocking is noted by a set of conventional symbols. *X* is used for cross and *DL, UR, DC* for down left, up right, and down center, for example. Other abbreviations and stage managerial shorthand may be used, together with symbols drawn on a ground plan. For example, "Cl xdr, sts ch 5" might mean "Claudius crosses downstage right, and sits in the number five chair"—a chair numbered on an accompanying diagram. Any method of shorthand is acceptable as long as it is coherent and can be readily passed on to a replacement stage manager.

SIX

Composition— Lighting

Lighting is the newest of the theatrical arts, and its sophisticated use since the discovery of electricity has paralleled the rise of the director. This has not been accidental. The development of incandescent lighting which could be regulated by remote control gave directors one of their most powerful tools, and much of the history of modern directing has been shaped by men who made important discoveries in lighting: Adolphe Appia, Gordon Craig, and Louis Jouvet. Some well-established contemporary directors, most notably Peter Hunt, began their careers as lighting designers.

Besides providing illumination and establishing locales, lighting can be used to create and maintain focus, to establish and change mood, and to amplify the rhythm of a performance. Lighting is a fluid, multicolored, four-dimensional medium that can work with or against the composition, acting, and interpretation of a play, and a director is well advised to understand its possibilities before he begins a full-scale production. The experienced director rarely makes a decision regarding scenery or blocking without considering the lighting consequences, and frequently designs composition specifically for certain lighting effects. In practice, the director often finds he must make concessions in blocking to get the lighting he

FIGURE 81. Lighting—and smoke, which provides a reflective medium so that light can be seen—creates the acting areas in this production of Goethe's *Iphegenia Auf Tauris,* directed by Hans Neuenfels at the Schauspiel Frankfurt (West Germany) in 1981. (*Pressbüro, Berliner Theatertreffen*)

wants, or vice versa, and the more he knows about the technical scope of the light designer, the more he can anticipate both the artistic possibilities and the adjustments that lighting may dictate.

Sunlight was the most common form of illumination for plays until the past two or three hundred years, and it is still a viable source in outdoor daytime productions. Sunlight is notoriously unregulatable, however, and if the production is to be lit by the sun, all the director can do is to orient the theater so that at the time of the performance the sun is at the audience's back rather than in its eyes.

Whereas oil lamps, calcium lamps (limelights), and gaslights were in use before the twentieth century, today virtually all stage lighting is provided by incandescent electric lamps, occasionally supplemented with carbon arc spotlights. Incandescent illumination can be remotely regulated in intensity, focused and aimed in a variety of lighting instruments, and colored by gelatin filters, and it provides steady illumination for hours without monitoring. Carbon arc lights are occasionally used today as followspots in large theaters; they can generate more illumination than ordinary incandescent instruments, but they require the continuous attention of an operator (to advance the carbon) and cannot be dimmed.

LIGHTING INSTRUMENTS

A lighting instrument consists of a light source (ordinarily an incandescent or a quartzlight bulb), a reflector, a lens, a housing, and a clamp; all lighting instruments are designed to get the most light possible to the desired place and the least light anywhere else. Each type of lighting instrument focuses light differently.

The ellipsoidal reflector spotlight, commonly known as a Leko, throws sharply focused beams over long distances. The Leko beam may be shuttered, or "goboed" (both processes involve the insertion of metal plates), to any shape desired, and if tightly focused, will throw a sharp circle, rectangle, or trapezoid of light on stage with clearly defined shadows.

The Fresnel light (named after its lens) throws a more diffuse beam and is ordinarily used for short throws. In a proscenium theater, Lekos ordinarily provide illumination that comes from the house so that there will be no "spill" of light into the audience, and Fresnels provide most or all of the spotlighting originating from the stage itself.

Striplights (including footlights and cyc lights) are groups of lights arranged in a row to provide a band of even illumination. They are ordinarily wired in three or four circuits, so that three or four colors can be mixed to provide differing tonal values to the stage.

Beam projectors, "scoops," "wizards," "P-C's," and a variety of trade-name instruments and specialty instruments are also used by the lighting expert, but the vast majority of lighting instruments fall into the three categories above.

Practical lights are ordinary household lamps or chandeliers that in realistic sets can be turned on by the actors and used for their illumination.

LIGHTING CONTROL

Lighting designers and directors look for maximum control in lighting, with the ultimate goal being independent control of every instrument used in the production. In practice this is rarely if ever accomplished and never absolutely necessary. Control is provided by the circuitry of the theater and the dimmers in the control room. The more circuits and dimmers, the more control.

Circuits are simply numbered wires. One end leads to the lighting instrument and the other to the dimmer board, usually through a "patch panel" which makes the proper connections. The dimmers are operated manually (in which case there are usually arrangements for operating several at a time), electronically, or in some modern installations, by computer. Electronic and computer dimmer boards afford the most control with the

FIGURE 82. White shirts of the actors catch the side lights for an effective tableau in the Denver Theatre Center production of *Moby Dick.* (*Courtesy, Denver Theatre Center*)

fewest operators, since a single move of the master switch can make literally a hundred (in a 100-dimmer board) intensity changes, some up, some down, precisely and simultaneously—a feat that is impossible manually without fifty sharp technicians.

EFFECTS OF LIGHTING

The director is interested in lighting techniques not as ends in themselves, of course, but as mechanisms of achieving directorial goals. Providing illumination is simply one of these goals, but it should not be too briefly passed over.

Illumination of what? Illumination of the action is the first but not the final answer. The action of a play must be illuminated to achieve visual clarity. In the illusionistic pictorial theater of the early part of our century, it was considered equally vital to keep light off the audience. The second position, however, may reasonably be questioned today. Until the days of English director Henry Irving, toward the end of the nineteenth century, the audience area was always as bright as the stage; in fact, records indicate that expensive and awesome chandeliers in the audience were lighted precisely as the play began, and not before. In other words, only recently have we abandoned the idea that the audience is part of the show. Some directors today feel that that idea is worth reviving. The Berliner Ensemble productions of Bertolt Brecht, for example, are performed in a nineteenth-century theater which is never fully darkened and which is filled with gilded cupids, cherubs, and rococo elaborations that remind the audience it is in a theater, not lost in a romantic imaginary fable. This, of course, was Brecht's intention. Arena staging makes the spectators aware of each other because the action takes place among them, and there is usually enough general illumination in the house to make that awareness part of the overall aesthetic effect. Modern playwrights occasionally "turn on the houselights" (for example, in Paul Foster's *Tom Paine*) to engender audience participation, and the directors of environmental productions frequently light their theaters evenly to disavow the "imaginary line" between actor and patron. The new all-black interiors of some proscenium theaters, such as the Ahmanson in Los Angeles, which were touted as light designers' dreams, have become for the most part audiences' headaches, since constantly peering at a brightly illuminated set from the back of a pitch-black auditorium is, after a while, like staring at the sun through a telescope. Lighting design should not *automatically* be directed to leave the audience in the dark.

LIGHTING THE ACTION

Besides providing adequate illumination for the set and the actors and creating credibility for the time and locale, lighting can be controlled to support the action in creating effective focus, mood, and rhythm. These interests are not always parallel, of course, and what might create effective focus might also destroy the credibility of the locale, so all lighting decisions must be coordinated at the directorial level, either by the director or by the lighting designer.

The director's prime decision is specifying the *amount* of moment-to-moment control: the amount of visible light shifting (cues) during the course of the action within a single continuous scene or act (that is, while the curtain, if there is one, is up). There are three basic ways of working with lights during a scene or act.

Static lighting. The lights come on at the beginning of the scene and do not shift, except to go off at the end of the scene. Traditionally this form of lighting is used for naturalistic plays (although practical lights may be turned on and off, and characters may let sunshine in through windows and doors), since it generally copies the lighting of everyday life. It is also used frequently for tight, fast farces and comedies and for realistic dramas.

It is also useful for Brechtian "epic" theater, which seeks to downplay the magic of the theater and to give straightforward productions of didactic lecturelike plays. Static lighting, of course, was the rule for many centuries, and many directors today swear by it for everything. "If you don't have to change the lights, why do it?" asks one, and a director who calls for light cues should be able to explain why.

Imperceptible light cueing.   The aesthetic of cueing lights imperceptibly is virtually the same as that of not cueing them at all—the creation of a natural stage action that does not call attention to itself or its theatrical contrivances. By imperceptibly shifting the lights, however, the director can have his cake and eat it, too. He can acquire mood changes and focal changes by very slowly shifting lights to emphasize new areas of the stage and perhaps new background coloring. A blue sky can redden over a five-minute period, so slowly that no one notices the change except by subliminal registration. An area in which principal characters are sitting can imperceptibly grow brighter, and background characters can be deftly faded out, as an important scene localizes in a small area. This sort of cueing, if done very subtly, can retain credibility and gain flexibility, and it is fre-

FIGURE 83.   Spears glisten in the lights for a bold theatrical effect in Jean-Louis Barrault's production of Shakespeare's *Julius Caesar* in Paris.   (*French Cultural Services; Photo Pic*)

quently used in realistic plays of great subtlety and/or atmosphere, such as those of Chekhov or Tennessee Williams.

Bold theatrical cueing.   The director can call for highly focused lighting effects to produce a nonnaturalistic style. Blackouts, single spotlights, followspots, and color shifts were originally considered expressionist in their serious theatrical applications. They create a theatrical effect that must be justified on its own terms. The overall effect of theatrical lighting, of course, is to emphasize the theatricality of the presentation; no attempt is made to disguise light changes as if realistically occurring by some natural process. Rather, the lighting changes are the director's and designer's interpolations into the script to enhance its inner action. A famous example is Fritz Erler's *Faust* (Munich, 1904), in which the walls turned red at the entrance of Mephistopheles.

Bold theatrical cueing is common today in multiscene plays like *Antony and Cleopatra,* or Ibsen's *Peer Gynt,* which demand many shifts in locale. It is also widely used on Broadway, for example, in the opulent Tom O'Horgan productions of *Hair, Jesus Christ Superstar,* and *Lenny,* and in Hal Prince's musicals, *Cabaret* and *Follies.*

FIGURE 84.   A variety of lighting systems were brilliantly integrated in Manfred Karge and Matthias Langhoff's 1980 production of Büchner's *Woyzeck* for the Bochum (West Germany) Schauspielhaus. Overhead stage lights, fluorescent striplights, industrial worklamps, bald tracing circus lights, a bare hanging bulb, and onstage followspots can all be seen in this photograph; also used were flashbulbs, footlights, candles, and offstage followspots. Each lighting system operated independently, and different systems, alone or in combination, were used in each of the play's twenty-six scenes.   (*Pressbüro, Berliner Theatertreffen; photo by Thomas Eichhorn*)

FIGURE 85. Stage smoke provides a reflective surface ranging from the near opaque to the near transparent, and thus becomes scenic when combined with lighting. This actor is framed in lit smoke, which serves as scenic backdrop and atmospheric environment. From the award-winning 1981 production of *Billy Bishop Goes to War*, produced by the Vancouver (Canada) East Cultural Center. (*Courtesy, World Theatre Festival, Denver*)

THE EFFECTS OF CONTROLLED LIGHTING

Lighting controls what the audience sees. Major differences in lighting intensity totally control the audience's "picture." For example, lighting the stage while keeping the house black directs attention to the stage, and blacking out the stage altogether terminates attention, just as does a falling curtain. Used more subtly, lighting operates totally independently of other compositional tools, for no matter how many focal principles may be at work, a major lighting change will always overrule them and is *never attributable to the actor or character upon whom the focus rests*. This principle may be extremely valuable when a director wishes to draw attention to a character who must in all other respects be nonattractive and noncharismatic. (Imagine, for example, a scene in which a character is dreaming, and the dream is being acted out for us—but we are asked to be aware of the dreamer as well. One way to stage this is to let the dreamer sleep in a pool of light, while the "dream" is performed on another level, in a slightly dimmer area, the rest of the stage being black.) The director guides the audience's attention with lighting, just as the film director does with alternation of closeups, long shots, and two-shots. Although many-cued theatrical lighting that tries to imitate film editing is an obvious contrivance, it can also be said that as in film, many-cued lighting tends to promote naturalistic acting, since the actor need do nothing out of character to attract the audience's attention when that attention is necessary. Thus, boldly expressive lighting, though it may create inconsistencies in an otherwise totally naturalistic *play,* is not at all inconsistent with the most naturalistic *acting.*

THE DIRECTOR WORKS ON LIGHTING THE PLAY

Depending on the resources of the theater company employing his services, the director works in conjunction with a lighting designer and/or lighting technicians, or does the design and work himself. If he collaborates with a lighting designer, however, he has more to do than just approve the designs. At the very least, a director is invariably held responsible for deciding (either in collaboration or not) what style of lighting will be used (the amount of control) and what actual cues will be taken. One way of doing this, of course, is to let the lighting designer come to rehearsals and prepare a suggested cue sheet. Another, more professional solution is for the director to plan at the blocking stage which light cues will be needed, which might be desirable, and which might be worth thinking about. In either case, the director should come to the first lighting rehearsal with a prepared cue sheet including all cues possible or desirable for inclusion in the production.

Lighting cues are set during special lighting rehearsals. During the lighting rehearsal, each cue is fixed, including notation of which instruments are patched to which dimmer, the intensity readings of each dimmer, and the manner of executing each cue. Manner of execution means which technician is to move which dimmers, how fast, and (where applicable) in what order. Cues are listed by number; on the sheet a characteristic cue would list all dimmer readings which are to change, who will change them, the cue for "taking" (either a visual cue, if the operator can see the stage and hear the dialogue, or a cue from the stage manager conveyed over an intercommunication system), and the "count" on which the cue is to be taken. Since there are literally hundreds of "items" per cue, and sometimes hundreds of cues per production, the lighting rehearsal may take many hours or days. The lighting and technical rehearsals for new Shakespearean productions of England's Royal Shakespeare Company can take not days but weeks, and the college or community theaters that try to squeeze complicated lighting rehearsals into a single afternoon or evening usually betray their amateur standing on opening night.

The full participation of the director during lighting rehearsals is essential to the artistic integration of the production. The director's participation at this stage of the production is similar to a film director's participation in editing the film. In both cases the director works with trained artists who presumably know more about the actual technical workings than the director, but only the director (again presumably) knows the total content and intended effect of the play or film. The stage director is responsible not only for working out with the technicians exactly what is required or desired at each point; he or she will also invariably remain on the scene to approve the nuances of each cue. Lighting rehearsals can be highly creative sessions, with suggestions flying back and forth from the director to the staff, and a director who leaves these decisions up to the technicians abandons some directorial responsibilities to them, too.

SEVEN

Composition—Sound

Stage composition is usually studied in terms of its visual effects alone, but this is only half the picture. The audience has eyes, but it also has ears, and the term *composition* applies to both senses. In fact, composition is also a musical term (a musical writer is a composer), and in theatrical usage it can indicate the orchestration of sounds the audience hears as well as the sights it sees.

There are many sounds in a play. Primarily, in most cases, there is spoken dialogue. Many plays also contain music, in the form of songs, background music (what in films is called "theme music"), onstage or pit orchestras, and sometimes *a capella* group singing. In more and more contemporary plays—for example, *Subject to Fits* and *Lenny*—perhaps in the tradition of Brecht's epic theater, music is intrinsic to the production, yet these plays are not considered musicals. This tradition is as old as Shakespeare and the Greeks. In addition to music, there are sound effects, either on stage or recorded, such as thunder, telephone rings, horn beeps, rainfall, and wind. Sound effects need not be realistic; for example, the last scene of Edward Albee's *Tiny Alice* is played against the amplified sound of a heartbeat. Then there are the sounds the actors make: footsteps down a corridor, the tinkling of ice cubes in a glass, the ad lib screams and grunts of a fight, the cutting of a coconut with a machete. Finally, there is the

FIGURE 86. Music is featured prominently in this amalgam of dramatic scenes by Sam Shepard produced by the Denver Theatre Center. Playwright Shepard considers himself as much a musician of the theater as a writer, and directors of his works must be especially sensitive to their music, rhythms, and sounds. (*Courtesy, Denver Theatre Center; photo by Nicholas de Sciose*)

sound of the theater's air conditioning, the hum of amplifiers and lighting instruments, the fidgeting while the audience gets comfortable after intermission. With the exception of unpredictable sounds (subways rattling underneath Broadway theaters, airplanes flying over outdoor ones), these are the audial components of a play.

Except for some attention to pace and rhythm, the goals of sound composition have usually been ignored by directors. They have felt that if the visual action is carefully worked out, the composition of sounds will be acceptable. But creating a composition of rhythms, intonations, music, and sound effects is a crucial directorial task.

RHYTHM

Speech is naturally rhythmic. Someone excitedly telling a story tends to speed up his or her delivery; someone speaking of a difficult subject to sensitive listeners tends to speak slowly. Ordinary conversations are punctuated by expletives and interjections, like "No!" and "For sure!" (or whatever is in fashion). We can describe any spoken sentence in terms of pitch, inflection, volume, tone, and the pauses that surround and punctuate it. The delivery of speeches creates the major rhythm of a spoken play.

Rhythms affect the communication level of the content of a speech. Listen to a television newscaster delivering a standard news item. He or she invariably begins rapidly, with an unusually high pitch on at least some of the first few syllables:

In Chi^{ca}go today, ^{twenty-}seven men were found guilty of destroying public property. . .

The rapid delivery secures the audience's attention. But by the end of the item, the announcer's voice has slowed and dropped in pitch, so that the final windup is more like this:

In all, they were sentenced to one hundred and eighty-six _{years.}

[and then] In ^{baseball} today, the Giants . . .

The audience's attention won, the newscaster can now make his or her points with heavy meaning, potency, and irony. Compare, in this regard, the measured delivery of David Brinkley or John Chancellor commenting after a regular newscast.

Directors also use rhythms to engage their audience's attention and to make points, but they must ordinarily justify their usage of rhythms by realistic means. Ordinarily this is not too difficult—characters simply play the intention of engaging each other's interest, and they will engage the audience's. The attention to rhythms in stage speech should not only provide an orchestrated sonic pattern but also reveal the workings of the play's inner action.

A useful image of the rhythms of speech is provided by the roller coaster. Imagine the three phases of a roller coaster's course: chugging slowly and with great power up the initial ramp, coasting at medium speed around the first curve, then plunging freely and furiously down the glide. The speed of the roller coaster is inversely proportional to the power expended in moving it. Speeches are similar. Those that take the most inner energy to deliver (such as a difficult confession, for example) can be delivered at the most ponderous (uphill) speed; those that are easiest to say (Undershaft's political philosophy in Shaw's *Major Barbara*, for example, which we imagine he has rattled off a hundred times before) are like the roller coaster hurtling freely down the track. And just as a roller coaster ride achieves its greatest excitement by a rhythm of ups and downs, so does a play become truly interesting when it has a changing, up and down rhythm.

Rhythm in speech is directly connected with the difference between inner and outer action. If a character has a line like "Well, I have to go now," and his intention is simply to go home because he has something to do (and his presence is no longer particularly desired), his inner action, outer action, and internal monologue are virtually identical. He can say the line rapidly and leave. If, however, he is a father leaving his son for perhaps the last time (he is going off to war, for example), then his outer action and inner monologue are quite different (he is probably thinking, "Will he miss me? Will I see him again?"), and he presumably gives the line slowly. However, if in the identical situation he wishes to disguise his feeling so that his son will not see that he is upset, he will again speak rapidly— probably too rapidly—to imitate the behavior of one whose inner monologue and outer action are the same. So there are at least three rhythmic possibilities of delivering that line, and for that matter, any line:

1. Rapidly—he has nothing particular on his mind.
2. Slowly—he has a lot on his mind.
3. Too rapidly—he has a lot on his mind but is trying to hide it.

Directors vary rhythms to create the greatest possible sonic texture. They punctuate the play with pauses—the ultimate of (2)—that are filled with internal conflict and inner monologues, and interjections which are the ultimate of (1) and (3). Again, even a blind person listening to a play in a foreign language should be able to note the character dynamics merely by listening to the rhythms of speech. The French theater, as a matter of fact, is noteworthy on this score; French directing is perhaps as much a matter of audial composition as of anything else.

PACE

Pace is the overall dynamic of the play. Most "minor league" drama critics seem to consider directing as no more than pacing, and fast pacing at that, and frequently mention the director only by way of saying that the play was "too slow" or "well paced" (by which they mean "fast"). For this we must simply blame the ignorance of such drama critics, while recognizing that *subtle* pacing of a play is indeed a concern of the director.

George Bernard Shaw said that if a play seems to be going too slowly, the director should slow it down some more. What he meant was that the director should slow the play down to examine its internal rhythms and inner action, that if a play seemed slow it was because it was improperly understood and directed to begin with. The problem in pacing a show, as Shaw correctly observed, is that inexperienced directors too often work for a fast result. Realizing that scenes in fine plays they have seen were performed at a rapid clip, such directors instruct actors from the first rehearsal onward to speed everything up. One old-school director of our acquaintance does little more than sit in the back of the theater during rehearsals and shout "Louder and faster!" at the actors, sometimes beating out the pace with a stick. Obviously, this can lead to very superficial results.

Undeniably, action which is loud and fast is initially more exciting than that which is low and slow, but masterpieces like Lindsay Anderson's production of *Home* stand in direct contrast to this principle. In *Home* the actors never raised their voices, never spoke rapidly. There is no absolute rule on pace. The only thing the director must always remember is that slow outer action must be exquisitely filled. If the characters speak slowly and monotonously, and if the audience can see nothing going on in their heads either, then the play is sunk.

Most directors try to break a play down, during the rehearsal period, into its separate beats, playing them slowly until the actors are fully comfortable with their moment-to-moment intentions and actions. Then, in the last week or two of rehearsal, the play is "paced up" to performance level, the fastest level at which all the beats can be clearly played and at which the rhythms are not hurried into a muddy merge. There is a final premium on speed: the audience does not want to waste its time, and the director should not let time elapse without some information being conveyed. *The real pace of the play is not the pace of sounds or movements but the pace of information flowing from the stage to the house.* In a badly paced play there are great informational silences where nothing is going on, or the information comes across too fast for the audience to understand it or for the actors to play it.

Directors almost always find that naturalistic actors are more comfortable at a slower pace than is theatrically desirable. This is natural for actors—just as a dancer feels rushed if the orchestra speeds up the tempo on her, as a secretary feels rushed if he must type ten letters before lunch. Actors like to have time enough to play all the things they want to and are instructed to, and of course they are getting information from each other even if the audience is not. In pacing a show, therefore, it is sometimes necessary for the director to push the actors a little, just as it is sometimes a choreographer's job to push the dancers, or a boss's job to push the secretary. No director should feel that his or her primary responsibility is to keep the actors comfortable and happy. The directors' primary responsibility is to the show and to the audience for whom it is intended. If in their judgment the flow of information to the audience is too slow, they must take measures to increase it or speed it up, while ensuring that the credibility of the show remains intact.

Even the best plays include dull passages that must be gotten through quickly. In his stage direction for the opening scene of *Henry IV*, the playwright Luigi Pirandello even cautions the director, "This scene should be played very rapidly." The scene consists of necessary, but rather boring, exposition, and Pirandello does not want the audience to leave the theater before the fireworks begin in Act II.

The audial and visual composition of a play work hand in hand, but they are not parallel. A character can be pacing the floor slowly and speaking rapidly, or she can be racing around and saying nothing at all. Imagine the orchestration of sights and sounds in the examples that follow.

In Anouilh's *Antigone,* Antigone sits awaiting death in a bare stage prison. The guard walks back and forth behind her, his heels beating a steady rhythm on the floor.

In Dürrenmatt's *The Visit,* the semicircle of townspeople silently converge and cover Anton Schill. After a pause, a piercing scream is heard.

In *Hamlet,* the king leaves the stage while Polonius shouts for lights. Forty people, all ad libbing and yelling, leave the stage by five different exits. Suddenly there is silence and Hamlet is alone on stage.

In *King Lear,* Lear is told while eating with his cohorts at a huge oaken table that he is to be denied his hundred knights. After two moments of silence he screams, "Darkness and devils!" and overturns the giant table. The table crashes to the floor along with a dozen pewter mugs, which clatter and tinkle for several seconds.

In *Measure for Measure* the curtain rises on about thirty nobles facing the duke, who is upstage. As the duke raises his hand, all the nobles simultaneously fall heavily to their knees with a huge "thud." After a pause, the duke begins to speak.

In Ionesco's *The Chairs* an orator ceremoniously walks onto an empty stage, unrolls a speech, gazes out to the audience, and squeaks, because he is a mute.

MUSIC

Music has long been used to create excitement and to enhance the emotional empathy of films, television, and radio shows. Early silent films were played with a "live" musical track provided by the local organist or pianist. Today theme music in films is developed by specialists who create splendid effects, such as the underlying theme music of *Love Story* or the pseudo-Scarlatti which enlivened *Tom Jones.* Radio and television shows use music extensively to add excitement and to punctuate key scenes; few of us have forgotten the Lone Ranger riding into the distance to the strains of Rossini's *William Tell Overture* and Liszt's *Preludes.* Soap operas often use music (which, in fact, is why they are called operas) to cover the virtual absence of plot and characterization.

Music is accepted in film, television, and radio partly because these are by definition technological media. After dealing with projectors, celluloid, and wave transmission, it is only a simple step to add a phonograph

FIGURE 87. Lee Breuer's 1981 experimental piece, *Sister Suzie Cinema,* utilizes a five-man *a capella* singing group as principal performers, singing on an airplane wing which slowly rises as they perform. The play, which was created for the New York Public Theatre Festival, was subsequently acclaimed at world theater festivals in France and in Colorado. *("Sister Suzie Cinema" written and directed by Lee Breuer, music by Bob Telson, featuring 14 Karat Soul & Ben Halley Jr., 1981. Photo by Carol Rosegg)*

and a sound system. In the theater, however, music is not immediately justified as an acceptable convention; it must be justified by style. For example, naturalistic plays which use live actors portraying true-to-life situations seem to resist the intrusion of recorded sound. There are, however, many ways to integrate music into stage productions.

Recorded music can be conventionally used in a naturalistic play when it is part of the play's natural environment. Countless American plays feature scenes in which an actor turns on some music—as in Arthur Miller's *A View from the Bridge,* where Rudolfo plays the phonograph, or in Saroyan's *The Time of Your Life,* where Joe plays the jukebox. Chekhov was the master at integrating offstage musicians into his plays, and the farewell scene of *The Three Sisters,* which is accompanied by an army band in the distance, is incredibly poignant. Even when music is not specified by the playwright, nothing prevents a director from having a character turn on a radio (which plays, of course, some preselected music timed to the action of the play) during the course of a scene. The effect of the music might be extremely helpful, and the effect of another character turning it off, suddenly, can also be telling.

Recorded music can be used without an apparent natural source in a play not tied to the strictures of realism. Tennessee Williams's *The Glass Menagerie* is described by its author as a "memory play" in which "atmospheric touches and subtleties of direction play a particularly important part." Williams calls for the use of music "to give emotional emphasis to suitable passages." Sample musical directions in that script are

> Music: "The Glass Menagerie" under faintly.
> Dance music: "All the world is waiting for the sunrise." The Dance Hall music
>   changes to a tango that has a minor and somewhat ominous tone.
> The violin rises and the stage dims out.
> Waltz music: "La Golondrina"
> Music changes
> Music swells tumultuously
> A tender waltz

Some of this music is justified realistically (a dance hall is presumably across the street), but most is not. As Tom, a character in the play, says to the audience, "The play is a memory. . . . In memory everything seems to happen to music. That explains the fiddle in the wings."

Stylized plays[1] in general can be effectively integrated with music. In William Ball's production of *Tiny Alice* for the American Conservatory Theater, Julian made his final, futile escape attempt to the cataclysmic sounds (hugely amplified) of the *Dies Irae* in Verdi's *Requiem.* When Verdi's fanfares climaxed, Julian fell down the giant stairway he had been attempting to climb, while red banners streamed from the doorway he could not open. Directors frequently turn to heroic scores to accompany scenes, grand entrances, and key moments of Elizabethan plays, or to Mozart for Restoration comedies. Mendelssohn wrote a rather famous score for *A Midsummer Night's Dream,* as did Sibelius for *The Tempest:* these are often played along with the dialogue, where they can be successfully integrated. Electronic music was successfully used to accompany Herbert Blau's production of *King Lear,* and rock music is used today (as will the contemporary music of any day be used) in nearly any play which admits musical additives.

Live music performed by a visible source[2] was a feature of original Greek and probably Elizabethan staging. It is still used in the Kabuki and Nō dramas of Japan. In such productions the playing of the musicians is a conventionally accepted aspect of the visual production. Some productions of modern plays have copied these models; *A Taste of Honey* (English) and *Subject to Fits* (American) have both used onstage orchestras of three to five pieces to accompany the action with both underlying theme music and musical punctuation. Many other plays, not written to include an orchestra,

---

[1]*Stylized* is a vague but accepted term used to describe departures from naturalism. See Chapter 9 for a fuller discussion.

[2]Music played by a live but hidden orchestra is considered in this chapter as though it were recorded. The effect is the same in both cases.

are produced as though they were. Ariane Mnouchkine's 1981 Paris production of *Richard II* used a two-piece kabuki orchestra which played
throughout the orientally staged production. Many plays include songs to
be sung (for example, *The Good Woman of Setzuan*), in which case it is the
director's option where the musical accompaniment should originate and
what it should consist of. In other plays or productions, the actors themselves play musical instruments (as in Tom O'Horgan's production of *Tom
Paine*). Finally, there are full-scale musical productions.

In all productions featuring live music, great attention must be paid
to the integration of the orchestra's (or musician's) presence with that of
the rest of the show. Seemingly inconsequential details like the need for
music stands and lights to read music by can cause giant problems in dress
rehearsals. Because a violinist executing a virtuoso cadenza can draw focus,
just as can an actor scratching his jawbone, problems of visual composition
are vitally affected by musicians. Decisions on where to put the orchestra
are matters not just of acoustics but of visual concern as well.

In general, the use of an onstage orchestra declares to the audience,
"We wish to entertain you" or "We wish to make sure you get our points";
the former merely by the natural enjoyment most people derive from
music, and the latter by making the stylistic admission that "We [the director, actors, and musicians] are openly and directly *presenting* our play to
you; we are not trying to pretend that we are simply copying life." Brecht,
for example, used songs to stop the action and present didactic pieces of
commentary (some would call them propaganda) evolved from the play's
dramatic content. The use of an onstage orchestra would certainly enhance
that effect, which is one of intentional intrusion into the story. The use of a
live orchestra on stage throughout Joan Littlewood's production of *A Taste
of Honey,* an otherwise naturalistic play, could have been counterproductive; however with sensitive direction Littlewood was able to use the music
with minimum intrusion and maximum enhancement.

The out-and-out musical play, such as *My Fair Lady*, presents a wide
variety of directorial options in the artistic integration of music with plot.
This is even more true when the theater is equipped with a flexible orchestra pit which may be raised or lowered automatically (ordinarily by
hydraulic lifts). The orchestra can be lifted to stage level, as it is occasionally
for an overture, or lowered completely; or it can be lowered so that only the
conductor is seen. The possible combinations multiply when there are both
a pit orchestra and an onstage orchestra, as in Hal Prince's production of
Cabaret. Music in the all-out musical can range from entirely presentational
(as in a "production number") to hidden background to the "realistic"
scenes in the play.

A final type of theater music is incidental or intermission music,
played while the curtain is down before the play begins, during intermis-

sions, and after it ends. Occasionally incidental music can "bleed" into the beginning of acts, recommencing as the lights dim at the end of acts. Incidental music does more than divert the audience while the stage is dark; it can be used to set the emotional tone in the play, to revive key themes played during the action, and to "set up" an audience for a theatrical opening at the beginning of the show.

The director's decisions regarding the use of music are broad in scope, as the following possibilities show.

- Should music be used at all? Silence is often effective where music is not. Music can be intrusive in a naturalistic play; if overused, it can be offensive in a stylized play.
- What is the music to do? To set the period? Mozart with Molière might establish a classical ambience, whereas John Cage with Molière might indicate a modern production and keep the audience alert to modern implications of the seventeenth-century play. Should music set the emotional tone? Convey excitement? Suspense? Jarring internal transitions? The effect of memory? Of time passing? Should it play against the emotional tone, as the bright marching music plays against the sadness of the departure of the soldiers in *The Three Sisters*, heightening the poignancy?
- What kind of music should be used? Classical? Pop? Jazz? Rock? If classical, what period? Should an original score be composed?
- From where does the music emanate? A sound system? Orchestra pit? Onstage? In a stage box in the audience?
- Do we see the musicians? The conductor? How much? At all times? Does the orchestra move?
- How is the music timed? How is it integrated with the action? Are the characters supposed to be aware of it? Do they play with it or against it? Is it just for the audience's benefit, with the characters oblivious of it (as in most films)?

These questions must all be answered, and in practice, not in theory. Music must be chosen carefully and timed perfectly. A speech that is to be spoken to music must be rehearsed with great precision, so that it ends when it is supposed to, generally at the same time the music ends, night after night. Recorded music, inflexible in performance, must be matched to the behavior of live actors (sometimes flexible) and to the situation. For these reasons music cannot be effectively added at the last minute to "beef up" a scene that was planned without it; it must be integrated early in the rehearsal period if it is to be a valuable part of the play's overall composition.

SOUND EFFECTS

Sound effects are both functional and creative. If the script calls for a telephone to ring or a horn to beep, the sound must enhance the telling of the story. In such cases, in realistic plays, it is desirable to imitate the sound as closely as possible. If when the phone rings it is clear that a stage manager is playing a sound-effects record offstage, the effect does more harm than good. "Realistic" sound effects must be just that, and it takes good equipment and good technicians to make realistic effects sound real.

Realistic sound effects need not be limited to functional ones. Sounds can be used to underline, much as music can. Continuous sounds such as wind or the falling of rain are often called for in scripts; if not called for, they frequently can be added. The sound of traffic can be used in a play that takes place near a busy street (for example, *My Sister Eileen*), both to set the locale and to underline the action. In such a case the sound effect can be modulated to be louder at certain moments, quieter at others, and even totally silent. If the effect is to be realistic, the modulation of continuous soundtracks must be subtle. Sounds can also punctuate action; for example, Tennessee Williams asks for a passing locomotive during certain abrupt moments in *A Streetcar Named Desire*. A character can sometimes put an "exclamation point" on a sentence by pounding a table or hitting a wall; if it can be safely done, he or she can throw a glass against a wall and let the sound of the crash be a counterpoint to the dialogue. Such sounds can come across as gimmicks, or they can be successful adjuncts to a play's sound composition, depending on the artistry with which they are handled.

Nonrealistic sound effects are rarely used, but they can be enormously effective in plays which admit a high degree of stylization. William Ball began his production of *Tiny Alice* with an ear-piercing siren blast. Drumbeats have been used to intensify fight scenes. The cadence of actors stamping their feet was effective in the Open Theatre production of Jean Claude Van Itallie's *The Serpent*.

We might mention at this point the amplification of stage sounds and speech. Most musical plays today are produced with electronic sound amplification, ordinarily with microphones placed at the footlight positions and hung from the flies. The sound is then projected into the audience by speakers located over or around the stage or even in the far reaches of the theater. Sometimes the actors even carry hand or body mikes. More and more spoken plays are using microphones and amplification. The use of such technological equipment simply to make the sound audible is generally undesirable if unnecessary. It sets up an intruding factor only to compensate for the actor's weakness; it makes softly spoken dialogue sound unnaturally loud, and loud dialogue tinny. Since it is vital that the actors' words reach the audience, the intrusion, if necessary, is better than the confusion which would result otherwise, but it is never preferable to non-amplified projection. The exception is when hand mikes are used by the actors as props, as in the rock opera version of *Othello*, in *Catch My Soul*, or in *Hair;* there the mikes are part of the overall style of the performance.

INTEGRATION OF SOUNDS
AND SIGHTS

The use of sounds is as vital a part of overall composition as the visual effects. The compilation of sounds and sights is complex. In one production of *The Night of the Iguana*, for example, the second act closed with an amalgam of the following sounds:

1. The actors' voices (live)
2. Bursts of thunder accentuating certain words of dialogue (recorded)
3. A marimba band in the background (recorded)
4. Wind (recorded)
5. Rain (recorded)
6. A broadcast in German over the portable radio (recorded)
7. Parrot screams (recorded)

and sights:

1. The lights blacking out as the power goes off
2. Shannon and Hannah illuminated by flashes of lightning
3. Maxine lighting a candle behind a slatted door, watching
4. The Nazis seen in the tiny light from their portable radio
5. Moonlight illuminating the foliage, bending in the wind, and the hanging lamps, swinging
6. Rain glistening in the moonlight
7. Shannon's hand, spotlighted (followspot) as he reached for rainwater to cool his head

Almost all these production elements are called for by the author (Tennessee Williams) himself, who, however, warns that despite these elements, the director must avoid an "effect curtain," seeking instead to portray the human values of the moment rather than the purely theatrical. This is sound advice.

In every style and kind of play, composition must remain subordinate to and supportive of the explication of the human actions, which are the stuff that all theatrical dreams are made of. Composition is never the play itself; it is only the outward manifestation of a production. But effective composition can make a strong play stronger, a funny play funnier, and a tragic play a searing theatrical experience. No director has ever had much impact in the theater, no matter how brilliant his or her interpretation of scripts or work with actors, without having an innate sense of composition and a conscious ability to use that innate sense.

EIGHT

Working with Actors

Dual Perspective

If the two basic ingredients of theatrical performance are actor and audience, those of the rehearsal period are actor and director. Working with actors in rehearsal is certainly the most visible of the director's functions, and that upon which he or she will spend the most time: anywhere from 100 hours on the typical university production to upwards of 200 hours on a professional production, or even the legendary year's work that directors such as Stanislavski and Brecht are known to have lavished on their productions.

Directors may have been actors themselves of more or less experience and competence; or they may, like many of the leading British and American directors today, have graduated from a university department with a strong literary and directorial understanding of drama but little acting experience. There are pros and cons to either path: the danger of actors turned directors is that they may never learn to stand outside the performances and see the production as a whole but tend to direct by performing the roles themselves and getting the actors to imitate them. On the other hand, directors with no acting experience may be unable to see a problem from the actor's point of view and get so caught up in their "concept" that they fail to recognize the actor as an individual, instead treating him or her like a puppet, with the possible consequence of hollow, wooden performances.

Ideally directors should have a double perspective: they should be able to see the totality of a production and yet not lose sight of the work of each individual actor—how it fits into the total artistic balance they are trying to achieve. To create a balanced production with a disparate group of actors, the director will need to sense how to approach different actors, tune into their rhythms, help them fit their working methods into a harmonious ensemble, and thus create a consistent style for the production.

The director's goal in any rehearsal must be to provide the best possible environment in which the actors can do their most creative work within the agreed parameters of the production. A director should always remember the fact, as put by Nemirovich-Danchenko, that "when the curtain rises and the actors come to life the director must die." Finally the performance rests with the actors. The difficulty and agony of cutting the umbilical cord, and giving the production over to the actors, will be less acute if the director bears in mind throughout the rehearsal period that he or she is helping the actors give their best performance—not creating a monument to his or her own directorial ego.

The Legacy of the Past

To work successfully with contemporary actors, the director will need to be familiar with the range of acting techniques and approaches which are the legacy of the twentieth century. This broad spectrum of possibilities for tapping into the actor's creative potential is, of course, one of the reasons for the expanded role of today's director. But it hasn't long been the case. It is a function of the twentieth century in which the impact of democratic psychology and technological sophistication has broken down preconceptions of artistic norms. In earlier centuries the concept of a "proper" way to perform a role tended to hold sway. As late as 1869 American actor Mark Smith was praised for his "most unexceptional Brabantio," the implication being that he had fulfilled the normal expectation of how the role should be performed, and was therefore excellent in the critic's eyes. Such an attitude didn't require much initiative from actors or directors; but it could still be found in acting manuals published in the 1940s, which stated that one should always kneel on the downstage knee, enter on the downstage foot, and pause at the door before exiting, and that "laborers" moved with a quick and jerky rhythm.

The academic, aesthetic, and commercial limitations on the actor's creativity can be traced back to the neoclassical attitudes of the seventeenth century and the bourgeois society of the eighteenth. During the historical development of acting methods, two major approaches tended to evolve: the representational or naturalistic tradition and the presentational or theatricalized. This dichotomy, sometimes categorized as inner versus external approach, or feeling versus technique, goes back to a basic paradox of theater: the actor is both him- or herself and a character (that is, another *persona*) at the same time. This paradox was first articulated in the eighteenth century by Denis Diderot, who supported the presentational position: the actor builds a mask which he manipulates and presents to the audience, objectively aware of everything he is doing, even when weeping real tears. The purpose of the "mask" actor is to engender emotion in the audience whether or not he is experiencing it himself.

The opposite position is that actors embody the role within themselves, experiencing the actual emotion of the action, which is revealed to the audience through their own *persona* or face. This internal method uses the actor's own psychological and physiological reality to reach feelings and reflexes such as the character would experience if the dramatic situation

FIGURE 88. Denis Diderot's essay "The Paradox of the Actor," is in dialogue form and is occasionally performed as a play, as here under the direction of Jacques Baillon for the Petit-Odeon (Paris) in 1977. The dramatization of Diderot's essay allows the debate about acting methods to be exemplified by the actors; it is a form popular in the French theater, where many dramatic authors—including Molière, Giraudoux, and Anouilh—have written plays that take place in rehearsal, and explore theatrical themes. (*French Cultural Services*)

were real—feelings that are not susceptible to technical control. To base their art in a truthful imitation of nature has, of course, been the long-standing aim of actors—an aim Aristotle recognized with the concept of *mimesis*. But to each century, "natural" has meant something different. To the seventeenth-century actor it meant neoclassical form: balance, perfection of verbal utterance, and character based on perceived and accepted norms of expected behavior; kings, for example, would always be noble in mind and regal in posture, never belching, scratching, or picking their noses; such mannerisms would be seen as the birthright of the lower classes. However, to the romantic actor of the early nineteenth century, "natural" would mean an extravagantly physical and dynamic exercise of emotional pyrotechnics. Both these approaches to acting, though centuries apart and based on differing contemporary perceptions of "natural," tended to external clichés—communicating the recognizable elements of a character by an accepted code of gestural shorthand.

By the end of the nineteenth century this tradition had become calcified, and stage mannerisms communicated without any depth of understanding or feeling tended to be the order of the day on the Broadway, Boulevard, and West End stages. This process was reinforced as theater became one of the commodities of bourgeois society—entrepreneurship dominating art, and performance merely copying an original that was known to sell. The star system, which was a function of this sensibility, led to a domination of theater by the actor-manager, whose productions were geared to the exhibition of his or her unique traits.[1]

Subordinated to the ego of a star performer, subject to the repetitious requirements of formula plays, economic hostage to bourgeois taste, it is little wonder that in the latter half of the nineteenth century, the actor's creative function was relegated to the facile employment of well-tried mannerisms. Any sense of the protean quality of the actor's art, ensemble relationships, or exploration of a text to arrive at dramatic truth was lost beneath a welter of commercial exploitation, self-display, and technological trickery. However, although this commercial role playing based on rigid social and aesthetic forms was predominant, it was coming into conflict with new philosophical and social perceptions. The development of "naturalism" as an aesthetic focused on the portrayal of the minutiae of the lives of lower-class individuals, with whom the stage had never previously been concerned. At the same time, Freudian psychology broadcast the concept that behavior is by no means as simple as its external appearance: true

---

[1]There is a story told of one of the last of the old-school actor-managers, who was playing Shylock in *The Merchant of Venice* when one of the younger actors fell sick and had to be replaced. The replacement arrived (sight unseen), reported to the manager, and asked, "Sir, how do you see our relationship in the scene we have together?" To which the great man replied, "Oh, don't you worry about that. Just stand by the back flat, and when I want you I'll come and get you."

meaning may only be determined from an understanding of the deepest thoughts and feelings—sometimes unconscious—of an individual.

Contemporary Virtuosity

The confrontation between a flexible, "naturalistic" social philosophy and a petrified, clichéd stage aesthetic, led at the end of the nineteenth century to the new stagecraft and art theater movements, and to a dialogue about the nature of the actor's work. Actors sought for a way to reveal on stage an organic expression of a character's deep-seated feelings and responses, rejecting all facile techniques which impersonated the form of emotion without including its content.

The significance of this dialogue, for the twentieth century, has been the virtual elimination of any further acceptance of the idea of rigid norms and the blossoming of a whole range of possibilities for the actor and director. There has been a merging and expansion of the naturalistic and theatricalized traditions, which are now seen as not only reconcilable but also mutually supportive. Approaches, methods, and techniques have evolved which encourage the actor to return to the kind of virtuoso playing once expected of the itinerant players of the Middle Ages, of the commedia dell'arte, and of the actors on Shakespeare's stage.

Today's young actors are multitalented and multiskilled, with a broad and eclectic range of training and techniques to draw from. To command the respect of and to be able to work effectively with these actors, a director must be able to draw from a broad palette, a varied toolbox of working methods which may include inner process, analytical approach to text, cybernetic relationships, alienation technique, physical exploration of text, ensemble work, mask work, and games and improvisations. The director must know when these techniques are appropriate: that working with actors on a play by Miller or Williams may need a different approach from working on those by Shepard, Congreve, Coward, Beckett, or Brecht. Eclecticism should be intelligent and informed. To help the director be more aware of the many approaches possible, and their implicit virtues and dangers, we are going to examine them in their original context.

SYSTEMS AND STUDIOS

The Stanislavski System

There has, in the twentieth century, been no more profound and catalytic effect on actors' approach to their craft than the work of Konstantin Stanislavski. Cofounder, leading actor, and artistic director of the Moscow Art Theatre, Stanislavski was the first to attempt to codify a scientific method for the actor; he also thought in terms of choices rather than

FIGURE 89. Konstantin Stanislavski as Dr. Astrov in Anton Chekhov's *Uncle Vanya*. (*Foreign Languages Publishing House, Moscow*)

givens, and his work led to further exploration of the actor's craft, both along similar lines and in reaction to his principles.

Nowhere has his influence been more significant than in the United States. The Moscow Art Theatre visited America in 1923, and two members of the company—Richard Boleslavsky and Maria Ouspenskya—remained in New York and taught Stanislavski's system. This led to the adoption of elements of the system by the Group Theatre in the 1930s, and ultimately to the founding of the New York Actors Studio and the evolution of the "method" as taught there by Lee Strasberg in the 1950s. Several members of the Actors Studio—notably Marlon Brando, Paul Newman, Rod Steiger, Julie Harris, and Geraldine Page—became internationally famous stage and screen actors, which lent dynamic to the spread of "method" techniques. Stanislavski's first book, *An Actor Prepares,* was also published in the United States and became almost a bible of the acting profession. For all these reasons it is likely that a director working in the United States will come up against actors whose approach to their craft is to some degree determined by an acquaintance with Stanislavski, or Strasberg's interpretation of his system.

Stanislavski's system enables actors to discover within themselves what their part requires of them—the inner truth—and to communicate that truth to the audience so that it will believe in the character and situation. The director must ensure that the actors understand the given circumstances of the role: what their character is trying to do or achieve; the character's situation in regard to time, place, and preceding events; the personal details of the character, and the attitudes of the other characters in the play. The director stimulates, refines, and shapes the actors' explorations of the dramatic action as it relates to the character's objective and is informed by the given circumstances of the play.

An outline of this cooperative process might be as follows. Several readings of the play will take place. The first one or two will simply be to understand the plot, catch the flavor of the play, and clarify the text (so that actors and director have the same understanding of ambiguities and foreign or unfamiliar words). At this stage the director may want to share with the actors his or her research into the play's background—any historical or unfamiliar context that needs discussing—which will probably lead to more general questions about the play's background to flesh out the given circumstances. With this information the actors can do research of their own with some agreed sense of the director's focus. Detailed questions of character relationship should probably not be discussed at this early stage.

At subsequent readings the director and actors will break the play up into units of action, with the function of the unit defined in terms of an active verb—to do, to want, to attain. Each of these unit objectives should relate to the main objective or "through line" of the play. For example, if the main objective of Chekhov's *The Cherry Orchard* is to show that a decadent aristocracy must inevitably give way to a more dynamic, if crass, peasant energy (we are not saying it *is*), the unit in which Ranevskya gives away her purse to an itinerant beggar reveals how her failure to have any real sense of the value of money contributes to the downfall of the family. The specific action of the unit fits directly into the main action of the play. One of the director's most important functions is to see that the actors have a clear understanding of the main action and how each unit and objective contributes to it: sometimes actors fail to look beyond their own part, and lacking a view of the whole play, consequently give narrow performances with little to offer to their fellow actors.

While maintaining the perspective of the whole, the individual actor should be encouraged to explore the units in which he or she is involved to find smaller facets of the larger objectives, which add color and variety to a character and avoid simplistic, one-dimensional caricature. So, when rehearsals begin on stage, all the actors should have a clear outline of their character's function within the play, of the circumstances that will determine how that function will be pursued, and some sense of the particular attributes that will enable them to build a sophisticated character.

During the rehearsals the director will work closely with the actors to help them deepen their understanding of their character and find within their resources the emotional and physical means of communicating its intentions. The director will probably do this by questioning the actors to remind them of all the possible ramifications of an action. Questions should not be lectures in disguise but be as simple as possible. To take another example from *The Cherry Orchard*, Varya has an entrance in Act IV, while Lopakhin is in the room; ostensibly she is looking for something. The director might ask, "Why does she make the entrance?" If the answer is, "To see if she has packed something," the next question might be,

"But isn't she very efficient?"
"Yes."
"Then is it likely she wouldn't remember what she's packed?"
"No."
"Then why else might she come in?"
"To see Lopakhin."
"Why does she want to see Lopakhin?"
"Because she is in love with him and he is leaving . . ."
"And?"
"She hopes he might ask her to marry him."
"So why does she pretend to be looking for something?"
"She would approach it obliquely, because she is a shy somewhat insecure person."
"Anything else?"
"Well, women would never make a direct approach at that time."
"And what about Lopakhin?"
"Well, he's pretty uncertain too, and a direct approach might frighten him off."

This is an overly extended example because an actor probably wouldn't need all that much prodding. But it illustrates how, by questions and suggestions, the director can elicit a great deal the actor may not have taken into account and reveal to the actor how the entrance will reflect the unspoken or "subtextual" nuances of the Varya-Lopakhin relationship.

A rehearsal tool Stanislavski employed to help his actors experience the life of the text was improvisation. We shall discuss it later in this chapter as a total approach to rehearsal; here we just want to mention a couple of ways Stanislavski used it. One form was virtually living the actual circumstances: working on *The Lower Depths,* Stanislavski took his actors to live in a skid-row environment so that they might soak up through their pores the experience of existing in dirt and degradation. At other times Stanislavski would tap into the actor's store of life experience by creating a situation analogous to the textual action yet more directly concerned with the actor's own situation. A simple example of this, in a contemporary context, might be to explore the balcony scene from *Romeo and Juliet* as a young girl, who had to be home by midnight, saying goodbye to a boy she had just met at a friend's party.

In all of these ways the director can help the actor in their joint search for the goal of the Stanislavski system—the honest portrayal of real life on the stage. Stanislavski focused acting on living, the feelings and choices involved in being alive.

The Stanislavski System and the Strasberg Method: Controversies

As we have suggested, Stanislavski's system was strongly adopted in the United States, especially by Lee Strasberg, whose teaching approach at the New York Actors Studio came to be known as "the method." However, the original Strasberg method was based on only the first half of Stanislavski's work, which stressed inner process. There were two reasons for this: first, Stanislavski's system was introduced to the United States by Boleslavsky, who was only familiar with Stanislavski's early work on "emotional memory"; second, the first part of Stanislavski's work to be published in the United States was *An Actor Prepares,* which emphasized inner process. Stanislavski's full system, putting more emphasis on physical techniques and the playing of physical actions, wasn't published until much later; by which time his approach had been given a somewhat unbalanced emphasis toward emotional rather than physical techniques.

Thus, directors working with method-trained actors are likely to find them relying considerably on self-exploration and emotional memory for their acting technique. Emotional memory teaches actors to recall personal experiences which affected them and to re-create that remembered emotion on the stage in a similar situation. The danger of emotional memory is that it is essentially secondhand, using emotion that does not arise spontaneously from the situation. It can lead to both irrelevance—the actors are busily involved with a past situation of their own rather than playing the action in the present—and the belittling of the part—the actors simply tailor the part to their own immediate emotional responses. In both instances the actors may tend to ignore the life the author has created in the action, substituting their own personal feelings.

FIGURE 90. Stanislavski as Vershinin in Chekhov's *The Three Sisters.* A comparison with his Astrov, p. 173, indicates Stanislavski's strong sense of the physical elements of characterization. (*Foreign Languages Publishing House, Moscow*)

This approach brings up another controversial aspect of "naturalistic" playing—to what degree an actor "plays himself" while creating a character. This is really a semantic problem, but it is still often fervently debated by theater practitioners. In one sense, of course, an actor always plays himself—what else does he have to communicate the action? But "himself" here stands in the same relationship as a violin to a violinist. It is an instrument and may be played in many different ways. In this sense an actor uses himself to discover those attributes that best suit a character in a given situation. Thus he isn't playing himself—i.e., only one tune on his instrument—so much as playing on himself, or from himself to provide a wide variety of characters. Method actors will sometimes use the character to explore their own emotional responses rather than start from the given circumstances of the text, and by playing the action, in character, find the emotional response the character would have to that situation.

One problem for a director is that some actors like to emote; they don't think they are really acting unless they are "feeling it." Spontaneity is also often regarded as a good in itself, and when you put these two things together it is sometimes difficult to restrain actors who are giving a tremendously spontaneous display of their personal emotions—they feel good, and their friends tell them they were terrific. It's real acting! Economy, selection, and refinement are harder to come by, and less obvious. So the director must look out for actors who overindulge their private emotion or try to bend the character to their own image by the use of such "naturalistic" techniques as broken speech rhythms. Robert Lewis tells of an actor he once directed who said "y' know" before every line. When asked why, he said, "Well, it makes it real for me—that's the way I talk." To which Lewis said, "Well, you're not going to be able to say 'y' know, to be or not to be.'" No director could improve on that succinct reply.

Having said all this, directors are, of course, free to use whatever of Stanislavski's or Strasberg's techniques that work for them. Emotional memory, for example, can be used judiciously as a rehearsal tool—which is what Stanislavski originally intended it to be. It may help actors who are failing to commit themselves to the emotional depth of a part; and it can get beneath immediate clichéd responses. It is, basically, a personal and private technique which is well suited to film and television work, where the camera probes the emotion through the eye of the actor, and the creation of a character response of high definition may be too strong for the medium. The stage director should be aware of the caveats expressed about method technique. Although the rehearsal process and performance are obviously connected, they are not necessarily the same: private moments in rehearsal may never achieve the energy and definition to cross the footlights; and the excessive exploration of the actor's psychical tripes may produce irrelevant emotion and extraneous action which has little or nothing to do with the playwright's intentions.

A Stanislavski Synopsis

Before leaving the discussion of naturalistic techniques, it might be useful to summarize those aspects of Stanislavski's system which are incontrovertible and likely to be part of the method and vocabulary of most contemporary actors—whether they know those aspects derive from Stanislavski or not. A director must, therefore, be aware of their meaning and utility.

1.   The objective. What characters want; what their actions are geared to achieve. These goals may not be the same as what they say they want (see *subtext*, below); the objective is the most basic reason for the character's presence in the scene. It is what actors play when they step onstage—the action or purpose of the scene (not the lines, not the feeling). It is complemented by the concept of the obstacle—what stands in the way of characters getting what they want—and tactics—how characters either change their objective slightly or go about getting around the obstacle.

2.   Subtext. The character's actual intention or meaning which may underlie a statement. When a character says "I love you," he may mean "I want you to think I

love you so you will go to bed with me"; or she may mean "I want you to think I love you so you will give me that penthouse apartment."

3.   Unit of action, or "beat." A unit of time bounded by a common preoccupation with a specific and consistent action. Some beats last for seconds; some go on for pages. The purpose of breaking a script down into units, or beats, is to avoid superficial acting—failure to recognize when the action focus of a scene has changed. Each individual unit will fit into the main action of the play (see examples on pages 24–28).

4.   Given circumstances. The details of situation and character that enable the actor to give a particular shape to the action. Stanley Kowalski in *A Streetcar Named Desire* and Horner in *The Countrywife* are great "studs"; but the way in which they play their action is quite different.

5.   The "if." This device enables actors to make appropriate choices by putting themselves into the character's situation: "What, given that I am Othello, would I do if I were in this situation?" The concept of "situation" is crucial here, as it implies consideration of all the given circumstances of the text: facts, events, epoch, conditions of life, and so on, as Stanislavski made clear in *An Actor Prepares*.[2] This process does not, of course, have to be as self-conscious as it sounds; many of the actors' choices will spring instinctively from their osmotic assimilation of the given circumstances. But it is a useful basis for a director to begin a discussion with an actor who seems not to be making good choices.

Physical Actions

As Stanislavski developed his acting system he concentrated less on inner process and more on the playing of physical actions, the idea being that any action directed toward the achievement of a desire or want will generate spontaneous supporting feeling: do the act and the feeling will follow. This is not, of course, a return to "external" acting but the recognition of the *gestalt* nature of the human makeup: mind and body are interrelated, not separate entities, and emotion and its muscular symptoms are reciprocal.

This concept provides a bridge from the naturalistic acting method—concentration on inner process and feeling the part which is embodied and represented by the actor's persona—to the more theatricalized tradition—creating a mask or score of physical actions and presenting this to the audience. Three of Stanislavski's disciples evolved a movement toward a more radically presentational form of acting. Eugene Vakhtangov used the concept of physical actions to approach more than purely realistic scripts; and Michael Chekhov and Vsevold Meyerhold provide useful tools for the modern director.

Michael Chekhov's most significant contribution to the acting process is the concept of the psychological gesture.[3] This is based on the idea that

[2]Constantin Stanislavski, *An Actor Prepares*, trans. Elizabeth Hapgood (New York: Theatre Arts Books, 1948), p. 48.

[3]See Michael Chekhov, *To the Actor* (New York: Harper and Row Publishers, Inc., 1951), chap. 5.

FIGURE 91. Psychological gesture as illustrated in Michael Chekhov's *To the Actor*. (*Drawing 5 by Nicolai Remisoff from* To the Actor on the Technique of Acting *by Michael Chekhov. Copyright 1953 by Michael Chekhov. Reprinted by permission of Harper & Row, Publishers, Inc.*)

the performance of a strong action will stimulate consistent supporting emotion. Chekhov gives, among others, the example of a character that is domineering, has a strong will, and a somewhat wrathful sensibility. Using these strong, basic characteristics the actor discovers an all-embracing physical gesture which expresses these basic dynamics. The gesture must be simple, strong, clean, and involve the whole body. The actor repeats the gesture several times, finding that it becomes stronger each time, and the qualities on which it is based become more powerful. The feelings of wrath and distaste well up to fill and sustain the gesture. Through the performance of the gesture the actor penetrates the psychology of the character. It works. Once the strong outline—the spine of the character—has been created and has tapped into its emotional base, the character can be given more subtlety and sophistication by further exploration of detail and adaptation to given circumstances. But it will now happen from a solid physical base.

This is a very useful tool for a director who is working with actors who are overly analytical and physically tight. Sometimes actors will know all there is to know about the feelings and desires of their character, but they simply can't express it—they are always censoring themselves, intellectually manipulating; their work is constipated. By plugging into physical imagination, bypassing the mind in the first instance, actors can loosen up and allow all their understanding to flow into physical expression. The exercise is also useful with actors who are spilling the character's emotions all over the place but can't give them shape and focus.

Meyerhold and Biomechanics

The disciple of Stanislavski who moved completely away from naturalism and emphasis on inner process was Vsevold Meyerhold. His emphasis was entirely on physical action, the dynamic communication that could be made by the movement of the actor's body in space. In one production,

FIGURE 92.   A Vsevolod Meyerhold set using swings, ropes, and pulleys on which actors performed their biomechanics in a gymnastic style of acting (1927). *(Deutsches Theatermuseum, Früher Clara Ziegler-Stiftung)*

for example, he had a young man express love for a young woman by making an entrance down a chute. Whistling down with a cry of glee he landed flat on top of his lover. The visual excitement of the scene conveyed the sexual excitement of the situation, expressing it at least as intensely as the most passionate, naturalistic statement of love would do.

Meyerhold always looked to express the essential action of a scene in terms of a physical metaphor. In his production of *The Government Inspector,* he used eleven doors to stage the scene in which the local officials bribe Khelestakov; in each door stood one official. At the same time, and with the same gesture, they all held out bribes while chanting their lines in unison, like an eleven-part fugue. The whole effect was to create a gigantic, robotlike bribe machine, to which Khelestakov responded with the mechanical movements of a clockwork doll, picking off bribes in rhythmic sequence.

To accomplish such integrated physical effects, Meyerhold trained his company in biomechanics—principles of movement he had evolved to accustom the actor to using the stage space three-dimensionally, rather than the flatter, linear approach of the naturalistic theater. Gymnastic exercises, tumbling, and circus skills were employed to help the actors gain a sense of the relationship of their body to space, time, and rhythm. In Meyerhold's

FIGURE 93. Meyerhold's production of *Turandot* in Moscow (1925). The total use of the stage and the choreography of the actors created a fluid, plastic, rhythmic picture. *(Deutsches Theatermuseum, Früher Clara Ziegler-Stiftung)*

theater the actor was a plastic part of a rhythmically harmonious whole in which other actors, properties, stage furnishings, and scenery were all coordinated.

Meyerhold exemplifies the theatricalized tradition, which reacted against the limitations of naturalism, and working in a physically metaphoric manner, sought to communicate aspects of human endeavor broader than the everyday trivia or private emotion of realistic drama. Based on the essentially physical nature of theatrical communication, and appealing as much to the audience's imagination as to emotion, the theatricalized tradition rested on simulation rather than embodiment of character, mask or score of actions more than face, and external physical action more than inner process.

A director working in this tradition may come across actors whose experience is limited to a naturalistic manner. The director may need to convince them that there is surface truth as well as inner truth in theater, that each event has its own truth of communication, and if that truth is discovered and played consistently, the audience will be completely convinced. Farce, for example, has its own truth. It is highly conventionalized, physical, and exaggerated. If the actor goes delving deeply into his character's psyche for intense emotion, or requires a "realistic" motivation for each action, then he or she may dampen the farcical fireworks. Truth in farce is, of course, based on or related to perceived human activity, but not in a direct, one-to-one manner. The director will have to convince the actor of the validity of conventions: that essence can be more important than detail, that rhythm can have more impact on an audience than lines, and that physical actions can communicate more than private emotions. Physical exploration of the textual action is always a good starting point for theatricalized theater, and some specific techniques for use in rehearsals appear later in this chapter.

Copeau and Poetic Physicality

The movement away from naturalistic detail toward spatial plasticity was continued by Jacques Copeau. However, Copeau took a much more reverent approach to the text than did Meyerhold, and he was concerned for the physical manifestation of the poetic values of a script. He also emphasized the importance of ensemble to the best performance: the growing together of a group of actors that enables them to intuit each other's life rhythms and emotional responses, and consequently to act on the same wavelength, not as a collection of individuals each locked into a separate, sealed compartment. To achieve his ensemble Copeau spent several months with his company in a country retreat where they could play games, read poetry, discuss art, and otherwise become familiar with each other as they absorbed their texts. However, the best a contemporary director may reasonably expect is to be associated with a regional repertory company that has a similar company of actors for a couple of seasons. But whatever the situation, some time spent on encouraging actors to be comfortable with each other, and therefore more willing to take risks, can achieve the kind of mutual intuition and reciprocity that enormously facilitate the rehearsal process. Of course, it depends how much time a director has. If he or she is pressed, then a couple of parties and an after-rehearsal cup of coffee or a drink or two is probably the best that can be done. If there is more time, some conscious effort to create an ensemble atmosphere may be attempted. (Again, some exercises appear in the section on rehearsal techniques later in this chapter.)

Apart from the emphasis on ensemble, Copeau is worth noting for the value he placed on explicating the text to the actor in terms other than the surface meaning of the line. This is especially important in verse plays or plays with a highly poetic content where rhythm, melody, and imagery are built into character and situation. A director should not approach a verse play without having some sense of scansion, of how variations among foot patterns, placement of caesuras, and the use of line in the formation of larger rhythmic structures all contribute to the creation of character. Alliteration and onomatopoeia add color to the line, and rhythm and color can convey emotional sense even without help from content.[4] A director must bring all this knowledge to the actor's attention to avoid a superficial approach to the text, and again, it is a useful exercise to have the actor explore the textual values in purely physical terms, acting out the images and stretching his or her imagination beyond the limits of the words.

Artaud—A Theater of Cruelty

Antonin Artaud was a contemporary of Copeau, but his influence on theater became most significant in the 1960s and 1970s. With Artaud's concept of a theater of cruelty, the reaction Stanislavski initiated against the physically clichéd, emotionally sterile, and verbally bombastic theater of the late nineteenth century was brought to its most extreme physical climax.

Because of his personal problems with mental disturbances and drug therapy, Artaud had little chance to practice his theater; and his writings, though copious, tend to be abstract and metaphysical. But the aesthetic and purpose of the theater of cruelty is clear: to smash through the veneer of bourgeois civilization to reach a more atavistic, organic, elemental culture. Artaud's theater would unleash human appetites and express the potentiality of life in its most transcendent form, including love, crime, war, incest, and revolution. In a famous image, Artaud likened his theater to a

---

[4]A useful practical discussion of this aspect may be found in John Harrop and Sabin Epstein, *Acting with Style* (Englewood Cliffs, N.J.: Prentice-Hall, Inc., 1982), chap. 3.

FIGURE 94. Artaudian physical intensity is demonstrated by Gerard Tcherka, the actor, adapter, and director of this theatricalization of Artaudian theories, produced in Paris in 1977. (*French Cultural Services*)

plague which breaks down normal human functions, leads to delirium and visions, and sends the last of the living howling through the streets committing gratuitous acts.

His emphasis upon the physical aspects of performance relates Artaud to Meyerhold, but with a much more apocalyptic sensibility. We deal more fully with the theater of cruelty in the chapter on style, but here we are briefly going to discuss its legacy for the contemporary actor and some ways a director may work with actors in an Artaudian mode.

Artaud left no details of an acting process; this has had to be explored by his disciples, such as Peter Brook, Joseph Chaikin, Richard Schechner, and especially Jerzy Grotowski. Grotowski suggested that the basic approach of the Artaudian actor must be *via negativa*. Rather than building up an accretion of attitudes, the actors chip away at themselves, removing the blocks and resistances that prevent them from fully acting out the personal responses they find when confronting a role. To achieve stillness at his or her center which allows all impulses to flow freely through; to be stripped of all physical masks that block the full expression of feeling—that is the actor's goal.

Such self-revelation must not be an egotistical act. It is a challenge, not an excuse for the easy gesture or for being carried along on a sentimental tide of emotion. The confrontation of the text, myth, idea—whatever the impulse for the event—must take place within a disciplined theatrical context, and the director must reinforce the actor's willingness to take risks while rejecting gratuitous self-indulgence.

The actors use their role as both scalpel and trampoline. They research the situation with their body, probing for responses, finding associations, making contacts. They then use these discoveries as a springboard to confront the spectator with the intensity of the action. In rehearsal the performers select from among their discoveries those responses which create the shape of the action with the greatest intensity and clarity. This is the "score" of the event. It is fixed but not restricting, the "signals through the flames," made up of physical gestures and hieroglyphs—physical metaphors of action. A hieroglyph is not a common gesture such as might be made over a cup of coffee or the flick of cigarette ash. It is a metaphysical statement, expressing in intense physical terms the actor's deepest response to a human situation. Hieroglyphs have the impact on the audience of silent blows, and they create a resonance far beyond the power of our detailed, realistic, everyday gestures.

Discovery through the body is the essential method of Artaudian actors, but at least two things stand in their way. The social training of many years cannot be quickly sloughed off; and the inevitable tendency to respond with the immediate, naturalistic gesture takes some time to overcome. Actors will first respond to the action with physical clichés. When the director rejects these, the second response is likely to be a new set of clichés. They will not be the socially trained "mask" responses but will reflect personal and idiosyncratic aspects of the actors' self. The director must encourage the actor to probe for a still deeper and more total response that finds its roots in the collective iconography of humanity—the shared unconsciousness residing in the solar plexus that is the evolutionary product of millenia.

How does a director work with actors on an Artaudian piece? Well, first of all he or she must presume a physically adept and open group. Grotowski worked for years with his actors to achieve the physical capacity he required.[5] Given the physical ability, we are going to suggest a few exercises and methods aimed at exploring the actor's physical and vocal facility beyond the limitations of normal human expression.

The director will find props very useful in stimulating the actor's physical exploration. Not the bric-à-brac of our everyday life such as cups, saucers, glasses, newspapers, or books, but properties with a less specific

---

[5]See Jerzy Grotowski, *Towards a Poor Theatre* (New York: Simon & Schuster, Inc., 1970), for a comprehensive discussion of his approach and exercises.

FIGURE 95. Note the intense physical and emotional commitment of actor Ryszard Cieslak in Jerzy Grotowski's production of *The Constant Prince*. (*Courtesy, Teatr Laboratorium, Wroclaw, Poland*)

identity. Colored ribbons, staffs, pieces of cloth, nets, rope, and beads may by the way in which they are used be given a highly symbolic value, just as the wafer and wine become the flesh and blood of Christ in the Christian mass. By the use of gesture an actor can transform a piece of blue cloth into a rippling sea, beads into teardrops, a piece of rope into a serpent or umbilical chord.

As sounds and rhythms are so fundamental to this form of theater an exercise which explores them is a good starting point. The director can give the actors various objects with which to produce sounds—sticks, stones, tin cans, boxes, and so on. The actors then explore the complete sound range of the instruments, muting them against the body, suspending them in the air, laying them in various positions on the ground. Then the director can introduce rhythms, enormously varied in pace and intensity. Groups of rhythms can be formed and complete conversations held by exploiting the sound and rhythmic range of the instruments. Scenes can be played by using the vocabulary of sounds the actors have discovered to convey the

FIGURE 96. Stripping an actor down—in this case with a revealing costume and a "bald wig"—and providing him with bold, symbolic props, such as the zigzag sword, can liberate great theatrical intensity, as exhibited here by Michael Mancuso as a Nubian slave in the Denver Theatre Center's 1982 production of Shaw's Androcles and the Lion. (*Courtesy, Denver Theatre Center; photo by Nicholas de Sciose*)

sense of the text. The purpose of this exercise is to let the actors experience the possibilities of rhythm and sound. This experience can then be transferred to the actor's voice and body, the voice producing sounds different from those of the normal human vocabulary, and the body expressing a language beyond the accepted psychological or social clichés of everyday behavior patterns.

As extensions of this basic exercise, improvisations can be performed which require the completely nonnaturalistic expression of emotional states. For example, a scene can be set up on a completely naturalistic basis, but at a certain point an incident can be introduced, by way of a message or a new character, which creates an emotional state in the actor. The actor is required to express this state by using sound and movement which are completely nonnaturalistic but which communicate to the audience the essential quality of the emotion. Scenes can be created to give the actor more assistance in finding and using essential sounds and movements. For example, say that two girls have been roommates for many years. One has a boyfriend who has developed a secret attachment for the other, and finally the first girl has to be told. The boy must tell the girl, but he wants to avoid hurting her or destroying the relationship between the two girls. The girl tries desperately to keep the boy, wants to maintain her pride, but cannot disguise her bitterness at her roommate. The scene can be improvised naturalistically at first, then played again using only the essential words which convey the idea. Finally, the actor chooses essential sounds which reflect the sense of the scene, and the scene is replayed using variations on these sounds. When the scene is reduced to a basic impulse, the sound and movement it creates convey its organic essence.

Another approach to an Artaudian form of theater is to start with the breath. Breathing and the heartbeat are the two fundamental human rhythms, and both affect and are affected by emotional states: a deep breath, for instance, can quiet a state of nervous tension. Actors can be shown how the manipulation of breath affects their body. Short, irregular, rapid breathing affects the muscle impulses and rhythms of movement, resulting in certain expressive qualities. Breath patterns also affect facial expression. The actor should explore the potential emotional responses of a variety of breathing rhythms and depths. Breathing can then be given vocal extension, creating nonverbal sounds supported by and communicating emotional states. Scenes can then be played by using only breath and its physical and vocal extensions to convey the essential quality of the scene.

A good nonverbal exercise is for the actors to work in pairs and select a simple human relationship, for example, boyfriend/girlfriend, cop/crook, teacher/pupil, salesperson/customer. Without exchanging ideas the actors move around the space exploring the relationship. No words are used and no realistic props. Actors should concentrate on the rhythms of character, expressing them through space to their partner. A pattern will emerge that expresses the nature of the relationship as both actors perceive it. At this stage of the exercise one partner should choose a simple but emotionally strong message to communicate to the partner—"the man you shot died," "I'm leaving you," and so on. Again, no words are to be used; the message is to be communicated through the body movements in the spatial pattern already developed. When the partner senses the nature of the message he or she replies in a similar manner—with body movement in spatial patterns. With a strong concentration and bodily commitment to the exercise, messages can be understood and dynamic conversations held. Some coaching will be needed to channel actors away from small, realistic gestures into more deeply seated, engaged movements of the whole body. As actors become familiar with the exercise, more complex transactions can take place on more fundamental issues.

Because creation of the imaginative and intelligible hieroglyph is the chief task of the actor working in this style, we are finishing this section with a couple of exercises a director might use to help the actor become familiar with it. First, the actors should scatter around the space, contacting it in a neutral manner. Within the space are various nonspecific props such

97.

98

98A.

100.

FIGURES 97–100. Patterns exercise.
(*Patrick Siefe*)

as sticks, ropes, colored ribbons, pieces of cloth, and so on. The director numbers off the actors and introduces opposing concepts to be explored, such as harmony/discord. The odd-numbered actors explore one concept; the even numbered, the other. Actors should work individually and physically at first, responding to an immediate sense of what the concept means to them. The response should be confronted and refined into a hieroglyph—a series of gestures or movement. When the actors seem to have discovered their hieroglyph, the director calls out pairs of numbers—one even, one odd—and these actors reveal their hieroglyph to each other, responding to each other's rhythms, confronting the opposite concept, and adjusting so that the two hieroglyphs become one, displaying the essence of the dichotomy. While working in pairs the actors may use any of the props around the space. There are many pairs of concepts that work for this exercise: goodness/evil, victory/defeat, truth/falsehood, freedom/restraint, self-interest/sacrifice, and so on. Actors should be coached to reject the realistic gestures they first employ and to discover deeper and more broadly meaningful images.

In the second exercise the actors begin by contacting space in a neutral manner. The "sin" concepts of gluttony, lust, avarice, envy, pride, sloth, and wrath, are introduced one at a time. The actors should follow

FIGURE 101. Actor working on "Sin" exercise. (*Patrick Siefe*)

their immediate physical response. At first there will be a certain amount of imitation, pantomime—sticking out the belly for gluttony, moving slowly for sloth. The actors must understand the full medieval significance of *sin*—not contemporary peccadilloes. They should be coached for a strong visceral reaction, a full body response from the feet up, a total physical exploration. When all actors seem to be working at this deep level, they should be helped to refine the physical discoveries into a rhythmical, disciplined, repetitive image which retains the intensity of feeling at its core. Between work on each concept the actors shake out and resume a neutral walk in space—necessary because of the intensity of the work involved. When all the sins have been individually explored, the director throws them all at the group and allows actors to work on one that they have a particular response to. After a few minutes' work the actors shake out and sit in a circle. Now each actor in turn performs his or her particular hieroglyph in the center of the circle. The other actors don't know the concept, but if the hieroglyph is valid they will soon sense it. As they get the idea they begin to whisper the concept: lust, envy, pride, and so on, in time with the center actor's rhythm, encouraging him or her to a peak of intensity. The exercise is excellent for achieving a visceral response to ideas and a refined, intensified image based on that response. It quickly reveals clichés and weak, realistic gestures.

The director working with actors in an Artaudian form must get across the point that a pure feeling can be far less dynamic in terms of theatrical communication than a stage image, gesture, or vocal impact. One pearl-drop tear on the cheek of a sightless, unemotional, madonnalike mask can convey as much about human emotions as the warmest flood down the face of a romantically transported actress. The director also must constantly be testing, proving, and encouraging the actor's exploration to avoid the two pitfalls of this form—the physically imaginative but unfocused and irrelevant image; and the clever, nonnaturalistic, physical cliché which looks interesting on the surface but avoids the deep confrontation of the action.

Brecht—Epic Theater and Alienation

We can't leave this consideration of contemporary acting systems without some discussion of the ideas of Bertolt Brecht. Brecht's work doesn't belong directly to either of the two traditions we have noted; but it rejects and accepts parts of both. In practice it was a presentational form of theater, in which the actors both embodied and simulated their character at the same time. Brecht felt that a purely theatricalized form was too removed from reality; but at the same time, a naturalistic imitation of life in whatever detail was formalistic if it didn't deal with social, economic, and political realities in such a way as to achieve the betterment of the human condition. Brecht's theater was geared to the instruction of the audience: an appeal to the mind rather than the emotions.

Brecht did not reject emotion per se but only the empathy it produces. Empathy can be defined as giving oneself up to sharing the emotional state of a character to the degree that the character's emotions become "real" and obscure all consciousness that one is at a theatrical event. It was to this effect that Brecht objected, for it meant that the spectator had suspended his or her capacity for critical judgment of the social reality behind the emotional state.

It was toward the breaking of empathy that Brecht used the alienation effect. Alienation prevents empathy by constantly reminding the audience that it is in a theater, breaking the illusion that what it is witnessing is "real" life. Alienation has nothing to do with direct attacks on the audience or with deliberate attempts to make the audience physically uncomfortable. We have seen this done by actors, but it is counterproductive to Brecht's intention, because it either makes the audience retreat into a protective attitude and reject what is being presented, or it angers the audience and stimulates a visceral, emotional response which clouds its intellectual capacity.

To achieve alienation the actors must carry the audience with them through the story, while presenting their character in such a way as to clarify and comment on the action—so that the audience recognizes the issues at stake rather than feels the emotions being generated. To achieve this effect the director must help the actors carefully examine their part to discover the political dialectics of the play and the function their character has in presenting them. The questions the actor must ask are not "Who am I?" but "What am I?"; not "Who does this action?" but "What does this action do?" It is the action and the consequences of that action in social and economic terms that concern Brecht, not the nature of the psychical self. Rather than try to develop an emotional *persona* for the character or draw up an imaginary biography of his or her past, the actor should be encouraged to make a skeletal outline of the events and action of the play and underline where his or her part fits.

Although it is impossible to avoid emotion—it comes as an automatic response to any action or attitude—Brechtian actors do not pump it up: they accept what is there, control it, and channel it into the objective playing of the action. And just as the actors objectify and rechannel the emotion, so they alienate themselves from—stand outside of—their character in order to pass comment on its actions. This technique essentially employs the basic dialectic of acting—the actors as themselves and as character. In the balance between the two traditions—embodiment and representation of character, and simulation and presentation—Brecht required emphasis on presentation, because criticism of the character's socioeconomic actions was his purpose.

FIGURE 102. A strong sense of pre-sentational "mask" in Edward Pason Call's production of Bertolt Brecht's *Mahagonny* at the Mark Taper Forum Theatre, Los Angeles. (*Center Theatre Group/Mark Taper Forum, Los Angeles. By permission*)

Here are a few specific approaches and exercises a director might employ to help actors come to terms with the demands of epic theater:

- Read the play more than usual; take a socially critical viewpoint on the characters and identify the political focus of the play.
- Don't let the actor jump into "living" the part; identification with the character should only be used in rehearsal as a method of exploration and observation of the character's socioeconomic responses.
- The actor should confront rather than assimilate the character.
- Make the actors conscious of their dual focus—that they are demonstrating the character's function to the audience; make sure that all actors know the nature of the political response they are trying to engender in the audience (for example, Mother Courage is not meant to be a marvelously heroic character but one corrupted by a false economic system that kills her children and reduces her to a beast of burden).

Brecht himself employed certain rehearsal techniques:

- Transposing the actions and remarks of the character into the third person

- Transposing the action into the past
- Speaking the stage directions

Thus a piece of action in rehearsal might go as follows: "Mother Courage slowly got down from her wagon, walked over to the officer, looked at him and said, '. . . .'"

Using the third person and the past tense enables the actors to achieve the right attitude of distance from the action. Putting the action in the past allows the actors to look back at their sentences and to make judgments on them. Speaking the stage directions in the third person has the effect of alienating them from the text itself.

These techniques may be varied and elaborated upon. The stage manager can call out the stage directions or narrate the action as the actor moves through it: "So then Mother Courage wearily sat down, took her daughter Kattrin's hand, and waited for the soldiers to bring in the stretcher bearing the body covered with a sheet." The actor may use the third-person alienation technique and add a comment on the action—the kind of critical comment that the *gestus* (the acting) should convey: "He

FIGURE 103. Helene Weigel reduced to a beast of burden in Brecht's *Mother Courage*, as produced by the Berliner Ensemble in East Berlin. (*Roth Berlow, Berliner Ensemble*)

stood up weakly; because of the soldiers taking the food, he had not eaten for three days, and facing the officer with bitterness, said, '. . . .'"

The following exercise is based on Brecht's own quintessential model for epic acting—the street scene.

A situation is set up in which one of the actors is relating to the rest of the group an incident he or she has seen. In Brecht's model the incident was an automobile accident at a street corner, but the possibilities are unlimited. The witness describes and acts out the circumstances of the situation so that observers are able to form an opinion. The witness demonstrates the actions of the persons involved in the incident, but only as him- or herself—there is no attempt to create an illusion or to become emotionally involved. If the witness wants to suggest that someone was angry, he or she will display the actions of the anger but will not assume the emotion him- or herself. The characters involved in the situation will become known to the observers by their actions, and only those actions which are absolutely necessary to describe the nature of the event. The witness will demonstrate the actions and talk directly to the observers. If he or she wishes to use props or costume elements it will be for gestic purposes; for example, a crooked hat may suggest that one of the characters was drunk, or a white stick that he or she was blind.

The object of the witness's demonstration is to show what part each individual played in the incident and enable the observers to form an opinion and fix responsibility. The actor who is the witness must always take an objective standpoint, using the "he did" and "she said" construction, so that the observers are aware of both the witness and the person he or she is demonstrating; the actions and opinions are never merged into one, although the witness may have his or her own point of view. The game may be placed in a courtroom environment with witnesses, jury, judge, and lawyers. A certain license will have to be allowed to enable the witnesses to demonstrate more physically than they would in a court of law, and the jury should be allowed to ask questions.

The following is an exercise in the demonstration of a task with a critical viewpoint. The actors pair off. One of them performs some everyday working task: digging a garden, washing up, changing a tire, changing bed linen, and so on. The focus should be on highly specific details, and the task should last about a couple of minutes. The other actor then repeats the partner's performance as accurately as possible. The second actor then repeats it a second time with whatever adjustments he or she thinks necessary to clarify the nature of the task: omitting some detail, adding other detail, changing rhythms, and so on. The actors then discuss the differences in their performance of the task, paying particular attention to accuracy of detail, clarity, and the essential actions necessary to the valid performance of the task. The exercise is now repeated with each actor taking a particular social or economic attitude to the task: a trade unionist changing the tire on a Rolls Royce, an out-of-work engineer digging the garden, an impoverished student changing the linen in an expensive hotel. Taking a critical attitude should not alter the basic detail of the task but only the way in which that detail is performed.

For this last exercise actors pair off and begin a simple mirror exercise, establishing good concentration and exchange of rhythms. When the game is well underway the director suggests broad characters to the actors—housewife, model, truck driver—and lets them base their mirror movements on a general physical sense of the gestures and rhythms of such a character. The actors shake out and change partners every few minutes to keep them relaxed as well as concentrated and to stimulate their imagination. They continue the game, the director now giving broad socioeconomic situations as the basis for the mirror movements—energy crisis, gas rationing, motherhood, feminism, whatever happens to be topical. Finally, still within the structure of the mirror exercise, the director gives the actors a character type, and when it is reflected in the mirror movements, adds a socioeconomic situation. The actors will now be presenting a movement gestus of a character: presenting it in such a way as to reflect that character's attitude to a socioeconomic situation. The exercise must be watched carefully, as there is a fine line between allowing actors time to develop their movements validly and tiring them out because of the intense physical concentration the game requires.

Synthesis

Brecht is a good point at which to conclude our discussion of systems; embodying in his approach a naturalistic basis with a strongly presentational sense of communication, he represents that synthesis of methods which typifies the state of the art for the contemporary actor.

Stanislavski is still the great mentor—not just because he was the first to attempt to codify an acting process but also because he was so right in much of what he said. It is really not his fault that his system was taken too rigidly and for too long thought to be the one true gospel. The narrow, normative attitude of the late nineteenth century that looked for one rational, scientific method for solving a problem—an immediate panacea or touchstone for success, *pace* the New York Studio—was responsible for narrowing the artistic scope of theater and using one recipe for all creative tasks. Stanislavski himself acknowledged the limitations of his approach. He admitted lack of success with plays in the grand and heroic manner: "Apparently it is not inner feeling but the technique of expression that prevents me from doing in the plays of Shakespeare, what we are able to do in Chekhov."[6]

[6]Constantin Stanislavski, *My Life in Art* (Moscow: Foreign Languages Publishing House, 1925), p. 400.

"Technique of expression" says it all. Although Stanislavski was on solid ground in insisting to his actors that art must be based on natural laws and human truths, he perhaps underestimated the need of art to express the inexpressible, to create a world larger than the earthbound one—a world of the imagination. Each work of art possesses its own truth; in the theater these require different modes of expression and different approaches from the actors and directors to communicate. This does not imply any fundamental contradiction between Stanislavski and, say, Artaud—to take perhaps extremes of inner and outer approaches. If there is any final truth, it may be that unless feeling is shaped into a communicative image it is "a passionate letter without postage"; and unless the image, gesture, or signal is connected to feeling it will lack force.

Today the ideas of Stanislavski, Meyerhold, Michael Chekhov, Brecht, and Artaud tend to operate in a free-market system. None of them is discrete; today an accomplished actor's method is likely to include elements from each, and may well alter with each role. It is essentially a question of what works for whom, where, and when—an informed eclecticism that has enabled the contemporary actor and director to take on the full range of the dramatic repertory and be limited neither to performing one style of drama nor to attempting to apply one method to a whole variety of theatrical demands.

Obviously some techniques are more directly applicable to some plays than to others. Stanislavski is probably a good starting point for *The Three Sisters* and Brecht for the *Caucasian Chalk Circle,* but the director who has a familiarity with the range of acting techniques available will not only be able to talk with actors in the relevant vocabulary or help them where their technique may be limited but also add interest to rehearsals and bring fresh insights to productions by the choice of techniques that may not seem immediately appropriate.

REHEARSAL TECHNIQUES

Apart from the major acting philosophies just discussed, there are a host of approaches and techniques that a director can use on a day-to-day basis in rehearsal. We are going to deal with some of these as practical additions to the director's technical toolbox.

Person to person

Beneath all the systems, philosophies, and techniques, the basic relationship of director to actor is on a one-to-one human level, and because of the intense nature of rehearsals it is not uncommon for the relationship to go through a stage of jockeying for position—who is going to trust whom; who is going to dominate whom; and so on. Sometimes this mistrust arises because the actor and director start out with different conceptions of a role. If, through discussion, a reasonable accommodation can't be reached, then the directors should assert their interpretation. They may well, of course, be wrong and that will show in the final product. Or it may be that the actor is unwilling to take a risk. Actors tend to cling for security to known effects, to what has worked for them. Many actors in a repertory situation will all too often begin by repeating the character they have just finished playing. Whatever the case, directors must ultimately assert themselves. Popularity with the actors is nice, and a congenial working environment highly to be desired, but not at the cost of the production's effectiveness.

Persuasion rather than bald directives is preferable. This can be done in several ways, and the director has to have a nice feeling for what will work when and with whom. The most common approach is for the director gently to shepherd the actor in the direction he or she wants the actor to go, allowing the actor to discover the solutions the director has carefully planted for him. In this way the actor has a more visceral connection with the character because he believes he created it entirely on his own. When the actor has solved a scene in the way the director had planned, the director smiles gratefully and congratulates the actor.

A slightly more risky method is to throw responsibility on the actor, either by suggestion—that there is a problem the director has been unable to solve and is thus relying entirely on the actor—or by implying that the actor is incapable of achieving the desired result, and thus, by indirectly impugning the actor's ability, catalyzing him or her into marvelous, and hitherto unsuspected, feats of creative activity. The risk is, of course, that the actor simply turns sulky and gives a performance that says "won't I be glad when this is over."

The preferable relationship is a reciprocal one of give and take with—at least at the outset—the director doing somewhat more giving and the actor more taking, in the pursuit of common solutions. But even this relationship will be influenced by the psychology of different actors. Some need constant reinforcement; others require a certain amount of browbeating or restraining. Reinforcement means building actors' confidence in what they are doing, allowing them the scope to take risks without fear of being slapped down. More than this, some actors need to feel that the director is there all the time, actually aware of what they are doing. It is easy to be thankful for the actor who is doing just fine and to concentrate on the others. But sometimes actors don't know they are doing well, and sometimes they don't believe it. A word of encouragement is never wasted, and even going as far as to invent a minor point of criticism just to assure some actors you are paying attention to them can give them confidence in their work.

Browbeating—a form of psychological intimidation—may be necessary to restrain actors who confidently go off in all the wrong directions.

Just as it takes a certain amount of physical force to stop a freely rolling automobile, it takes a similar amount of psychical or spiritual force to get a strong performer off one track and onto another. This necessity is not as harsh as it sounds; it is unlikely to harm the highly self-confident actor, and some actors actually thrive on it. However, when it is a cover for a director's own insecurity—just as reinforcement can be used out of timidity or laziness—it can be a dangerous aberration in the rehearsal relationship.

Suggestion and discussion are the best bases for a comfortable and dynamic working relationship with the actor. A suggestion is psychologically neutral. It neither praises the actors nor criticizes them; it simply opens the possibility of another way of playing a moment or scene. "Try going to the window on that line," a director might offer. "How about playing against the line here?" "What would happen if . . . ?" All this will encourage the actors' own voluntary responses which they will perform better than if they had been summarily handed them. Mixed with a pinch of correction when time is short, and a pound of encouragement throughout, suggestion offers the director the best chance of having a peaceful and profitable rehearsal.

A few final suggestions:

- If the actor believes he has a problem then, as far as the director is concerned, he *does* have one. "No, no it's just fine," might do for a first answer; but if the actor comes back, listen carefully. Sometimes an actor cannot express the problem well, he just feels something is wrong. It's worth taking rehearsal time to get at it, for a good actor is often the best judge of the inner chemistry of the production; and it's not going to work if the director pursues his brilliant concept against the actors' instincts for the inherent rhythms of the action.

- Make sure actors know what *you* are talking about—sense their vocabulary as well as their rhythms. Images such as "move from third into top here," "push here, pull there," or "let it simmer a little" are sometimes better than all the technical vocabulary with sage references to Diderot or Grotowski. Good actors are seldom unintelligent, but they often mistrust intellectualism; they are instinctive and intuitive, and this, as long as there is a good basis of rational process, should not be ignored.

- Always try to throw in something positive when giving notes. Again, under pressure of time it is easy simply to point out what is wrong and take what is working for granted. Never try to fool actors by playing the glad game with something everyone knows is wrong, but don't give abrupt, unhelpful notes such as "that was lousy." An exception might be an occasion when everything has gone wrong, and the atmosphere can be lightened by making a joke of it—a kind of reverse confidence which suggests that "we all know it isn't really as bad as that." Notes should become more positive—that is, pick out the good points—as the opening nears, and don't suddenly change direction on your actors at the last minute. We have been in situations when the director hardly gives the actors a note, then at a late dress rehearsal suddenly tears a scene apart. This simply destroys the actors' confidence, and at that late stage a problem is your fault and not the actors'.

• A director has achieved his best results—particularly in realistic theater— when his work is invisible in the performance. When a reviewer praises a production and commends only its excellent acting, a director should sit back, look happy, and count the full seats. Directors are not in competition with actors for plaudits and attention. A production should be integrated and seamless. Anything that can't be convincingly played by the cast should be eliminated in rehearsal. If the director forces an actor to go through with it, it is likely to be an embarrassment to the production. Further, and finally, a director should have the humility to realize that when an actor cannot play an effect, it may well be a poor choice from the start. No director alive hasn't made some unworkable decisions in the prerehearsal period; good directors recognize them and don't force their actors to pursue them.

Warming Up and Cementing the Ensemble

To come to practical grips with the rehearsal process, and to begin at the beginning, it is useful to start a rehearsal with a warm-up period. This has at least two advantages: as the term suggests, it warms up the actors' muscles and limbers them for the practical work ahead; it is also a time when the actors can focus on their instrument, the body, and get it and the mind geared toward the rehearsal, forgetting all thoughts of quarrels with friends, where the next meal is coming from, and so on. You might want to give the actors some time on their own to do basic physical exercises, and then use some games to complete the warm-up and help the ensemble to gel—to get people loose and used to relating to each other at a high level of energy. The theory behind the use of games is that a major obstacle to relating to one another is the "adult" human reaction to emotional involvement—dissimulation and suppression. Even the recent relaxation of former puritanical attitudes toward the body and its functions has not entirely freed people of inhibitions and moral phobias, and a certain amount of work with any group of actors can probably make them more open with each other, so that they can approach any relationship required of them with greater freedom and flexibility.

Openness and freedom of response are, of course, the essential attributes of children before contact with the adult world encourages them to build defensive barriers around their imagination and emotions. The child's capacity for play and the creation of games is unbounded. Part of the philosophy behind the use of games as a theatrical tool is geared precisely to releasing in the adult that spontaneous capacity for human interaction which was his or her birthright. How the games succeed with actors depends to some degree on their maturity and experience. The director may encounter resistance from experienced professionals who have their own "tried and true" methods. We were once associated with a production in which a seasoned professional actor told the director that he knew what he was doing and "don't need your kiddie's games." This may have been true. At all events directors should avoid using games as an end in themselves. A professional repertory company that has worked together for many months (if you are lucky enough to find one) is less likely to need ensemble work than a scratch cast of university students coming together for the first time. However, if imaginatively and purposefully used, games are always interesting rehearsal tools and, in most instances, a good way of helping actors to work with each other. Some games we have found useful for warm-up and ensemble purposes follow.

Plastique.   Take one part of the body and allow the rest of the body to follow this specific part with complete plasticity through 360 degrees of space. Start, say, with the shoulder; it is better not to use arms or legs until the exercise is well under way. Let the shoulder move in any direction and lead the rest of the body with it. Then transfer the leading point to the head, the pelvis, the hip, the knee, and so on. The change is not abrupt, but the plastic energy flows through the body from one leading point to another. The body follows and the center of balance is constantly adjusted to remain the fulcrum of whatever position is taken up from moment to moment in the adjusting flow. The feet may be moved, but it is better to keep them firmly planted until some skill has been gained at finding and adjusting the center of balance. The exercise should never jerk; the body should never overbalance; all parts of the body should lead at some time, and a full 360 degrees should be used.

Machine game.   This is one of the oldest chestnuts in the theatrical bag, but that doesn't diminish its value. One actor begins a rhythmical and repetitive physical action and is joined, in turn, by each of the other actors, who relates his or her action to what is already developing. At first there will be tendencies to linearity and perpendicularity. Play several games until interesting and varied machines are produced. The game is good for warm-up, physical ensemble relationships, and physical imagination.

Red Rover.   This is a form of tag, and all of the many varieties of tag are good warm-up games. Players line up at one end of the space with one player in the middle. All players fold their arms across their body. Now players have to hop on one leg to the other end of the space. They may change legs, but only one leg may be in contact with the ground at any one time. The player in the center has to intercept by knocking the crossers off balance. This is done with the folded arms. The center player must also hop when intercepting. The game continues until all players have been intercepted.

Three deep.   This is another good high-energy, physical-control game. Players form two circles, one immediately behind the other, so that

FIGURES 104, 105, 106, 107. Machine game. *(Patrick Siefe)*

they are standing two deep. Two players are outside the circle. One chases the other around the outside of the circle until he or she is caught, whereupon the situation is reversed—the chaser becomes the chasee—or the chasee moves into the circle and stands in front of one of the twosomes, making it three deep. When this happens the rear member of the group becomes the chasee, and the game continues as described.

Dropping the handkerchief. This is a somewhat similar game. Players form one circle. One player walks around the outside of the circle with a handkerchief. At some juncture he or she drops the handkerchief at the heels of one of the players in the circle. This player must pick up the handkerchief and chase the other player around the circle, attempting to tag this player before he or she can get back into the space of the chaser. If tagged, the handkerchief dropper continues dropping the handkerchief at another pair of heels. If he or she gets to the empty space, the game continues with the new dropper. The trick to this game is nonchalance on the part of the dropper and alertness on the part of the players in the circle.

Touch-me-not. In this game, players stand in a circle about the size of a boxing ring. Two players are in the middle. Each has to try to touch the other's back. They may use the whole of the circle, but they may not leave it; nor may they touch any other part of their opponent's body (some arm contact is inevitable). They play the best of three "hits." Whoever wins takes on the next player. This is a good game for alertness, physical imagination, agility, and finesse. It also encourages concentration on and response to every move made by the person one is playing with.

Zap. Players form a circle or two lines opposite each other. One player throws an imaginary bolt of energy with a particular body movement and sound at another player. The second player must accept the energy bolt, repeat the movement and sound, and then transform it into his or her own movement and sound and zap it at another player. There should be no gap between receiving the bolt, performing the movement, and then transforming it. The game is played with high energy and fast pace. Players may need to be coached at first to use their whole bodies, rather than just their arms and legs, in performing the movements. The game is a good warm-up and encourages the use of physical imagination.

Numbers change. Players sit in a circle and number off. One player, in the middle of the circle, calls two numbers. Those called must change places before the caller can take one of their places. The dispossessed player is now in the middle and must call numbers.

Explosion—no motion.   A good energy and concentration exercise is to have the whole group of actors walk the performing space and, on a hand clap, drum bang, or whatever, explode out of itself into any physical position that happens. Now each player must imperceptibly alter the pose while concentrating on not moving. As in the machine game, players will at first adopt boring horizontal or vertical positions; play the game until they explode through 360 degrees.

Finger painting.   This game helps actors lose their inhibitions about touching each other. (How often has one seen young actors engaged in the passionate kiss which touches at the lips only, the bodies embarrassedly straining to avoid contact?) Using the hand as a palette and fingers as a brush, one actor first whitewashes his or her partner all over and then, on this blank canvas, paints in a character. The partner, eyes closed, tries to sense the character from the touch and then adopts the rhythms and characteristics associated with what he or she has sensed. When the game is played with concentration a remarkable degree of accuracy can be achieved in transmitting the character through touch.

Discovering the Action

The use of games and physical exercises is not restricted to a warm-up or ensemble process. The approach may be validly employed to explore the script to discover the intrinsic action and to develop character. Physical exploration of the dramatic action is based on two perceptions. One is that the body both learns physically and communicates physically. The whole rehearsal process is, in fact, geared to the translation of the script into flesh and blood—the physical absorption of it by the actors. The blocking, the lines, the understanding of subtext, the character detail all become second nature, so that the actor doesn't go out and consciously play them but instead plays the action they have shaped and responds directly to the stimuli of the stage moment. The actors' response is physical—they play physical (including verbal) actions—which brings us all the way back to Stanislavski. Charles Marowitz[7] tells an instructive story of Stanislavski being unable to get the right playfulness and naiveté he wanted from one of his actors. He invited the actor to his house to talk it over; but when the actor arrived Stanislavski was seated on the floor in the midst of a bunch of toys. Warily the actor began by humoring Stanislavski and tentatively playing with him and the toys. After a while, however, a genuine fascination began and the two men became completely engrossed in play, at which point Stanislavski gleefully said, "There, now you have it. That's what your character is like."

[7]Charles Marowitz, *The Act of Being* (New York: Taplinger Publishing Co., 1978), p. 22.

FIGURES 108, 109, 110. Explosions—No motion exercise. (*Patrick Siefe*)

FIGURES 110A, 111, 112. Explosions—No motion exercise. *(Patrick Siefe)*

Here, Stanislavski was not only using a physical rather than an intellectual or analytical approach to a problem but was also working with the play or game structure that is the second of the two perceptions we mentioned: the sense of human transactions taking the form of games people play. Playscripts have the structure of a series of these human games, many of which are based on learned human experience that we all carry around with us. However, they almost all contain some suppressed drive to action, and if actors can physically plug into this element and play it out, then they have a much stronger sense of the dramatic action. By confronting the action physically, actors will find that their bodies spontaneously react to the game, based on human experience, that theater essentially is. Through the physicality of the game the emotional content of the action can also be released. Searching for inner feeling can often be a static process and can bottle up an actor's energy. Attacking a role physically, with gusto, releases energy, breaks down inhibitions, and discovers the parameters of an action. It is usually easier to tone down a performance than to bring an actor who is locked into his or her private emotions up to performance size.

We are going to illustrate the process of physical exploration of the action by showing its application to situations from a spectrum of plays; as a technique it is not limited to any one form. To look, again, at *The Cherry Orchard,* there is a scene at the end of Act III in which Lopahin reveals that he has bought the estate, finally crushing any hopes Mme. Ranevskya might have had of saving it, meaning that she must leave her home forever. Chekhov's direction is that Mme. Ranevskya is collapsed, weeping bitterly. What is actually happening is that her past and her present are being destroyed. To help the actress get a strong sense of this action, Lopahin can actually go around the house breaking it up—overturning furniture, throwing out ornaments, and so on—while Ranevskya follows him around trying to put it back together and to restrain him from total destruction. This activity will give the actress a very strong physical sense of her emotional state. It also helps the actor, for although Lopahin's action is not vicious or bent on deliberate destruction, the breaking up of the room will help him to get out the drunken, physical euphoria he is feeling. After such a rehearsal both actors will return to the action with a much stronger hold on it.

The Cherry Orchard is one of the classics of naturalism, with its deeply rooted subtext, and the physical approach helps to get this aspect to the surface. In contrast, verse plays with densely poetic language often trap actors into rhetorical delivery of surface values. Here again a physical approach to the text will help the actor to discover a scene is not about verse or poetic imagery but about action. There are a couple of scenes in *Othello* (III, iii and IV. i) in which Iago is tempting Othello, or poisoning him against Cassio and Desdemona. The kinds of physical metaphors that come to mind to encapsulate the essential action of the scenes might include a bullfight, a spider enmeshing its victim, or an angler playing a fish. Actually the scenes are subtly different: in the first scene Iago is more tempting Othello; in the second, more goading him. Taking the angling image for the first scene (this might be reinforced by saying that Iago has Othello "on a string") the actors can discover the physical dynamics of the scene if a rope is tied around Othello and put into the hands of Iago, who now, literally, has Othello on a string and can play him like a fish. As he pulls on the rope, plays it out when he meets resistance, discovers when to strike and when to play along, Iago will discover the physical property of the lines and get a very strong sense of the physical relationship in space that the ebb and flow of the scene's action demand. Othello will also physically experience the pull of Iago's temptation, how strongly he needs to resist, and the way in which he is pulled into Iago's net.

A similar exercise may be done for IV. i, using the bullfight image. Rehearsing in a confined space—a good warm-up exercise might be Touch-Me-Not (see page 204)—Iago is given a cape and a stick with a padded end with which to physically goad Othello as the lines suggest. The image of a trapped, maddened bull is also a useful one for Othello in this scene and will help the actor rise to the full dynamics. Physical exploration in this manner is particularly useful for verse plays and prevents the action from becoming stuck in or lost beneath the poetry or emotion.

As a last example we are going to take a play from a genre different from either verse tragedy or naturalism. *Blithe Spirit* is a comedy of manners with a farcical premise. Problems for an actor here include linguistic repartée and finding the right level of comic believability, especially in the "quarrel" scenes. Here again the use of physical objects gives the actor a stronger hold on the scene. Repartée is, essentially, verbal fencing, and a useful exercise is to give the actors foils, in the form of padded sticks, which they can use to make their points (we speak of pointing a line), parry, riposte, and so on. The handling of the line and the handling of the stick, the weight of the line and the strength of the thrust, are related, and the actor gets a strong sense of the line as an active weapon.

In the quarrel scenes where the characters verbally assault each other, it is important to discover the level of aggression which maintains believability but does not destroy the comic effect. If the actors become too serious, too emotionally involved, the scene will fall flat and lose all humor. In *Blithe Spirit*, Charles and Ruth and Charles and Elvira have several scenes of recrimination, which have a serious basis but are comic from the audience's perspective because of the childish way in which these eminently sophisticated adults behave. Beneath the social patina of the scene the characters would like to kick, slap, pull each other's hair, and throw tantrums like a spoiled child. One way we have found useful—which makes the action physical, allows the characters to vent their childlike anger, and yet doesn't inflict any serious hurt (hurt in comedy must never be serious but rather like the puny ineffectuality of the child's punch)—is to give the actors cushions, rolled-up newspapers, and balloons with which to attack each other, and thereby illustrate the physical intention beneath the line. None of these implements can inflict serious hurt; the actors appreciate the ridiculousness of what they are doing and it gives them an audience's perspective; most important it gives the actors a strong sense of the value of a line, as they have to choose what weapon to emphasize it with and how hard to strike: the choice of prodding, bopping, or knocking on any given line is a practical analysis of the dynamics of the scene. A feather duster, for the lightest teasing, and the padded stick previously mentioned may be added to the arsenal of comedy rehearsal weapons.

It will be evident from this discussion that physical confrontation has at least two functions: it cuts through language to reveal the essential action of a scene, and it allows the actors to experience it in their bodies; that is, it enables actors to experience the subtext of their part, and it builds a strong physical infrastructure to the lines. There is also, in the process, a slight distinction between the actual physical confrontation of the action—breaking up the props to express the physical intention of a rage that has to be bottled up inside—and turning the action into a game, such as the bullfight suggested for *Othello*. Both achieve the physical experience of the action; which is more appropriate will depend on the nature of any scene.

Developing Character

Games can be used to help actors discover a broader range of possibilities for their character. Sometimes actors get stuck in a particular set of physical rhythms: it may be their own, a character they have recently played, gimmicks they fall back on when they are uncertain of what they are doing, or preconceptions about the part that other productions have given them—all of which limits the full exploration of the role. Discussion, character analysis, and biography are all very well in their way, but they may not get beyond intellectual understanding into physical response. Sometimes one physical element that feels right can release an actor into a full characterization. It may be how the character holds his head, sits in a chair, tugs at his beard. Alec Guinness likes to start from how his character walks; Laurence Olivier had a penchant for false noses; Gielgud works from vocal rhythms. Now actors can, and should, do much of this work for themselves—it is their job. But if some actors seem blocked, are having difficulty with physical characterization, or seem to be content with what first came to hand, it can be useful to take out an evening in rehearsal, or some time after a warm-up on a couple of occasions, to do some exercises which help the actors explore a broader range of possibilities.

A very basic and widely used character exercise is Animal Attitudes. Actors are asked to pick any animal and then walk around the rehearsal

FIGURES 113, 114, 115, 116.   Animal attitudes.   (*Patrick Siefe*)

space exploring its basic rhythms and qualities of movement. Actors should be allowed to take their time and coached to focus on these questions: "Where is the center of energy?" "Does it balance with a tail?" "Does it dart, trot, or glide?" The aim is not to imitate the animal so much as to assume its essential properties of movement. From here actors are coached to build the physical mask of a human character, using the rhythms, centers of energy, and patterns of movement they have discovered. Actors should be encouraged not to get too sophisticated at first—two or three basic characteristics, strongly and cleanly defined, are all that are necessary. In and of itself this exercise helps actors to slough off personal rhythms; but it can be more closely related to a textual situation by having them begin with an animal they believe their character most closely resembles.

Another exercise, similar to the preceding one, takes a quality or attitude as its starting point. Players are asked to take a quality such as miserliness, gluttony, or lechery and try to discover what response they find to it in their bodies. That is, what rhythms, what physical attitudes, what disposal of energies are suggested by these qualities? Again players should be coached to take their time, repeating the idea to themselves and using whatever images come to mind, until the body gradually takes the quality into itself. Having discovered the outline of the mask, players are coached to play with it, exaggerating aspects of movements, gestures, rhythms, and so on, to explore the possibilities. What will be achieved is a series of gestures and physical attitudes which illustrates the particular quality the player started with, and at the same time, gives a broadly defined character. Again, this exercise can be directly related to a text by having actors choose a basic character trait as a starting point. It is especially useful in plays where characters have eponymous names such as Fidget, Tattle, Horner, and so forth.

Another exercise is based on the use of physical deformities to create character masks. Players should walk about the workshop space with an easy consciousness of their own physical rhythms and centers of energy, achieving a comfortable neutrality. Players are then coached to adopt various abnormalities: their legs become two feet longer; their feet double in size; their arms touch the floor; their nose is a foot long; and so on. Each time they adopt the physical deformity they are coached to explore what it does to their body rhythm, posture, and center of energy. Players should return to neutral between each abnormality. After exploring various abnormalities and the rhythms associated with them, players are coached to build a character mask by adopting two or three of the physical attributes they discovered when exploring the deformities. This should be done gradually, one at a time, until a strong, integrated physical outline of character is created.

The preceding exercises, and many like them, are not intended to create complete characters, nor, necessarily, produce clues that a director or actor will build on—although they usually do so. But at the very simplest level they are a starting point, a means of exploration, a way of letting actors work within a larger scope than their own physical personality or a few tricks that have worked for them in the past.

Improvisation

Discussion of the use of games and physical exercises in the rehearsal process leads directly to the directorial method of working with actors on a text in a totally improvisatory manner. As with games, improvisation is a way of approaching a textual problem indirectly, by using an actor's direct personal experience in a somewhat analogous situation and then channeling the discoveries made back into the textual action. It should be mentioned that improvisation can be a theatrical form in its own right, as with the commedia dell'arte, in which actors, using their own skills, developed whole plays from skeletal synopses. Also complete plays can be derived from improvisation, a popular technique in the 1960s and 1970s. A company would improvise around a theme, and a playwright would then develop a script from their discoveries. *The Serpent* by Jean Van Italie was created in this way, indeed, on the theme of the Creation.

We are going to discuss improvisation as a rehearsal tool and offer a model of how a play may be rehearsed totally in an improvisatory manner. There are three basic uses of improvisation as a rehearsal technique. The first is to approach a text by setting up an analogous situation closer to the actors' own experience. The approach to the balcony scene we suggested on page 176, using a "good night" between a newly met boy and girl, is an example of this technique. Second, subtext may be made more immediate and dynamic by improvisational exploration, for example, the approach to the scene from *The Cherry Orchard* suggested on page 208. A third use of improvisation is to flesh out an actor's understanding of both situation and character by playing out circumstances which are outside of the textual action but inform the life of the play and influence character. An example would be an improvisation we might call "at home with the Brabantios." Brabantio is Desdemona's father in *Othello;* in the first act of the play there is a great deal of reference to how Othello was a guest at Brabantio's house and how he wooed Desdemona—all of which occurs before the play begins. However, it is crucial to the relationships of Brabantio, Desdemona, and Othello in the first act. Improvising the situation adds a great deal of depth and reality to the playing of the first act: not only to Brabantio's feeling of being betrayed but also to Desdemona's long speech describing the wooing circumstances. It also enables Othello and Desdemona to explore their relationship to each other before it falls apart—something which isn't developed in the text.

Improvisation makes great demands on an actor's imagination and ability to give and take with fellow actors in an immediate and spontaneous manner. The director's job is to maintain a secure (that is, no fear of failure), open, and stimulating atmosphere and, ultimately, to select and refine the choices from the many possibilities that are suggested. Improvisation sessions should probably start—certainly in early rehearsals—with games and exercises such as those suggested on pages 202–5. These exercises help members of a group to get to know and trust each other, familiarize actors and director with individual rhythms and potentialities, release nervous tension and encourage concentration, and tap energy sources and spontaneity. Further, the syntax of the production can be embedded in the games and exercises: the actors can be gaining an experience of some of the demands of the action and the style without being consciously aware of it.

Directors should always have a sense of what they are trying to obtain by using an improvisation, but they should not have too rigid a notion of what the solution will be. One of the virtues of improvisation is the new light it can shed on apparently clichéd situations. A director should also develop a fine sense of when an improvisation has broken down and when the actors are simply taking time to explore the situation before coming up with fresh actions. Improvisations shouldn't be rushed; nor, however, should they be allowed to ramble on when they have outrun their usefulness. A director can stimulate and influence the course of an improvisation by sending an actor into the situation to play an objective that will set up a conflict; by introducing new props; or by changing some of the given circumstances, such as climate, time of day, or location. What should not be done is to alter an actor's character or objective in mid-improvisation, as this will inevitably make the actor self-conscious of his or her responses and block spontaneity.

Spontaneity is fundamental to improvisation, and it is a vital part of a performance. Ideally the playwright's words and actions should have so totally become those of the actors that the playing is spontaneous within the learned structure. Spontaneity is often blocked by tension, however, which can arise in various ways: feeling pressure to "perform" before the actors have a visceral sense of their part; consciously realizing that they are "on stage"; being physically hampered by holding a script and reading lines rather than making eye-to-eye contact; being locked into a playwright's words without sensing the actions from which they arise; being blocked into rigid patterns of movement by a director who has a firmly preconceived idea of the *only* shape of the play's action. A non-script-holding, non-preblocking improvisational approach can free the actor from some of these inhibitions. (It can also, of course, set up some problems of its own, as we shall discuss.)

Any text is the reduction into words on paper of the flesh-and-blood action felt by the author in his or her creative state. In producing a play a director has to rediscover that organic action. This may not happen if the actors learn lines by rote and move through spatial patterns, which however sensitively and scrupulously thought out by the director are still limited by one person's imagination, as opposed to the collective creativity of all the players. Improvisation also allows the actor to experience in a primal way the thoughts, actions, emotions, and ideas which will give life to the production. These elements become the actor's own because they have arisen from a direct confrontation of the impulses behind the text. It may be said by actors that they already have an awareness of the textual qualities and don't need to indulge in improvisation. In one sense this is true; intelligent actors will usually have an intellectual understanding of their part. The point of exercises and improvisations is to turn that understanding into a palpable experience uninhibited by the structural obstacles of rehearsal, such as scripts, preblocking, preconceptions, and physical tensions. The actors should be able to explore and come to understand the text with their whole person, physical and emotional as well as intellectual. Some say that this is hopelessly idealistic, that professional theater allows no time for such extraneous activity. Indeed, in the old weekly repertory system in which the actors were performing one play, rehearsing another, and learning a third in any given week, they could do little more than to pull number 21 from their bag of tricks and hope that they remembered enough to get by (in itself this is a game of some improvisatory potential). But today the average three- or four-week rehearsal time permits exploration and improvisation. Even so, some actors and directors feel that learning lines is boring. "Get them out of the way, and then get down to the play." They ignore the fact that the lines are their only indication of what the play is and that they cannot learn lines in a vacuum—a character attitude is learned with the lines. Such an attitude, then tends to circumscribe further exploration of the possibilities beneath and around the lines. Nor does it allow free character interaction in a rehearsal.

Improvising in rehearsal: a possible model.   During the first stage in improvising around a text, the actors gain an overall grasp of the play. All cast members should be fully aware of every aspect of the text so that they may play their part not as an isolated series of actions but in relationship to the rest of the play. Actors too often have no interest in scenes in which their characters do not appear and only marginal interest in characters to which they do not directly relate in their scenes. The first reading of the play should, then, be geared to gaining a sense of it as a whole. Actors should not read the parts they will ultimately be playing, and parts can be changed frequently as the play is read through.

During the second reading of the play the same principle concerning the distribution of parts can hold, but the reading will be interrupted by discussion of how the play works. This discussion is an examination not of psychological attitudes and subtextual motivations but of how the playwright has built the play: why certain scenes follow others, what the crucial actions are, on how many levels the play is operating, how the climax and denouement are achieved. Attention is concentrated on essentials, and notes should be kept, perhaps by the stage manager, of the points agreed on by the group. The actors should keep notes of the progression of the play; key words will give the actors the essential clue to the action of the scene—reference to which refreshes their memory of the scene's action and enables them to improvise the circumstances. The key words can be kept on six-inch by four-inch index cards which are legible without hampering the actor. The notes will help the actor in later rehearsals by marking the significant actions, conflicts, and tensions in the text as they create the flow of the work. Each actor should also take notes on the whole play, the nature of the notes depending on individual preference, except that the significance of the actions should be generally agreed on.

Rehearsals can now begin without scripts in hand, the actors having their simple key outline to refer to if necessary. Scenes are worked through with improvised dialogue and movement, again, at first, with no actor playing exclusively his or her final part. It is also interesting and useful to break the cast into groups, each working separately on the same scenes, which they later present to each other. In this way enormously varied possibilities can be found for any part of the text. Although the actors should be encouraged to rely as much as possible only on their key outlines, there will at first be times when the actors stray too far from the textual skeleton or get lost and dry up. At such times the text itself should be consulted, not in terms of what *lines* come next but what *action*. The actors should approach the text with questions such as these: "Why are we in this situation?" "How do we get from here to such and such a climax?"

When the actors are reasonably familiar with the flow of the play and can run through it in their own words with only brief reference to their key outlines, improvisations should be undertaken to create the general atmosphere of the play and of actions which relate to but do not occur within the text. For example, with a play such as *The Importance of Being Earnest*, which requires truthful representation of social manners and conventions, a general discussion of these, based on period research into upper-class life, would have taken place during the first readings. Now improvisations can be played out to create the atmosphere of tea parties (with cucumber sandwiches), dinners, soirées, and formal balls. More specific improvisations could include Miss Prism creating the circumstances of the loss of the baby, John Worthing (which will make her final speech much more real for her); Canon Chasuble preaching one of his "unpublished sermons" at his country church; and John and Algy on a night out at their club. In these specific circumstances the actors who are actually to play the characters would adopt their roles.

The improvisations can include games where appropriate. For example, in *Earnest*, Act I, where Algy is refusing to return John's cigarette case until he finds out who Cecily is, blocking a chase and then having the actors continually repeat it will become boring, and the scene will be lifeless. It may better be approached by playing varieties of tag games or Donkey in the Middle, with John in a circle trying to catch objects tossed to each other over his head by other members of the cast. If you wished to go further toward character in the action, the belt could be removed from John's pants so that he would have to try to maintain his dignity—that is, keep up his pants—during the chase.

The language in verse plays—Shakespearean or otherwise—can be worked on through games, as in the following examples:

Players pair off and begin with a simple mirror exercise—performing physical gestures exactly copied by the partner. When concentration and fluidity are established, the director throws some simple images at the pairs, for example, birch trees, waving flags, or fountains. The pairs now use these images as a basis for the mirror exercise. When this exercise is working, the pairs split up and the director gives the individuals more abstract or complex images to work with, such as yellow, Monday morning, or vanilla ice cream with butterscotch topping. The players must have time to explore and establish an image before moving on. When the players are committing themselves fully to the exercise and exploring with their whole bodies (this will need some coaching), the director starts to introduce some literary images and specific images from the play. The players are encouraged to avoid literal interpretations, to go for the poetic meaning of an image—to let the image speak to their bodies, not to the mind. The point of the exercise is not to discover physical gestures for the specific communication of images but to feel the images so that the physical sense of them will inform the actors' speech, although they may well not use a gesture at all to illustrate a particular image in performance. This is quite an intense exercise, physically and emotionally, and should probably not be played for more than twenty minutes at a time. It is an exercise that may be developed over a long period of time, coming back to it at each rehearsal.

An extension of this exercise is to create a dance out of a speech, one that might take two or three minutes to speak. The director chooses a dance style, such as classical ballet, modern, jazz, Spanish, disco. One player now reads the speech while the other players interpret it according to the chosen style. The exercise is repeated in different styles of dance. The players should stick fairly closely to the form of dance chosen and not go off into abstractions; the dance form gives a structure and discipline to the exercise. Finally, the players interpret the speech with any combination of the dance forms that seems appropriate to them. When each player has choreographed the speech, the dance should be performed to the other players *while* the dancer is speaking the lines. This step gives the players a

FIGURES 117, 118, 119, 120. Mirror exercise. (*Patrick Siefe*)

tremendous experience of the physical shape, rhythms, and dimensions of the speech.

As work on character begins, Animal Attitudes or any of the exercises suggested in the section on developing character can provide a basis for improvisational work. Again, discoveries from these exercises should be discussed collectively by the cast so that all the actors become familiar with all aspects of all characters. Another group game useful for character exploration is Essences. Characters are discussed in terms of nonhuman qualities: what texture of cloth, fruit, color, musical instrument, food, and so on brings the essential nature of the character to mind. For example Canon Chasuble in *Earnest* might suggest the color purple (not just because of the religious rank) and plum as a fruit, because of his floridity, rotundity, and unctious voice. In this way a collage is created which might give the individual actors practical insights into their character they would not have discovered without the different perspectives of the group.

This kind of exploratory work might take up a third of the total rehearsal period, depending on how far the director is driving rehearsals along as opposed to having no preconceptions and working entirely from what arises in rehearsal. Both methods are valid, but experience suggests that actors work more efficiently, even in improvisation, if each rehearsal session has a focus and a definite, if loose, guidance from the director. This does not mean that directors refuse to alter the ideas they come in with; it simply means that they should have some basic but flexible attitudes toward what they are seeking from the play.

At this juncture in rehearsal the director should tell the cast when he or she expects them to be thoroughly conversant with the playwright's lines. While the improvisatory sessions have been taking place the actors have been reading the text on their own time, so that their physical and emotional understanding of it, gained from improvisation, is channeled into the playwright's lines as they are assimilated, rather than committed to memory, by the actors. For the next rehearsal period more specific work on character is done—concentration on smaller units of the play at greater depth. Actions are still being explored improvisationally to discover their most organic and truthful spatial representation, but increasingly the scenes will take a specific form as the actors fall comfortably into the movements and relationships arising from their now visceral understanding of the action.

Problems continue to arise during this period, and as questions are asked, the text must be constantly searched for answers. The director, too, asks questions to make the actors clarify their understanding of motivations, actions, and physical responses. The actors may come up with answers which differ from the director's understanding of the circumstances. Then the director decides whether the actors' natural responses have given them a correct intuition or whether they have misunderstood the situation, in which case further questioning may correct their approach. Letting the actors find the answer by asking them pertinent questions is always preferable to giving them a solution which they may perform but not understand. Suggesting that the actors try an action again with a different objective is also a good way of confirming the validity of a solution.

The last third of the rehearsal period is devoted to running through the play for continuity, flow, and pace, and to introducing the final settings, properties, and costumes. It is important, however, that fairly accurate simulations of these final elements have been employed throughout the rehearsal period. The same principle applies to lighting and sound, which should be integrated gradually, not suddenly lumped on at a mammoth "tech" rehearsal a few days before opening night. If possible, members of the stage management and technical staff should have been involved in early improvisations so that they too will have had the experience of discovering the play's needs, as did the actors. The technical elements of the play should then be built into the production in the same rhythm and flow as are the actors and the text.

If the organic assimilation of lines with actions has been complete, there should be no need for prompting during the last rehearsals; in fact, there should be no prompter. The company should know that when a difficulty arises, all the actors must help the one whose concentration has lapsed. Their complete knowledge of the play will facilitate this aid, but if a complete blank occurs, then the run should be stopped and the action—not the words—examined to determine the problem.

As always, one of the director's prime tasks in relation to the actors is to maintain a relaxed yet positive atmosphere. One of the dangers inherent in the improvisational approach is that focus on the final purpose—a performance—can be lost. Actors can become self-indulgent and idle if the game sense predominates rather than being used as a tool or structure for a clearly defined purpose. So the director must be sensitive to the working climate, constantly able to relax tensions or to stimulate creativity by introducing new ideas and challenges. The discipline of an improvisatory group is not imposed from without but arises from the concentration on and enthusiasm for the task at hand. Should there be any tendency toward boredom or repetitive work in the last rehearsal days, when the actor feels the need of an audience but the production is not quite ready for one, then the director can run part of the play in another style: melodrama, opera, Nō. This freshens interest and often, even at a late rehearsal stage, leads the actor to new discoveries.

Working on a text improvisationally can be said to have the advantages of establishing immediate contact among actors and with the pulse of the play. Holding scripts inevitably hinders physical exploration and eye contact. Words get in the way of the sense. The mechanical process of keeping one's place and watching for cues dominates the organic process of listening, feeling, and responding. Texts which are improvised on should become more vital and fully fleshed, and actors should be more aware of the play as a totality rather than just of their part.

There are caveats to this technique. Improvisation tended to become a cult a few years ago. There is no law of theater which says "thou shalt improvise." Perfectly good productions are created without the use of the technique at all. There is always the danger of improvisation for the sake of improvisation. It can degenerate into pseudocreative, party shtick: ego trips in a sandbox. Sometimes actors like it because it appears to be creative but actually avoids coming to grips with the hard problems of the script. A director should not improvise simply because he or she doesn't know how to come to terms with the play. As fun for fun's sake, it should at best be used at the beginning of the rehearsal period as a getting-to-know-you technique and a way of generating energy; the energy should then be focused on solving the problems of the script.

Even when improvisation is validly used there are still some problems. Actors—with no lines or blocking to hold onto—at first feel a lack of security. Directors must furnish that security by getting the actors to believe they know what they are doing; they must earn the actors' trust. They should be able to provide a wealth of creative challenges, moving the play forward and not allowing rehearsals to deteriorate into aimless meanderings without any real progress. The director must always know what an improvisation is attempting to solve. The outcome may be different from expectation, but it will at least be significant. And perhaps the biggest caveat of all about this technique, the director must make sure that the improvisation has some relationship to a textual situation and that the solutions discovered carry over to the text. Situations occur in which actors are doing, say, Animal Attitudes, and interesting discoveries are made in terms of character; then, everyone takes a ten-minute break, comes back to the text, and falls back into their day-to-day personal rhythms with no carry-over of the discoveries. But all caveats aside, when improvisation is well used it can produce highly creative results, and it must be accounted a significant tool at the disposal of the contemporary director.

Mask work

One final technique a director might employ to get at the physicality of a text, and develop character, is the use of masks in rehearsal. Masks have various potentials: they break actors out of their own personal rhythms and centers, expand preconceptions about a role, stimulate physical imagination, and bring greater physical variety to a character. Mask work cannot be done quickly; a director must be prepared to devote time to its use. The theory of mask is a theory of absorption or body learning,

FIGURE 121. The legendary French director Jean-Louis Barrault pioneered in mime and mask applications to the theater. (*French Cultural Services*)

FIGURES 121 A B C D. Mask exercise. Actor Douglas Kaback adopting character mask at mirror and developing character. (*Patrick Siefe*)

A

B

C

D

based on the integration of physiognomy and body rhythms and centers of energy. When the face is altered, the body will alter to balance and integrate that face and, in a gestalt fashion, the psychology and inner responses will also adapt to support the new physicality. To take a very simplistic example: suppose an actor adopted a mask with a long thin nose and pointed chin; there is a strong likelihood that the actor will develop sharp pecking rhythms, an inquisitive lean of the head, and a somewhat quizzical, possibly narrow-minded attitude. Now this is not necessarily the case; and it is simplistic. But what is absolutely the case is that if mask work is done properly, strong, consistent, and inner-supported characters develop.

If you have the time and your actors are unfamiliar with mask work, you may want to start with the neutral mask. The basic props are a number of full-length mirrors and a table for the masks. The mask should be put on in front of the mirror, with a certain reverence, a knowledge that something is going to happen; it is, perhaps, too much to say "going to be possessed by another spirit"; but indeed that is precisely what happened in mankind's earliest, shamanistic mask rites. With the mask in place the actors should observe their whole body in the mirror until the sense of the mask starts to permeate the whole body; this sense will start with the face and work down. The relaxed, serene, nondefined qualities of the neutral mask will help the body achieve a neutral posture. Personal quirks will drop away, and a well-balanced, centered, relaxed energy will be present; this won't happen in five minutes or even the first time the exercise is done. It has to be persisted in, believed in, and it will work—more quickly with some actors than others. The actors must never push; they should absorb, should let the mask tell the body what to do, and not let the body impose on the mask. The basic properties of the neutral mask emphasize more the body as opposed to facial expression, physical economy, and simplicity; the mask throws into high relief any busy or unnecessary gestures and actions.

The neutral mask is a good introduction to mask work, but it is the character mask that has most utility in rehearsing a text. Again, what are required are some full-length mirrors and a table with masks. Two or three actors at a time (depending on the number of mirrors you use) select a mask and adopt it at the mirror. It doesn't matter which mask; anything will do at first as long as it is comfortable and generates some response. Let the actors try different masks until something starts to feel right in the context of what they have already discovered about their characters. All actors should have enough time with the masks to begin to develop some physical character. Now the exercise may be expanded with some props or pieces of costuming the actors may explore. A range which seems appropriate to the play should be available, but the actors should make their own choices while working in the masks. Limited physical environments—tables, chairs, and so on—can be added which the actors explore. The director throws in a line from an actor's part and lets him or her explore it in the mask. Other characters then throw in one or two of their lines, and the actor in the mask responds. Small situational improvisations can be developed in this way, with a limited basis in the text.

At the conclusion of such an exercise or even a simple mask session—which should, we reemphasize, last not less than an hour when actors have some competence, and several hours in the early stages of mask work—it is very useful to have actors discuss their reactions to what they saw of each other in the masks. This examination puts the actors in touch with the play in the context of each other's choices; it is based on a physical reality, not intellectual discussion about psychology and emotion.

A director will need to encourage the actors, at first, to explore freely, to accept that there are no mistakes, only better choices. If the text is to be used, the elements should be introduced slowly so that the actors absorb and react to them rather than feel them as restrictions. And during exercises, the actors should be encouraged to go back to the mirrors to reinforce their discoveries and find further inspiration.

The mask is essentially a rehearsal tool; it will be discarded when detailed work on a text proceeds. Gains can be made at all levels, from the simplest release of an actor from personal rhythms and physical preconceptions to the development of a strong character base which can be sophisticated and refined and ultimately used in performance.

AUDITIONS AND CASTING

Before rehearsals begin, a director has to go through the crucial and often time-consuming and agonizing (in terms of the finality of choices made—one can make changes in action up to the last minute, but with actors usually what you choose is what you have to live with) process of casting the play. To make the situation more difficult, unless directors are working with a permanent repertory—and that means about twelve months at best—or are very old hands in the business so that they have some acquaintance with most actors, the audition is the moment at which they know the least about the actors. As in any other aspect of the work, each director will have his or her own approach to auditions, but there are some general truths. First of all directors must know, at least in general terms, what they are looking for. This means having done a good deal of homework so they aren't relying on superficial impressions or on the fact that they once saw Meryl Streep play the part and so are looking for a Meryl Streep type. Without being rigid about it, knowing what they are looking for will save a great deal of time by enabling them to exclude certain actors immediately. This will allow them to take as much time as possible distinguishing among the actors who are within the range. Sometimes, of course, directors will be in the "cattle call" situation, where they have a couple of minutes to see each actor. The danger of the snap judgments needed there is not so much missing a real talent who reads badly as being fooled by a slick cold reader who has little else to give. Auditions can flatter to deceive; directors must not trust what they see on the surface, especially if it seems perfect.

There is a certain truth in the saying that with a good ground plan and a good cast a director is 90 percent of the way to a successful production. Part of that proposition has been more cynically expressed: "Directing is the art of compensating for the mistakes made in casting." With so much at stake, therefore, whenever possible at an audition the director should try to penetrate beyond the actor's prepared reading by asking him or her to redo it with a different objective, to work against the text, or simply to physicalize the situation without dialogue. Small improvisations can also test an actor's imagination and reveal his or her emotional and physical range. Obvious physical suitability for a part is not enough, by itself. Ours is, after all, a craft of tricks and illusions; things can become other than they seem.

Of course, physical suitability must be a part of casting; it is unlikely that a 130-pound stripling would be cast as Falstaff even though, as the adage has it, in every thin man there is a fat man trying to get out (and John Gielgud, a comparative lightweight, has played the part with distinction). Actual physical attributes should be weighed against actable physical attributes and the actor's essential, *qua* person, suitability for a part. Nor is the director casting any single part in isolation from the others; the total physical and temperamental balance of the cast must be considered. In one production of *The Taming of the Shrew,* both Petruchio and Katherina were very small people with enormous energy. Their very lack of stature gave a definiton to their relationship in unusual terms—they constantly stood out from the much bigger and calmer actors who surrounded them.

By clever casting directors can add dimensions to the production. However, they should beware of casting decisions which seem amusing at first but finally destroy some of the values of the play. For example, if Petruchio were very small while Katherina towered above him, this would initially increase the farcical elements of certain scenes, but ultimately it would destroy the truth of their relationship in the play as a whole. Unless, of course, the director happened to be doing a feminist extrinsic interpretation (see the section on style), which turned the play on its head and had Katherina finishing up triumphant.

It is usually safer, of course, to cast by type, as long as the director is sure of a minimal level of talent. Stanley Kowalski, for example, demands an actor with a strong physique and an obvious sexual magnetism: a donnish, puny Stanley would be laughable. This joke is, indeed, what Woody Allen used for laughs in his play and film *Play it Again, Sam.* His fantasy of being Humphrey Bogart was so far removed from his own bumbling ineptness and nonmacho physicality that it formed the basis of the play's humor—which is fine in a comedy. If a director knows what he or she is looking for, casting against type can work in the cause of particular interpretative or stylistic choices, the ramifications of which are clearly understood from the start.

One problem in casting a director will have today in our increasingly multiracial society is that of casting against ethnic type in plays originally written for particular ethnic groups. Finally this dilemma can only be solved by a director in the light of his or her own sensibility and idea of theater. But the director should not naively pretend that black, white, and brown people are the same color or that color does not carry associations for an audience. For example, would Shakespeare's *Othello* be the same if Othello were played as Anglo-Saxon with an all-black supporting cast? Does not color have a special significance in this play? A similar issue would arise in Imamu Amiri Baraka's *The Dutchman* if the director chose to cast a black girl and a white man instead of in the original way.

It may well be that we will one day achieve a social climate in which color has absolutely no significance, but we wonder if that day is quite with us yet and whether an audience's suspension of disbelief will extend so far as to accept a family of two white parents and a black child, or vice versa. Perhaps a rough rule of thumb is that realistic plays demand respect for genetic possibilities; otherwise their conventions are too severely disturbed. It may be better to completely recast these plays with, for example, an all-black cast, as was recently done with *A Long Day's Journey Into Night*.

On the other hand, there seems no reason why classical works or those with a theatricalized style cannot be cast entirely irrespective of color. Shakespeare's heroes could be played by nonwhite actors: that Henry V was historically white seems not as important as the statement Shakespeare was making about heroism and kingship. Expressionistic plays, surrealistic plays, plays which deal with macrocosmic issues, and plays in which characters personify broad human qualities as much as individuals (for example, *Everyman* and its modern equivalent, *Waiting for Godot*) can equally be cast without racial consciousness, and indeed, without limitation by sex—that other burning issue today when women are demanding more roles. *Everyman* could be cast as all women or as men and women of mixed racial types. *Godot* can and has been performed with only women. A 1981 production of Marlowe's *Doctor Faustus,* done by Giles Havergal of the Glasgow Citizen's Theatre, had Faustus split between a male and female actor, each portraying different aspects of this humanistic character.

Given the complex nature of casting, there are some very practical things directors can do to help the auditioning process. First they should take a careful look at an actor's portfolio to get some sense of the range of his or her work and assess the audition against this broader background. Should the director recognize any of the other directors or actors the auditioning actor has worked with, a moment's chat about shared experience can break tension and reveal some sense of the actor as a person. An impressive list of credits with persons known to you should carry more weight than a poor cold reading.

In a university or other nonprofessional situation, where actors don't have portfolios, get them to fill out an audition sheet giving particulars, including, where applicable, whether they are willing to cut hair and shave beards or appear nude. At the bottom of this sheet there should be a space for the director to make notes on the actor's vocal and physical qualities and potential for casting. Its also useful to have a master casting sheet on which you jot down names for possible call-back. As you go through the audition you will probably eliminate some early names as more suitable actors appear.

Eliminate as much as you can at auditions and call back the absolute minimum. This makes the call-back process easier and avoids wasting any actor's time. At call-back you are looking, obviously, for the best actor for a part; but you are also concerned with ensemble and balances. Maybe if you make a certain choice you have to surround that actor with second choices because of balances; so on the whole, it might be better to make a different choice and have a better overall ensemble. However, try to make certain

FIGURE 122.   Text in hand, British director Peter Hall coaches actress Peggy Ashcroft in a delicate scene. Notice the makeshift rehearsal furniture; all the emphasis here is on the acting.   (*Courtesy, National Theatre of Great Britain*)

FIGURE 123.   American director Gordon Davidson, at left, gives encouragement to actors during rehearsal for *Children of a Lesser God.*   (*Center Theatre Group/Mark Taper Forum, Los Angeles. By permission*)

anchor choices so that you have a basis for fitting together the cast. Don't read actors longer than you need to, but don't be afraid to read until you are satisfied. Try to get the book out of the actor's hands for a while, so you can get a sense of their physical range. If you know and trust the judgment of a fellow director with whom an actor has worked, it is often useful to get some first-hand background on the actor's ability and methods of working. Finally, when in doubt take a risk; go for the actor, not the type.

REHEARSAL RHYTHMS

This section might be entitled "Notes from a Director's Diary, or, You'll Probably Have to Make the Mistakes for Yourself, Just as We Did." It is really a grab bag of afterthoughts deriving from directing, being directed, and teaching directors.

A rehearsal period, like a performance itself (and, indeed, any human activity), has its own rhythms. The pace of activity will vary; there are exciting moments of great discovery and periods of quiet gestation. Free exploration is balanced by disciplined focus on a problem. A director should not expect the same energy all the time, but should be aware when the cast is not working and when some activity to create energy or achieve concentrated effort is required (this is especially the case with nonprofessional actors who sometimes bring the weariness and assorted human cares of the day to evening rehearsals—hence the warm-up period). Never come to a rehearsal without some fairly clear sense of what is to be worked on. But don't be afraid to change focus if it doesn't work or to go with a rehearsal that takes off on another, useful, direction. As long as some progress is made, then nothing is lost.

Perhaps the three greatest mistakes made by young (and not so young) directors are: (1) letting rehearsals become boring by failing to produce new challenges and repeating work already done; (2) working superficially on the surface of the text, producing a great deal of energy which is never focused on the hard problems; and (3) expecting actors to give a performance before they know what the play is about. This last is, of course, a function of experience; in his first productions a director is terribly aware of opening night and the possibility of "failure." So he wants to make sure he will have *something,* and is desperately anxious to get the production shaped up and the characters working. Alas! What happens is that he pushes too hard, knocks the breath out of the production, has it all sewn up in the first two weeks, and then sits back and runs it, wondering why it gets more and more lifeless.

Experience teaches the pace at which a production comes together— that the last act, for example, is much more quickly shaped up than the early acts, because the actors have solved the problems of their characters and the play's overall action, and all that work flows into the last act. Similarily, comedies and farces will be terribly flat in the middle rehearsal period. Everyone has heard the jokes many times; actors are struggling with lines, uncertain of shape, exploring action. Timing, on which the humor rests, simply isn't there; and there is no life yet in the action, in which the jokes are actually contained. The director sits in horror, thinking "Oh, God! It isn't funny." The worst thing he or she can then do is concentrate on the jokes, making the actors work at "being funny." If the action is right, if the actors are comfortable, it will start to be funny once again, as they relax, enjoy the action, and allow the humor to come through.

The director should not be in too great a hurry. He or she should know where the production is at all times (and it doesn't have to be ready until opening night), what it is necessary to achieve, and what it is possible

FIGURE 124. John Barton gives critique to Marjorie Bland, as Titania, in Barton's 1977 production of *A Midsummer Night's Dream* at the Royal Shakespeare Company. (*Courtesy, Royal Shakespeare Company; photo by Anthony Crickmay*)

FIGURE 125. Alan Schneider, one of America's leading directors, coaches Hal Holbrook and Lillian Gish in the Broadway production of *I Never Sang for My Father.* (*Courtesy, Martha Swope*)

to achieve. Don't accept the wrong solution to a scene simply for the sake of getting something concrete. Choices have to be firmed up, but some decisions can be left fairly late, once actors thoroughly understand the action of the play and their character's part in it.

Give the actors a little breathing space. Don't try to work on everything at the same time or concentrate on details before there is a basic shape. Don't confuse the actors with business while they still have the book in their hands and are trying to come to terms with blocking. We once heard a young director tell the actors to "pick up the cues" when they were reading from held scripts. Make sure an actor knows what you want before you rerun a scene; and don't just keep running a scene for the sake of it—have a purpose, a problem to work on. Try to have enough rehearsal props to give an actor a feel of the situation; constant miming of props can lead to bad habits.

There are, of course, a million other do's and dont's which all directors have to find out for themselves. When all the alternatives have been discussed, and the ramifications of all the possible choices explained, the director will only have learned how he or she *can* work with actors, not how he or she *should*. This will always be a personal relationship which cannot be

FIGURE 126. Antoine Vitez, celebrated for his innovative productions of Molière, here adjusts an actor's costume while offering advice toward the first performance of his production of Victor Hugo's *The Burgraves* at the Théâtre de Gennevilliers on the outskirts of Paris. (*French Cultural Services*)

FIGURE 127.   William Ball, founding director of the San Francisco American Conservatory Theatre, issues a directive from the back of the house during dress rehearsal.   (*Courtesy, American Conservatory Theatre; photo by Hank Kranzler*)

prescribed. Each director's approach will finally be a function of his or her personality, as is each actor's. A director, always conscious of the final needs of the play, should try to work with an actor in the actor's own rhythm—not forcing the slow boilers, while keeping the quick workers from going stale.

Drawing a performance from actors is always preferable to imposing an interpretation on them. The director's aim should be to create the best possible environment in which actors can produce their best work. Let actors discover as much as possible in their own way. A director should provide support, security, encouragement, suggestions, energy, structure—it is, by definition, an impossible job. Directors should constantly explore and question the process themselves and question the actor when necessary. A positive, not inquisitorial "why?" is a very useful word for the director. The director and actor are both on the same side. They are trying to achieve a mutual understanding, not always stated, and work together for the final good of the play and satisfaction of each other's creative needs. But, it is worth remembering, when push comes to shove, that it is the actor who is going to do it for you.

NINE

Styling the Play

We all use the term *style* and believe we know what we mean by it, but no two persons are likely to give it the same definition. Among some ten possibilities, the dictionary tells us it is a "distinction or characteristic of some group or period" and "an individual's typical way of life." This latter sense is consistent with the adage that "style is the man": the revelation in action of essential inner character. When we speak of people's life-styles, we mean everything from the food they eat through the people with whom they associate to the clothes they wear and the moral choices they make. Style is related to, but should not be confused with, form. Form is the recognizable externals; style is the way they are arranged to communicate a certain essential quality or to create a particular effect (this definition suggests the possibility of intrinsic and extrinsic style, to which we shall return). It is not the cars a person drives, the food a person eats, or the clothes a person wears that, by themselves, create his or her style (although the choices do reveal something of the person) as much as the way in which they are driven, eaten, or worn. As an old song tells us, "It ain't what you do, it's the way that you do it." For example, a woman with a given body (form) can project erotic, athletic, maternal, or androgynous qualities depending on how she perceives, clothes, and uses her body. Her sense of self, her expression of an inner essence, is revealed by the externals—

clothes, body rhythms, hair style, and so on—but it is the essence that animates the external; they, alone, do not create the essence.

The recognition or identification of essence through externals is, however, contingent on the understanding of changing conventions: the criteria of female attractiveness, for instance, have undergone many changes in the present century. The Edwardian period admired a round-bosomed, full-hipped amplitude in women, who were bedecked in a finery that celebrated material abundance, delineated social status, and proved the wealth of the men who supported them. The alluring woman of the 1950s projected her quality with lighter but tighter and body-emphasizing clothing, heavy makeup, and bouffant hair styles. Her attractive sister in the late 1960s and 1970s wore flowing garments, lightly emphasizing her body's freedom, utterly simple hair, and a face bare of makeup but shining with "organic" health. In the 1980s, the "health" quality of the 1970s has become an obsession. The current style is an impeccably jogged, aero-bicized, and jacuzzied body, covered either by the second skin of tights and leotards or the athletic emblems of tank tops, running shorts, and warm-up suits. The attractive female form has a slim, tensile strength; athletic and androgynous, it is closer to the received male ideal, reflecting the influence of feminism on the female sense of self. A male appendage at the beginning of the century, the contemporary woman now defines herself against the male. But where the external evidence of the strong, independent, self-sufficient female is clearly defined, it tends to be in conflict with the inner essence: the mannish, gray flannel, "lady executive" suit will have a thigh-high slit. There is a mixed, ironic, ambivalent sense of personal style, which reflects the nature of current social attitudes.

"You can be whatever you want to be," is the catch phrase of our present neohumanistic period, in which the only fixed criterion is that of the fluctuating self. To the individual today style is an elective; and the style of the age is eclecticism—a contradiction in terms. Reflecting social trends, we find that theater, over the past eighty years, has moved toward greater eclecticism of style, until style in theater today is, to some degree, a matter of choice. Before this century, style in theater tended to be associated with the accepted way in which a certain type of play should be performed. Terms such as Greek style, Shakespearean style, or more broadly still, "classical" style were bandied about without meaning the same thing to any two actors or directors, being loosely based on conventions handed down through the centuries as to how plays were originally performed or had come to be performed in the tradition of the theater. Even in the twentieth century, in English theater, for example, Shakespearean style all too often meant the adoption of an artificially rhetorical manner of speaking and the striking of heroic poses. Mummified Molière was a disease of the French theater, and calcified Chekhov was to be found in Russia. Stylistic disease can set in very quickly. In the American theater, not many years after the

FIGURES 128, 129, 130, 131. A portfolio of fashionable women throughout the ages. Figure 128: Lily Langtry, the Edwardian beauty. (*The Bettmann Archive, Inc.*) Figure 129: Marilyn Monroe, surrounded by admirers (including Clark Gable, John Huston, Eli Wallach, Montgomery Clift, and at top, husband Arthur Miller). Monroe was the sex symbol of the 1950s and early 1960s. (*Magnum Photos, Inc.*) Figure 130: A "flower child" of the late 1960s. (*San Francisco Chronicle*) Figure 131: Cheryl Tiegs, the "modern woman" of the 1980s. (*Pendleton Woolen Mills*)

preeminence of the New York Actors Studio, a Brandoesque deformity, or method mimicry, began to distort productions of contemporary plays. All these examples illustrate the tendency to imitate form without relationship to its content. Such approaches are nothing more than the use of empty, contrived mannerisms: they are not based in any theatrical truth, and they are certainly not "style."

The point we are making is not that, say, the Greek, Shakespearean, or French neoclassical theater had no identifiable style, but that, at best, we can only make an educated guess at what it was, and at worst, by attempting to resurrect the skeletons of the theatrical past, we embalm our productions in the present. Our world is very different from those earlier periods when both theater and the society it depicted were homogeneous, and the combination of a fixed set of social and moral attitudes with a given dramatic form and theatrical space is likely to have produced a clearly defined, consistent style in each period—the intrinsic essence matching the extrinsic production. We, however, both profit from and are victims of our history. We can choose from a wide variety of theatrical spaces with sophisticated technological facilities; a wide repertory of plays from many periods and countries is at our disposal; our audiences bring a vast spectrum of social, political, and moral attitudes to the event. Theatrical style may once have been a given, but as we suggested with social styles today, it is now an elective, responding to the rhythms of our faithless, fractured, and highly variegated age which rejects rather than respects tradition.

The contemporary director must recognize not only that it is redundant to speak of a "correct" or definitive production but also that any production of a classical play will bear some stamp of the current time because actors (and directors) inevitably bring something of their contemporary selves to their work. Thus, the responsible theater artist will interpret a play from the standpoint of his or her day, while making every effort to understand the intrinsic values of a playwright's work: combining his or her sense of the present with an appreciation of the social and theatrical reality of the time in which the play was written.

As with interpretation, therefore, there will be an intrinsic and an extrinsic style for a given play. The intrinsic style is to be found within the text and will be a reflection of what we know of the original theater architecture, technical sophistication, costuming, and so on—all the concrete elements which would have affected its performance. Added to these will be the somewhat more subjective elements which will have affected the values the playwright wrote into the text: the social, political, philosophical, and moral attitudes of the day, as he or she perceived them. The shape and sound of a text will be influenced by all these elements, which also help to distinguish one text from another.

As an example of intrinsic differences let us look at the work of Shakespeare and of Racine, the French neoclassical dramatist. Shakespeare wrote in a flexible, powerful, blank verse; his sense of life was wide-ranging, reflected in the many scenes and sweeping focus of his structure. His plays were performed out of doors, between heaven and hell, surrounded by a teeming, democratic audience. The occasion was full of noise, color, smell, and activity. Racine's work was written in the more balanced Alexandrine verse form, within the confines of neoclassical structure. It was performed before a small, elite audience in a wooden auditorium, where the tone and pitch of the voice and the economy of movement gave the performance the quality of chamber music. There is clearly a distinct difference between the intrinsic performance values of the two playwright's works: each has its particular theatrical truth. Directors need not feel restricted by this fact, but they should be aware of it before they attempt to produce Racine in an outdoor amphitheater with actors whose experience is restricted to naturalistic dialogue.

Although saying that every play contains an intrinsic truth that the director will do well to recognize, we are not suggesting that a play can simply speak for itself. Today the words of any classical text are no more than ciphers on a piece of paper: they cannot tell us how the play was brought to life. If we could allow the text to speak for itself it would say different things to different actors and directors. Words are simply the lifeless end of the dramatist's creative process; to turn them back into theatrical flesh and blood, we need to understand something of the attitudes and theatrical conventions of the playwright's day and how the words were intended to sound in the mouths of living actors. We look for the intrinsic truth of any play not because we wish to re-create the precise historical details of its style—as we have already suggested, this would be impossible—we do it because, without some understanding of what a play was intended to say, we run the risk of creating a warped, meretricious, or hollow production, being unaware that we have dressed a surfer in preppie's clothing!

With an understanding of what a play might have been intended to say in its own time, we can move on with some confidence to what it might best have to say for us—the creation of an extrinsic stylistic statement. The recognition of extrinsic style accepts the theater as a living thing, its function being communication in the present, not preservation of the past. Certain elements are constant and certain fundamental truths present in all dramatic activity, but life is constantly moving and actors and audience are subject to the influences of their day: the amending of moral postulates, the alteration of social attitudes, and the influence of technology on art, in television, cinema, and other media. A director is a product of the period in which he or she lives, and a conscious attempt to re-create the original style of a play must contain subjective elements. If this were not so directors wouldn't be necessary, for it is the directors' function to use their creative faculties, and in so doing they inevitably express their sense of the world in the choices they make. Creative directors do not suppress this subjectivity but examine it and use it in achieving their play's style of presentation.

Extrinsic style is, then, the manner in which directors project to the audience what they wish to say through the vehicle of the play. It is interpretation in action. The style of a production will communicate the directors' response to what the play has to say for themselves, their audience, and their time. It is not in any sense arbitrary; it relates to the intrinsic values of the text without being bound by them and projects, in a vital and contemporaneous manner, what directors feel is of interest and moment in the play.

To make a clear statement through style, directors must have a consistent idea of what that style is to be. They do not simply break eggs into a bowl, whip them up, and pour them into a pan without knowing whether they want an omelet, a soufflé, or plain scrambled eggs. A clean, effective style is achieved only by the consistent interrelationship of the world of the play, the world of the audience, and the world of the stage. The world of the play is its intrinsic style. To understand the world of the play, the director must research into its historical background and the background of the author. The research should cover both the time in which the play was first produced and the period in which it is set. It should cover not only the nature of the stage at that time—costumes and physical plant—but also the social, political, and philosophical attitudes of the day. Research will help the director gain a sense of the playwright's background; knowing something of his or her personal tastes and feelings will be useful in gaining a sense of how and why the play was written. Works of criticism can be useful by suggesting levels of interpretation that may not be immediately apparent. They should be used discriminatingly, however, and rejected if they appear to be imposing, rather than deriving, interpretation. Criticism can also help the director understand the structure of the play: whether it has a dynamic build, with a series of short scenes all driving toward a climax, as in *Macbeth;* or whether the tendency is toward circularity, as in *Waiting for Godot,* with steady, repetitive, harmonic progression. The director can reflect this essential quality of the play's form in patterns of movement, creating a part of the style of the performance.

Another part of the world of the play which must be explored in any attempt to derive its intrinsic style is the actual content: what the text tells us. The characters' mode of life is indicated by the environment suggested by the playwright; this can be very explicit, as with Shaw and Ibsen, or simply implicit in the historical period and social stratum of the characters. The language of the play may be naturalistic or poetic, as may the action, which can depend on the amassing of detail or the creation of symbolic effects. The language of the play may be more important than physical action (as in Racine). The action itself may be inherently comic, tragic, or melodramatic. Directors must at least be aware of all these factors if they wish to gain a sense of the intrinsic style of the play. Just as the nature of a production depends on a series of choices made by the director, so the intrinsic style of the play is the result of a series of choices, conscious and unconscious, made by the playwright. The unconscious choices result from the playwright's reaction to society, and we may determine them through research; the conscious choices appear in the play and must be derived from analysis of all its components. No matter when the play was written, the process for gaining a sense of its intrinsic style is the same. Once directors understand or have a feeling for this essence, they can translate it into whatever style they believe will best relate it to the world of their audience.

The world of the audience is partly a given, but there are certain variables. The givens are that set of circumstances and attitudes which compose the contemporary social character, in the broadest sense. In the United States in the 1980s this might be a complex of concern for the state of the economy and inflation, the conflict between energy needs and environmental or antinuclear sentiment, a continuing desire for self-definition on the part of minorities and women, the assertion of the values of the "moral majority," and an overall loss of social purpose compensated for by the emphasis on self-fulfillment. It will also reflect the physical mode of living: houses and furnishings, clothes, omnipresence of television, more economical cars, increasing use of computers, and the paraphernalia of a "high tec" society.

Aside from these givens there will be variables, depending on the more or less esoteric nature of any specific audience at a play. For example, the attitude toward disarmament is likely to differ between a middle-aged, middle-class Republican audience and a youthful, idealistic student audience. Again, a black ghetto audience is apt to find values in *Othello* which may be missed by an all-white audience. Equally a feminist audience may not find *The Taming of the Shrew* as funny as will a stag dinner-theater group. As they determine what sort of impact they wish to make, and thus the style of the production, directors must consider both the given and the variable circumstances in their audience's world—otherwise they may find that the result is contrary to the intention.

Directors can create a style which relates to both the world of the play and the world of the audience and reveal the statement they wish to make, not by warping the text, but by translating its intrinsic essence into terms which will be readily understood and assimilated by the audience. Their means of translation is, of course, the world of the stage.

The world of the stage includes all the elements which physically constitute a production: the scenic space; the settings; the lighting; the costumes; the music or sound effects; and the actors' bodies, voices, and gestures. The director's task in molding all these elements into a production is to see that they are all consistent with each other and with the style chosen to convey his or her idea of the play. Any inconsistency makes a specific statement of its own. Directors may wish to depart from the consistent pattern, in which case the aberration becomes part of their style, and they must be consistent in creating inconsistencies.

Unwitting inconsistency will work against the impact and the success of the production. For example, suppose the director of a Shakespearean production has chosen to play up the poetic values of the verse, and all but one of the actors are achieving a Gielgud-like, mellifluous flow. If one actor attempts to turn the verse into prose with "natural" breaks and nonmetrical intervals, he will obviously stand out from the rest and break the style. Even if his deviation were intended to make a character statement, it is a very crude way of doing so.

We do not, of course, mean to imply that a director cannot choose to play down the impact of the verse in a Shakespearean production; Nicol Williamson spoke Hamlet with a "natural" quality some years ago, and he was highly acclaimed in some quarters. What we are saying is that directors should be aware of the impression created by their choices. They should not, to return to our image of the 1980s executive woman, unwittingly let the intrinsic thigh flash through the mannish gray flannel skirt.

Once determined, style should inform the entire production, down to the manner of accomplishing scene changes and whether the audience is allowed to leave the play for a ten-minute cup of coffee. Directors cannot work from scene to scene and from element to element, hoping for the best. They cannot achieve the best without a clear sense of what they want to say and how they propose to say it. Again, this is not to say that a rigid concept and style are determined before rehearsals begin and imposed on the production. The style may well best evolve from exploration of the text by actors, designers, and director working in concert during rehearsals. Assuming the luxury of unlimited rehearsal time, this would be a way of ensuring a highly integrated production; but the exploration would still take the path of discovering the intrinsic values of the text and relating them to how the actors and production staff feel about *their* world and what they wish to convey to the audience. The procedure is different but the purpose is the same, whether one is putting on *King Lear* in three and a half weeks or *The Room* in three and a half months. The director must discover the intrinsic values of a play and communicate them in a manner to which the contemporary audience can relate and respond. To do this with clarity and dynamic impact requires the consistent relationship of all the elements of production in the creation of the style which has evolved from all the other considerations.

We are now going to discuss various stylistic possibilities and attempt to show the consequences of various directorial choices in the creation of style.

FITTING THE STYLE TO THE PERIOD
IN WHICH THE PLAY IS SET

Setting Shakespeare's *Julius Caesar* in Roman times, or Racine's *Phaedre* in ancient Greece, means that the intrinsic style of the play would not be the same as that chosen for its production. Shakespeare's play was written for an Elizabethan stage, for performance in Elizabethan costume (possibly with minor "Roman" accents), by actors who were observing the vocal and gestural conventions of their day. The values of the play are Elizabethan, and no attempt would have been made to achieve any realism of Roman effect. Thus directors who attempt a production of *Julius Caesar* set authentically in the first century B.C. have a great deal of extrinsic work ahead. We presume that they have a clear idea of the values they wish to enhance by setting the play in a chronologically exact period; to do this merely as a historical exercise is to do little more than present the costume designer with a limited challenge and to court a boring production. Perhaps the directors feel that the poetry of the play is weak, that greater realism will enhance and project the action of a physically dynamic play and will make a stronger statement, for a contemporary audience, about the nature of political power.

To create the authentic effect they are seeking, the directors will need to explore the architecture, sculpture, music, clothing, weapons, food—in short, the whole social climate of the period—as well as its moral and political attitudes. Knowledge of the tastes and feelings of the historical Caesar, Brutus, Anthony, and Cassius will help the directors flesh out both the characters and the action. The acting style for such a production might attempt a seeming naturalness within the costume and scenery, making the actors appear at home there. This would be different in nature, but not in effect, from their seeming at home in a contemporary living room; they would forgo heroic pose and rhetorical delivery, for after all, in their day Caesar and his contemporaries were men, not legends inflated by the passage of 2,000 years.

As they make stylistic choices in terms of costume, setting, acting style, and so on, directors know that they are emphasizing certain elements of Shakespeare's play to the exclusion of others. In a Roman *Julius Caesar*, they are likely to lose poetry and an absolute sense of stature for a more immediate, physically dynamic, and solid impact, but they do it consciously. Such a production does not ignore the intrinsic values of the play; it is balancing them off against extrinsic gains. Although there may be a tension between the intrinsic quality of the play's language and its delivery in the production, tension between Elizabethan costume and a presumed Roman environment may well be removed for a modern audience more used to realism of effect. There seems no immediate reason, today, why plays of a specific historical period should not be set and costumed in that period, rather than following the Elizabethan convention. By their choice of style directors, in this instance, may hope to project the import of the play in more immediately recognizable and dynamic terms.

SETTING THE PLAY IN THE PERIOD
IN WHICH IT WAS WRITTEN

By contrast, rather than setting a production of *Henry V* in the early fifteenth century, a director may decide to produce it as it might have been done at the Globe Theatre in Shakespeare's day, re-creating as nearly as possible the conditions of Elizabethan performance. Indeed, the intrinsic values of the play may be enhanced by such an approach. The play deals with heroism and kingship, rather than any particular king, and is as much about Elizabeth and her rule, praising her by extolling her ancestry, as the period of Henry V. The weight and masculinity of Tudor costuming probably support the values of political power in the play better than those of the lighter early Renaissance period. For a contemporary audience the universality of historical remove is probably as well created by Elizabethan costuming as by Plantagenet. In all these terms the intrinsic values of the play may be supported by what might otherwise be seen as an historical experiment. Added to this, the director would probably hope to rediscover some of the atmosphere which attended the original performance of the play, giving a further dimension to the audience's participation in the event and reaching out to them with the color, pageantry, vigorous action, and patriotic sentiment both within the play and the Globe Theatre itself.

In his film version of *Henry V,* which began in the Globe Theatre and then reached out to include the field of Agincourt itself, Laurence Olivier made the world of the play so alive and vital that it reached its contemporary audience and swept it along on the flood of events. Summer Shakespeare festivals in the United States, such as Ashland in Oregon and the Utah Festival, take pains to create as authentic an Elizabethan atmosphere as research and scholarship allow. Besides using outdoor stages which are reconstructions of the Elizabethan stage, with direct actor-audience contact, these festivals entertain their audiences with Elizabethan dancing and music; and suitably clad "wenches" sell oranges, horehounds, and other Elizabethan delicacies. When such effects are executed sincerely and with artistic purpose, as is usually the case at Shakespeare festivals, they can help greatly to set the mood for an audience and introduce it more fully into the world of the play and the style of the total theatrical event. In such cases style is created by the atmospheric adjuncts as much as by the play itself, and the stage and its surroundings should be stylistically consistent.

The danger of this kind of stylistic choice is that the external trimmings will overshadow the play. In a Los Angeles production of *The Way of the World,* the director splendidly captured the presumed atmosphere of a Restoration theatrical performance: claques alternately cheered and argued with the actors; orange girls were ogled; fops preened themselves and strutted from the audience onto the stage to interrupt the performance. Meanwhile the unfortunate actors struggled valiantly with the intricate language and complicated plot. The audience found the occasion amusing but gained little experience of the play: the event succeeded; the play didn't. A director must be aware of the implications of his or her choices when making a radical stylistic gesture—it can lead to closer communication of the world of the play to a contemporary audience, or it can bury the play beneath external eccentricities.

CONTEMPORIZING THE PLAY

A play can be directly contemporized by dressing the characters in up-to-date clothes and giving them contemporary mannerisms, speech patterns, props, and so on; or it can be done indirectly by emphasizing elements of contemporary significance within the values of the play.

The presumed advantage of modern-dress productions of classics is the creation of a physical environment to which the audience can immediately relate: the removal of an historical barrier which might create a problem of communication with a modern audience. There is some truth to this statement; but a contrary argument could be advanced which suggests that it is the universality of values that communicates in a classic play, not the details of the surface environment. Moreover, the very fact of an historical remove can possibly set the intrinsic values of a play in high relief for a contemporary audience. It would be invalid to generalize, and a director who is looking to contemporize a classical work must take each play on its own terms. If a director has a valid sense of the intrinsic style of his play and then feels that it has an essential quality that can best be communicated to the audience by contemporization, and if he then does this consistently, matching the intrinsic values to the extrinsic style, the production should succeed. Even the language, which is a very real problem with Shakespeare and other plays written in verse: Is it stylistically consistent for actors dressed in contemporary clothes to speak a language completely removed from contemporary form? Of course, one response is that the man in the street didn't speak in verse in Shakespeare's day either. As we have suggested, each director must make his or her own choice in terms of each play; but we would emphasize that contemporizing a play requires a more total rethinking than dressing actors in modern clothes and adding a few contemporary gestures and behavior patterns.

Classical comedies, perhaps because of the lightness of their content, their conventional structure, the uncomplicated nature of their values, and the similarity of lover's problems throughout the ages, lend themselves well to contemporization. In the early 1970s, *Two Gentlemen of Verona,* one of Shakespeare's earliest, slightest, yet most pleasant comedies, was given highly contemporized, yet stylistically quite different, productions by the Royal Shakespeare Company and the New York Shakespeare Festival. The English production was jet-set mod and took no liberties with the verse, which sat well upon the lips of the upper-class socialites the characters had become. The American production was New York ethnic, highly physical and with strong emphasis on song and dance, and took great liberties with the text, changing lines and updating allusions—for example, the duke didn't banish Valentine; he had him drafted.

Both productions, though quite different in style, were highly successful in conveying the intrinsic quality of the play to the audience for which each performed. It is likely that neither production would have been

FIGURE 132.   The ethnic and athletic *Two Gentlemen of Verona,* directed by Mel Shapiro for the 1971 New York Shakespeare Festival in Central Park (and later on Broadway). Notice the contemporary yet timeless costuming, the open scaffolding nature of the set, and the emphasis on physicality.   (*Friedman-Abeles*)

successful in the other environment. The productions are proof that externals alone do not determine style: verse, costumes, properties, and so on can vary and yet project to the audience for which they have been selected the same essential values.

Ten years later, in the early 1980s, the New York Shakespeare Festival is still looking to contemporize classical works, with varying degrees of success. Gilbert and Sullivan's *Pirates of Penzance* has been cleaned of all the encrustations with which a hundred years of adulation and tradition can suffocate a "classic." Directed by Wilford Leach, it has been given a bright and breezy production in, again, a physically athletic, loose-jointed American style. The gentle satire of Victorian mores, written by Gilbert and Sullivan in a musical style that mocked the conventions of Italian grand opera, has been revamped to satirize its own Victorianness and given a fresh lease on life in this electronically amplified, rock-influenced, energetically ephemeral late-twentieth century version. The rowdy, campy, circus ring of a production uses the media icons of our time as the subjects of its satire, taking affectionate swipes at swashbuckling-movie clichés and silent comedy routines and introducing a ballet of Keystone Kops. The production has been highly successful because although purists could condemn its every external gesture, it puts its finger on the essential intrinsic sense of fun and whimsy and satire of Gilbert and Sullivan, and communicates them through the brasher, brassier values of our day: it is a Pirates of Pizazz.

The New York Shakespeare Festival was less successful with Lee Breuer's production of *The Tempest,* mainly because its extrinsic values were not sufficiently related to the intrinsic qualities of the play. The orientation toward style was similar to that of the *Pirates of Penzance*—to turn the characters and images of the play into an idiomatic glossary of our time. Popular culture supplies the heroes, and technology the vehicle. The ship in the storm scene becomes a helicopter; Trinculo and Stefano become Mae West and W. C. Fields; the villains of the court are mafiosos; the background music is from old Disney movies. The problem is that this is a pot pourri, a media mess. The cultural parallels are recognizable instantly, but they stand alone, making no coherent statement among themselves, let alone relating to the intrinsic values of the play. Relentless invention does not constitute a style; the shock of recognition soon becomes predictable, and the clever surface begins to look thin as there is little true action taking place to sustain the audience as its waits for the next glib gimmick.

The Tempest is probably a play with too much substance, too much depth, to treat in such a facile manner. On the other hand *The Taming of the Shrew* perhaps lends itself to a radical approach; and the Royal Shakespeare Company had some success with a highly contemporized version directed in the late 1970s by Michael Bogdanov. Set in a modern but nonchronologically specific Italy, the play was put within rusty metal frames, catwalks, and staircases and began with an altercation between an

FIGURE 133. Petruchio "bikes" to his wedding in Michael Bogdanov's production of *The Taming of the Shrew* at the Royal Shakespeare Company, 1978–79. (*Courtesy, Royal Shakespeare Company*)

usherette and a drunk member of the audience, who jumped on the stage shouting, "No bloody woman is going to tell me what to do." This was of course Christopher Sly, who becomes Petruchio, and who set the basic tone of the play—a strong, crude emphasis on male domination. In this world women are seen as property and assessed for their material value. The idea is carried through by making Baptista a wealthy tycoon surrounded by servants in morning suits, while the lord and his huntsmen are in smugly superior hunting pink. The updating of the play is consistent and appropriate and related to character: Baptista briskly calculates the rival dowry offers on his adding machine; Petruchio arrives at the smart wedding on a motorbike; befitting Petruchio's eye for women, his housekeeper wears a short-skirted costume of the air hostess ilk.

The final scene encapsulates the whole statement, with dinner-jacketed speculators sitting around a green-baize gambling table, with brandy and cigars, speculating on their latest assets—wives. This scene enabled Katherina to deliver the "submission" speech ironically and thus make a final comment on the nature of male domination. This is, of course, to stand Shakespeare's intention on its head, but the inversion was totally consistent and, by clever extrinsic transformations, kept the intrinsic values intact while passing an ironically relevant comment for our own time.

An interesting production, which underlines the danger of a bright idea not entirely thought through, attempted to transpose *Miss Julie* to South Africa in 1980. This London production, directed by Eric Hillyard, made the play's class statement into a racial statement with a black Jean and white Miss Julie. The production altered the lines about the servant's inferiority to make a racial reference, but Miss Julie's nobility was left in class terms—no reference was made to her being white. Too many of Strindberg's references to the class structure of his own time are too particular and don't fit a South African environment: when Miss Julie says that Jean could "almost pass for a gentleman dressed like that," it is patently not true of South Africa where a black is a black no matter how dressed. The production failed to be thorough and consistent in relating its extrinsic interpretation to the intrinsic values, and as such, remained a well-meaning hodgepodge not sufficiently well thought through. The interesting idea remains for another director to test.

It is not, of course, necessary to dress a play in modern costume or set it in a present-day environment to contemporize its values. During the 1960s the Royal Shakespeare Company under the direction of Peter Hall had a fairly consistent policy of "democratizing" Shakespeare. This was a function of Hall's personal beliefs, the egalitarian nature of the ensemble

FIGURE 134.   Peter Hall's 1966 production of *Henry V* for the Royal Shakespeare Company. The plain and worn look of the costumes and the simple, unheroic staging create the aura of World War I trenches. (*Courtesy, Royal Shakespeare Theatre, Stratford-upon-Avon; photo by Holte Photographics*)

he created, and a general social tendency in Britain at that time—the old middle-class establishment was under attack, and the rise of the "meritocracy" was at hand. Hall felt that his audience was very much concerned with the issues of social democracy, and this belief influenced his approach to Shakespeare's work.

The democratic interpretation was especially apparent in Hall's 1966 production of *Henry V*, which was utterly different in style from Olivier's production some sixteen years before (see page 242), which had been created for the Festival of Britain and was bathed in the heroic overtones of Churchillianism and victory in World War II. Gone were the magnificent costumes; Hall's Henry was dressed in dun brown, the color of mud and modern battle dress. He was a workmanlike leader who might have risen through the ranks. The military events were unpleasant, painful, and blood-bespattered. A ragged army was led by a tired leader, to whom it owed allegiance not so much because he was king but because he had proved himself in battle.

At about this same time, the British National Theatre was performing a similar exercise with Restoration comedy. Perhaps nowhere in theater has the term *style* been more bandied about than in connection with Restoration comedy. The life-style of the rather esoteric group of people with whom Restoration drama is concerned appears so conventionalized and removed from contemporary experience that to come to grips with this problem, a litany of mannered characteristics became part of the tradition of British theater, becoming known as "Restoration style." This style was varnished over the surface of the plays, giving them a brittle, superficial veneer that hardly took into account distinctions between plays or differences in character. What the directors of the National Theatre, such as John Dexter and William Gaskill, did in the 1960s was to strip away conventional encrustations to discover the true nature of the plays. Their perspective was influenced by Brechtianism (see pages 260–63), a strong theatrical force at the time which laid special emphasis on economic motivations, and by the social democracy previously mentioned. The actors were helped to understand the significance of class and economic attitudes; the costumes were treated as everyday dress, lived in with the somewhat lax hygiene of the time; the earthy, often diseased reality was revealed beneath the meretricious mask. The approach was really a very simple but thorough exercise in interpretation, starting from an honest attempt to come to grips with the physical, social, and economic world of the play, seen from the inside, not through a scrim of accumulated conventions and misconceptions.

The Country Wife was given a quite different production by the Acting Company of Washington D.C. in 1981, but one which stemmed from an equally thorough and consistent reading of the play. Directed by Garland Wright, the company was not so much concerned with the economic or social values of the time—these it took for granted while it reflected them

FIGURE 135. *Love for Love* at the British National Theatre, with Laurence Olivier as Tattle (left). Notice the creased, unglamorous costumes, the lived-in set and worn furnishings, and the relative simplicity of the actor's manner. Directed by Peter Wood. (*National Theatre Company of Great Britain*)

in costumes and settings; instead it played up the hollow meretriciousness of the sexual games of the period and showed the unsatisfactory consequences. The production was very dynamic and playful, fitting its physical style to the intrinsic sense of sex as a game played on an everlasting carousel, which produces a hyperkinetic, circular chase that can never bring satisfaction. The actors created strongly delineated facial masks, based on exaggerated but consistent facets of realistic detail. The production was more mannered and glib than those of the National Theatre some ten to fifteen years before—it used the text as a trampoline for theatrical gymnastics—but it consistently and coherently bounced off the intrinsic values it had discovered in the text and, in its own way, was equally as truthful to the text as the earlier productions. Its style was its own, discovered by an examination of the play, not borrowed from a petrified tradition with no intrinsic value.

The twenty-year period between 1960 and 1980 has been very significant in terms of the development of contemporary theatrical styles. The period overlapped the existential gestures of absurdism, confirmed the major influence of Brecht, and felt the shock waves of Artaud. We deal more specifically with the aesthetics of Brecht and Artaud later in this chapter, but it might be instructive here to touch briefly on how they

FIGURE 136. Strong delineation of character facial masks in The Acting Company's production of Wycherly's *The Country Wife*, directed by Garland Wright, 1981. (*Photo by Diane Gorodnitzki*)

influenced production styles during the period: how "contemporization" can mean the response to aesthetic movements as well as to social and political trends. (We recognize this as a somewhat false distinction as, of course, both Brecht and Artaud were responding to and reflecting certain social and political attitudes of their day.)

The lifetime of the Royal Shakespeare Company exactly coincides with the post-1960 period, and if we continue to use its work extensively to illustrate our discussion of style, it is because its development is a stylistic history of the period; it is a major English-speaking company that has attempted both to respond to its times and to create a coherent production policy, and its principal work—Shakespeare—is tensile, virtually indestructible, and has the breadth of values that lends itself to a wide spectrum of interpretations.

The social democratic sensibility of the early 1960s led the company to develop a style that was simple, uncluttered, and neutral, a style from which rhetorical varnish had been stripped and baroque embellishments banished. This style, especially in terms of what came to be called its "black box" settings, was highly suited to the Brechtian quality which was the next influence on the company. There was a logic to this: the political sensibility of social democracy was not far removed from Brecht; and the simplicity and austerity Brecht demanded in his productions—so that the political message might be enhanced—equally suited the democratic sensibility and emphasis on the unembellished word which underlay the company's approach: the text was to be revealed, unembroidered and unhindered by rhetorical or social formality.

Peter Brook's *King Lear,* heavily influenced by Brecht and the Polish critic Jan Kott, was perhaps the prime example of this period. It is Brook, too, always attuned to contemporary sensibility, who was responsible for the productions of *The Tempest, Marat/Sade, A Midsummer Night's Dream,* and Seneca's *Oedipus,* which led the company out of the 1960s into the 1970s and the incorporation of Artaudian elements into its work. The production of *A Midsummer Night's Dream* probably marks the highpoint of extrinsic interpretation to contemporize the intrinsic values of a Shakespearean work. The production incorporated the gymnastic physicality and virtuosity Artaud demanded of the theater into the clarity, discipline, and focus of Brechtianism. The play took place within a bare, brightly lit, white set (the black box had become a white gymnasium), where the actors performed acrobatics, trapeze work, and circus tricks which were both consistent with their characters as magic makers and a celebration of the actors' total skills. Brook made his magic fit the intention of the play, which succeeded because although he had one foot in the circus, he had both hands on the intrinsic values of Shakespeare's text.

From the 1960s and 1970s and their hallmark productions, showing how classical works can be made to respond to the aesthetic as well as social and political sensibility of their time, the Royal Shakespeare Company has entered the 1980s, reflecting the eclecticism now current. The existential, Brechtian, and Artaudian gestures have been distilled into the mainstream of theatrical production, intermingled with and supporting other values. There is no one aesthetic or social formula to challenge the creative director, and no particular stylistic pattern is revealed. The 1980 production of *The Greeks,* a ten-hour retelling of the fall of the house of Atreus and the causes, course, and consequences of the Trojan war, culled from Aeschylus and Euripides, is an example of a company taking on major challenges but not focusing on a specific extrinsic value. It is an attempt to tell the story for our time, to remind audiences of one of the great myths of Western culture, without any ritualistic mumbo jumbo or political allegorization.

The production follows the tradition of simple staging—as befitting both its Greek ancestry and its Shakespearean adoption—and is costumed in a nonspecific Greco-modern style. The clarity and strongly physical quality of the company's acting owes something both to Brecht and to Artaud, but it is absolutely unselfconscious. The production is focused on the moral and legal issues inherent in the plays—"Who is to blame?" is the first line uttered—and on the telling of the story, clarifying the conflicts and refreshing the myths. If any "contemporary" reference does stand out, it is a function of Euripides' emphasis on women's social status—which

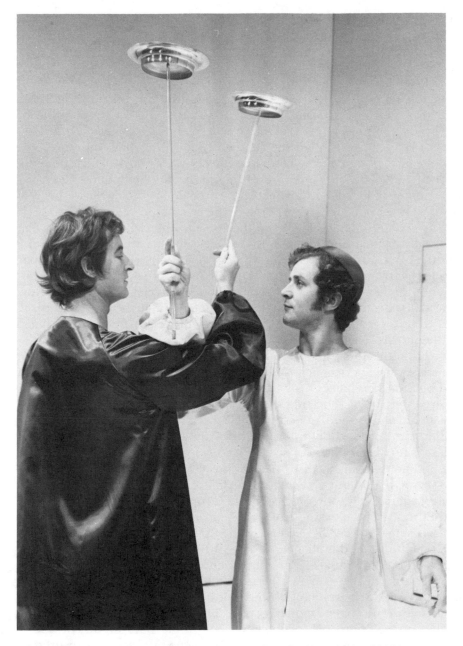

FIGURE 137.   Puck and Oberon performing circus tricks in Peter Brook's production of *A Midsummer Night's Dream*.   (*Courtesy, Royal Shakespeare Company, Stratford-upon-Avon; photo by Holte Photographics*)

FIGURE 138. Agamemnon with captive Cassandra in John Barton's 1980 production of *The Greeks* for the Royal Shakespeare Company. (*Courtesy, Royal Shakespeare Company; photo by Donald Cooper*)

gives the production a feminist slant. But that is not conscious contemporization; it is an intrinsic quality of the plays which responds, as any production will, to the contemporary concerns of its audience.

SETTING THE PLAY IN AN ARBITRARY PERIOD

So far we have dealt with stylistic interpretations which contemporize plays either by putting them in modern dress and environments or by enhancing certain contemporary values while setting the play in its own period. There is another option open to directors: choosing a physical style that is neither contemporary nor intrinsically suggested by the play—for example, setting *The Taming of the Shrew* in the American "wild West," as was done by the Stratford, Ontario, company, or setting *Much Ado About Nothing* in the

Edwardian period, as was done for the New York Shakespeare Festival by A. J. Antoon.

The logic for such a choice is that the director believes that there is something in the social, moral, or simply physical climate of the chosen period that will enhance certain qualities he or she wishes to emphasize in the play. It can be a dangerous choice. The director has not only to reconcile the style of the play to the world of the audience but also to reconcile the chosen style with both. An arbitrary setting can give added dimensions to a production—making it an intellectual adventure tour of Western civilization—or it can lead to problems of interpretation for the actors and confusion for the audience, who is asked to look at the play through two pairs of eyeglasses.

In 1977, a highly successful Royal Shakespeare production, directed by John Barton, transposed *Much Ado About Nothing* to Victorian India at the height of the British Raj. One of the fundamental intrinsic qualities of the play is the "battle of the sexes," Beatrice and Benedick being "at point," both supported by a platoon of male or female combat troops. The social structure of late-Victorian India could hardly provide a more rigidly stratified and sex-streamed environment: the quite separate quarters of the

FIGURE 139.   Dogberry and Verges in John Barton's "British Raj" production of *Much Ado About Nothing* for the Royal Shakespeare Company.   (*Courtesy, Royal Shakespeare Company*)

male club and the female household; the officer's mess and the memsahib's drawing room. These are appropriately separate habitats for the silly pranks of the men and the tittle-tattle of the women, which form part of the fabric of Shakespeare's play.

The Indian setting also created an aristocratically idle, sportive, relaxed off-duty life-style in which the intrigues, jealousies, and backbitings of Shakespeare's plot become almost inevitable in the indolent heat. The whole environment was marvelously realized, with sun-blinds revealing and obscuring the "notings" of the plot, grass mats, the sounds of a cricket match offstage, and the windy pomposity of the regimental band. But perhaps the most brilliant transliteration of all was that of the constable, Dogberry, into a Kiplingesque Indian petty officer. The humor of Dogberry has worn a little thin for modern audiences. It is based on the premise that he is inordinately proud of his verbal capacity but always gets it wrong. This is precisely the case today with certain Indians who still owe dated allegiance to the British Raj in a kowtowing kind of way and proudly air their facility with English, which is always overliteral and slightly back to front. It is the stereotype which Peter Sellers popularized, but nonetheless true for that, and makes a perfect modern equivalent of Dogberry; as such it is a brilliant *aperçu* on the part of the director.

The late 1970s saw two quite different "arbitrary" productions of *Measure for Measure* based on similar perceptions of the intrinsic quality of the play. Jonathan Miller, who had previously set *The Merchant of Venice* in late nineteenth-century Italy, set his production of *Measure* in Vienna just before it succumbed to Nazi rule in the 1930s. The play's environment became that of a petty bourgeois bureaucracy, the entire action taking place in a long corridor with a series of doors, including the one to Claudio's cell. The only furniture was a table around which the legalistic arguments of the play unfolded, presided over by Angelo, a narrow-minded bureaucrat whose life revolved around the law book permanently on the table. The play deals with a gloomy, amoral society in which power is easily abused—easy prey for the *anschluss* to come.

To make his political point Miller did take certain liberties with Shakespeare's text—making the duke a calculating politician who finally manipulates Isabella into bed—but not nearly as many as another production of the time which found contemporary political values in the play. Set in a modern Italy, this production made Communist and feminist statements with the play, which opened with programs distributed like propaganda pamphlets and an actress spraying "I belong to myself" on a wall with aerosol paint. A subtext was introduced, dealing with state secrecy, police brutality, and the social oppression of women. Although the details of Shakespeare's text do not always sit easily with this idea, the intrinsic political values and the use and abuse of women by men are clearly part of Shakespeare's enquiry. To reinforce the point, the production changed

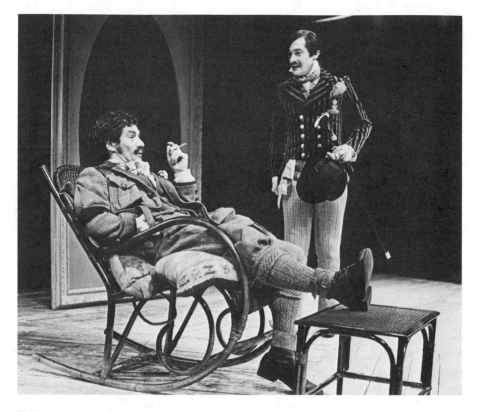

FIGURE 140.   An eclectically costumed production of Shakespeare's *Twelfth Night,* directed by Jon Amiel for the Royal Shakespeare Company in 1978.   (*Courtesy, Royal Shakespeare Company*)

Claudio to Claudia, which makes the famous cell scene that of a woman who saw no wrong in premarital sex asking a "sister," inhibited by religious values communism doesn't recognize, to give her body to save the spirit of the revolution—a neatly consistent twist of the situation. The play ended with a spirited rendering of the "Red Flag," which is superbly irrelevant to Shakespeare but a highly effective coda in the context of the production: the people will ultimately triumph in the face of political injustice.

The production, though heavily extrinsic, succeeded because it could find some support for its statement in Shakespeare's text, and it built consistently on that premise. The dangers of "arbitrary" interpretation, however, were exemplified by Charles Marowitz's production, in 1977, of *The Merchant of Venice.* The production was set in post-World War II British-governed Palestine. Shylock became the leader of the Zionist liberation movement; Jessica's marriage became an infiltration plot—she is sent as an *agent provocateur* into the enemy camp. The enemy, in the persons of Antonio, Bassanio, and so on, are Western businessmen and British military.

As an intellectual idea, the production gave Shylock much more moti-

FIGURE 141. A modern-dress production of *The Merchant of Venice* at the American Conservatory Theatre, San Francisco. (*Courtesy, American Conservatory Theatre*)

vation than Shakespeare did. Within the shadow of the holocaust he is fighting for a homeland for his people—in 1947 justice must seem inevitably on his side—the anti-Semitism of the play could hardly be more clearly underlined. But the production failed in two aspects: 1977 was a long way from 1947, and a contemporary audience might have a different perspective on the Israeli/Palestine situation—the oppressed might now be seen as oppressors. And almost more important, the production did not bother to try to make a coherent statement with the problems it brought up. How far can an audience accept caftaned Jews and English judges discussing Venetian law in Palestine, with a jet-set Portia surrounded by art deco furniture and massaged by a West Indian maid? The production is an example of an interesting concept which failed entirely to work because the director either failed to, or found that he couldn't, coherently interrelate the three worlds of style: that of the playwright, the audience, and the stage.

AESTHETIC STYLES

By aesthetic styles we mean those which neither rely for their definition on a historical setting nor are realistic (a term we will discuss later) in intention. The early part of the twentieth century saw a strong reaction against realism in all forms of art; it might be termed the era of the "isms." Impressionism, symbolism, futurism, dadaism, constructivism, expressionism, surrealism were all aspects of the attempt to break out of the limiting, rational form of realism which tended to recapitulate the surface of life rather than come to terms with the irrational, noncoherent condition of human existence. The artist's evocative imagination was now thought to be better able to reveal fundamental truths than the realist's "slice of life." The grotesque, the fantastical, the nonsensical, the stuff of dreams were all used to liberate the human mind from the restrictions of rational form and social conventions.

Many of the isms were short-lived as independent forms, and the more significant ideas have been absorbed into the mainstream of artistic perceptions. In the theater, these ideas have catalyzed the rediscovery of theatricality, liberating theater from the confines of the proscenium fourth wall and the concept that it stood in a one-to-one relationship with "real" life. Of the "isms," possibly constructivism and expressionism have had the most direct influence on theater, being more socially concerned than other aesthetic styles.

Constructivism, possibly the most concrete of the "isms," was based on sets made of naked technological artifacts: scaffolding, planks, ladders, slides, wheels. It was a theater built on engineering principles, affirming the materials and rhythms of a twentieth-century industrial society and reflecting humans in a machine age—and to some degree man as a machine. Acting within this style required a highly physical and acrobatic facility, with actions illustrated by cartwheels, somersaults, and tumbling. The Russian director Meyerhold was an exponent of constructivism, and his production of *The Magnificent Cuckold* was a classic example of its highly physical potential.

Modern productions which, perhaps unconsciously, owe something to constructivism would include Peter Brook's *A Midsummer Night's Dream* (see page 251), with its highly acrobatic style of trapezes in a circuslike set. The New York Shakespeare Festival's *Two Gentlemen of Verona* (see page 244) was also a highly physical production, using scaffolding and step levels which recapitulated the environment of a modern city with its quality of being either half built or half torn down. The Living Theater's production of *Frankenstein* went even further, showing the construction on stage of a man/monster of our industrial age by using all the paraphernalia of modern technology. The main danger in this style of production is that the physical theatricality will obscure the text, presenting nothing more than a bag of tricks with little relationship to the intrinsic action of the play.

Expressionism, born of a vehement sense of social indignation, took the shape of an attack on bourgeois forms and attitudes and a rejection of that "realism" in the theater which seemed to be a detailed perpetuation of those attitudes. Extremism of emotion, language, and stagecraft was its hallmark, combining the distorted, the grotesque, and the bizarre to project concrete images of the world of dreams and psychic fantasy.

FIGURE 142. Constructivist set for *The Man Who Was Thursday*, directed by Alexander Tairov. *(Deutsches Theatermuseum, Früher Clara Ziegler-Stiftung)*

FIGURE 143. Expressionistic staging of Ernst Toller's *Transfiguration*. *(Deutsches Theatermuseum, Früher Clara Ziegler-Stiftung)*

The theatrical style of expressionism is achieved by very specific scenic, lighting, acting, and vocal effects to make direct social statements within a structure based on the disjointed patterns of the human mind in dream. Staging is very fluid, using lighting to focus on this area and now that in no seemingly logical order. It is a form of Shakespearean or epic staging without the sequential progression; themes are used to make a nexus of impressions on the audience, rather than the logical, incremental building of actions toward a climax.

Language is less important to the creation of an expressionist style than are gesture and mask. The appeal to the audience is visual and emotional rather than conceptual, and the approach to acting is almost entirely opposed to detailed naturalism based on inner process; that is, the external manifestation is more important than inner motivation. The style of expressionism cannot be truly achieved without a feeling for the social vehemence behind it. Simply to employ its techniques without the fervor would be to produce a possibly clever but inevitably hollow imitation.

In some respects, reviving today plays of the expressionist period would be a redundant exercise. Many of the most significant stylistic gestures of expressionism were incorporated into the post-1950s avant-garde, and the true value of expressionism—as with most of the "isms"—lies in those new stylistic perceptions that it opened up to the theater. One of the most important modern styles, which incorporates elements of both expressionism and constructivism, is Brechtian, or epic, theater. This style shows its debt to the two "isms" in the technological emphasis of its settings, nonrealistic presentation, use of mask, fluid plot structure, and strong sense of social concern.

Epic style has two fundamental assumptions: first, theater is theater, and it is worthless to try to fool people into believing they are witnessing a "slice of life"; second, theater must be more than escapism, a "culinary" artifact; it must also serve a sociopolitical purpose. Theater must be didactic; it must confront people with the true reality of their condition, make them think about the way in which their lives are structured and governed and, specifically, reveal the superior virtue of a Marxist political and economic society. These two principles determine the intrinsic style of epic theater, and although the framework of extrinsic choices leaves many possibilities open, a director cannot truly communicate the values of a Brechtian play without taking cognizance of them.

Epic style is highly theatrical, discarding realistic settings and frankly acknowledging the presence of technological equipment on the stage. There is no attempt to hide the lighting instruments or the means by which scenic changes are achieved. Locations are created by the actors themselves with a minimum of props and furniture, so that the action can flow from scene to scene with complete continuity. Emblematic scenery is often used, and an orange box with a sign above it saying "bar" becomes as much a bar

FIGURE 144. Epic production of Brecht's *Mahagonny* at East Berlin's Komische Oper. (*Photo by Arvid Lagenpusch*)

as Belasco's most realistic creations. A director is not obliged to use all these techniques in an epic production, but he or she must be aware that Brecht perceives theater as a technological tool kit as much as a box of magic tricks.

The staging, which deliberately attempts not to fool the audience, reinforces the second principle of epic theater: it is a tool for social improvement. The audience must be encouraged to think about the stage action, not sucked into an empathic response. This remove is achieved by acting, music, media, and content. These are combined, with the scenic effects previously described, to keep the audiences always intellectually aware of what is being performed on stage, to challenge them to think about the play, and to prevent them from becoming so emotionally involved with the action that they lose their objectivity. The acting style of epic theater has been discussed in Chapter 8; we will only emphasize here that the remove the actor maintains from the character is in keeping with the total stylistic principle of objectifying the stage events.

Music, media, and content may be used to make a direct statement, or they may be conjoined for ironic purposes. In *Mother Courage* and *The Threepenny Opera,* harsh and grating music give a distinctively sardonic flavor to these productions. Posters and projections may comment directly on the action, for example, to show mangled bodies in a scene deploring war; more often, and more effectively, they make an ironic statement. Joan

Littlewood's production of *Oh, What a Lovely War* included an electric marquee that listed the mounting casualty figures while the characters talked gaily of what a "jolly affair" war is. Littlewood also used music ironically, staging song and dance acts with the thoughtless, insouciant lyrics of the day in front of film projections of the actual horror of war.

The purpose of epic style is to make a direct social or political statement which will challenge audiences and stimulate them to action. This is what *alienation* means when applied to the Brechtian method. It does *not* mean that the director makes the audience dislike the play and the actors or sets up a mutual antipathy; directors who attempt to do so are stylistically wrong. The aim of the epic style is to create objectivity, to break the audience out of its accepted way of viewing life, to confront it intellectually with the playwright's point of view. The content of the play may at times consist of direct preachment, for example, the plays written by Brecht in his middle period—the *Lehrstücke* or teaching plays. The physical and acting style of these plays is in the epic vein, but there is little employment of irony, and the theater is treated as a lecture hall in which a direct political moral (usually Marxist) is driven home. More usually in plays by Brecht and other epic playwrights, the moral appears in more of a parable form, the playwright's statement made through an ironic confrontation of the apparent action with setting, music, media, and costume, which combine to reveal a complacently accepted attitude in a new light.

Although the use of some or all of the artifacts and techniques just discussed is necessary to create an epic style, it is not a sufficient condition if they are not used with the clear purpose of breaking the audience's empathy and making it objectively consider an issue. The artifacts and techniques by themselves merely create the form; the intrinsic intention is necessary to create the style. There have been extremely romantic productions of *Mother Courage* in which an unduly sympathetic performance of the title role has created empathy in audiences, who are bathed in maudlin regrets at her misfortunes and lose the playwright's social statement about how she has allowed herself to be corrupted by capitalism.

On the other hand, Joan Littlewood created an epic style and effect without using an alienation style of acting, and with a much less consciously structured sense of theater than Brecht, whose training in Marxist dialectic is apparent in his dramatic form. In her production of *Oh, What a Lovely War,* the actors did not need to take an objective approach to their characters because the total form of the production was an ironic comment on its subject, World War I. Littlewood created a vaudeville circus form with a basic ensemble of actors, dressed as Pierrots, who played a number of different parts in a series of olios, or circus acts. There was no possibility for the audience to identify with any of the characters, who were distinguished only by hats and props, but the audience did identify with the cheerful actors who played to them as people. This was all part of Littlewood's plan, for the more audiences were emotionally drawn in by the actors, the harder they were then hit by the alienating effects of the projections, posters, and data, not to mention the ironic text. The audiences were brought up short and made to see themselves as susceptible to all the chauvinistic superficialities of war—colorful uniforms, patriotic speeches, brave music—while ignoring the horrific realities. This was exactly the point Littlewood wished to make. Thus, the essential point about epic, as about all style, is the intention behind the form: the intrinsic nature of the impact the director desires.

ALTERNATIVE THEATER

In the first edition of this book, published in 1974, we said, "No discussion of the art of directing today can be complete without some examination of the aesthetic principles and practices of what is known as 'New Theater.'" The statement still holds good, except that the principles are no longer new, and the forms of theater we referred to have come to be called "alternative theater." In a mere eight years many of these principles have become a part of the normal practice of mainstream theater; and the alternative theater, in its various forms, still makes significant contributions around the fringes of the world's major theatrical centers—be it New York, Berlin, Paris, or London—although operating today at a much lower profile.

We are, briefly, going to discuss some of the basic principles of the alternative theater aesthetic; not only is working in one of the forms still a very real possibility for the aspiring director, but also some of the principles tend to be part of the common currency of choices open to a director today in whatever area of theater he or she might work.

The aesthetic of the alternative theater was brewing throughout the early part of the twentieth century, and it found different expressions in the various "isms" discussed on pages 258–60. In the 1960s the social and political sensibility behind the artistic avant-garde—which, by definition, must be ahead of its time—found its manifestation in the various protest movements of that period. That desire to break out of the rational formality of social structures and the sense of indignation at the morally and economically inequitable nature of human existence, which underlay the gestures of the theatrical experimentation of the early twentieth century, now found itself in tune with real sociopolitical sensibility. Art had performed its function of encouraging social revolution and was now reflecting it. An alternative form of society was being demanded, and an alternative set of artistic aesthetics produced an alternative theater to support this demand.

The sociopolitical revolution of the 1960s was, for the most part, an

attempt to destroy the moral values, economic inequities, and social structures of the industrial and capitalist bourgeois organization of the mid-
twentieth century, with what were perceived as its overly formalized, morally restrictive, and emotionally repressive influences on humanity. Freud
in his *Civilization and Its Discontents*[1] had suggested that mankind had given
up much of its sensual birthright and holistic relationship to life in exchange for the security and material comforts of civilization. The desire for
an alternative society as reflected in alternative theater took some of its
dynamic from a wish to free humanity from the suffocating encrustations
of Western civilization. There was an emphasis on experience rather than
explanation, a rejection of the cerebral in favor of the visceral and tactile, a
sense that life should not simply be interpreted but felt and that the feeling
should be holistic and all-embracing. Life is in the living, and theater is in
the performance. There was a democratic rejection of the concept of masterpieces: an egalitarian society could not allow one dominating set of
values. Emphasis was to be on subjective feeling rather than objective
assessment.

The theatrical expression of some of these values had been practiced
by the avant-garde long before the total aesthetic came together in the
1960s. Dada had emphasized the concept of simultaneous events embracing and confronting its audience from many directions and with many
stimuli at the same time. In a landmark presentation at Black Mountain
College in North Carolina in 1952, composer John Cage combined a lecture, a recitation from a ladder, a piano recital, movie projections, and a
dance performance into one simultaneous event which took place in and
around the audience.[2]

Meanwhile, the Bauhaus experimenters of the 1920s were trying to
escape the idea of the physical theater as a defined space with complete
separation of audience and performer. They made use of technology—
which we noted as having a significant impact on the style of Brecht at
about the same time—to mechanize all the physical aspects of theatrical
space. The actor-spectator relationship could thus be made completely
flexible, molded into whatever shape the action of any play demanded.
Although the efforts of the Bauhaus designers themselves were cut short
by the political circumstances in Germany in the 1930s, their sense of
flexible, nonspecific, all-embracing theatrical space was an important aspect of the aesthetic of the later alternative theater.

Changes in the approach to painting reinforced the new spatial dynamics of theater. After the cubists broke down the accepted classical har-

---

[1]Sigmund Freud, *Civilization and Its Discontents,* trans. James Strachey (New York: W.
W. Norton & Co., Inc., 1962).

[2]Theatrical folklore relates that a dog began to follow dancer Merce Cunningham
around the room and, in the spirit of the piece, became part of the performance.

monies and created the concept of collage it was only a matter of time before everything that had hitherto been regarded as foreign to paint and canvas would be involved in the creative act. From pieces of paper extending the space of the canvas into three dimensions, the artwork reached farther into the space of the room until finally it came to fill it completely and to include not only the artist but also anyone visiting the environment thus created. People as moving, colored shapes became part of the artistic event. Mechanically moving parts were then added, and the created surroundings could be rearranged at the artist's or spectators' discretion. Sound and speech, both mechanical and recorded, became part of the artwork and environment. The artwork now appeared to many artists more an arena in which to act, so action painting and flexible environments took the place of canvas. As art came closer to theater, so theater incorporated its spatial perspective into its own aesthetics.

An important event in the evolution of experimental theatrical ideas into a coherent pattern that might be termed an alternative theater aesthetic was the publication in English in 1958 of *The Theatre and Its Double* by Antonin Artaud, a French visionary of the 1930s who had been influenced by Dada, surrealism, Asian theater, and drugs. Artaud called for a theater of intense physical and emotional impact, to explore and release humanity's most primitive passions and instincts, calcified and repressed by modern civilization. In this belief, of course, he was at one with Freud: Artaud's spiritual apocalypticism was matched by his political sensibility, as he believed that bourgeois social structures were to blame for humanity's oppression. In specific terms Artaud sought a theater which rejected domination by text and totally surrounded and involved its audience with the searing nature of its physical and aural impact. It must create "a language in space, a language of sounds, cries, lights, onomatopoeia, the theatre must organize into veritable hieroglyphs, with the help of characters and objects and make use of their symbolism and interconnections in relation to all organs and on all levels."[3]

A nontheatrical aesthetician who interrelated many of these revolutionary concepts in his perception of the nature of contemporary culture was Marshall McLuhan. He envisaged a "retribalization" of humanity in a culture which emphasized involvement, physical sensation, and plastic values. McLuhan believed that the printed word had limited a human being's capacity for total sensory experience but that the contemporary proliferation of imagistic and aural media would return that all-embracing experience of human existence which had been sacrificed to rationality, and linear forms of perception and expression. Philosophically, McLuhan is at one with the propounders of environmentally embracing, participatory

[3]Antonin Artaud, *The Theatre and Its Double*, trans. Mary Richards (New York: Grove Press, 1958), p. 90.

theater in which information and sensory experience are integrated and communicated on the more abstract level of the hieroglyph.

The three basic principles underlying the aesthetics of alternative theater are, thus, environmental, media, and Artaudian. Most alternative theater productions will use all these effects, but not necessarily so: media productions are invariably environmental, but environmental productions do not have to employ media; any attempt to surround the audience with sensory imput must have some Artaudian impact, but media can be used for strictly political effect, as in Brechtian theater.

The Environmental Principle

The basic stylistic principle of the environmental use of space is that it should be regarded as a totality, embracing both actors and audience in one continuous whole. The action takes place around, above, behind, below, and among the audience. (This does produce problems in terms of focus; one production solved the problems by seating the audience in the middle of the space on swivel chairs.) The purpose of this technique is to create a totally shared experience, where bodily contact can occur between actor and audience; spectators are drawn into and become an integral part of the event. Some proponents regard it as a return to the essence of predramatic ritual in which all participants were both themselves and actors, and no division existed between actors and spectators.

The definition of space in an environmental production is not predetermined but organic and dynamic. There are two kinds of space: transformed and found. *Transformed space* is an environment created for the production by the designing of *all* the space, not a separation of the space into an area for performance and another area for audience. Spatial design should arise organically from the exploration of the action and serve its needs. The action should not be made to fit the needs of a predetermined space. Ideally the nature of the spatial definition should evolve with the production itself and be created spontaneously and gradually by the interplay of director, actors, designers, and technicians.

Found space is a given environment which is explored, not altered; the performance adjusts to the environment and copes with its given elements. A production occurs in found space, for example, if it is given in the streets or other public places or taken into a building and performed in the space as given. In both transformed and found space, it is a principle of performance that spectators may, by their movements, unexpectedly redefine the space and that performers must be prepared to adapt to and take advantage of this flexibility of environment.

Flexibility of environment is related to another principle of environmental production, flexible and variable focus. Unlike "formal" theater, where one of the director's tasks is to create a specific focus and to ensure that the audience sees what it is supposed to, when it is supposed to, environmental theater can offer a choice of focuses. More than one event can take place at the same time; indeed, because of the all-encompassing nature of the environment events can occur all around the spectators, who may choose what to look at and in what order. Of course, the director does decide what range of alternatives to give the spectators, and by relating the simultaneous events to one sensory totality he or she can provide the audience with a greater depth of experience of a given action than is possible in single-focus structure.

The multifocal principle derives from the idea of people as beings who, in their daily life, are surrounded by a plethora of impressions which they absorb through eyes, ears, nose, and fingertips, and whose experience is not linear—particularly in the modern urban confusion of lights, movements, and sounds, some distinct and some only faintly heard—but an ever-changing totality. The experience creates the impression; "the medium is the message."

Environmental staging is often used in productions in which the text is not held as sacrosanct but is "confronted" to discover which of its values have significance for a contemporary audience. In such situations the text is cut, expanded, or rearranged to emphasize relationships and attitudes that may be more pertinent than at the time of its writing. It shows the influence of film technique on theater and can add new dimensions to a text by intercutting, or playing simultaneously, scenes that were written sequentially, thereby achieving interesting results in terms of understanding an action or through ironic juxtaposition.

Although there are profits from environmental staging, there are also some caveats the director should bear in mind. The idea that the creation of one space common to performer and audience will lead to a shared experience as in predramatic ritual doesn't always work out in practice: our highly fragmented modern society does not have the shared religious and social beliefs on which rituals were based. Again, as long as there are people who know they are actors and people who know they are spectators, there will be an aesthetic division between the two, and the violation of audience space by the actor simply becomes another part of the structure of the event; it doesn't necessarily make it more integrated and informal. To put one's arms around a person is not necessarily to embrace him or her in the emotional connotation of the term; to surround the audience with the performance does not necessarily mean touching it at any greater depth than in a proscenium theater.

The Media Principle

The use of media in contemporary theatrical events is the ultimate logic of the theater's assimilation of human technology, which goes back at least as far as the *deus ex machina*. The specific exploration of the contemporary theatrical possibilities of multimedia can perhaps be dated from 1958 when Josef Svoboda produced his *Laterna Magika* at the Brussels Exposition. *Laterna Magika* featured eight mobile screens and five projectors of both slides and film. There was interplay between projections and live actors, augmented by various treadmills, lifts, and other mechanical stage devices, the whole being audially embraced by stereophonic sound. The performance, which had a disconnected revue-type structure, created a pluralistic field of vision and a dynamic montage of simultaneous images much in keeping with mid-twentieth-century modes of perception. Multimedia may or may not be used with live performers and may or may not have an informational structure. The light shows which were a popular form of entertainment in the 1960s may be regarded as a form of multimedia theater, employing amplified stereophonic music and the projection of slides and film of changing colored patterns, together with strobe lights and other visual effects. These were directed, in the sense that a choice of relationships had to be made among the various elements, and geared toward the achievement of a particular emotional mood or physical response in the audience.

A more calculated and informational use of media is often used in

FIGURE 145.   A Josef Svoboda montage for Werle's *Die Reise*, produced in Hamburg by Lars Runsten (1969).   (*Art Centrum, Prague*)

productions wishing to make a social or political statement. For example, to create an antinuclear event, a director could use the sound of atomic explosions, projections of victims of the attack on Hiroshima, television commentary from the Three Mile Island meltdown, stills of cancer victims and sounds of the dying, blinding lighting effects, and shots of clean solar energy intercut with the pollution of nuclear waste. These elements could be connected by a narrative commentary or be simply an aural and visual collage. Irony can be introduced by playing lyrical and pastoral music against the sound of explosions and projecting children at play onto the cancer victims; this technique is, of course, what Brecht used, in a more formally theatrical way, with his alienation effect; his epic style as a whole also made considerable use of media.

Directors using media to heighten a production will employ the same techniques discussed in environmental style: intercutting, superimposition, simultaneity. But in addition they must deal with the relationship between film and live performers. Here the question of focus becomes important if they are working on a plot-oriented production. Experience suggests that other things being equal, a live performer will tend to dominate film or projections; but the problem of actor and image competing for attention is probably best solved by interrelating the actor and the image.

In a plot-oriented production, media can be used to create scenic atmosphere, such as the projection of a cherry orchard in Chekhov's play—making the metaphor more evident to the audience. It can also illustrate subtext, making visual the actual thoughts of a character; represent past situations and experiences; pass commentary on a character's action; and altogether create a denser experience of the text.

Television, specifically, brings added dimensions. It can help solve the problems of audience focus—scenes can be televised as they are acted and viewed on monitors throughout the theater. Television can show the progress of an outside event that is going to impinge on the play's action; for example, if the entrance of an individual is a climactic point in the plot, he can be shown preparing for the entrance, heightening the onstage tension. Television can also show different aspects of an action—from the rear, above, below—or it can focus in on and emphasize small detail.

This discussion by no means exhausts the uses of media but indicates the very real possibilities it affords the contemporary director; it is not simply an ephemeral gimmick of the 1960s. Media can produce new rhythms, densities, and associations. They can be used to key audience reactions both intellectually, by visual information, and emotionally, by the use of changing visual and aural images. More than ever, in using media, directors must have a strong sense of the impact they wish to produce and of the need to create an integrated focal impression. The danger of overstatement awaits the unwary director, especially in classical plays where poetry was intended to do much of the work that media can now do. The director should take care not to overelaborate. The story is told that Tyrone Guthrie, directing *Hamlet*, was asked by an actor for some help with the lines "The morn, in russet mantle clad, walks o'er the dew of yon high eastern hill," to which Guthrie responded, "What do you want, a pink light?" Just as a physical action onstage should reveal an idea within the text and not call attention to itself, so should media enhance the implicit, not the explicit; it should add a dimension, not be redundant repetition.

The Artaudian Principle

Artaud's concept of a "theater of cruelty" was one of the most dynamic influences on the aesthetic of alternative theater. Cruelty implies an intensity and severity of emotional attack which is calculated to drain the ulcer of humanity's repressed desires and instincts—the aggressions, lusts hates, and sadistic impulses which Artaud believed to be held in, suppurating beneath the mask of civilized behavior. Cruelty is above all rigor. It does not necessarily involve sadism and bloodshed, but it does not shun them if they serve the violent intention of the attack on the senses. Artaud called for intense physical images which would crush and hypnotize the spectators, and he suggested that actors should be like martyrs, burnt alive but still signaling through the flames. In a famous image Artaud likened his theater to a plague which breaks down normal human functions; leads to delirium, visions, and bizarre images; and then leaves people cleansed and peacefully accommodated to their normal existence. Thus "cruelty" purges all the repressed primitive instincts that lead to war, murder, rape, and incest.

Artaud dismissed realistic theater as trivial, and he was equally offhand with overly literary, psychological, or intellectual values in texts. Most directors working in an Artaudian style have originated events from metaphysical concepts or myths or have adapted certain classical texts. The intrinsic style of Jacobean and Senecan tragedies and early romantic plays with gothic values (Artaud himself did a production of Shelley's *Cenci*) have been found well suited to an Artaudian approach, as have Euripidean tragedies such as *The Bacchae, Medea,* and *The Trojan Women.* One of the classics of Artaudian theater was Peter Brook's production of Peter Weiss's play, known in the shortened title as *Marat/Sade.*

The form of the Artaudian event is frequently that of a ritual or rite of passage. It is not so much the telling of a story as the exploration of a theme which touches the core of Man's identity. The shape is unlikely to be narrative and logical but rather nuclear and imagistic: full of sights and sounds that—like the Christian mass with its smell of incense, incantations, symbolic sharing of flesh and blood, and raising of the host—physically and spiritually embrace the participants. Artaudian theater cannot be kept within a proscenium. Its shape must be articulated to match the patterns

FIGURE 146. De Sade, and inmates, in stage trap in Peter Brook's 1965 production of *Marat/Sade* for the Royal Shakespeare Company.   (*Courtesy, Royal Shakespeare Company, Stratford-upon-Avon; photo by Holte Photographics*)

and rhythms of the event. The Performance Group, directed by Richard Schechner, discovered a circular shape for its *Dionysus in '69,* whereas its *Makbeth* finished up angular. Jerzy Grotowski's company built its setting for *Akropolis* among the audience, out of stovepipes.

The shape of an Artaudian performance will determine the degree of direct audience participation. Grotowski solved the problem in the most sophisticated manner, especially in his production of *Faustus* where the spectators sat around a table as guests at a last supper before Faustus's damnation. In *The Constant Prince* Grotowski again had the spectators surrounding the event, this time as around a bullring or an operating table, watching the surgical procedure of the revelation of the actor/character's self. Schechner often took the concept of audience involvement further, with a great deal of body contact between actor and spectator and the performance of "embracing" rituals.

In keeping with his distaste for literary values, Artaud subordinated language to action, but he did not dismiss the effect of sound. Groans, roars, liturgical chants, folk songs, declamations—the whole gamut of human vocal possibility is used. These sounds would go together with those produced by a whole range of nonmusical means—feet on the ground, hands on the body, sticks, metal boxes, anything that might produce in-

FIGURE 147.   Notice the intensity of the actors in jute sack costumes in Jerry Grotowski's *Akropolis.*   (*Courtesy, Theatr Laboratorium, Wroclaw, Poland*)

tense aural effects. Lighting was intended to produce an equally forceful impression on the spectator. Threatening, penetrating, vibrating, the light, like the sound, should move the audience to intense experiences of terror, eroticism, pain, or passion.

The style of costuming in Artaudian theater serves the total focus of the event, with no restriction in terms of historical accuracy or detail. Artaud himself rejected modern dress because of its limited connotation, but directors have run the gamut from the simplest body coverings, such as T-shirts and leotards, to resplendent and ritualistic dress. The qualities of costuming should be body-enhancing, timeless, and symbolic. The Performance Group first used T-shirts in *Dionysus in '69* and then progressed to nakedness. Grotowski used a loincloth for his principal actor in *The Constant Prince* and jute sacks with holes for the arms in *Akropolis.* The function of costume is not essentially to delimit a situation or define a character; it is to reinforce the total *mise en scène* in visual impact and broad meaning.

The basic stage image of Artaudian style is in the form of a hieroglyph. Created by the actor's gestures and use of props, hieroglyphs are not psychological or pantomimic but archetypal, containing a poetic rather than realistic quality. A hieroglyph, at its best, is a refinement of intense human experience turned into physical image. In his production of *Marat/Sade,* for example, Peter Brook had Charlotte Corday flagellate de Sade with her hair. This is an essentially Artaudian image, more interesting, intense in impact, and of broader dramatic significance than any literal or staged whipping could be.

In another production a white sheet was used as a symbol throughout the piece, connecting images and denoting the action of the event. At different times the sheet was a cloak, the removal of which represented a physical stripping and metaphorical transfer of dominance. It was a serpent, representing sensuality and threat; a whip, tantalizing and punishing; and a shroud, creating the image of death. It was also an umbilical cord, and passing through the crotch of one player to the crotch of another, it became the passage of semen in the sexual act.

Actors' bodies may also be used to create collective hieroglyphs, such as the womb and vaginal passage created by the Performance Group in *Dionysus in '69*. In this image Dionysus was born through a passageway made up of naked actors pulsating and groaning in expulsive rhythms. Here the naked body of the mother, the image of birth, and a literal rite of passage is combined in one active hieroglyph compounded of the bodies of many actors who experience the event as individuals and blend their bodies in a group image at the same time. The serpent in the Open Theatre's production of that name was created in a similar manner, with a line of actors performing in a serpentine way to create the image. There was no attempt to imitate a serpent (that is, a snake), but the qualities of evil and

FIGURE 148.   Birth of Dionysus hieroglyph from *Dionysus in '69*. Note close relationship of actors to audience.   (*Courtesy, Richard Schechner*)

temptation—the serpent's action in the Garden of Eden—were blended into a poetic hieroglyph—far more interesting and dynamic than any literal imitation.

In creating an Artaudian style, lights, sounds, costumes, and the plasticity of the actors' bodies must be interrelated to create an all-embracing *mise en scène*. Images and movements enmesh with objects, silences, and aural rhythms, physically surrounding the spectators and immersing them in a constant but ever-changing bath of light, sound, and imagery to create an intense sensual impact—the experience of cruelty. It is not an easy effect to achieve, and it leaves itself open to gimmickry and self-indulgence. We have been witness to orgiastic couplings with no relationship to any dramatic action, which have left the spectators surrounding them bored, glum, and frustrated. Performers have urinated on spectators in the false belief that any display of taboo functions will have an Artaudian effect. This is equivalent to the fallacy concerning Brechtian theater, that "alienation" means insulting the audience. The Artaudian theater, as the Brechtian, provokes the audience, not offends it. It wishes to involve the audience in the event in such a way as to give it a new, holistic experience of its sensual human potential. This will only be achieved by deep commitment to the intention on the part of both actors and director—a clear sense of purpose, sincerity, discipline, and skill.

The Contemporary Influence

Though more visible in the 1960s and early 1970s, alternative theater still forms a significant part of theatrical activity today and carries the torch of theatrical experimentation. The Living Theatre, the longest-standing alternative company in the United States added, in 1979, a *Prometheus* to its long repertory of experimental work. The piece is still involved with the great human myths, a vast labyrinth of images sweeping imaginatively across the surface of human culture. The set is a central triangular scaffold and a metallic tunnel, which serves as a birth canal from which history delivers its misshapen progeny. The company discovers some magnificent hieroglyphic images, as when Prometheus is revealed as a spiderman in one of the dark geometrical caverns of the set, visible only by lights attached to his body so that when he swings and hangs upside down it is like a huge moving constellation of the heavens—an image straight out of Blake and in the finest tradition of Artaudianism.

The alternative theater in Britain has had a somewhat political cast, reflecting social and economic concerns and thereby giving it a Brechtian form, as represented by groups such as Belt and Braces, Foco Novo, and The Monstrous Regiment—this last being a feminist group dealing specifically with the place of women in society. Groups such as the 7/84, although political in orientation, have incorporated rock-and-roll music, masks, media, and direct audience confrontation into their recent work. Perhaps the Pip Simmons Theatre Group is the British company with the most radical and broadest alternative credentials. In the late 1970s the company created a production based on the work of Edgar Allen Poe, *Mask of the Red Death*. The audience was dressed in white hooded cloaks as the inmates of Prince Prospero's Gothic castle, witnessing scenes of lust and debauchery as Poe moved to his death through a moonlit graveyard. The production involved various locations and huge moving screens and incorporated many of the techniques of alternative aesthetics. In a similar mode the company's production of Shakespeare's *Tempest* saw the play as being about murder, rape, and revolution, and it was performed in a highly physical fashion with considerable nudity.

In Europe, and in Germany in particular, many elements associated with alternative theater have been incorporated into the mainstream as directorial interpretation continues to be radical. Peter Stein, a leading German director, created a highly environmental production of *As You Like It* in 1978. Set in a large open space, designed to suit the geography of the production, Stein edited the early scenes in the play cinematically, overlapping and intercutting so that the characters were seen in immediate confrontation by an audience which itself formed the court crowds. To move into the Forest of Arden, the audience walked through a long wooded labyrinth into a complete forest environment and was totally incorporated into the action. By his environment Stein fully realized the physical world of the play and made the audience a direct participant.

At the Berlin Theatertreffen in 1981, Stein produced the entirety of Aeschylus's *Oresteia* with primitive and ritualistic staging. The chorus worked within the audience space, at one time laying tracks on which Agamemnon's hand-winched chariot moved through the audience's midst. Shouts, mutterings, and prayers from the choral men were matched by elegant rituals of fire, water, and ceremonial syrups performed by the women. The performance was punctuated by the murders, in which cascades of gore were pumped from the corpses to splash in great puddles on the floor.

The Artaudian values of this production were matched, at the same festival, by a production of *Woyzeck*, retitled *Woyzeck Marie*, which explored the deepest recesses of the human soul and body. Urine, sweat, vomit, and blood were constant features of the production. Steam rose persistently from a grating in the floor of the setting, which itself underwent constant defilement. A midget in a fecal-brown baby suit cavorted around, while atop a construction hoist a bald soprano delivered a part of the throbbing, audience-jarring score. Eight lighting systems illuminated the action and represented the technology that finally destroys the title characters.

Wherever one tends to look today, there is evidence of the influence of alternative theater aesthetics—whether it be in a successful commercial

FIGURE 149. A bloodied and revengeful Clytemnestra poised above the brutalized bodies of Agamemnon and Cassandra in Peter Stein's Artaudian-influenced production of the *Oresteia,* Berlin, 1981. (*Pressbüro, Berliner Theatertreffen; photo by Ruth Walz*)

production such as *Equus,* with its physicality, nudity, and imaginative staging; an off-Broadway production such as *Strider* (directed by Robert Kalfin), in which dance, mime, and music are mixed to relate the life and hard times of a horse that metaphorically represents the Russian peasantry; or the more audacious rock-and-roll concerts, with their electronic media, assaults of light and sound, and often violent and sexual styles of performance.

Discounting the continued experimentation of the more deliberately and consciously "alternative" companies on the contemporary theatrical scene, the mainstream has, at the very least, absorbed the following elements of alternative theater aesthetics: a more physical and theatrically imaginative use of the body, less acceptance of verbal and physical taboos, the acceptance and confrontation of the audience, more flexible use of space, and the use of media effects. Thus, the contemporary director,

FIGURE 150. Mime and the actors' physicality create the "horse" in Robert Kalfin's 1979 production of *Strider.*   (*The Chelsea Theatre Center*)

whether or not he or she is working directly within the latitude of alternative theater, must be aware of and understand the stylistic possibilities and limitations of these techniques.

EXAMPLE—*MACBETH*

Before we conclude our exploration of the nature of style with some discussion of realism and naturalism, it might be useful to look at one play in terms of a range of possible stylistic interpretations, thus bringing into immediate perspective the potentialities and consequences of choices open to a director.

Looking at *Macbeth* from the viewpoint of its intrinsic givens, we know that it was written to be performed on an open thrust stage, which allowed dynamic movement and sweep of action yet also enabled an individual actor to be in a close relationship to the audience. We suspect that costuming was elaborate but restricted to the period in which the play was written, that is, early Jacobean Britain. Setting would be minimal, allowing the poetry of the play to work on the audience's imagination, and some setting may have been emblematic or heraldic. The play was written about a primitive period of Scottish history, around the eleventh century; it is filled with religious imagery as well as darkness, death, blood, and evil. There is a thrusting perpendicularity about the quality and rhythms of the play, which tends to upset the natural order—social, moral, and political. Interpretations of the play may be various but probably take into account such elements as the existence of a natural moral order, which includes the divine right of kingship; the responsibilities of a ruler to secure the state; the ethical priorities of a society; free will versus determinism; the destructiveness of ambition; and simplistically, the struggle in a man's life between good and evil and the personal responsibility for choices in moral terms.

To attempt a totally intrinsic stylistic interpretation would be to use a similar space, period costuming, and so on and to reveal the religious, moral, and political values in the play. However, probably a straightforward triumph of good over evil could seem melodramatic to a somewhat more cynical contemporary audience. A director might, therefore, wish to keep close to the play's intrinsic values but make a slightly more ambivalent statement about the nature of moral and political choices, retaining, however, the ultimately optimistic moral statement of the play. To do so might mean setting the play slightly later in the Jacobean period to emphasize physically the darker morality of that time. Elizabethan costuming might be too colorful, solid, and self-assured for the darker values of *Macbeth;* to use more blacks, grays, and silvers, overlaid with meretricious jewelery, especially for Macbeth and his wife, might emphasize the false values they embody. The setting could use black and weathered oak and some of the manorial qualities of the Jacobean period, with thrusting gables, yet remain somewhat heavy, black and gray, and oppressive. Cavernous interiors could include shadowy places and staircases, an incipient decadence relieved by shafts of light. Physically this interpretation might lend itself more to a proscenium than to an open thrust stage. Lady Macbeth's influence over Macbeth might be couched strongly in sexual terms; he has to prove his virility in terms of political power. The idea of religious ambivalence might be emphasized by costuming the weird sisters as ancient nuns; the unchanging nature of the nuns' dress over the centuries will make it easily identifiable to a contemporary audience but not anachronistic within the style of the production. Ambivalence might further be played up by making Malcolm less wholly virtuous but more politically motivated; thus the ending of the play could be optimistic without being romantic.

In some respects *Macbeth* represents a conflict between medieval and humanistic religious and moral values, and if our first interpretation shows a slightly ambivalent humanistic bias, the power and impact of medieval religiosity and superstition could be enhanced by setting the play in the eleventh century—the time in which the historical events of the play take place. *Macbeth* contains a strong intrinsic sense of primitive force, supernatural agencies, and naked power—all of which lend themselves to costuming with animal skins, leather, heavy bronze weaponry, rough woven textures, and adornment by emblems of the hunt. Open staging could emphasize the barren, rocky space of the Scottish highlands with a lot of levels and granite values. The levels would both signify the thrusting ambition of the play and provide the potential for strong, physical acting— leaping from level to level in the battle scenes, which would be violent, coarse, and bloody. The physical heroism of the play, the necessity for strength in a ruler, and the warrior values of Macbeth, Macduff, and Malcolm could be evenly balanced, which would both help the tragic values of the play and throw the final judgement onto moral superiority. In this context Lady Macbeth could clearly be seen as playing on Macbeth's sense of male pride as determined by military prowess and physical courage. An eleventh-century environment, associated in the contemporary mind with superstition and the prescientific belief in supernatural powers, would bring out the witchcraft in the play. The sense of fear, dread, and uncertainty could be played up by the use of darkness, shadowy figures, sudden apparitions, the call of wolves and hooting of owls, all of which would make believable and reinforce the power of the weird sisters, who could be played as strange and fearful old crones, emanations of the unnatural forces surrounding the play:

> but in the night, imagining some fear,
> how often doth a bush become a bear.

The importance of the supernatural, and specifically the fact of the weird sisters in the play, is one of the problems a director has to deal with in interpreting it for a modern audience. Orson Welles approached the problem, in a famous 1936 production, by setting *Macbeth* in an environment in which witchcraft, or black magic, was still a functional part of the society's beliefs. The production had a black cast and was set in nineteenth-century Haiti—which produced an immediate clash between a strong but primitive culture and the ill-fitting overlay of the values of Western civilization. It also provided a perfect location for the witchcraft in the play, as voodoo continues to be a strong element of Caribbean culture. The production utilized a naked witch doctor and primitive native masks. Five goats were sacrificed in the theater and their skins used for the drums whose constant throbbing underlined the black magic in the play: when Macbeth and Lady Macbeth were planning their murder of Duncan the drums drove them on to the deed and then accompanied Macbeth's thoughts throughout the play, like the insistent beating of a guilty conscience, conveying to him the memory of past black deeds or the suggestion of new atrocities. Set in a proscenium space, the production used a darkly threatening, lush jungle-green background out of which Macduff's barefoot native soldiers came to overthrow the ambitious Macbeth, who had given up the truth of his own cultural background to adopt the ill-fitting, garish trappings of a mere-

FIGURE 151. American Indian influence in the costuming of *Warrior*, an Artaudian adaptation of Shakespeare's *Macbeth*, conceived and directed by Laird Williamson at the Pacific Conservatory for the Performing Arts. (*Pacific Conservatory for the Performing Arts*)

tricious Western civilization. Luminous death masks for the ghosts were only one of the effects that used the chosen environment to reveal the intrinsic demands of the play; the production was highly consistent in marrying its extrinsic style to Shakespeare's theme, finding the precise equivalents of the political struggle, religious values, and superstitious aura of the play.

A more recent production, directed by Laird Williamson for the P.C.P.A. (Pacific Conservatory for the Performing Arts), which addressed the problem of a modern equivalent of medieval witchcraft chose the shamanistic religious rites of the American Indian. The production as a whole, heavily influenced by Artaudian aesthetics, was set on an open stage with a close environmental relationship to the audience. Costumed with strong overtones of American Indian dress, it approached the play as a mythic ritual, heavily emphasizing physical imagery and subordinating language. A chorus alternately illustrated the action with sounds and spoke a narrative reduced to essential elements of Shakespeare's verse. The director created some imaginative and dynamic physical hieroglyphs to communicate essential moments of action: a carousel of skeletal horses bore the ghostly Banquo and his progeny around a mesmerized Macbeth; Duncan ritualistically passed among his keening followers, red ribbons spewing from his dead and gaping mouth; Lady Macbeth was "spotted" by long talons of red wool; Macbeth was tantalized by a chorus of daggers held just beyond his reach. The production captured the primitive dynamics of the play, found a strong contemporary rationale for the witchcraft, and discovered some marvelous visual imagery to communicate part of the poetic action. But the emphasis on physicality did reduce the effect of the play's verbal poetry and sacrificed some moral resonances to external effects. This is a problem any director taking an Artaudian approach to a classical text must be aware of: one is not simply cutting language; it is poetry in which the action and themes of the play are inextricably bound up.

As political ambition is an ever-present truth of human society, *Macbeth* perhaps lends itself to modern-dress interpretations that deal with dictatorship, political corruption, and the ethical structure of a society. Costuming could run the gamut of drab battlefield dress, gray-suited bureaucracy, and formal evening dress. The dignity and elegance of evening dress would provide an accommodating milieu for the speaking of verse—always a problem in modern-dress productions. One could also visualize Lady Macbeth in a striking deep red gown, urging on the tuxedoed Macbeth to murder. Faceless, bureaucratic hit men in pinstripe suits could eliminate Banquo and the Macduff family. The weird sisters could be battlefield molls, fortune tellers, or any of the strange assortment of displaced camp followers that modern warfare throws up. Staging could be a modern equivalent of Elizabethan: bare forestage with levels achieved by scaffolding. Perhaps the stage could gradually accumulate the technological bric-à-brac, half-destroyed, to be found around any modern battlefield, giving a sense of the breakdown of the society based on military power; this could be cleared up when Malcolm succeeds at the end of the play. If the director wished to press home political analogies, he or she could choose a very specific environment in which political ambition ran riot. There is no lack of contemporary examples, from a Watergate to a White House in which an ambitious political general was involved in a power struggle with the president.

A director who wished to concentrate on the political values of the play might also decide to take a Brechtian approach. This would be perfectly possible but we should, in all honesty, suggest that if a director were interested in a Brechtian production dealing with political ambition and moral corruption, he or she should probably do *The Resistible Rise of Arturo Ui*. The epic structure of *Macbeth* equates with Brecht's sense of plot progression, but the demands of Brechtian staging are likely to place the production on a proscenium rather than a thrust stage. Here, again, the stark, nonillusionistic nature of Brecht's settings—with overt technology, a steely perpendicular space with glaring light and shadow—will create a modern Elizabethan equivalent and serve many of the intrinsic values of this play. Costuming would probably be nonspecific in historical terms, with recognizable modern overtones; masks might be used to good effect if the ghost and apparition scenes were handled that way. Another way to handle the ghost scenes is by the use of projections and media; and it is probably here that the givens of a Brechtian style are most useful to a production of *Macbeth*. The witchcraft in the play, the apparitions, and the battlefield scenes could all be handled by media. Whether the director decides to make the witches an emanation of Macbeth's inner psyche, or actually to have a visual presence in more concrete terms, the use of film and projections adds a dimension that equates with the supernatural. Moreoever, in terms of reinforcing the themes of the play, the battle sequences could be played against a background film of carnage caused by military ambition; and Macbeth's recollection of his past sins as they close in on him could be given broader resonances by a collage of contemporary political assassination, or more broadly still, political martyrs throughout human history.

We have briefly discussed six possible stylistic approaches to *Macbeth*. This by no means exhausts the potential of this tensile dynamic play which lends itself to a strong interpretational approach. The play could, for example, be looked at expressionistically, as an exploration of the psychological imbalance of Macbeth's mind. It could be set against black drapes with one central blood-red carpeted staircase, on which the action of ambition rises and finally falls. Three huge shamanistic masks could be the sources of light, probing the action and Macbeth's mind. Any interpretation will enhance certain values of the play and give less weight to others. We believe all the interpretations we have suggested to be possible and valid, though we acknowledge that some are closer to the perceived intrinsic qualities of the play. It is the director's task to find the right means, for that time and place, with which to express the essential idea of the play. If directors interpret the play responsibly, and not capriciously, and evolve their stylistic choices consistently from their premise, their production should succeed in engaging the audience in a fresh and stimulating theatrical experience.

REALISM AND NATURALISM

We have consciously left realism and naturalism to the end of this discussion of style, not because we feel them to be any less significant, but on the contrary, because—being the predominant modes of the twentieth century—they are likely to be the styles most familiar to actors and directors and, therefore, need the least explication. Not only are they the styles most familiar to young directors—certainly through the all-pervading impact of film and television—but because they purport to be based on contemporary life experiences, they are apt to need less contrivance from both actors and directors to create the necessary effect.

Realism is a somewhat catchall term applied fairly generally to those productions in which all the actions are more or less drawn from life; the settings are a reasonable approximation of a "real" environment; the language is not unduly contrived or rhetorical; and the director interposes himself enough to keep the actors in informal yet open positions, the characters tolerably believable, and the pace fluent and snappy. As a genre it has prospered since the mid-nineteenth century when Madame Vestris started to use box sets to narrow down the theater's purview into the room in which democratic people lived most of their lives. Into this room Tom Robertson introduced "cup and saucer" realism, and he was followed by Ibsen who brought in the social problems of the middle class. This development was based on the principle that the impact of the play's discussions on the audience would be enhanced if placed within an environment to which the individual could immediately relate, saying, "Oh, yes, my drawing room [or parlor] is just like that." Realism has tended to become the style in which one produces Lanford Wilson, Peter Schaeffer, Neil Simon, and most other commercial playwrights.

One of the problems with realism is that life constantly moves on. If directors were to do *Plaza Suite* or *Barefoot in the Park* in the year 2001, would they set it in New York in the 1970s or update it to the twenty-first century. Similarly, the realistic elements that drew an immediate response

FIGURE 152.   External realism in *The Whip,* London, 1909.   (*Crown Copyright Theatre Museum Victoria & Albert Museum*)

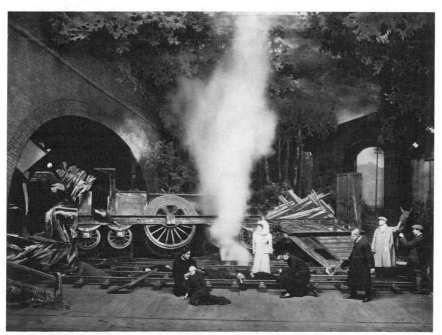

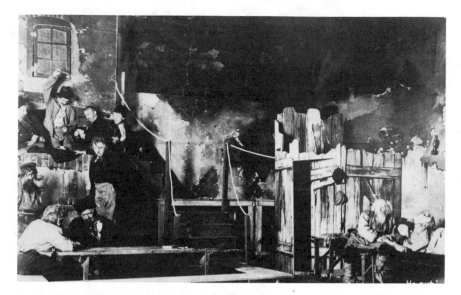

FIGURE 153. Naturalism in a 1903 Berlin production of Maxim Gorki's *The Lower Depths*. *(Deutsches Theatermuseum, Früher Clara Ziegler-Stiftung)*

from Ibsen's audience in the 1880s might seem somewhat archaic in the 1980s. Realism is partly a genre and partly a contemporary style, and a director will have to decide how far the specific furnishings, costumes, manners, and so on of a particular period are an intrinsic structure necessary to reveal the play's social themes and how far they may or should be updated. For example, does *A Doll's House* have more impact on a contemporary audience if it is given a modern setting; or does its relevance to the women's movement depend on the very fact that it relates to the social condition of women in an earlier period? On the other hand, a play such as *Barefoot in the Park,* which does not rely on historical background for thematic impact but is concerned with human relationships at a more general level, may seem hopelessly dated unless set in the period for which it is being performed, for example, 2001.

 Realism works from the premise that the stage environment is a correct illusionistic representation of real-life circumstances, but it may not be deeply concerned with the inner workings of character. External detail can predominate in a production, as when Belasco re-created the detail of Child's Restaurant on the New York stage. Realism can go for effect more than motivation. *Naturalism,* on the other hand, takes the position that what is happening on the stage *is* life, or at least a highly selected "slice of life," which the audience simply happens to be looking in on.

 Theoretically no concession should be made to the presence of an audience at a naturalistic production: staging is geared to produce the effect that the stage is simply a room with its fourth wall removed. This requirement will still involve exercising a number of directorial options, and the logic of the director's choices will determine where the production lies along the realism-naturalism continuum. For example, lighting in naturalistic productions should emanate from actual sources in the set; it should avoid hard edges and artificial shadows, blending the textures of the set and the figures of the actors into a lifelike whole. The set itself should appear lived in, not newly built and painted for the theatrical occasion; there should be no cut-out trees that wobble when touched or flats that shake when doors are slammed; doors should be slammable. Similarly, costumes should show appropriate wear (no beggars in clean, pressed rags), contain no obvious "character detail," and work with the physical environment.

As with the physical environment of the production, so with the staging of the action. Balance will be informal—no creation of stage pictures for aesthetic effect—and movement apparently random, recapitulating the casual patterns of life. Actors will not be conscious of working in open positions, and they may turn their backs to the audience. The first great naturalistic theater, Antoine's Théâtre Libre, was sometimes known as "the theater of Antoine's back!" There is likely to be a good deal of small business in naturalistic productions, with characters smoking cigarettes, drinking coffee, swinging their legs, and playing with their hair or moustache. It should be remembered, however, that such business should not be simply gratuitous but should have some relationship to character or action.

As to acting, we have already dealt with methods and approaches at some length in Chapter 8, and we will simply mention here a few likely stylistic options of naturalism. Dialect, rather than pure stage speech, will probably be used; lines may overlap, and some small ad-libbing is possible. Line delivery is almost certain to have a broken pattern, with lines split up and interjections used. Gestures can be small—depending on the size of the house—and somewhat intimate or private. As naturalism is concerned with the sociopsychology of ordinary human beings in everyday situations, it seeks to reveal what makes people tick—inner truths—and will thus tend to be introspective, inner working, and emotionally understated.

The very attempt to create on the stage the appearance of nonstaged action is a great challenge to a director, and perhaps the finest tribute he or she can be paid is that the play did not seem "directed" at all. Naturalism is, finally, theater as free from art and artifice as art and artifice can make it.

SUMMARY

John Gielgud once said of style that it was "knowing what kind of play you are in." Style might also be defined as the realism of a particular period as communicated through the theatrical conventions of that period. Taking these two statements together provides an excellent starting point for approaching style: the necessity of knowing the given circumstances of the text and the theater for which it was written, so as to avoid the distortion that comes from ignorance. In other words, discovering the intrinsic style of a play provides the soundest basis for a production. On the other hand, as John Barton has suggested, every time a director does a new production of a play he or she inevitably reinterprets it to some degree. The style of any production does not have to—indeed cannot—slavishly reproduce the focus and detail of the first production. Extrinsic stylistic interpretations can project the intrinsic values of a play in new directions and new guises to keep up with changing technology and social, political, and moral attitudes.

Style may run the gamut of the theatrical spectrum; it may be many things, but it should not be arbitrary. It should be responsible in relating the production values of the event to the intrinsic values of the text; and it should be consistent in relating the two worlds of the stage and the play to the world of the audience. Each theatrical event contains its own truth, which is communicated through its style; the same truth may be revealed in many different ways, but if it is not present, the event will fail. Peter Brook wrote in *The Empty Space,*

> All the different elements of staging—the shorthands of behavior that stand for certain emotions: gestures, gesticulations, tones of voice—are fluctuating on an invisible stock exchange all the time. Life is moving, influences are playing on actor and audience, and other plays, other arts, the cinema, television, current events join in the constant rewriting of history and the amending of the daily truth. . . . A living theatre that thinks it can stand aloof from anything so trivial as fashion will wilt. In the theatre, every form once born is mortal; every form must be reconceived, and its new conception will bear the marks of all the influences that surround it. In this sense the theatre is relativity. Yet a great theatre is not a fashion house; perpetual elements do recur and certain fundamental issues do underlie all dramatic activity. The deadly trap is to divide the eternal truths from the subtle variations; this is a form of snobbery and it is fatal.[4]

"The deadly trap is to divide the eternal truths from the subtle variations." The contemporary director's challenge is to avoid the "deadly trap." He or she does so by insightful understanding of the playwright's work and responsible and creative translation of this work into an imaginative, meaningful, and dynamic stylistic statement for his or her own time.

---

[4]Peter Brook, *The Empty Space* (New York: Atheneum Publishers, 1968), p. 16.

TEN

Putting It Together

In the previous chapters we have discussed the general areas of directorial concern—areas where directors play a vital role in the process of putting on a play.

In this chapter we would like to suggest something of a schedule of directorial acts: the orderly process of directorial creativity as it is usually carried out.

There is, of course, no set schedule of directorial duties, nor could there be. Directors vary in their skills and temperaments; plays generate different sorts of demands; actors, designers, theater companies, and local cultural traditions impose scheduling priorities that run roughshod over any "model" timetable. Nonetheless, there is a general order of production development (both for the preparation of full-length plays and directed classroom scenes) that can be abstracted from the practice of most American and European professional companies, one that holds true for most academic and community theaters as well, and which will prove to be a useful "standard" for the beginning director to start from.

This order of production can be divided into twelve identifiable phases prior to opening night, phases that themselves divide into four general periods:

FIRST PERIOD: *SPECULATING*

1. Selecting the play
2. Researching
3. Conceptualizing

SECOND PERIOD: *PLANNING*

4. Budgeting*
5. Scheduling
6. Staffing*
7. Designing
8. Casting

THIRD PERIOD: *CREATING*

9. Rehearsing
10. Building*

FOURTH PERIOD: *CONSOLIDATING*

11. "Teching"*
12. Dressing

Although there is nothing sacred about this order, its logic is obvious. It is impossible to cast a play that has not been selected or to rehearse a play that has not been cast. And directors who decide to conceptualize their material after it has been designed and built will inspire something less than confidence from their coworkers. We will take a look at each of these phases in some detail in the coming pages, breaking them down into the various steps by which a director will turn thoughts into action and speculation into a complete and well-worked-out production.

FIRST PERIOD: *SPECULATING*

The period of speculation takes place entirely in the director's mind; it is therefore a period of great freedom, where the imagination may be relatively unbridled and the creativity may be relatively unrestrained. In this

---

*(Phases marked with an asterisk are *not* ordinarily involved in the direction of class-room scenes).

period there are few deadlines; no anxious coworkers awaiting instructions; and no pressures to get platforms built, lights set, or cue sheets written.

Instead the director is wrestling with his or her own ideas and impulses. Shall it be a modern dress *Macbeth?* An outdoor *Bacchae?* An in-the-round *Endgame?* An improvisation in the streets? A new play? A definitive reconstruction of a nineteenth-century melodrama on the high school auditorium stage? A repertory of Shaw in a rented metropolitan theater? A scene from Chekhov for directing class? What do I want to *do* with the material? Why present it at all? What is *important* about the material? What is *entertaining* about it?

The speculative period, naturally, is a period of questions. It is also a period of research, of investigation, and of the formulation of working solutions—or, at least—of starting points toward solutions. The period may take anywhere from a week to several years; often directors speculate on plays for more than a decade before committing themselves to production. Sometimes it takes a decade to generate the opportunity to direct a certain play, and much of that decade can be spent in such speculations. On the other hand, directing opportunities (or challenges) can also arise quite suddenly, in which case the speculative period is quite compressed. In either case, the comprehensiveness of the director's speculative inquiry will prove to be a mark of the final complexity and depth of the work.

Phase One: Selecting the Play

Most play productions begin with a director choosing dramatic material—not *all* play productions, of course; professionally, plays are more generally selected by producers or artistic directors, who then hire directors to direct them. A notable case in point was the 1981 Broadway production of *The Little Foxes,* which was selected after Elizabeth Taylor had been chosen to play a role on Broadway. In that situation, the "star" preceded both the play and the director (Austin Pendleton): a clear case of drama-as-vehicle, which is a common Broadway arrangement.

Still, the preponderance of play productions feature material chosen and shaped by the directors who are entrusted with their realization, and would-be directors are well advised to carry in their heads a selection of plays, both old and new, that are "in speculative preparation" while the directors await the opportunity to turn "speculative" into "active."

The staging of *new* plays is of immense benefit to a director's career, in that the director not only interprets material but "discovers" it as well, enjoying the opportunity to work with the playwright in revisions and to determine to some extent the shaping of the play's initial theatrical appearance. Most American directors of importance earned their reputations through stagings of original works, including Elia Kazan (*Death of a Sales-*

man, A Streetcar Named Desire, Tea and Sympathy, The Skin of Our Teeth) and Harold Prince (*Sweeney Todd, Company, Follies*). Many European directors, by contrast, develop their careers through exciting revivals of classic works; many of the leading German directors, for example, specialize entirely in the classics, and England's Trevor Nunn, artistic director of the Royal Shakespeare Company, has reportedly never directed an original play in his life. (Nicholas Nickleby being an adaptation.)

How do directors go about choosing a play to direct? Or a scene for directing class? There is usually one overriding reason—because the material appeals to them. That appeal may be artistic or commercial; we would hope that it is both. The play appeals as a work of insight, intelligence, sensuality, theatricality, humor, and/or dramatic impact, and these values encourage the director to think that others would be interested in supporting the production by investing time and money as financial backers, producers, actors, technicians, and—most important—members of the audience.

For the audience is the other main concern in choosing a play; there simply is no theater without an audience to attend it. The audience may be a small one; it may even be a compelled one (as is the audience of fellow students in a directing class); but there must be a reasonable expectation of attracting an acceptable audience before a production idea becomes viable. Neil Simon on Broadway? Experience suggests "yes." *Troilus and Cressida* in a dinner theater? Experience suggests "no." But one can never be sure. *Waiting for Godot* in San Quentin prison seemed dubious at best, but Herbert Blau's 1957 production there proved legendary. Chekhov and Euripides in summer stock seemed out of the question, but Nikos Psacharopolous's Williamstown Summer Theater demonstrated the triumph of the unthinkable time and time again in the 1970s and 1980s.

Adapting nondramatic material.   The selection of *nondramatic material* is an option more and more directors are turning to. Trevor Nunn's brilliant adaptation of Charles Dickens's novel, *Nicholas Nickleby* (London, 1981) and Eric Bentley's cutting and pasting of the House Un-American Activities Committee transcripts (*Are You Now or Have You Ever Been,* 1975) are two examples of directorially inspired productions adapted from narrative material with outstanding success. Director Frederick Newmann's stage adaptation of Beckett's novel *Mercier and Camier,* produced by Mabou Mines at the New York Public Theatre in 1979, departed from the novel while remaining based on it—sort of a directorial extrapolation of a novelist's characters and themes. There is nothing to prevent directors from taking an active role in the creation of material, as opposed to the mere selection of plays: some of the finest theatrical experiences of recent years have been the shapings of actor-improvisations, novelists' narratives, and newsworthy transcripts and documents, with the resulting "play" something that is only

FIGURE 154. A scene from Trevor Nunn's *Nicholas Nickleby,* which was adapted by the Royal Shake-spear Company from Dickens's novel to great success in 1981. (*Photo by Chris Davies*)

published, if at all, after the production that provides its crucial theatrical form.

Acquiring rights.   Selected material does not necessarily mean acquired material. For any production where audiences are solicited, legal rights to produce the material must be acquired, usually through negotiation. Although this requirement does not apply to scenes presented in a directing class—ordinarily—understanding the reality of rights acquisition is vital for a director.

Dramatic works—as well as novels or published nonfiction works that might be adaptable to the stage—are protected by copyright and are the property of their authors; permission of the authors, or the authors' representatives, is therefore required for the production of any play other than those in the "public domain," that is, those written before the copyright laws were written or those whose copyrights have expired. Present copyright laws protect dramatic works for the lifetime of the author plus twenty-five years; earlier laws protected works for two consecutive twenty-eight year terms (fifty-six years in all); therefore, in general, material written in the previous three or four decades is ordinarily subject to copyright restrictions.

Most published plays, following their initial commercial runs, are leased to one of the major play-leasing companies (Samuel French Inc. and the Dramatists' Play Service are the largest of these), which make them available to amateur producers on a fixed royalty basis. Commercial rights for professional productions are negotiated, normally, directly with the author's personal agent. Rights to musical plays are generally held by specialized leasing companies (Music Theater International and Tams-Witmark, Inc., are the major ones in the United States), whose royalties are figured on a sliding scale, depending on the size of the theater and the price of admission. Musical royalties often include a required rental fee for scripts and scores, which generally exist only in privately printed or mimeographed form.

Obviously a director's first task is to secure the permission to present a play. *New plays* can often be acquired for production directly from the author; professionally this is done through agents and with the payment of an option fee, which permits the director to produce the play within a certain period of time, usually six months. Option contracts can be complicated, and various constraints are often put on them by the actor's union; still, the option to produce a new play is a worthwhile investment for a would-be director in that it presents splendid opportunities for creating an original theatrical experience.

Translating, adapting, and revising. Most often, directors select finished playscripts that are already stageworthy. However, there are many situations in which the director will choose material that still requires substantial alteration before further steps may be taken toward production. The material may be a play in a foreign language, for example, in which case it must first be translated. Or the material may be a nondramatic work that requires rewriting in a dramatic format. Or the play may be a new one, and the director may wish to collaborate with the author on revisions. All of these are opportunities for major creative shaping by the director at the earliest stages of production.

Bilingual directors may wish to translate plays themselves, if they feel they have the appropriate literary gifts. This would insure that they have the final voice in the play's tone and interpretation, and they can shape the play definitively in its major climaxes, comic bits, and confrontations. A director who translates a play in the public domain (that is, unprotected by copyright) then "owns" the rights to that translation and need not negotiate further with play-leasing houses or authors—an important consideration professionally. Lacking the translator's facility, directors can choose from available translations or commission someone to translate in collaboration;

occasionally, when two or more translations are in the public domain, directors can collate what they consider the best parts of two or more translations. *It makes a difference.* Translations vary markedly in meaning, wit, power, speakability, and eloquence. Some published translations, designed for the Broadway stage of past decades, alter fundamental concepts of the original scripts; others, intended for reading audiences only, are hopelessly wooden. Indeed, few translators have the gift of *theater* that dramatic authors flourish by; rare is the translation that does not diminish the original. ("Translator—Traitor!" goes the Italian expression.) With more than a dozen published translations of some classic plays (*Oedipus Rex,* for example), directors may well spend several weeks choosing the translation most suitable to their overall design.

Dramatic adaptations of nondramatic works will almost always fall to the directors themselves, since it is fundamentally the *idea* of adapting such and such a literary or documentary property to the stage that must inspire both the dramatizing and the directing. For major projects, outside writers are often brought in (as with *Nicholas Nickleby*), but in most cases directors will spend many hours at the typewriter putting their ideas into dialogue, speech headings, and stage directions. André Gregory's *Alice and Wonderland* and Paul Sills's *Story Theater* were notable director-created pieces in this country; and director Peter Zadek's extraordinary *Jeder stribt für sich allein,* adapted from the World War II novel by Hans Fallada into a five-hour extravaganza with scathingly satirical review sketches (for example, "Nazis are so sexy"), was one of the great successes of the 1981 Berlin theatrical season.

Directors who adapt works have the same high level of control over the shaping of their material as director-translators do; they also "own" the works they create (provided that the original sources are not protected by copyright) and can therefore move their productions to larger and/or more professional theaters if original engagements prove successful.

But the most common involvement for the director at this step of script development does not involve "owning" a script but collaborating with a playwright in the creation of a new play. It is this directorial function which has distinguished fine directors like Louis Jouvet, Elia Kazan, Gordon Davidson, Mike Nichols, Harold Prince, Marshall Mason, and John Dexter, and which gives directors a lasting place in the history of dramatic literature.

Often the director's participation involves only the play's premiere production, although on some occasions playwrights rework their plays during the first three or four productions, usually as they go "up" the ladder from showcase to regional theater to Broadway productions. Sometimes, too, a playwright will rework a long successful play that seems to have further potential; Tennessee Williams, for example, continually revised works more than three decades old. The director works with the playwright, of course, only at the playwright's prerogative; the playwright, both in the ethics and the contracts of the theater, has the last word on the play's text. But that prerogative is usually given: positive directorial influence on playscripts is a generally accepted fact.

The director-playwright collaboration is often carried on by correspondence, which gives us the advantage of peering into it when those discussions are later published. The letters between Elia Kazan and Archibald MacLeish concerning Kazan's suggested revisions for the poet's *J.B.* are a beautiful example of the methods by which directors can shape the scripts they direct before the rehearsal period.[1] More often, the collaboration is carried off in informal discussions, with a good deal of give and take on both sides.

In translating (or choosing a translation), adapting, and collaborating with the playwright, directors virtually assume a quasi-playwriting role themselves, and a background of playwriting is certainly worthwhile for would-be directors. The director shares with the playwright a centrality in the theater's creative structure; both are individuals who *generate* productions and who must be able to envision overall theatrical effects and designs while still working in the privacy of their own heads. Perhaps the director will never write a play or translate a play or even adapt a play, but the feeling that he or she is creating theater out of nothing—a feeling that the playwright must share—must be part of his or her imaginative powers.

Phase Two: Researching

The director's research begins with the play and then extends to the world of the play, the world of the playwright, and the play's fundamental themes and ideas. Beyond that it may extend into pertinent areas of politics, history, psychology, aesthetics, theater history, dramatic theory, and theater technology. It may involve, as well as reading, looking through art books and listening to records. It may be an immersion that lasts for weeks or months or even years.

The directors must be *experts* on the plays they direct; not only that, they must be *perceived* as experts. Their ideas must be capable of articulate expression; their plans must be translatable into concrete detail. The breadth of a director's knowledge must encompass all those peripheral areas from which actors and designers will find inspiration; the director's research must not simply focus on the narrow issues that the play makes explicit but must also provide a solid foundation for wide-ranging discovery within the text and the theatrical experiments and improvisation that will implement the text in rehearsal.

Reading the play is, naturally, the starting point for directorial re-

[1]*Esquire Magazine*, May 1960.

search. A solid background knowledge of the author's works, if the author is established, is also expected, as is an understanding in depth of the play's period. Ignorant in these areas, directors will have to remedy their insufficiencies quickly, for designers and cast members will expect (and have a right to expect) directorial authority in these subjects.

Breaking down the script.   This is the time to break the script down into its given constituent units, uncovering the underlying dramatic structure and anticipating the demands of production. How many intermissions are suggested? How many sets? How many actors? How many costumes? The answers at this point are merely speculative, but the director is beginning to take apart the script so as to explore its separate ingredients.

The script breakdown goes on to outline the acts, scenes, French scenes, and sometimes, the action units of the play (see pages 25–27). This outline becomes the raw material for developing the conceptualization and planning; it also suggests the full scope of the production and the breadth of the creative options open to the director. The outline can extend into analysis of the play's dramaturgy: where are the climaxes and high points? where does the play turn? where are the major "builds"?

This is also the time to study the play's language, to look up unfamiliar words and references, to research the play's allusions and speech patterns. Why is the syntax of the speeches just so? What is the dialect? The extent of the play's vocabulary? Its speaking style?

Many directors annotate their working scripts quite heavily prior to rehearsals, so as to have the fruits of their research at immediate recall in the coming weeks. Some directors use this time to write formal or informal essays on the play which can serve later as opening remarks to the cast or as program notes or published articles.

Outside sources of research.   Literary and dramatic criticism, including reviews of previous productions, form a secondary body of material for directorial research: what does the play mean to other people? What have other critics and directors found interesting about the play? Found difficult? Found wanting? The author's own remarks may be consulted: what did the playwright intend this work to say? What did he or she like about its original production? What did he or she dislike? No opinion, of course, is sacrosanct—even the author's. No critical evaluation, and no production, can be considered absolutely "definitive," despite the fact that some are likely to be considered especially memorable. The director's interpretation will, in the end, be unique and personal, certainly not a product of research alone, but research can help to inform and clarify that interpretation.

Visual, musical, and technological research forms a third body of material. What kind of *colors* seem to suit the play: Rembrandt gold? Picasso rose? Chartres blue? What kind of music? Many directors turn quickly to new theatrical technologies for inspiration: what is happening with holograms, plastics, or body microphones?

Naturally, in all these areas, a director's background knowledge is the first step, but directorial research takes those first steps in new directions and to greater ends. A play should not simply be "done" off the top of the director's head: every play, every directed scene, should be studied freshly, explored creatively, and imagined in terms of an *advancing* theater rather than a static one: a theater that breaks boundaries rather than accedes to them. Active, creative research is the foundation for these advances.

The dramaturg.   Some directors have the good fortune to work in collaboration with a *dramaturg*, a literary advisor attached to some repertory theaters, particularly in Germany where the term developed more than two hundred years ago. The *dramaturg*, in addition to providing the director with the fruits of his or her extensive research, is often expected to supply program notes and background essays in support of the production and its interpretation. More often, at least in America, directors will do this themselves.

Indeed, the results of directorial research often develop a life of their own, coming to public attention through published articles or books following the production itself. In the German theater, publication of texts, together with directorial commentaries, is fairly standard as an accompaniment to dramatic revivals; usually these publications are sold in the lobby, and often they are available in bookstores as significant editions of the plays themselves. At the Colorado Shakespeare Festival, directors of each season's works are expected to write an article on their views of the play in the festival's own journal, *On Stage.* The published criticism and commentaries of leading directors, particularly Peter Brook, Richard Schechner, Tyrone Guthrie, and Harold Clurman are important works in their own right. Therefore the director-as-*dramaturg* affects not only the immediate information fed into the production but also the context, the intellectual climate, in which the production will be received and in which the play will, in the future, be understood.

Phase Three: Conceptualizing

As the research proceeds, conceptualizing overtakes it. From studying the play, the playwright's world, and the visual and aural adjuncts that may play a part in that world, the director begins to visualize, to imagine, and to shape the eventual production. The process of conceptualization is a step from *passive* to *active* concentration, from *understanding* to *creating* a piece of theater.

Conceptualizing does not simply mean reducing a play to a single stated concept ("Dreaded word—'concept,'" said one important reviewer after a refreshingly plain 1981 *Macbeth*); it *does* mean putting into articulate form those elements that distinguish one production of a play from another. It is *defining:* what the play is about, what the general look of the production is likely to be, how the characters will relate to each other, and how the actors will relate to the text and to the characters they play. It combines interpretations, design, and style; it is the starting point in communicating production goals to designers, actors, and staff.

Clearly the first step in conceptualizing is deriving an intrinsic interpretation of the text: what happens in the play and what it means. Concision is crucial here, determining the *main* lines of action and the *overriding* meanings of the play, for these will be the focal points of the entire theatrical realization.

From there the director may wish to develop an *extrinsic* interpretation: what should be consciously emphasized in *this* production, what is particularly important for *this* audience, what is particularly fascinating to *this* director. Are there glimmers of intrinsic meaning that seem touched on too lightly in the text—meanings that could be brought out more openly by particularly forthright staging or cutting or casting or lighting? What kind of people are the play's characters? How *could* they be cast? What kind of person is going to play *this* Hamlet? A teenager? A Renaissance courtier? An overweight intellectual? A woman? Three different people in alternation? And why?

What will be emphasized in the play's look and feel? In *Hamlet,* for example, should the courtly pageantry be played up? The Senecan revenge elements? The existential fatalism? The supernatural appearances? The eroticism of thwarted sexual relationships? Should the play suggest Viking Denmark? Gothic Europe? Northern Renaissance humanism?

Where will the play be staged? Outdoors? In the round? Behind a proscenium? On a bare stage? On platforms? What *kind* of staging? Extravagant? Lavish? Spartan? Cold? Romantic? Sensual? Earthy? Improvisational? In the audience? Militant? Polemical? Lush? Profound? Violent? Rambunctious? Mile-a-minute? Three-ring-circus? Grandiose? Epic? Cruel? Naked? Animalistic? Dirty? Wet? Brittle? Austere? Gaudy? Cacophonous? Absurd? Madhouse? Ritualistic? Metaphysical? Demonic?

The conceptualization may be defined by association. If a director says, "I'm going to direct *Macbeth* like a Wagnerian opera," the designers will have a vivid shorthand reference to the director's conceptual intentions; that phrase alone (provided the director and designers have comparable understandings of Wagnerian operas) is perhaps enough to stimulate some first working drawings toward an eventual production. Or the conceptualization may be more direct: "*Hamlet* in modern dress, emphasizing the issues of political tyranny and rebellion." "*Oedipus* in the round, in primitive dress, with the chorus surrounding the audience. Focus on the paradox: to find oneself is to blind oneself." "A lush production of *A*

Streetcar Named Desire, emphasizing the romanticism of the New Orleans environment, the late 1940s era, and the affectations of Williams's southern heroines." All of these are clear, concise, and provocative.

Preparing the script.   At about this time, the director is working on the script. Already the script has been pasted into a promptbook, allowing for extensive marginal notes derived from the director's research; now into the promptbook are entered ideas for staging certain moments, first notes for costumes and lighting, and most important, initial decisions on the script itself. Characters can be added; others can be deleted or combined. Scene changes can be made so as to either require or eliminate intermissions. A basic scenery and costume plan for the production should be determined: multiple sets, single sets, unit sets, or no sets, as the conception suggests and the expected budget delimits.

If there is cutting to be done, this is the time to do it—before roles are assigned to actors who may resent intrusion into "their" parts. Cutting may highlight or emphasize certain elements in a text or merely shorten the time of production, allowing the audience to get home by midnight, for example. An uncut production of *Hamlet* would run at least five hours, and few directors are willing to extend the audience's patience with the Danish prince for that duration. (Hamlet himself speaks of cutting the play-within-the-play: when Polonius complains that a speech of the player is "too long," Hamlet replies, "It shall to the barber's, with your beard." Shakespeare quite probably approved of cutting *Hamlet* in performance too.)

Cutting must be accomplished without violating the sense of the scene or the rhythm of the play; inexpert cutting often distorts characters, spoils climaxes, and aborts dramatic poetry. Effective cutting, on the other hand, trims repetitive material and no longer meaningful references in such a way as to tighten and intensify a play's power and meaning. Cutting a text is a painstaking job requiring great dramatic and literary flair on the part of the director; mistakes can be disastrous. (Gerald Freedman's *Peer Gynt* production in Central Park retained the play's funeral scene but not the previous scene explaining who the buried man was—thus making the retained scene incomprehensible.) Cutting, therefore, should be considered very carefully, with the cut text read aloud at every juncture, making certain that the cutting in fact improves the script and doesn't simply butcher it.

Script frontmatter—lists.   The final step in script preparation is a series of lists and notes, which ordinarily go into the front of the production book as working documents. The script breakdown of acts, scenes, and French scenes is entered into the book as a table of contents and paginated so that the director can find each scene immediately in the text. A firm list of characters can be assembled, which will shortly become the casting call, determining what roles will be sought in auditions. A costume list and a property list can be made; also a list of musical numbers, a list of musical cues, a list of sound cues, and a list of special effects. These lists are all "working" lists—they will be modified several times as the work proceeds—but they create the raw material from which budgeting and planning can go forward. And the director's preliminary staging notes, or rough ideas for ground plans, can be entered into the book as well, along with the ideas and concepts that the director has managed to put in writing during the conceptualizing phase.

SECOND PERIOD: *PLANNING*

To this point, the director's work has been entirely speculative: that is to say, the director has worked entirely in his or her own mind, has not engaged any coworkers, and with the exception of purchasing a copy of the play and a looseleaf notebook, has not spent any money. No production may ensue from all this work; indeed, the bookshelves of many directors are well filled with such hypothetical promptbooks, or production proposals, that have not yet been put into actual use. All this work has been done, to a certain extent, at leisure: there have yet been no deadlines to meet and no pressure of time on the decision-making process. And all this work has been "artistic" in the purest sense. No compromises have had to be forged—thus far. No leadership battles, no communication breakdowns, no budgetary binds, no illnesses or accidents, and no equipment breakdowns have marred the process. But it is time to become practical. From this point on, the production leaves the director's mind and becomes involved with people, money, space, and time—*real* time, with time's demands.

The *planning period* is one in which people and space are engaged, money is raised, and timetables are established. It is basically the period in which the conceptualization is given its implementing forces, and in which ideas become decisions and decisions become commitments. The planning period can be short or long, depending on many factors, but the universal truth of this period is that decisions once made and committed cannot be subsequently changed without the gravest of consequences. So it becomes a period of great directorial responsibility; virtually every decision made in these days or weeks will show up on the stage months later.

Phase Four: Budgeting

The practicalities of the theater are never so apparent as when a budget must be considered, for the theater can rarely operate apart from a fiscal base. Even the first known theater, that of ancient Greece, was depen-

dent on local patrons selected by the state to provide funds for the costumes and properties of Greek tragedies.

In the professional theater, the budgeting function falls to a producer
and his or her staff, but the budget proposals are based, ultimately, on
some sort of directorial conceptualization. In college and community theaters, the director often takes the producer's role as well; therefore an
understanding of budgeting is essential for every director.

The costs of production include the rental of theater and rehearsal
space; utilities; dramatic royalties; salaries; allocations for scenery, costumes, props, sound, and lighting; scripts; and publicity. In the professional theater, salaries and publicity will be the dominant items; in amateur
theater, scenery and costumes usually prove the chief expenses. College
students, who are used to assuming the availability of theaters, equipment,
air conditioning, and a large pool of volunteer actors and technicians, often
forget that they are blessed in the use of facilities and personnel that would
cost dearly in the outside world. Budgets for major professional theatrical
productions have exceeded two million dollars and continue to rise. No
director should be oblivious to the costs of play production, including the
hidden costs that are "free" in some situations but shall have to be reckoned
with if the play is to move to another theater.

Dealing with a production budget makes a director come to grips with
the fundamental compromises and trade-offs that are an inevitable part of
theater practice. There is no such thing as an unlimited budget; directors
are continually forced to decide, for example, whether it is more important
to use real linen in the costumes or hire a "name" actor for a certain role—
items that have nothing in common but their cost. Budgeting starts, of
course, at the selection process: the royalties for a Broadway comedy are
higher than for Shakespeare; but then the costs for costumes in Shakespeare, ordinarily, are higher than for a Broadway comedy. Conceptualization can never be divorced from money: an austere modern-dress *Tartuffe*
will almost certainly cause fewer financial problems than an historically
based production of the same play,—where wigging costs alone could
prove exorbitant. Budgeting decisions seem at first glance to be inartistic
and limiting, and to an extent they are; still, the production budget is the
foundation of theatrical *reality*, and no director can, in practice, ignore its
constraints.

Budgeting takes place gradually, as the production moves from the
speculative to the planning period; naturally the actual budget cannot be
precisely determined until the play has been designed and individual design elements are costed out, a process that takes place continually in the
planning period. But the initial budgetary allocations, or limits, should be
set as early as possible. Directors should know, for example, whether it is
more important to have lavish costumes or to hire live musicians—if they
can't have both. They should know whether they're planning on having a

$50 set or a $10,000 set, for this figure will certainly play a part in whom they will be able to attract as the scene designer. They should know whether there will be funds and staff available to build costumes or to rent them or to gather them out of actors' wardrobes and costume storage outlets. And they should know that they have the kind of money available to direct the kind of production they are planning to put on.

Phase Five: Scheduling

Productions develop in time, and as more and more people become involved during the course of production work, time becomes more and more precious as the work proceeds. Some theaters enjoy fairly casual scheduling. Subsidized European theaters, particularly, often give directors several months of rehearsal and preparation time before opening; indeed, they may even leave the opening date undetermined until the director feels the show is ready. Since these theaters present a repertory of plays, they can maintain a fairly flexible schedule of performances, substituting other shows in the repertory until the new play is able to face an audience; also these theaters maintain permanent artistic staffs whose employment includes work on several productions simultaneously. The American theater, both professional and amateur, is ordinarily more rigidly scheduled. Normally a director will first determine an opening date and schedule backwards from that point to establish other deadlines.

Production scheduling is an intricate process. Time must be allotted for the construction of scenery and costumes even before the scenery and costumes have been designed, and frequently before the designers have been selected. Rehearsal time must include ample time for the actors to be onstage, or else a stage simulation must be built to duplicate the features of the eventual setting. The technical staff will need much time in the theater itself to position scenery, hang and focus the lights, and make the machinery operable.

In professional productions, where actors' salaries are paid during rehearsals as well as performances, rehearsal time is usually compressed into three or four forty-hour weeks. In college and community productions, rehearsal time is spread over four to ten weeks, with rehearsals occurring mainly in the evenings for two-and-a-half to four hours each. No scheduling system is mandatory. Summer stock productions are frequently put together in a single week of daytime rehearsals, while the actors perform another play at night. European, subsidized theaters, as noted, may rehearse a play for several months.

Do not assume that the quality of a production correlates directly with the time spent in rehearsal. Plays can be overrehearsed, particularly with amateur actors whose interest and enthusiasm may wane over a protracted period, and performances grow stale long before opening night. Even professionals are not immune to creeping ennui resulting from overlong, unstimulating rehearsal schedules.

When the production dates have been set and the theater hired for the run, the director can work backward to schedule the other crucial stages of production. The most important of these is the start of the rehearsal period, for by that time the casting and most of the work on the script must be complete. The director then needs to schedule design completion dates, by which time approved designs will have gone to the scene shop, the costume shop, and the property room, and then the dates for technical and dress rehearsals. Normally a production manager helps the director coordinate and establish this part of the timetable, but the director is finally responsible for seeing that the schedule is adhered to, and he should keep an eye on the progress of technical areas if he wishes to exercise genuine control over the production.

Those critical dates once set, the director then proceeds to set other target dates: for auditions, casting, publicity releases and interviews, photographs, and specific rehearsal accomplishments. If the director is doing a dialect play and wishes to engage the cast in a three-day "crash course" in Irish brogue, now is the time to set aside those days on a calendar. If the play requires juggling, dancing, fencing, or any other special effect that the actors may not be accomplished at, periods of special coaching should be worked into the schedule. Gordon Davidson had to allocate eight weeks of "prerehearsal" time for actors in *Children of a Lesser God* (1980) to learn sign language. Finally, the director should allow some time for himself, before the production begins, in which he is free to elaborate on his conceptualization and to make his plans more sophisticated.

Phase Six: Staffing

Those on the production staff, numbering from one to two dozen or more, are the director's chief associates in the planning stages and later in the building period. The staff may consist of separate scenery, costume, lighting, property, makeup, and sound designers; stage and production managers; a technical director; a musical director; a choreographer; an assistant director; a personal assistant; and a host of technical operators and technicians. There will be a house staff—ushers, house managers, box office personnel—and a publicity staff accountable to the director's basic plan for the production's public face. There will also be an office staff, including secretaries and accountants. Rarely will a director select all these people, since many of them will be staff personnel at a given theater, but involvement in the selection of the designers, the music director, and the choreographer is ordinarily crucial for the ultimate implementation of the director's concepts and plans.

Considerations in the selection of a staff, beyond the obvious requirement of the artists' availabilites, are their skills at working within the planned production schedule and anticipated production organization, and most important, their consonance with the director's conceptualization and working methods. For this reason, an articulated directorial concept is most useful in assembling a harmonious and creative artistic staff. A working schedule and working budget are also vital, in that they set limits within which designers, musical directors, and choreographers can make their own decisions and plans.

Personal *rapport* is a basic requirement for effective collaboration, and the director must choose a staff with an eye to each member's potential for creating unity or conflict. A production staff is not a social club; nonetheless each individual artist must be a contributing member to a whole enterprise, and the director plays a crucial role in selecting artists who can collaborate well with each other and can create imaginatively, and express themselves candidly, within a climate of shared artistic initiative. The director will seek people, therefore, who are talented, interested in the specific goals of the production, helpful in offering creative ideas of their own, amenable to the director and each other, and available within the time schedule and financial budget of the production.

Phase Seven: Designing

The director's responsibility for design does not end with the approval of a designer (see Chapter 3). The collaboration between director and design staff determines in great measure the stylistic consistency of the production. Design consultation usually begins as soon as a designer has been selected, when the director explains the concept and receives a preliminary response from the designer. The designer then begins research and creative projections. The director should by this time be able to point the designer toward various sources that are in keeping with the overall interpretation of the play and with the stylistic guidelines he has in mind. It is equally vital that specific dates be agreed on, by which the director may expect to see preliminary sketches, final sketches, set models, and finished products. It is rarely desirable for the director to set these dates arbitrarily; in almost every situation the deadline is agreed on by all involved. They should then be written in a formal memorandum, copies of which are distributed to the entire technical and production staff.

The extent of the models and designs to be provided by the designers is also subject to agreement. Some directors can visualize a setting from only a ground plan and an elevation sketch; others require a scale model to get the "feel" of the set. Similarly, some directors feel satisfied with color renderings of costumes; others prefer exacting sketches accompanied by color swatches of material. The more work designers are asked to do in presenting models of their designs, the less time they will have (or the shops will have) to execute the actual settings or costumes. Some designers are adept at making models; others, at drafting plans and elevations; the choices should be fairly and reasonably worked out by the individuals involved.

Unfortunately, the lighting designer and the sound engineer are frequently not consulted until later stages of the production period. This is often a grave mistake. It is always desirable to involve these people at the preproduction stage along with the other designers, since their scope can be greatly enlarged and enhanced by approaches to the settings or costumes which can be made only at this time. A lighting designer cannot, however, draw up any but the most general lighting plot until the set design has been approved, and the director should not expect a final light plot until the scenery is constructed and the lighting designer has had ample opportunity to work on it.

During this stage the property master and makeup designer should also be consulted and prop and makeup lists compiled. The property list is one preproduction aspect that may change a great deal during rehearsals; it is wise, therefore, that props be acquired (and designed, if necessary) as far ahead of schedule as possible, to allow them to be tested in rehearsal and modified if need be. Makeup, by contrast, can be finalized shortly before technical rehearsals unless special circumstances require earlier attention.

At various stages during the preproduction planning the director must approve the designs. He or she is ruled by deadlines and does not have an indefinite time to respond to the designers' proposals or sketches. Ordinarily, once general concepts for settings, costumes, and lighting have been agreed on by director and designers, and the designers have submitted sets of renderings, models, or draftings to the director, the director looks at each proposed design and approves them individually or sends single items back for revision. Eventually a complete scenery system will be approved, along with costumes, props, and a lighting plan.

Once final approval has been given, the director is pretty much bound to what has been agreed on. Certainly changes after this point are expensive; they are also demoralizing if they seem arbitrary or capricious. Naturally, directors will discover things in rehearsal that had not occurred to them in their study, and they will occasionally decide to demand redesigns in various elements; but these can only be accomplished amid a rising tide of frustration and bewilderment from coworkers who may simply conclude that the directors failed to "do their homework in the first place." Peter Brook, the celebrated English director, for this reason refuses to have his productions designed until rehearsals are well under way, but Brook earned this luxury (and a luxury it certainly is, from an economic standpoint) only after achieving a worldwide reputation for brilliant experimentalism. Until a director can sustain a production company on the basis of such a reputation—together with a generous funding source—he or she had better be prepared to plan well, commit decisively, and follow through consistently.

Phase Eight: Casting

Actors can be cast early or late in the planning period; professionally, leading actors may be cast as the very first step in the production process, as with Elizabeth Taylor in *The Little Foxes* previously mentioned. Alternatively, actors are sometimes cast after rehearsals have begun, either to replace actors who have not worked out or to perform roles written in during the rehearsal process.

In either case, casting decisions are both critical to a production's success and emotionally harrowing for the actors and directors who are weighing artistic values against personal ones, and career interests against those of pleasure, in a flux of high-pressure decision making that will have long-term consequences. Casting may not be 90 percent of directing, as an old Broadway adage would have us believe, but mistakes at the casting stage can rarely be eradicated by even the most brilliant actor coaching or staging.

Developing a pool of actors is often the director's first task. Professionally, directors enjoy a buyer's market, as a single listing in trade magazines will bring forth hundreds of applicants for paying roles; in the collegiate or community theater, however, the director may not always attract a satisfactory response to an audition. Obviously a director's reputation is critical in attracting actors, because actors, in general, prefer to work under directors known to be expert, experienced, and creative. The prestige of the theater company, the ambience of the working conditions, and the general excitement generated by the project are other factors in attracting talented actors to a casting pool. No director should be oblivious to the need to attract actors to the production, and every director needs to think imaginatively about soliciting the very best auditions possible. One way is an audition poster, usually handmade, which can be placed on appropriate call-boards and around local gathering places. The audition poster should make clear what the production is, when it will be performed, when it will be rehearsed, and who the director is going to be; or it should give a telephone number where such information will be available. In the community theater, directors also may place audition announcements in local newspapers. Directors should follow up their announcements with freely distributed fact sheets that give complete information on the play, the cast of characters, what will be expected at auditions, what the rehearsal commitment will be, and what personnel, if any, are already commited to the production. It is unethical to post audition notices that suggest roles are available if they have already been cast, but it is not unethical for directors to discuss the play with potential auditionees and suggest roles that they might audition for.

An *open audition,* the normal format for initial casting decisions, is a posted call for all interested actors (limited, in some situations, to members of a dramatic club or students of a drama school or holders of a union card). Auditionees at such an open call should be asked either to present a prepared (memorized) piece from any play or from the play being cast or to read "cold" from the script along with the stage manager or other auditionees. Sometimes the director will ask auditionees to sing, dance, improvise, speak extemporaneously on a subject, or any combination of these activities. The audition poster and/or advertisement and listing should make clear what is to be expected, and if a song is expected, what is to be provided in the way of accompaniment. Some directors prefer to hold these open auditions in private, with actors ushered onstage one at a time by the stage manager; other directors allow auditionees to watch each other audition (the former practice is standard professionally).

Normally, initial auditions are quite short, two to five minutes per actor, and often less if the acting pool is a large one. The director must make fast decisions—often on tangential or vague evidence—trying to estimate, for example, how well the actor will play Hamlet on the basis of his delivery of a monologue from *Richard II* (in which the actor had been directed by somebody else) or else on his ability to sight-read from a script. Some actors simply can't read (actors with dyslexia, for example, which inhibits reading ability but in no way inhibits performance). The director's task, obviously, is to see through the (in his or her view, misdirected) prepared audition from *Richard II,* and through the sight-reading difficulties, and see instead the performance, eight weeks from now, of Hamlet in the planned production.

Most directors take information from the actor at the time of the audition; perhaps the actor is asked to fill out an *information sheet,* with height, weight, dramatic training, and experience in résumé form. Many directors take instant photographs of the actor to attach to these sheets, and more and more professional directors videotape principal auditions. These methods help directors remember actors when the audition pool is large—say a hundred or more.

Following the initial auditions, top candidates are invited to call-back auditions, which most usually involve readings from the script together with other actors being considered for the play. Important things to look for at the call-backs, which are the final auditions before casting (although there may be several of them before decisions can be made), are the rapport actors seem to have with each other and with the director; the actor's apparent directability; the actor's apparent growth during the auditioning process; and the balance and blend of voices, sizes, appearances, temperaments, emotions, and skills that the director senses coming out of the readings.

Some directors at this point cast on impulse. Others are more careful; they may interview actors privately, telephone previous directors with whom the actors have worked for augmented recommendations, and/or ask members of the production staff involved in auditions for advisory opinions. Occasionally even other actors are asked, although this step can endanger cast morale if it appears to elevate certain cast members as an elite clique, with special access to the director.

Eventually, casting decisions are made and announced in appropriate fashion. The professional "announcement" is in the form of a contract; the nonprofessional practice is a simple agreement signified by the director posting a cast list, and the actors initialing their willingness to perform as cast. It is important to establish, however, that the casting process does result in a "contract"—ethically if not legally binding—in that the director has made a commitment to the actor, and the actor, by accepting the role, to the director, and that this contract cannot be unilaterally broken by mere whim or change of heart. For the director, the casting decision is an acutely responsible act, particularly insofar as it takes place in one of the most emotionally laden phases of the theater, a phase in which hearts are broken and acts of revenge prepared. Every director must learn to cast fairly, (and to make the casting *seem* fair), to make decisions aboveboard, and to make casting announcements with extreme tact and graciousness.

THIRD PERIOD: *CREATING*

Up to this point, the director has been working essentially out of a study or office, which for that matter, might be a corner of a local cafeteria or a friend's living room. And the work is mostly private: one-on-one conferences with staff members, small meetings, and casting sessions in an audition hall. But the third period changes all this: it is the transition to creative work that is highly public, highly visible, and with continually escalating demands on time. The speculative and planning periods are now considered "homework," and woe to any director facing a cast suspicious that he or she has not done the homework assiduously. Indeed, few directors feel that they come to their first rehearsals adequately prepared. Whether this is a case of practice denying an overly idealistic theory or simply that few creative people ever feel entirely satisfied with their efforts is impossible to say. Still, the homework period is over, and at whatever stage directors find themselves regarding their preparedness, the work-in-progress period inevitably begins.

Phase Nine: Rehearsing

Rehearsing may not be the most important phase of directing, but it is certainly *thought* to be the most important phase by most observers, and it is unquestionably the phase in which the directors spend the bulk of their scheduled time.

Directors are the sole master of rehearsals and can schedule them in any way they wish. Some directors spend relatively large blocks of time on exercises designed to create cast ensemble spirit; others prefer lengthy discussion and analysis sessions in which the play is quite minutely taken apart and put back together; others prefer to "block and run," giving the actors their movements and then running the scenes over and over again. Moreover, directors may adopt different schedules for different plays, in part sensing the receptivity of the cast to various techniques and procedures.

Several things *have* to happen in rehearsals: the actors have to understand the play; they have to learn their dialogue and at least certain stage movements; they have to feel at least fairly secure (intellectually and emotionally) in what they are doing; they have to develop such virtuosity as they can and as the production demands; they have to interact effectively with the other actors; they have to learn how to use and work with the costumes, props, scenery, furniture, and sound and lighting effects designed to support their performances; and they have to create, in ensemble, the rhythm of the play in a pattern sufficiently "fixed" in rehearsal to be properly cued and lit by the stage manager and the technical crew. They may also, if they are amateurs, have to learn fundamentals of theater ethics, backstage behavior, and artistic discipline. All of these become the direct responsibility of the director, whose tools are nothing other than personal encouragement, persuasion, and inspiration.

Rehearsal schedule.   The first step in rehearsing a play is to prepare a plan, the implementation of which is a rehearsal schedule. How much time for learning dialect? How much for learning lines? How much for analysis? How much for perfecting blocking? The *amount* of time—given an opening night already scheduled—is inflexible; hours wasted early on cannot be made up in the later, and more urgent, rehearsal days. Moreoever, time must always be held in reserve for illnesses; cast replacements; technical holdups; and even for thefts, power failures, and other emergencies. The schedule assures that work begins immediately and proceeds continuously toward a given end.

To prepare a rehearsal schedule, directors first break the production into rehearsal units. Using the French scene list developed in the planning period, they collate the scenes with the same actors into separate units; for example, all the Macbeth–Lady Macbeth scenes form one unit, and all the witch scenes form a second unit. By rehearsing a play in units rather than in sequential scenes, actors can consolidate their rehearsal time, giving them large chunks of "free time" that can be spent learning lines and working on their roles away from the rehearsal hall. In the early rehearsals, where continuity is not yet a factor, most directors prefer to work in rehearsal units rather than in whole acts or sequential scenes.

With a play broken into units, a tentative rehearsal schedule can be made up. Such a model follows, presuming a two-act play broken into six rehearsal units, which will be rehearsed in thirty four-hour time slots (that means six weeks of evening rehearsals or three weeks of all-day rehearsals).

Slot 1: First reading. General concept, clarification of text.
Slot 2: Second reading. Designers present renderings or models. Exercises. Party.
Slot 3: Block and work unit 1.
       4: Block and work unit 2.
       5: Block and work units 1 and 2.
       6: Block and work unit 3.
       7: Block and work unit 4.
       8: Block and work units 1 and 2.
       9: Block and work units 3 and 4.
      10: Work Act I (includes only material from units 1–4)
      11: Block and work unit 5.
      12: Block and work unit 6.
      13: Block and work units 5 and 6.
      14: Work Act II.
      15: Work Act I (ALL LINES MEMORIZED).
      16: Work Act II (ALL LINES MEMORIZED).
      17: Work units 5 and 6.
      18: Work units 3 and 4.
      19: Work units 1 and 2.
      20: Run Act I. Work problem areas and run again.
      21: Run Act II. Work problem areas and run again.
      22: Run entire play.
      23: Work problem areas.
      24: Run entire play.
      25: Work problem areas and run entire play.
      26: Technical rehearsal.
      27: Second technical rehearsal.
      28: First dress rehearsal.
      29: Polishing rehearsal.
      30: Final dress rehearsal.

This model allows the play to be rehearsed from convenient units to sequential scenes and acts, to run-throughs of the entire play, to the integration of technical and design elements, and to final polishing and dress rehearsals. Notice that the schedule reaches a "premature peak" at about midpoint, with run-throughs of each act at slots 15 and 16; this is to give the director an indication of the entire production before going back over the individual units a final time in rehearsals 17 through 19. If there is any reconceptualizing or redirecting to be done, this is clearly the time to see it and to do it. By the first run-through at rehearsal 22, the basic form of the production must be in fairly solid shape, for the work beyond that point will mainly be perfecting what has been sought and achieved in previous planning and rehearsing.

The polishing rehearsal at slot 29 is often a luxury in the amateur theater but a critical phase of the professional; indeed, the Royal Shakespeare Company and other European companies often take weeks rather than hours for polishing. In a polishing rehearsal the cast reports onstage in costume and makeup, and key staging points are perfected, with full lights, sound, and scenery, to absolute precision. This rehearsal must be securely placed in the rehearsal schedule at the outset; it cannot be added at the last minute, as the dress rehearsal cannot be arbitrarily moved ahead.

A rehearsal schedule is almost like a play itself; it begins slowly, progresses to a premature peak halfway through, gets a bit shaky as technical elements are added, and then climaxes in dress rehearsals and performances. The overall structure of the rehearsal schedule is not merely functional; it creates a growing sense of excitement and of artistic "build." As each new element comes into the rehearsals—memorized lines, working scenery pieces, sound effects, costumes, and props—the actors (even hardened professional actors) develop more and more the theatrical spirit that makes live drama a vivid art; the thrill becomes almost palpable when lighting comes into play. The director must be sensitive to this structural building of excitement and should fight a conservative tendency to begin run-throughs too early, which may sometimes leave the actors bored with the production before it opens—making the "premature" peak into a preemptive one.

Rehearsal discipline.   The director is responsible for establishing a basic discipline for all rehearsals, and the earlier this is accomplished the easier it is maintained. Even professional actors occasionally need guidance from the director concerning what grace period, if any, will be allowed for traffic holdups, doctor's appointments, and "unavoidable" rehearsal conflicts, and a cast will quite likely include several members whose previous experience with rehearsal discipline varies from that which the director expects.

Therefore the director should be very clear at the beginning of rehearsals about precisely what sort of discipline will be imposed: what grace period, if any, shelters actors who may be tied up in traffic on their way to rehearsal or too overburdened to learn their lines by the scheduled dates. The director should know that *absolute* discipline ordinarily obtains in the professional theater: actors may not be even one minute late, they may not

FIGURE 155. Director Mike Nichols, right, sits around the table with playwright Murray Schisgal (left) and the cast of Luv for a first reading of the text.

talk offstage during rehearsals, and they may not miss rehearsals without genuine physical disability. Amateur directors who fail to maintain that level of professional discipline risk alienating the professional or professionally oriented actors in their casts, as well as risking a deteriorating rehearsal morale. On the other hand, overly demanding, overly rigid directors in the amateur theater do run a risk of creating autocratic and noncreative rehearsal climates, particularly when working with actors unused to professional discipline. With some plays, a loose improvisational environment is required for generating an appropriate level of creative freedom among the cast; and the director should be cautious in insisting on an arbitrarily inflexible discipline that is out of keeping with the material (textual and human) he or she is working with.

Text discussion.   In the first rehearsals, discussion of the play is probably the dominant working mode. Many directors begin rehearsals with an extensive verbal presentation of the play, the production conceptualization, the interpretations that will guide the rehearsals—at least at the outset—and the world in which the play is considered to take place. This presentation may be a formal lecture, accompanied by slide presentations, recordings, or other devices calculated to stimulate and unify the cast in back of the production's aims. Design presentations further explain and illustrate the direction of the production, so that the cast knows where the show is going before actual rehearsals begin. Some directors continue text discussion in "sit down" rehearsals for days or weeks. Jean Vilar, the late director of France's Théâtre Nationale Populaire, spent more than half the rehearsal period in this fashion; and Marshall Mason, the fine American director, refuses to even begin blocking his productions until the actors have memorized their entire parts in such discussion sessions.

Text discussion usually takes place during readings, where the play is read aloud and analyzed, point by point, by the director and the cast. Often, in a first reading, the director may have the play read "around the table," with each actor reading a speech in turn, regardless of what role the actor will be playing; this has the advantage of involving all the actors equally and of permitting the initial discussions to be less result-oriented than if the actors were to begin performing their roles immediately. Often directors request that the actors read their parts "without acting," or without excessive emotion, so that the rehearsal can be more easily interrupted for analysis and explanation.

Blocking.   Jean Vilar and Marshall Mason notwithstanding, most directors like to get a play "on its feet" by the second or third rehearsal. This must be preceded by marking the outlines of the setting on the rehearsal hall floor, usually with colored tape, and by setting out such rehearsal furniture as may be available—three folding chairs to represent a sofa, an overturned chair to represent a statue, and so forth. Then the actors, while still reading their parts, can walk through movements the director gives them and note their blocking in their hand-carried scripts. Alternatively, the director can simply invite the actors to improvise movement as they wish, guided by the action of the play and their own spontaneous impulses, with the idea that blocking will be "set" from the improvised movements later on (see also Chapter 4).

During the blocking stage, the actors are ordinarily still learning lines; indeed, most actors prefer to learn their lines after the blocking is established, so that they can tie the lines to their movements. Major blocking (that is, entrances, exits, long crosses, and special business like lying on a bed or jumping over a rail) is usually set as early as possible, so that minor moves (standing, sitting, turning, countering, and so on) can be developed more improvisationally later and adjusted without changing the major pattern.

No matter how well preblocked or how improvisationally derived, some blocking patterns simply fail to work. Good directors remain as open-minded as possible about "their" blocking and are sensitive to the actors' complaints—expressed directly or just through noticeable discomfort—that the blocking hurts rather than helps the play's dramatic development. Often a scene is blocked, completely reblocked, and reblocked again in as many rehearsals; directors must be free to experiment and to find patterns of movement that work both for the actors and for the audience. Actors also have to "believe" in the blocking in order to give it their full emotional commitment, and directors must be able to judge when reblocking the scene can unblock the actor—even when the actor may be unaware of it. Too much reblocking, on some occasions, can threaten cast morale (as can too much rewriting during the rehearsal period); actors need change during rehearsals, but they also need the sense of progress and the knowledge that material learned in one rehearsal will not be arbitrarily discarded in the next. As long as the reblocking implies improvement, it will be accepted; when it begins to imply directorial desperation, the production may begin to fall apart.

Coaching actors.   Actors *want* to be coached. Even among experienced professionals, the statement, "I never got any direction!" is a common complaint. Rehearsals, for an actor, are fundamentally lonely times; the actor is onstage, being looked at, unable to look "out" at the audience most of the time. Actors are notoriously insecure, professionals no less than amateurs (and perhaps even more so, insofar as their careers are at stake with every new role). Actors, therefore, quite literally need a director's encouragement, advice, guidance, and—frankly—instructions. That doesn't necessarily mean they want a particular director's instructions. Coaching actors depends, primarily, on the actor's confidence in the director and on the director's methods.

There are many ways to coach actors, of course, most of which are described in Chapter 8. All of them involve a firm but fair use of directorial authority and a reliance on the director as outside observer and objective evaluator of the actor's work in progress. Plain criticism of an actor is certainly a useful, if primitive, directorial technique, particularly when dealing with simple and understandable problems. "You're grabbing her too tightly" or "I can't hear you" are the kinds of directorial intrusion that virtually every actor can respond to immediately, making the appropriate adjustment.

Working with actors on a more personal and constructive level, however, is the guts of great directing. This can vary from very gentle suggesting, prodding, and inducing of behavior to downright psychological invasion of the actor's personality. In theory, a director wants to be gentle, supportive, and rational in dealing with actors; in practice, astounding directorial results have often come out of stormy sessions in which both actors and directors have wrestled with their own inhibitions, fears, ideals, cravings, and passions. Let us never rest on the assumption that directing actors is reducible to rational or scientific principles. Nor should we say it is always hair-raising and tempestuous. The fact is that the best directing is probing and profound, and it engages actors and directors in the deepest explorations of both the characters and the artists that create and portray them. It is not sufficient for the actors to *understand* their characters; it is necessary that they *enact* them, which may require resources well beyond their superficial skills at vocal projection and mimicry. And those hidden resources are often the medium in which the finest directors work, directors who bring performances out of actors that the actors themselves never believed possible.

Directing actors, therefore, is not a fit occupation for the timid. Even in quite "unprofound" plays, the personal confrontations between actor and director may be harrowing. In one famous example director Moss Hart bullied, cajoled, and absolutely tyrannized actress Julie Andrews in a New York hotel room for the twenty-four hours preceding the opening night of *My Fair Lady;* and nobody, least of all Miss Andrews, found fault with the procedure after the next day's reviews. There are, of course, ethical (and legal) restrictions on what directors may do in provoking—or coaxing—the actor's best possible performance; and there are also tremendous disadvantages to any directors who seem to be working toward selfish, inartistic, or unhealthy ends, thereby abusing their directorial authority. Still directors who are willing to get their hands dirty, and who are knowledgeable and sensitive enough to bring out an actor's hidden powers and unexpected skills, will in the end excite the admiration of actors and audiences alike.

Shaping.   Giving final shape to the ensemble of performances—before the introduction of scenery and technical effects—occupies the director in the later stages of rehearsals, that is, partial run-throughs, reworkings, and polishing sessions. This is often the most difficult period in rehearsals because the initial excitement of the actors discovering their parts, and each other, is over, but the excitement of lighting, sound effects, and audience reaction is yet to come. Nonprofessionals are particularly uncomfortable at this stage in that they cannot envision the growth that's yet to come; inevitably, in amateur theater, someone will say "what this show needs now is an audience" long before that situation is actually realized.

It is at this point that the director must introduce new challenges to the cast: the challenge of creating a play's subtlety and complexity, of performing pieces of business with great precision, of timing punch lines and curtain lines with maximum effect, and of creating a play's moments of highest impact with breathtaking—not just competent—authority.

In these rehearsals the director must provide a catalytic excitement. In Tyrone Guthrie's words, "The all important thing for a director is not to let rehearsals be a bore. The chief practical means to this end is to keep people busy . . . seeing that work proceeds at a good brisk pace, not at that of the slowest wits. Better to rush the dullards off their feet than to bore and frustrate the brighter spirits."[2] This statement is never more true than at these later stages of rehearsal.

Run-throughs and notes.   Most of the rehearsals at the end of this period are run-throughs, where the entire play is rehearsed without stopping, except for intermissions. The goal of run-throughs is to give the actors the sense of the play's continuity and to duplicate as much as possible the actual performance conditions, when stopping for correction is impossible. At these rehearsals the director communicates to the cast mainly through notes, notes the director takes during the run-through and delivers to the cast—either individually or in a group meeting—after the rehearsal. Some directors prefer to write up their notes and give them to the actors the following day. It is important, in giving notes, to be thorough and demanding, and at the same time, to be respectful of the actors' time; it is deadening for actors playing small parts to sit through two hours of note-giving sessions knowing all the time that nothing said will pertain to them. It is probably a good idea for directors to spend a few minutes consolidating their notes before gathering the cast, so that they can give their whole-company notes first, keeping the principal actors for individual notes after releasing the majority of the actors and crews.

Phase Ten: Building

More or less simultaneously with the play's rehearsal, the production is being built in the various shops and studios. Scenery is being constructed and painted; costumes are being cut, stitched, and fitted; lighting instruments are being rented or assembled; and sound cues are being recorded or transcribed. Although none of this is necessarily a director's own job, all of it comes under the director's overall supervision.

Where possible, the director should visit the shops regularly, examining platforms and scenery as they are built, checking the fabrics of the costumes, going over the sound cues as they are created, and in general, trying to anticipate problems that may arise and working toward complete communication between what's happening in rehearsals and what's happening in the shops. Props added in rehearsal must be added to the official prop list; unexpected staging decisions might require scenery to be re-engineered for safety reasons; actors' business may require pockets to be added to costumes or quick-change fasteners to be built in. More serious redesigns, although undesirable, may be necessary and must be negotiated between the director and the designers and/or the production manager

---

[2]Tyrone Guthrie, *A Life in the Theatre* (New York: McGraw-Hill, 1959), p. 153.

and shop supervisors. The scheduling of technical rehearsals, costume parades, and pretechnical discussions must be precisely arranged.

Ordinarily, the lighting designer will attend early partial run-throughs of the play to get a firm idea of the patterns of movement initially staged and the lighting potentials and possibilities. The sound designer, special effects designer, and scenery and costume designers will also wish to attend many of these rehearsals, and they should be specifically invited to rehearsals that involve special considerations they should be aware of. The director may play an active role in some of the technical planning and building that goes on in this period; many directors, for example, act as their own sound designer and develop, during nonrehearsal hours, the sound tapes that will be used in the production.

The basic goal of the director during the building period is to understand *in full* what the show is going to look like and sound like technically, and to communicate such understanding among the actors, designers, and technicians, who at this point are working in separate environments. Only the directors have the entire production in their heads, and only they can prevent surprises when actors and scenery and operators finally come together in the few days before opening. There are literally thousands of details in even the most modest production, and the director's comprehensive understanding of the production elements as they are being assembled is the only key to their eventual smooth integration.

The building period culminates in a series of "pretech" meetings and "pretech" rehearsals involving the director, the design and technical staff, the technicians, and in some cases, stand-ins for the actors. (The latter, in amateur theater, are ordinarily the actors themselves while "off-duty.") At these meetings the initial promptbook and cue sheets are prepared—in pencil—listing all light cues, sound cues, shift cues, curtain cues, and prop placement cues. The cues are marked in the script precisely where they occur and are separately recorded on cue sheets, which will be given to the technicians charged with operating them. A costume list and quick-change list is also included when necessary, together with the indication of where quick-change costumes will be located backstage. A schedule of technicians will be made, determining who will move what scenery pieces or properties and when. Often the offstage positions for scenery pieces will be marked on the stage floor. When the promptbook is made and the technical elements ready to be operated, pretech rehearsals may take place, with an assistant reading appropriate lines from the script, the stage manager calling cues, and the stage technicians and operators taking the cues as they would in performance, often with stand-ins "walking" the stage to judge the effectiveness of the still-tentative lighting. The pretech rehearsals are designed to give the stage manager and the technicians experience in giving and taking cues, roughly timed, so that technical rehearsals with the actors present can proceed more smoothly. The pretech rehearsals also provide the director with a reasonably unhurried opportunity to examine the technical effects closely, making certain that they are working well. In full technical rehearsals it will be unwieldly, to say the least, to make fundamental changes in the agreed-on lighting patterns or sound cues. Also, from a morale standpoint, the pretech rehearsals give the technical crews an opportunity to rehearse before meeting with the actors—as the actors have had opportunity to rehearse before meeting the crews. Certainly no body of theatrical artists wants to expose its first efforts to the scrutiny of other—possibly impatient—colleagues.

FOURTH PERIOD: *CONSOLIDATING*

In the production's final period, the play and its ingredients come together. The rough edges are smoothed out, the disharmonies are realigned, the polishing given a final gloss, and the play is ready to face its audience for good or bad.

This is a time for looking at a production very carefully and objectively. The whole picture is what counts here, as well as the individual elements; most directors like to invite friends uninvolved with the production at this point to regain some of the original objectivity now lost beneath the patina of thousands of individual details.

Although little can be done to reconceptualize a production at this stage, much can be done to put a play back into focus—or to achieve a focus that has not yet occurred—by the intensive attention to specific details. Is a plot line obscured? Is a characterization confusing? Is there an actor who is playing out of style? Does the show run too long? Is everything too dark? Bold directorial strokes can be effective in dealing with problems—even serious problems—at this point. Scenes can be cut down, and irrelevancies can be eliminated. It may have been better to do so five weeks ago, but often there's no way to know until the final period what is irrelevant and what is not. In a particularly daring move, British director Michael Bogdanov eliminated the entire set for *The Mayor of Zalamea* during previews of his 1982 production, restaging the play on a bare, trapped floor. "It was no time to be timid," he explained; "the set just got in the way!" Such last-minute changes inevitably cause hurt feelings and consternation among the director's coworkers, but the director's first responsibility at these final moments must be to the artistry of the theatrical product; rigor and uncompromising artistic integrity are never more crucial than at this stage, when the thousands of hours of preparation must come together to create a true theatrical impact. It is at this point that directing can become the world's loneliest profession.

FIGURE 156. The Mayor of Zalamea, produced by the National Theatre in 1982 on a bare stage, after director Michael Bogdanov dispensed with the setting during previews. (*Courtesy, World Theatre Festival, Denver*)

Phase Eleven: "Teching"

Technical rehearsals are laborious and absolutely necessary for the success of a complex production. They are frequently agony for inexperienced actors and less so for experienced ones only because these actors have grown accustomed to them. The point of technical rehearsals is to ensure that every technical effect—every shift of lights; cue of sound; movement of scenery; and special effect emanating from the floor, wings, traps, or flies—works absolutely as it is intended to all of the time.

The length and complexity of technical rehearsals vary with the production. A one-set realistic drama with no special music or lighting effects can probably be "teched" in little more time than it takes to run the play. A highly sophisticated musical, on the other hand, may have to be technically put together over several days. Whatever time it takes, we must emphasize that technical rehearsals are needed to perfect technical effects, and they must be run and rerun until the technician is completely secure in what he or she is doing. Some directors try to do a run-through in conjunction with a tech rehearsal. In our experience this is disastrous. It is of no profit to the actors, whose rhythm is constantly being upset, and it wastes the technicians' time. Tech rehearsals are for technical effects; if a director feels the production needs a run-through at this juncture, then the schedule has probably been wrong, and this is no time for it.

The stage manager takes over.   During technical rehearsals the director shifts his or her responsibilities gradually to the stage manager. At the first technical rehearsal, when actual intensities and volumes are being set, the director assumes full charge and responsibility in consultation with the designers involved. As the technical rehearsals proceed to the operational stage, and the problems become the precise working out of prearranged timings, the stage manager must take over the responsibility for conducting the technicians' work. When in the fourth tech the actors enter the rehearsal, the stage manager must be able to exercise authority over them as well; once a production is in this stage, the stage manager must be given full control of the show. Many directors are unwilling to hand over "their" production to a less experienced stage manager, but only chaos will result if it is not done: directors will probably find themselves forced to remain backstage for every performance if they cannot hand over the reins of the production during technical rehearsals.

Phase Twelve: "Dressing"

Dress rehearsals are run entirely by the stage manager, and all technical instructions to the cast are usually relayed by the director through the stage manager. In the dress rehearsal everything comes together: sound, lights, costumes, scenery, acting, props, special effects, and makeup. If the technical rehearsals have been thorough and well organized, the first dress rehearsal can be a nonstop run-through of the play, with few hitches. It seldom, if ever, is, however.

The first dress rehearsal is often a disaster. This is not entirely surprising. The newness of the final costumes throws the actors' timing off, even when rehearsal costumes have been used; the actors are suddenly more aware of "things"; the lighting changes all perspectives; dialogue and carefully rehearsed action suddenly become unfamiliar; and concentration is dissipated on the surroundings rather than focused on the action. The director must learn to accept this occurrence in the faith that the second dress rehearsal will bring the production back up to performance level. Of course, this will happen only if enough work has been put into the production before technical rehearsals, and directors must learn to distinguish between a performance which is down because of external technical factors and one which is not sufficiently tight and cleanly rehearsed. While they are entangled in wires, headsets, light booths, and so on during the technical period, directors must keep their other eyes, ears, and hands on the specific needs of certain scenes and actors, to ensure that they remain at the necessary level or are finally brought up to it.

In professional situations the directors will call polishing rehearsals between the dresses. Here they can revivify scenes deadened by techs and cure problems brought up by scenery and costumes. College and community theaters rarely afford themselves this time, but they could profit from it. Second dress and all dresses following the first (there is frequently only one dress rehearsal, and rarely more than three) simply repeat the first and try to better its record. They undoubtedly will unless something unexpected goes wrong in the meantime. Directors ordinarily take notes during dress rehearsals and convey their comments to the cast through a full meeting after the rehearsal or before the next rehearsal, through individual written notes, or through dressing-room aside comments.

Final Phase: Opening Night

No one is more helpless than a director on opening night. The stage manager has control of the show, and anticipation has control of the actors. Most directors feel utterly useless on this day, and most *are* utterly useless. If it has not been done by opening night, chances are that there is absolutely no way to get it except by that magical adrenalized luck that seems so infectious at this time. But don't count on it.

Continuing rehearsals.   One of the unfortunate things about much amateur theater is that it seems to be directed solely toward an opening night, after which serious work on the production is abandoned in favor of cast parties and mutual self-congratulation. This is especially unfortunate because some of the most useful artistic work can be done only after opening night, when the production finally includes its missing ingredient: an audience. Certainly an audience is absolutely indispensable for the successful playing of a farce or comedy, because an audience's laughter is virtually written into the script. But even in a tragedy or serious drama the response of the audience, and the response to that response by the actors, is a fundamental part of the theatrical experience and can be gauged only in performance.

It is unthinkable to premiere a professional play in New York without at least one or two weeks of paid preview performances, during which the show is "shaken down," its ineffective parts tightened or pruned out, its climaxes heightened, and its timing honed to perfection. These previews are accompanied by regular daytime rehearsals to run over and improve the weaknesses which appeared the night before. In the case of a new play there is frequently a great deal of script revision at this point.

Similarly, it should be possible in amateur theater to hold preview performances, or at least to have continuing rehearsals and criticism by the director during the actual performance run. Truly artistic directors work on the show until they have the maximum result they can achieve, even if it does not come until closing night. It is the duty of the director, even after the production has come under the technical control of the stage manager, to supervise the run of the play, the morale of the company, and the consistency of the performances.

DIRECTING A SCENE FOR CLASS

The phases leading up to the production of a complete play are naturally abbreviated in the preparation of a scene for directing class, but the basic structure of directorial effort is not fundamentally different. True, there will ordinarily be no budgeting, staffing, or building to speak of, and rarely anything resembling a technical rehearsal; still there are just about as many considerations to pursue for the director who aspires to more than mere classroom competence.

The speculative period can be just as intense for a scene as for an entire production. Indeed, it can often be more so, for where else can the beginning director tackle the gentleman caller scene from *The Glass Menagerie,* for example, with more creative audacity and flair than in the freedom of directing class? Certainly in the areas of selecting and researching a script and in conceptualizing a production the director of a classroom scene may work with all the care and creative imagination of professional directors with their big budgets and renowned colleagues. Moreover, it is in the speculative period that directorial brilliance can first show up; the very quality of directorial speculation, reaching the right hands, may result in a budgeted professional production.

Normally classroom directors are their own staff. They will design their own scenery, costumes, and props, using pretty much what they can find in the classroom, in their own living quarters, and in the wardrobes and possessions of their actors. The limitations of the classroom may be explored creatively, however, within the limits set down by the instructor or by departmental policy. Chairs may be rearranged to perform in the round or in a proscenium format; the action may take place around audiences or behind them. Portable lights, tape recorders, musical instruments, and other special effects or apparatus may be brought into the room; conversely, the director may request permission to stage the piece outdoors or in another location.

Classroom scenes should be given a structured rehearsal schedule just like a play, with time slots firmly established at the time of casting, and with actors cast with the understanding that they will be available at all those times. The establishment of rehearsal discipline is particularly critical to the scene director, who must be on the lookout for actors unwilling to commit themselves to a set rehearsal schedule. Directors working with student actors may be well advised to cast persons not simultaneously involved in other "major" productions; it is far better to use actors eager to work than "better-known" actors whose greater involvement is elsewhere.

Working with actors in a classroom can be more difficult than in a fully staged major production, partly because the actors are not as fully committed as when they are in daily four-hour or eight-hour rehearsals, and partly because they may recognize that they are "only" in a classroom scene, perhaps one of many in the school year. Also there is less automatic authority vested in the director, who is "only" a fellow student, and perhaps a less experienced theater student than the actors he or she casts. All of these difficulties can be overcome, however, by the serious director, no matter how inexperienced, by the demonstration of directorial preparation, concern for the script, understanding of the complexity of the characters, and compassion for the actors and the acting process. Genuine directorial idealism—a passion for theatrical excellence—will inspire any actor and create a more humane creative environment, as well as a more disciplined one, than any kind of directorial ranting, threatening, or tattletaling. No student director should pretend to be a know-it-all; instead the would-be director must study, must care, must create, and must communicate feelings and ideas carefully, forcefully, and sensitively to his or her fellow artists.

The ratio of rehearsal time to performance time in the American professional theater is usually about sixty to one, that is, 120 hours of rehearsal for a two-hour production. This means about one hour of rehearsal for each playing minute, which is a fair average to spend on classroom scenes: ten rehearsal hours for a ten-minute scene, twenty hours for a twenty-minute scene, and so on. There should be at least one dress rehearsal for every scene—in the classroom itself if at all possible—using costumes and properties as they will be used in the actual presentation. This requirement includes consumable items (for example, food and drink, matches and cigarettes); many a presentation scene has been all but destroyed as actors choked on real biscuits which they had only mimed in rehearsal. The dress rehearsal should make such use of the room's lighting as can best be arranged, and directors should think creatively about the beginning and end of their scenes: how the scene should be introduced, how it should end (with a blackout? with the director saying "curtain"? with the actors bowing?), and how the actors should enter and leave the staging area.

Directing scenes is a basic directorial training ground, used in drama schools and universities the world around. It is also the workshop format of most professional studios, such as the Actors' Studio Director's Unit in New York. It demands the same skills in coaching actors that directing plays does and many of the same abilities in staging and coordination. But beginning directors must not mistake directing scenes for the more comprehensive tasks of directing complete plays, or assume that the direction of a play is nothing more than the directing of a number of individual scenes, strung end to end. When directors tackle a scene in class, they should always confront—at least in hypothesis—the entire production of which the scene would be a part. It is often useful, in directing a scene from a play, to prepare an entire proposal and/or hypothetical production book for the full play and to evaluate the produced scene in the light of the directorial plan for an entire production.

DIRECTING A MUSICAL PRODUCTION

Directing a musical production—which might be an American musical comedy, an opera, an operetta, or a Brechtian play with songs—requires all the skills of "straight" directing, plus additional managerial adeptness. The musical play is actually directed by three individuals: the musical director, the choreographer, and the stage director, any one of whom might become the "first among equals," given the particulars of the situation. In opera, for example, the musical director (who conducts the orchestra) usually has the more demanding position (and the top billing as well), and in American musicals of the past two decades, the choreographer has assumed a dominant role. Indeed, the rising importance of choreography has led to a cadre of choreographer-turned-director notables in this country, including the late Gower Champion, Jerome Robbins, and Tommy Tune, most of whom have moved easily between musical and nonmusical theater.

Often, then, in a musical production, the director's responsibility is largely administrative; he or she is the organizational link among music director, choreographer, designers, stage managers, and cast, and his or her major responsibilities are essentially supervisory in nature. The director's one irreducible function, artistically, is to stage the "book" (that is, nonmusical) scenes, but these may account for only a small fraction of the musical production's stage time, and a relatively unimportant fraction at that. Obviously, therefore, the director must have a keen knowledge and feeling about music and dance, as well as a fruitful rapport with musicians and dancers, in order to provide effective conceptual guidelines and direction to coworkers in a musical theater production.

Musical productions are ordinarily rehearsed in two or more theaters simultaneously, with music rehearsals, dance rehearsals, and "book" rehearsals going on at the same time. Naturally, this requires adroit scheduling and well-integrated stage management staffs; the director, in those cases, will collaborate with the music director and choreographer on the main lines of their work and will visit the separate rehearsals as much as possible to keep the show's main lines well in hand. The director's work during the final "consolidating" period of rehearsals is perhaps the most crucial, for here the director must assume the final responsibility over the music and the choreography, ensuring that the play's separate elements come together in a fruitful and effective manner. A director who has been largely absent from music and choreographic rehearsals at the earlier stages may find this very difficult to do.

Musicals are hard work for a director, and frequently unrewarding for those used to the more flexible and improvisational modes of the non-musical theater. Music demands fixed tempos (for the choreography) and rigid rehearsal hours (for the musician's unions); often the music is fixed on tape or the musicians are unavailable until dress rehearsal, which add further frustrations. But the musical theater has close ties to the world's first dramas; the Aeschylean choruses were both sung and danced, and the Shakespearean tragedies were written to include song as well as speech. Directors owe it to themselves to try to rise to the challenge of the musical rather than to avoid it because of its more obvious problems and difficulties.

A Sample Countdown: Conception to Production

PHASE	BEGINS	WITH
1. Selecting	anytime	Self
2. Researching	opening minus 16 weeks	*Dramaturg*
3. Conceptualizing	14 weeks	Self
4. Budgeting	12 weeks	Producer
		Production manager
5. Scheduling	12 weeks	Production manager
6. Staffing	12 weeks	Producer
7. Designing	11 weeks	Scene designer
		Costume designer
		Lighting designer
		Sound designer
8. Casting	9 weeks	Stage manager
9. Rehearsing	6 weeks	Stage manager
		Cast
10. Building	6 weeks	Designers, Crews
11. Teching	1 week	Everybody
12. Dressing	3 days	Everybody
OPENING	—	Everybody
		House staff

This is a model schedule for a college or community production, allowing four months from the time of selection to the opening, with starting dates listed as weeks or days before opening (Opening minus nine weeks, and so on). Some productions, to be sure, are put together in considerably less time: the Williamstown Summer Theater, a highly professional operation, put together a production of *The Fantasticks* in eight days after losing the rights to produce the play it had planned. Conversely, some productions are in preparation for a year or more; this schedule can only serve as one possible (although fairly common) timetable.

The director's collaborators, of course, will depend on the theater company and the budget; those listed should be considered only the *possible* collaborators. Often directors are their own *dramaturg* and producer; at other times they are their own designer(s) as well.

Bibliography

This bibliography is highly selective for two reasons. First, rather than providing a bald list of works in the area, we wish to give neophyte directors some indication of what they might find useful in the most influential works. Second, the possible sources the contemporary director might be referred to are as comprehensive as the spectrum of human activity itself. Our listing is, therefore, the nucleus of a library for directors, to which they may add books on theater, sociology, art, politics, or psychology as their interest and capacity allow.

ANTOINE, ANDRÉ. *Memories of the Théâtre-Libre*. Miami, Fla.: University of Miami Press, 1964. Autobiographical work by the great exponent of naturalism. Interesting for its views on the theater as a minute recapitulation of life and on how this can be achieved.

ARTAUD, ANTONIN. *The Theater and Its Double*. New York: Grove Press, Inc., 1958. The classic collection of the ideas and aesthetic of perhaps the most influential spiritual force behind the alternative theater.

BARRAULT, JEAN-LOUIS. *Reflections on the Theatre*. London: Rockliff Press, 1951. A highly personal autobiographical series of essays by France's leading actor-director.

BROOK, PETER. *The Empty Space: A Book About Theatre—Deadly, Holy, Rough, Immediate*. New York: Atheneum Publishers, 1968. A brilliant discussion by Britain's leading experimental director of how theater can and must be a dynamic contemporary force.

BURIAN, JARKA. *The Scenography of Josef Svoboda*. Middletown, Conn.: Wesleyan University Press, 1971. A discussion of the work of this leading European designer, plus marvelous production photographs of his work.

BURRIS-MEYER, HAROLD, and EDWARD COLE. *Theaters and Auditoriums* (2nd ed.). New York: Van Nostrand Reinhold Company, 1964. The standard reference work on theater buildings and stages.

CLURMAN, HAROLD. *On Directing*. New York: The Macmillan Company, 1972. The considered views and consolidated technique of forty years' experience in the American theater. Important for an understanding of the basically naturalistic approach of the American director.

COHEN, ROBERT. *Acting Power*. Palo Alto, Cal.: Mayfield Publishing Co., 1978. Highly contemporary examination of the acting process, relating Stanislavski to modern theories of psychology and communications.

COLE, TOBY, and HELEN CHINOY (eds.). *Directors on Directing* (rev. ed.). Indianapolis: The Bobbs-Merrill Co., Inc., 1963. An excellent historical review of the emergence of the director, plus a brief selection of the ideas of the principal directors from Saxe-Meiningen to Elia Kazan.

FELSENSTEIN, WALTER. *The Music Theater of Walter Felsenstein* (trans. Peter Paul Fuchs). New York: W. W. Norton & Co., Inc., 1975. The principles and craft of Germany's outstanding opera director.

GOLDMAN, MICHAEL. *The Actor's Freedom*. New York: The Viking Press, 1975. Perhaps the most significant contemporary rethinking of the nature of theater and the actor's function.

GROTOWSKI, JERZY. *Towards a Poor Theater*. New York: Simon & Schuster, Inc., 1969. Principles and techniques of acting described by the best-known practitioner of the theatrical spirit of Artaud.

GUTHRIE, SIR TYRONE. *A Life in the Theatre*. New York: McGraw-Hill Book Company, 1959. Anecdotes, attitudes, and achievements of the great director of classical theater. Interesting because of Guthrie's dynamic and innovative approach to Shakespeare.

————. *Tyrone Guthrie on Acting*. New York: The Viking Press, 1971. A practical and to the point treatise on acting from a director's perspective.

HAGEN, UTA. *Respect for Acting*. New York: Macmillan, Inc., 1973. The methodology of one of America's leading actors.

HARROP, JOHN, AND SABIN EPSTEIN. *Acting with Style*. Englewood Cliffs, N.J.: Prentice-Hall, Inc., 1982. A comprehensive discussion of the demands and dynamics of the major theatrical styles.

HETHMON, ROBERT (ed.). *Strasberg at the Actors' Studio*. New York: The Viking Press, 1965. Transcribed tape recordings of Strasberg's teaching, with comment by Hethmon. Does much to set the record straight about what the "method" actually is.

HODGSON, JOHN, and ERNEST RICHARDS. *Improvisation: Discovery and Creativity in Drama*. London: Eyre Methuen, 1966. Excellent practical discussion of how a director can employ improvisational methods in any production.

HOUGHTON, NORRIS. *Moscow Rehearsals*. New York: Harcourt Brace Jovanovich, Inc., 1936. The classic work on the methods of the great Russian directors in the period of Russian theatrical supremacy and experimentation.

KIRBY, E. T. (ed.). *Total Theater: A Critical Anthology*. New York: E. P. Dutton, 1969. A collection of essays on the roots and aesthetic of media incorporation in theater, from Wagner to McLuhan.

LEWIS, ROBERT. *Method—or Madness*. New York: French & European Publications, Inc., 1958. Fine commonsense discussion of some of the virtues and shortcomings of the Strasberg system.

LOGAN, JOSHUA.   *Josh, My Up and Down In and Out Life*. New York: Delacorte Press, 1976. Fascinating and instructive reminiscences by one of America's leading directors.

McLUHAN, H. MARSHALL.   *Understanding Media: The Extensions of Man*. New York: McGraw-Hill Book Company, 1964. Classic examination of the effect of technological advances in communication on how people now look at their world.

MAROWITZ, CHARLES.   *The Act of Being*. London: Secker and Warburg, 1978. Approaches to acting and directing by one of the most successful of experimental directors.

MUNK, ERIKA (ed.).   *Stanislavski and America*. New York: Fawcett World Library, 1966. A collection of the important commentaries on the influence of the great Russian actor and director on the American theater.

PILBROW, RICHARD.   *Stage Lighting*. New York: Van Nostrand Reinhold Company, 1970. An approach to stage lighting by the successful British designer.

PRINCE, HAL.   *Contradictions: Notes on Twenty-Six Years in the Theater*. New York: Dodd, Mead & Company, 1974. The experience of a lifetime as distilled by America's most succesful contemporary director.

REDFIELD, WILLIAM.   *Letters from an Actor*. New York: The Viking Press, 1966. The classic reflections on working with John Gielgud and Richard Burton in *Hamlet*.

ST. DENIS, MICHEL.   *The Rediscovery of Style*. New York: Theatre Arts Books, 1960. An examination of style seen as the distillation of the spirit of a text. Also includes a brief discussion of actor-training methods.

SCHECHNER, RICHARD (ed.).   *Dionysus in '69*. New York: Farrar, Straus & Giroux, Inc., 1970. A pictorial edition of The Performance Group's environmental production of *The Bacchae*.

SPOLIN, VIOLA.   *Improvisation for the Theater: A Handbook of Teaching and Directing Techniques*. Evanston, Ill.: Northwestern University Press, 1963. The classic handbook of games and exercises for actor training and play improvisation.

STANISLAVSKI, KONSTANTIN.   *My Life in Art*. New York: Theatre Arts Books, n.d. Personal memoirs, including discussions of Stanislavski's approach to acting and directing.

TAPLIN, OLIVER.   *Greek Tragedy in Action*. Berkeley: University of California Press, 1978. Useful, practical discussion on producing Greek tragedy.

WILLETT, JOHN (ed.).   *Brecht on Theatre*. New York: Hill and Wang, 1964. An essential compendium of Brecht's theories.

Index

A

Abstract effects with blocking, 135–36
Abstract scenery, 63–64, 66–71
Acting Company, 248–50
Acting exercises:
  for Artaudian theater, 186–92
  biomechanics, 182–83
  character development, 210–13
  for epic theater, 194–97
  improvisation and, 217–19
  with masks, 223–24
  physical exploration of action, 205,
    208–10
  warm-up, 201–7
Acting techniques and approaches, 169–98
  Artaud and Theater of Cruelty, 184–92
  Brecht and epic theater, 192–97
  Copeau and poetic physicality, 183–84
  evolution of, 169–72
  Meyerhold and biomechanics, 181–83
  naturalistic, 170–79
  physical actions concept, 179–92
  Stanislavski system, 172–78, 197–98
  Strasberg method, 176–79
Action units, 25, 27–29

Actor-managers, 3–6
Actor Prepares, An (Stanislavski), 174, 176
Actors, working with, 168–232
  acting techniques and approaches (*see*
    Acting techniques and approaches)
  auditions, 224–28, 305–7
  coaching, 313–14
  in directing class, 321–23
  dual perspective, 168–69
  rehearsals (*see* Rehearsals)
Actors' Studio, 55, 58, 61, 173–74, 176, 236
Adaptations, 293, 294
Aeschylus, 2, 56, 275
Aesthetic effects with blocking, 127, 130–35
Aesthetic styles, 257–63
Akropolis, 271, 272
Albee, Edward, 32, 156
Alice and Wonderland, 293
Alienation, 193, 262, 274
Alternative theater, 263–77
American Buffalo, 63
American Conservatory Theatre, 98, 100,
  257
Amphitheaters, 47, 50–52
Anderson, Lindsay, 160
Andrews, Julie, 314

Androcles and the Lion, 188
Anouilh, Jean, 74, 161, 170
Antigone (Anouilh), 74, 107, 161
Antigone (Sophocles), 35
Antoine, André, 6, 8, 70, 285
Antony and Cleopatra, 152
Antoon, A. J., 254
Appia, Adolphe, 9, 70, 146
Aragon, Louis, 129
Arbitrary style, 253–57
Arena Stage, 46, 48, 49
Arena theater, 46–48
Are You Now or Have You Ever Been, 290
Aristotle, 171
Arkin, Alan, 139
Artaud, Antonin, 184–85, 249–50, 265
Artaudian theater, 184–92, 265, 266,
    270–74
Arturo Ui, 118
Ashcroft, Peggy, 227
Asolo State Theater, 52
Asymmetrical balance, 131
As You Like It, 275
Audience:
    arena stage and, 46
    illusionistic theater and, 59–60
    lighting and, 149–50
    play selection and, 290
    proscenium stage and, 43–44
    style and, 239
    thrust stage and, 45
    violated stage space and, 60–63
Auditions, 224–28, 305–7
Authentic style, 241–43
Author-director collaborations, 17–18,
    293–94
Authoritarian blocking, 137–39
A vista scene changes, 72, 79, 81

B

Bacchae, The, 270
Bailey, Pearl, 61, 62
Balance:
    blocking and, 130–35
    ground plan and, 98
    in naturalistic productions, 285
Ball, William, 9, 98, 163, 166, 232
Baraka, Imamu Amiri, 226
Barefoot in the Park, 92, 283, 284
Bare stage theater, 63, 76–79
Barrault, Jean-Louis, 9, 17, 151, 222
Barton, John, 230, 253, 254–55
Bauhaus experimenters, 264
Beaton, Cecil, 73
Beats, 25, 28–29, 105, 179
Beck, Julian, 9

Beckett, Samuel, 31, 36, 66–67, 94, 135,
    290
Behan, Brendan, 30, 92
Behavior creation, 123–26
Belasco, David, 65
Belt and Braces Company, 274
Benedetti, Robert, 77
Bentley, Eric, 36, 290
Berliner Ensemble, 33, 59, 150
Berlin Theatertreffen, 275
Besson, Benno, 16
Billy Bishop Goes to War, 153
Biomechanics, 182–83
Bland, Majorie, 230
Blau, Herbert, 163, 290
Blin, Roger, 67
Blithe Spirit, 209
Blocking, 41, 102–43, 312–13
    abstract effects, 135–36
    aesthetic effects, 127, 130–35
    authoritarian, 137–39
    balance and, 130–35
    behavior creation, 123–26
    called-for stage actions, 103–4
    chosen actions, 104
    clarity and, 104–6
    credibility in, 115–19
    defined, 102
    focus and, 106–15
    improvisational, 137–40
    inner action and, 119–23
    lighting and, 146–47
    preblocking, 138–39
    recording of, 140–43
    special effects, 126–28
    symbolic patterns, 135–36
    terms, 102, 137
    tools of, 136–37
    variety and, 135
    (*see also* Ground plan)
Bogdanov, Michael, 117, 245, 246, 317, 318
Bold theatrical cueing, 152
Boleslavsky, Richard, 173
Bonnard, Pierre, 70
Booth, Edwin, 5–6
Bourgeois Follies, 128
Bourgeois Gentleman, The, 126
Box set, 43, 68
Brando, Marlon, 174
"Breaking the proscenium arch," 59
Breathing exercises, 189
Brecht, Bertolt, 32, 33, 59, 60, 70, 88, 118,
    122, 150, 156, 164, 192–93, 249–50
Brechtian theater, 192–97, 260–62, 274
Breuer, Lee, 162, 245
Britannicus, 115
British National Theatre, 248
Broadway theaters, 42

Brook Peter, 9, 15, 36, 37, 38, 52, 64, 67, 68, 127, 135, 185, 252, 253, 258, 270–73, 286, 296, 304
Browbeating, 199–200
Büchner, Georg, 152
Budgeting, 299–301
Building phase, 315–17
Burgraves, The, 231
Business, 102

C

Cabaret, 152, 164
Cage, John, 264
Call, Edward Pason, 194
Called-for stage actions, 103–4
Capek, Karel, 84
Carbon arc lights, 147, 148
Carra, L., 98*n*
Carter Barron Amphitheatre, 47
Casting, 224–28, 305–7
Catharsis, 23
Cat on a Hot Tin Roof, 35
Caucasian Chalk Circle, 198
Chaikin, Joseph, 185
Chairs, The, 64, 161
Champion, Gower, 62, 323
Changeling, The, 117
Character development, 210–13
Chekhov, Anton, 17, 73, 98, 122, 162
Chekhov, Michael, 179–81
Cherry Orchard, The, 114, 174, 175, 208
Children of a Lesser God, 302
Chronegk, Ludwig, 6
Circuits, 148
Civilization and Its Discontents (Freud), 264
Clarity, 36, 104–6
Classroom scenes, 321–23
Claudel, Paul, 17
Clift, Montgomery, 235
Climax, 22–25
Clocks of Basle, The, 129
Clurman, Harold, 296
Coaching actors, 313–14
Cocteau, Jean, 67
Colorado Shakespeare Festival, 296
Comédie Française, 3
Company, 290
Company Theatre, 61, 63, 77, 78
Composition, 40–167
    defined, 46
    sound (*see* Sound composition)
    stage (*see* Blocking; Ground plan; Lighting; Scenery systems; Stage composition; Theaters)
Compositional aesthetics, 130–35

Conceptualization stage of production development, 296–99
Consolidation stage of production development, 317–21
Constant Prince, The, 52, 55, 71, 272
Constructivism, 258, 259
Contemporization, 243–53
Copeau, Jacques, 9, 15, 70, 71, 77, 183–84
Copyright law, 291–92
Costume design, 84, 86, 285, 303
Country Wife, The, 248–50
Craig, Gordon, 9, 10, 70, 146
Creation stage of production development, 307–17
Credibility, 115–19
Criticism, 32–33, 238, 296
Crucible, The, 142
Cues, 150–52, 154, 316
Cutting, 37, 38, 298
Cyc lights, 148

D

Das Kleine Mahagonny, 59
Davidson, Gordon, 72, 228, 293, 302
Dean, Alexander, 91, 98*n*
Death of a Salesman, 36, 74, 92, 125, 289–90
Deductive ground plan design, 92–93
Denise, Maurice, 70
Denver Theatre Center, 66, 128, 149, 157
Designing phase, 303–5
Dexter, John, 9, 85, 248, 293
Dictionaries, 29–30
Diderot, Denis, 170
Dimmer boards, 148–49
Dionysus in '69, 54, 55, 271, 272, 273
Directing class, 321–23
Director-author collaborations, 17–18, 293–94
Director-designer relationship, 84, 86, 303–4
Directorial function, 1–11
    defined, 10–11
    evolution of, 2–10
    range of, 1–2
Directorial Image, The (McMullan), 34
Director-managers, 6–9
Discipline, in rehearsals, 310–11
Dr. Faustus, 52, 226, 271
Doll's House, A, 284
Dramatist's Guild, 18
Dramatists' Play Service, 292
Dramaturg, 296
Dramaturgical analysis, 22–25
Dress rehearsals, 319–20
Dürrenmatt, Friedrich, 32, 135, 161

Dutchman, The, 226
Dynamism, ground plan and, 101

E

*Effect of Gamma Rays on Man in the Moon
    Marigolds, The,* 95, 96
Eliot, T. S., 31
Elizabethan theater, 2–3, 41–43, 45, 61, 68,
    242
El Teatro Campesino, 50
Emergence, The, 77, 78, 81
Emotional memory, 176, 177
Emphasis:
    blocking and, 114
    overall interpretation as, 35–37
Empty Space, The (Brook), 286
Endgame, 63
Ensemble work, 201–7
Entertainer, The, 32
Environmental theater, 54, 55, 266–67
Epic theater, 192–97, 260–62
Epstein, Sabin, 184n
Equus, 276
Erler, Fritz, 152
Eumenides, The, 2
Everyman, 77, 226
Exposition, 22–24
Expressionism, 258–60
Extrinsic interpretation, 37–39, 297
    defined, 14
    justification of, 14–15
    relationship to intrinsic interpretation,
        15–19
    working with, 38–39
Extrinsic style, 236–38

F

Fantasticks, The, 79, 324–25
Farcical effects, 127
Faust, 152
Feydeau, Georges, 100
Floor plan (*see* Ground plan)
Fly galleries, 72, 76
Foco Novo, 274
Focus:
    blocking and, 106–15
    in environmental theater, 266–67
    ground plan and, 98, 100–101
    lighting and, 155–56
    in media theater, 269
    overall interpretation and, 36
    in rehearsals, 229
Follies, 152, 290

Followspots, 147, 148
Footlights, 148
Ford's Theater, 52
Forefathers' Eve, 53, 55
Form vs. style, 233
Fort, Paul, 70
Foster, Paul, 150
Found space, 266
Frankenstein, 258
Freedman, Gerald, 76, 298
Freelance directors, 9–10
French scenes, 25–27, 29
Fresnel light, 148
Freud, Sigmund, 264
Fuchs, George, 9
Fundamentals of Play Directing (Dean and
    Carra), 98n

G

Gable, Clark, 235
Games, 201–13, 217
Gaskill, William, 248
Gémier, Firmin, 51
George II, Duke of Saxe-Meiningen, 6
Gielgud, John, 29, 122, 135, 210, 225, 285
Gilroy, Frank, 65
Giraudoux, Jean, 17, 31, 125, 170
Gish, Lillian, 230
Given circumstances, 179
Glass Managerie, The, 23–25, 162–63
Globe Theatre, 42, 45, 47, 242
Goodale, Katherine, 4n
Goodspeed Opera House, 52
Good Woman of Setzuan, The, 73–74, 164
Gorki, Maxim, 284
Government Inspector, The, 182
Granville-Barker, Harley, 9
Greeks, The, 251–53
Greek theater, ancient, 2–3, 31–32, 41, 61,
    67, 81
Gregory, André, 293
Grotowski, Jerzy, 9, 52–53, 55, 58, 127,
    185, 186, 271, 272
Ground plan, 41, 87–101
    accommodation of action and, 90
    atmosphere and, 101
    choice of, 90
    deductive design, 92–93
    defined, 87
    director-designer relationship and, 87, 89
    dynamism and, 101
    focus and, 98, 100–101
    improvisation and, 99–100
    inductive design, 92
    pattern of movement and, 94–96

projection of action and, 90–93
tableaux and, 97–98
Guinness, Alec, 210
Guthrie, Tyrone, 10, 16–17, 86, 87, 270, 296, 314
Guthrie Theater, 44, 45

H

Hair, 58, 152
Hall, Peter, 9, 17, 114, 227
Hamlet, 14, 15, 19–21, 34–38, 64, 67, 83, 85, 92, 103–5, 116, 125, 161, 270, 298
Hands, Terry, 117
Harris, Julie, 174
Harrop, John, 184*n*
Hart, Moss, 314
Havergal, Giles, 226
Hearst Theatre, 47
Heartbreak House, 63
Hello, Dolly, 61, 62
Henry IV, 160–61
Henry IV, Part I, 72
Henry V, 132, 242, 247–48
Henry VIII, 4
Hillyard, Eric, 247
Historical research sources, 32
Hochhuth, Rolf, 32
Holbrook, Hal, 230
Hollywood Bowl, 47
Home, 122, 135, 160
Horizontal emphasis, 114
Hostage, The, 92, 93
Hotel Paradiso, 100
Hugo, Victor, 231
Hunt, Peter, 40–41, 146
Huston, John, 235

I

Ibsen, Henrik, 101, 152, 284
"If" device, 179
Illusionistic theater, 59–60
Imperceptible light cueing, 151–52
Importance of Being Earnest, The, 216–17
Impromptu, 76
Improvisation, 213–21
around a text, 214–21
Artaudian, 188–89
basic uses of, 213
ground plan and, 99–100
plays derived from, 213
spontaneity in, 214
in Stanislavski system, 176
Improvisational blocking, 137–40

Incandescent illumination, 147
Incidental music, 164–65
Inciting action, 22–25
Inductive ground plan design, 92
I Never Sang for My Father, 230
Information sheet, 306
Inner action (subtext), 22
blocking and, 119–23
in Stanislavski system, 178–79
Insect Play, The, 84
Inspector General, The, 100
Intermission music, 164–65
Interpretation (*see* Script interpretation)
Intimate Relations, 63
Intrinsic interpretation, 297
breakdown of script, 25–29
defined, 14
dramaturgical analysis and, 22–25
example of, 19–21
overall interpretation and, 34–37
relationship to extrinsic interpretation, 15–19
study resources for, 29–34
Intrinsic style, 236–39
Ionesco, Eugene, 32, 161
Irving, Henry, 149

J

J.B., 294
Jackson, Anne, 139
Jacob, Sally, 68
James Joyce Liquid Memorial Theatre, The, 61, 63
Japanese theater, 93, 163
Jarry Alfred, 67
Jeder stribt für sich allein, 293
Jessner, Leopold, 70
Jesus Christ Superstar, 152
Jones, Robert Edmond, 70
Jonson, Ben, 42, 51–52
Jouvet, Louis, 2, 17, 146, 293
Julius Caesar, 7, 132, 151, 241–42
Jumpers, 116

K

Kaback, Douglas, 222
Kabuki theater, 79, 93, 163
Kalfin, Robert, 276
Karge, Manfred, 17, 152
Kazan, Elia, 9, 17, 74, 92, 123, 289–90, 294
Kean, Charles, 4–5
King Lear, 14, 15, 37, 64, 67, 107, 161, 163
Kommissarzhevskaya, Vera, 9

Kordian, 53
Kott, Jan, 251
Krannert Center, 55, 57
Krejca, Otomar, 85

L

Ladyhouse Blues, 63
Langhoff, Matthias, 17, 152
Langtry, Lily, 235
Laterna Magika, 268
Layton, Joe, 76
Lazzi, 127
Leach, Wilford, 245
Leadership, 1
Leko light, 148
Lenny, 152, 156
Lewis, Robert, 178
Lighting, 146–55
  in Artaudian theater, 272
  bold cueing, 152
  control in, 148–49, 153–55
  director-designer relationship, 154–55
  effects of, 149–50
  imperceptible cueing, 151–52
  in naturalistic productions, 285
  in preproduction phase, 304, 316
  instruments, 147–48
  rehearsals, 154–55, 318–19
  static, 150–51
  use of, 146–47
Little Foxes, The, 289
Little Mary Sunshine, 63
Little Murders, 58
Littlewood, Joan, 9, 164, 261–63
Living Theater, 258, 274
Long Day's Journey Into Night, A, 226
Long Wharf Theatre, 44
Lower Depths, The, 284
Lugné-Poë, Aurélien-Marie, 8
Luv, 139, 311

M

Macbeth, 26–28, 132, 277–82
Macklin, Charles, 4
MacLeish, Archibald, 294
McMullan, Frank, 34
Madwoman of Chaillot, The, 125
Magnificent Cuckold, The, 258
Mahagonny, 194, 261
Major Barbara, 158
Makbeth, 271
Makeup designer, 304
Malina, Judith, 9

Mancuso, Michael, 188
Marathon 33, 55, 58, 61
Marat/Sade, 127, 251, 270–73
Mark Taper Forum, 44
Marowitz, Charles, 205, 256–57
Mary Rippon Theatre, 47
Mask work, 221–24
Mason, Marshall, 17, 293, 312
Mayor of Zalemea, The, 137, 318
Measure for Measure, 161, 255
Mechanical scene shifting, 81
Medea, 270
Media theater, 266–70
Meiningen Players, 6
Merchant of Venice, The, 4, 5–6, 13–14, 35, 256–57
Mercier and Camier, 290
"Method," the, 174, 176–79
Metropolitan Opera, 58
Meyerhold, Vseveold, 9, 179, 181–83, 258
Mickiewicz, Adam, 53
Midsummer Night's Dream, A, 15, 33, 67, 68, 163, 230, 252, 253
Mielziner, Jo, 74, 75, 92
Miller, Arthur, 18, 32, 36, 74, 125, 162, 235
Miller, Jonathan, 255
Mines, Mabou, 290
Ming Cho Lee, 76
Misanthrope, The, 34
Miss Julie, 247
Mnouchkine, Ariane, 164
Moby Dick, 128, 149
Modellbücher, 33
Molière, 92, 126, 170
Moment-to-moment interpretation:
  breakdown of script, 25–29
  defined, 13
  dramaturgical analysis, 22–25
  example of, 19–21
  inner action, 22
  vs. overall interpretation, 13–14
Monroe, Marilyn, 235
Monstrous Regiment Company, 274
Morley, Christopher, 74, 86
Moscow Art Theatre, 8, 22, 173
Mosievitch, Tanya, 86
Mother Courage, 261
Movement:
  compositional aesthetics, 134–35
  defined, 102
  ground plan and, 94–96
Much Ado About Nothing, 253–55
Multiple sets, 63, 64, 71–76, 80, 82–83
Music, 156, 157, 161–65
Musical productions, 323–25
Music Theater International, 292
Muzeeka, 79

My Fair Lady, 63, 73, 164
My Sister Eileen, 166

N

Naturalism, 282, 284–85
Naturalistic acting approaches, 170–79
Nemirovich-Danchenko, Vladimir, 8, 169
Newman, Paul, 174
Newmann, Frederick, 290
New York Performance Group, 55
New York Public Theatre, 59
New York Shakespeare Festival, 51, 244, 245, 254, 258
New York Times, The, 32
Nicholas Nickleby, 290, 293
Nichols, Mike, 139, 293, 311
Night of the Iguana, The, 125
Nondramatic material, 290–91
No Strings, 76
Notes, 315
Nō theater, 79, 163
Nunn, Trevor, 9, 32, 74, 82, 86, 290

O

Objective, 178
Obligatory stage actions, 94
O'Casey, Sean, 30
Oedipus, 251
Oedipus Rex, 293
O'Horgan, Tom, 9, 152, 164
Oh, What a Lovely War, 261–63
Oklahoma!, 63
Olivier, Laurence, 210, 242
O'Neill, Eugene, 32, 100
Open audition, 306
Opening night, 320–21
Open Theatre, 273–74
Orchestra, onstage, 164
Oregon Shakespeare Festival Theater, 52
Oresteia, 67, 69, 275, 276
Organically multiple settings, 73–76
Orlando Furioso, 56
Orphée, 67
Osborne, John, 32
Othello, 5, 14, 30, 35, 120–21, 124, 208–9, 226
Our Town, 76
Ouspenskya, Maria, 173
Outdoor theaters, 47, 50–52
Overall interpretation:
    defined, 13
    as emphasis, 35–37
    instrinsically derived, 34–37
    vs. moment-to-moment interpretation, 13–14
Oxford English Dictionary, 30

P

P.C.P.A. (Pacific Conservatory for the Performing Arts), 44, 280–81
Pace, 159–61, 229, 231
Page, Geraldine, 174
Painter's Palace of Pleasure, 118
Papp, Joseph, 37–38
"Paradox of the Actor, The," 170
Participatory theater, 60
Peer Gynt, 76, 152, 298
Pendleton, Austin, 289
Performance Garage, 58
Performance Group, 272
Persuasion, 199
Phaedre, 241
Phelps, Samuel, 4–5
Physical actions concept, 179–92
Physical exploration of action, 205, 208–10
Pinter, Harold, 17
Pip Simmons Theatre Group, 275
Pirandello, Luigi, 32, 91, 160–61
Pirates of Penzance, 245
Planchon, Roger, 128
Planning stage of production development, 299–307
Play, 135
Plays:
    other productions of, as research source, 33–34
    selection of, 289–94
Plaza Suite, 283
Poetic physicality, 183–84
Practical lights, 148
Pratfalls, 128
Preblocking, 138–39
Preproduction planning, 299–307
Pretech rehearsals, 316–17
Preview performances, 320
Price, The, 18
Prince, Harold, 9, 80, 152, 164, 293
Production design (*see* Blocking; Costume design; Lighting; Scenery systems; Sound composition; Theaters)
Production development, 288–325
    budgeting, 299–301
    building, 315–17
    casting, 224–28, 305–7
    conceptualization, 296–99
    consolidation stage, 317–21
    creation stage, 307–17

Production development (*cont.*)
  designing, 303–5
  dress rehearsal, 319–20
  musical production, 323–25
  opening night, 320–21
  planning stage, 299–307
  play selection, 289–94
  rehearsals (*see* Rehearsals)
  research, 238–39, 294–96
  scene for class, 321–23
  scheduling, 301–2, 308–10
  speculation stage, 288–99
  staffing, 302–3
  "teching," 154–55, 318–19
Prometheus, 274
Prometheus Bound, 56
Promptbook, 316
Properties design, 84, 86
Property master, 304
Proscenium stage, 42–44, 55
Prowse, Philip, 118
Psacharopolous, Nikos, 290
Psychological gesture, 179–81
Public domain, 291
Public theaters, 41–42, 45

Q

Quarry Theatre, 47

R

Rabb, Ellis, 13–14
Racine, Jean Baptiste, 115, 241
Radio City Music Hall, 42
Raphael, 127
Realism, 6, 8, 282–84
  blocking and, 122–23
  credibility, 115–16
  ground plan and, 93, 94
  scenery, 63–66
Redon, Odillon, 70
Red Rocks Amphitheatre, 47
Rehearsals, 168–232, 307–15
  blocking (*see* Blocking)
  character development, 210–13
  classroom scenes, 321–23
  coaching actors, 313–14
  continuing, 320–21
  discipline in, 310–11
  discovering the action, 205, 208–10
  dress, 319–20
  ensemble work, 201–7
  focus of, 229
  goals in, 169
  improvisation (*see* Improvisation)
  mask work, 221–24
  musical production, 323–25
  notes, 315
  pace of, 229, 231
  person-to-person technique, 198–201
  run-throughs, 315
  scheduling, 301–2, 308–10
  shaping, 314–15
  technical, 154–55, 318–19
  text discussion, 311–12
  warming up, 201–7
  (*see also* Acting techniques and
    approaches)
Reinforcement, 199
Reinhardt, Max, 9, 33, 51
Research, 238–39, 282–84, 294–96
Resolution, 22–25
Restoration comedy, 248
Reviews, as research source, 33
Revision, 293–94
Rhythm, 157–59
Richard II, 164
Richardson, Ralph, 122
Rights, acquisition of, 291–92
Rising action, 22–25
Robbins, Jerome, 323
Rojo, Jerry N., 54
Roman Baths of Caracalla, 51
Romeo and Juliet, 30, 86, 125
Rouché, Jacques, 8
Royal Shakespeare Company, 82, 154,
    244–47, 250–51, 254, 310
Run-throughs, 315

S

St. James Theatre, 62
St. Joan, 92, 100
Samuel French Inc., 292
San Francisco Mime Troupe, 51
Saroyan, William, 30, 162
Sartre, Jean-Paul, 32
Scene changes, 72–73, 79–81
Scenery systems, 63–86
  abstract, 63–64, 66–71
  bare stage, 63, 76–79
  building phase, 315–17
  categories of, 63
  multiple, 63, 64, 71–76, 80, 82–83
  quality of design, 84–86
  realistic, 63–66
  scene changes, 72–73, 79–81
  of Shakespearean plays, 64
Schaeffer, Peter, 283

Schechner, Richard, 54, 55, 58, 185, 271, 296
Scheduling, 301–2, 308–10
Schisgal, Murray, 311
Schneider, Alan, 9, 230
School of Athens, The, 127
Script:
  breakdown of, 25–29, 295
  frontmatter (lists), 298–99
  interpretation of (*see* Script interpretation)
  preparation of, 298–99
Script interpretation, 12–39
  categories of (*see* Moment-to-moment interpretation; Overall interpretation)
  ethical considerations, 18
  "right" vs. "vital," 15–17
  sources of (*see* Extrinsic interpretation; Intrinsic interpretation)
  summary of, 39
Self-exploration, 176
Seneca, 251
Sequential settings, 72–73
Serpent, The, 76, 166, 213
Sets (*see* Scenery systems)
7/84 Company, 274–75
1776, 40–41
Shakespearean plays, 3–6, 30, 32
  aesthetic styles for, 258
  arbitrary settings for, 253–57
  contemporization of, 243–48, 250–52
  interpretation of, 4, 13–16, 19–21, 26–30, 32, 33, 35, 37
  scenery systems of, 64
  theaters for, 42
  (*see also* names of plays)
Shaping, 314–15
Shapiro, Mel, 125, 244
Shaw, George Bernard, 32, 92, 122, 158, 159, 188
Shepard, Sam, 157
Sicilian Vespers, 85
Sill, Paul, 67, 293
Simon, Neil, 92
Simonson, Lee, 70
Simultaneous setting, 73–75
Sister Susie Cinema, 162
Six Characters in Search of an Author, 76, 91
Skin of Our Teeth, The, 290
Smith, Mark, 169
Sophocles, 35
Sound composition, 41, 156–67
  music, 156, 157, 161–65
  pace, 159–61
  rhythm, 157–59
  sound effects, 165–66
  sound/sight integration, 165–67
Sound designer, 316

Sound effects, 165–66
Sound engineer, 304
Special effects with blocking, 126–28
Specific theaters, 52
Speculation stage of production development, 288–99
Speech, rhythms of, 157–59
Staffing, 302–3
Stage actions:
  called-for, 103–4
  obligatory, 94
Stage composition, 40–155
  defined, 40
  goals of, 40–41
  integration with sound composition, 165–67
  (*see also* Blocking; Ground plan; Lighting; Scenery systems; Theaters)
Stage hands, 79
Stage manager, 319
Staging area, 58–59
Stanislavski, Konstantin, 6, 8, 17, 22, 172–77, 197–98, 205, 208
Stanislavski system, 172–78, 197–98
Static lighting, 150–51
Steiger, Rod, 174
Stein, Peter, 9, 67, 69, 275, 276
Stomp, 59
Stoppard, Tom, 116
Story Theatre, 67, 293
Strasberg, Lee, 174, 176–79
Stratford Shakespeare Festival Theatre of Ontario, 44
Stratton, Charlotte, 95, 96
Streetcar Named Desire, A, 35, 166, 290
Street theater, 50
Strider, 276
Striplights, 148
Style, 233–86
  aesthetic, 257–63
  alternative theater, 263–77
  arbitrary, 253–57
  audience and, 239
  authenticity, 241–43
  consistency and, 238, 240
  contemporization, 243–53
  defined, 233
  example of range of approaches to, 277–82
  extrinsic, 236–38
  vs. form, 233–36
  inner essence and, 233–34
  intrinsic, 236–39
  naturalism, 282, 284–85
  research and, 238, 282–84
  stage elements and, 239–40
  summary of, 285–86
  text and, 238–39

Subject to Fits, 156, 163
Subject Was Roses, The, 65
Subtext (*see* Inner action)
Svoboda, Josef, 83, 84, 268
Sweeney Todd, 80, 290
Symbolic patterns, 135–36
Symmetrical balance, 130–31

T

Tableaux, 97–98
Tale Told, A, 63
Taming of the Shrew, The, 74, 117, 225, 245–46, 253
Tams-Witmark, Inc., 292
Tartuffe, 92
Taste of Honey, A, 163, 164
Taylor, Elizabeth, 289
Tea and Sympathy, 290
Technical rehearsals, 154–55, 318–19
Television, 269
Tempest, The, 163, 245, 251, 275
Tent theaters, 46–47
Text:
  discussion of, 311–12
  intrinsic style and, 238–39
  (*see also* Script: Script interpretation)
Theater of Cruelty, 184–92, 270–74
"Theater of the fourth wall removed, the," 59
Theaters, 41–63
  arena, 46–48
  choice of, 55–58
  outdoor, 47, 50–52
  proscenium stage, 42–44, 55
  specific, 52
  staging area, 58–59
  thrust stage, 44–49
  uniquely designed, 52–56
  "violating the stage," 59–63
Theatre and Its Double (Artaud), 265
Théâtre d'Art, 70
Théâtre de L'Est Parisien, 56
Théâtre du Vieux-Colombier, 70, 71, 77
Théâtre Libre, 8, 70
Théâtre Nationale Populaire, 51, 128
Threepenny Opera, 88, 261
Three Sisters, The, 63, 73, 98, 112, 162, 198
Thrust stage, 44–49
Tiegs, Cheryl, 235
Time of Your Life, The, 30, 162
Tiny Alice, 156, 163, 166
Toller, Ernst, 259
Tom Paine, 61, 150, 164
To the Actor (Chekhov), 179*n*, 180
Touch of the Poet, 100
Transfiguration, 259

Transformed space, 266
Translations, 31–32, 292–93, 294
Trestle stages, 51
Triangularity, 112, 113
Trojan Women, The, 15, 270
Tune, Tommy, 323
Turntables, 72, 76
Two Gentlemen of Verona, 244, 258

U

Ubu Roi, 67
University theaters, 44–46
Unlocalized sets, 63–64, 66–71
Upstaging, 112
Utah Shakespearean Theatre, 51

V

Vakhtangov, Eugene, 179
Van Itallie, Jean Claude, 166, 213
Variant editions, 30–31
Variety, blocking and, 135
Verfremdungseffekt, 60
Vertical emphasis, 114
View from the Bridge, A, 162
Vilar, Jean, 51, 312
"Violating the stage," 59–63
Visit, The, 135–36, 161
Vitez, Antoine, 231
Vomitoria, 44

W

Wagons, 72–73, 76
Waiting for Godot, 31, 36, 67, 94, 226, 290
Wallach, Eli, 139, 235
Waller, D. W., 6
Warm-up period, 201–7
Way of the World, The, 243
Webster, John, 42
Weill, Kurt, 88
Weiss, Peter, 32, 270
What the Babe Said, 66
Whip, The, 283
Wild Duck, The, 101
Williams, Tennessee, 17, 23, 35, 125, 162–63, 166, 167, 293
Williamson, Laird, 280
Williamson, Nicol, 240
Williamstown Summer Theater, 290, 324
Wilson, Lanford, 17, 283
Woyzeck, 152
Woyzeck Marie, 275
Wright, Garland, 248–49

Y

Yale Drama School, 91

Z

Zadek, Peter, 293
Zeffirelli, Franco, 86
Zindel, Paul, 95